C++ Classes and Data Structures

Jeffrey S. Childs

Clarion University of Pennsylvania

PEARSON

Prentice
Hall

Upper Saddle River, NJ
The Software originally published with this text is No Longer Available.

Library of Congress Cataloging-in-Publication Data on File

Vice President and Editorial Director, ECS: *Marcia J. Horton*
Executive Editor: *Tracy Dunkelberger*
Assistant Editor: *Carole Snyder*
Editorial Assistants: *Christianna Lee and ReeAnne Davis*
Managing Editor: *Camille Trentacoste*
Production Editor: *Rose Kernan*
Director of Creative Services: *Paul Belfanti*
Creative Designer: *Bruce Kenselaar*
Cover Designer: *Jayne Conte*
Managing Editor, AV Management and Production: *Patricia Burns*
Art Editor: *Gregory Dulles*
Director, Image Resource Center: *Melinda Reo*
Manager, Rights and Permissions: *Zina Arabia*
Manager, Visual Research: *Beth Brenzel*
Manager, Cover Visual Research and Permissions: *Karen Sanatar*
Manufacturing Manager, ESM: *Alexis Heydt-Long*
Manufacturing Buyer: *Lisa McDowell*
Marketing Manager: *Mack Patterson*

© 2008 Pearson Education, Inc.
Pearson Prentice Hall
Pearson Education, Inc.
Upper Saddle River, NJ 07458

Printed in the United States of America

ISBN: 0-13-158051-5
        978-0-13-158051-0

Pearson Education Ltd., *London*
Pearson Education Australia Pty. Ltd., *Sydney*
Pearson Education Singapore, Pte. Ltd.
Pearson Education North Asia Ltd., *Hong Kong*
Pearson Education Canada, Inc., *Toronto*

Pearson Educación de Mexico, S. A. de C. V.
Pearson Education—Japan, *Tokyo*
Pearson Education Malaysia, Pte. Ltd.
Pearson Education, Inc., *Upper Saddle River, New Jersey*

This book is dedicated to my wonderful wife, Analisa, and my sons, William and Edward, for their unending patience while I completed this task.

Jeffrey Childs

Contents

Preface

The reason for this book is very simple. When I teach a course on data structures, I usually don't have all the topics that I like to teach in one book. And the topics are not usually arranged the way I like to teach them. And the data structures aren't always made the way I like to see them made. So I finally did something about it, and here it is. And I am convinced that it is a good book. Simple enough?

Well, maybe it's a little too simple. And the publishers would scowl at me if I just wrote a one-paragraph preface, so let me go into a little more detail which might convince you that this is a good book, too. Let's begin with my approach to the subject of data structures.

APPROACH

C++ is a great language for data structures, but how do we, as instructors, teach clearly those concepts of C++ which are so difficult to grasp? Indeed, this difficulty has been one of the few drawbacks of C++. My approach here is to first motivate the student to learn the concept. Anyone who has taught anything for a year knows that if concepts don't seem to have any purpose, the motivation to learn them goes flat. Throughout this book, you will find such motivations presented, and I encourage you to use them in your classroom.

I also know that you will be pleased with the clear explanations throughout this book of those concepts which so many have struggled so hard to teach; they are written in a student-friendly, conversational style. The basic concepts are presented without worrying whether they are 100% technically correct; they will be technically correct for the most part, but you know the kind of correctness that I am talking about—the kind that transforms a student-friendly presentation into something that may as well have been written in Greek. Students won't read it! I'm writing this textbook for students, not for other professors of computer science. The slides that accompany the book will also make these concepts more clear; I call them "action slides". Many of them are like those old movie book pages that you flip through to see things moving, like horses running. Except here you see code and data structures in operation as you flip through them.

In addition to the approach of teaching C++ more clearly, I also take the approach of putting the focus on the client—the programmer who uses the class or data structure. Hopefully, in their first course or two on programming, students asked themselves questions such as "What can I do to make this program more user friendly?" or

"What can I do to make the output neater?" In this book, I want students to ask, "How can I make this class (or data structure) more convenient for the client to use?" or "What can I do to make this class (or data structure) as flexible as possible for the client?" There is a shift of attention that needs to take place from the computer user to the client programmer. So, throughout the book, the client is given consideration when it comes to implementation issues.

All of the programs, classes, and data structures in this book have been written from scratch with the client in mind. The code was compiled and tested with Microsoft Visual Studio 2005 C++. Throughout the book, the code has line numbers that are referenced in the text. I recommend that students make use of the line numbers by first looking at the code and seeing if they can understand it. If there is a line or two that they don't quite get, they should look for the line numbers in the text and read the discussion of those lines. The *entire* discussion, should be read, however, to see if what they are reading agrees with what they understand.

Throughout the book, information is presented to help students select the appropriate data structure for an application and the appropriate implementation for the data structure. Speed issues are strongly considered, of course, but so are memory issues. The amount of memory used in overhead for implementations is weighed carefully. It is true that computers have much memory today, but throughout history, when the average memory capacity of a computer has increased, the average program size has increased as well. Memory issues are important, and they will continue to be important.

In this book, every attempt has been made to keep the exercises as meaningful as possible. As an example of an exercise that doesn't have much meaning, consider the instruction "Reverse the elements on a stack so that the element at the top is on the bottom." Toward what end? What's the purpose? I try to make sure that exercises have some kind of purpose, so that students don't get turned off and think that data structures are pointless.

Throughout the text, I emphasize that when one writes a class function, it should be written so that it can't crash, regardless of whether or not the client misuses the function. This is a lofty goal, but it is something to strive for, because—let's face it—a client has a harder time debugging code if the cause of a program crash isn't found within a line of execution of the client's code.

In my mind, the main reason for showing how a class or data structure is designed is so that students will know what issues to think about when they design their own specialized data structures. If we didn't have the goal of making it possible for them to design their own data structures, there would be no need to show them code for data structures, just use them. For this reason, issues involving the client, memory, and speed are raised throughout the text as the data structures are presented. These are all important elements of design.

One thing I think will be pleasing to students and instructors alike is that I've tried to keep the size of the book down; instructors might actually have a chance to teach everything in it, and students might actually be able to afford it. There are so many different topics that can be examined in a course in data structures that a book intended to please everyone ends up being a mile wide; but then, in a sense, it ends up pleasing no one.

Although my focus is on using C++, I recognize that when students get into the work environment, they are going to need to program data structures in other languages.

Therefore, a student who cannot think of a data structure as something independent of the C++ language will be in for a hard time. So I have tried to avoid talking about data structures in C++ terms until it comes time for their actual implementation.

I won't take the approach of starting with a simple (but perhaps impractical) implementation of a data structure like a stack and then gradually build on it, adding more and more capability. I find that many students are turned off by this approach; they struggle to understand a data structure, then they realize the design isn't that great, and they are presented with a better design. It doesn't help much to tell students you are starting off simple so that they can understand the ideas presented; they get the impression that anything they are learning at any particular time might not be any good. In a sense, though, I actually do take this approach; I just have a different way of doing it. I teach them everything they need to know in order to understand a sophisticated stack, for example, but I do it with ordinary, run-of-the-mill classes in the first chapters.

HOW TO USE THIS BOOK

This book should be used for a first course in data structures, and it can be used for either a second- or third-semester course, depending on the curriculum. Chapters 1–6 focus on understanding classes as a strong foundation for understanding data structures — more so than in most textbooks on data structures. If the book is used for a second-semester course, the student should already have a basic knowledge of C++ or Java. In that case, one would want to cover Chapters 1–10 thoroughly and then cover selected topics or basics in Chapters 11–15. If the book is used for a third-semester course, you will probably be at a level where you want to cover Chapters 1–5 lightly, perhaps as a review, and then cover Chapters 6–15 heavily.

For a second-semester course, I think you will appreciate the fact that I take the approach of teaching classes before I teach data structures; that is, I don't teach classes in a few pages and then jump into data structures. If the two topics are combined at one time, students are initially very confused, trying to grapple with the concept of what a class is and what a data structure is at the same time. Meanwhile, in the backs of their minds, they are wondering why stacks aren't made *without* using a class; it would be so much easier. And then, students come to believe that classes are used only for data structures, which isn't good either. So five chapters of the book are devoted to classes even before data structures are introduced. The advantages of classes are shown clearly in these five chapters, so there is no question about why they should be used for data structures when the time comes to do so. And this is mostly material that is taught when we teach data structures anyway, so we are not wasting much time by separating the two subjects.

For a third-semester course, you might want to take a close look at Chapters 1–5 and cover those essentials which may have been lightly covered in the second course, because the later chapters build on these earlier ones. You are going to want to pay attention to design decisions that are based on the client, because, as stated earlier, throughout the book the focus is on the client, and this is not done too often in most textbooks today; frequently, it is left to the employer to teach. You can probably fly through these first five chapters fairly fast (but don't get me wrong and fly like a bat out of hell!).

You may have a need to teach composition, inheritance, and polymorphism in your course. Alternatively, the curriculum may be designed to present these topics for the first time in a course in object-oriented programming. Chapter 6 contains optional sections on inheritance and polymorphism. Although these topics are not used throughout the entire text, there are exercises throughout that require using inheritance. (These are marked with an asterisk.) This arrangement should fit your needs, whether or not you use inheritance or polymorphism in your data structures course.

CONTENT AND ORGANIZATION

Classes are first presented in a simple way in Chapter 1—like structs, but with functions added. No const specifiers or constructors are used. This gives students a solid base for understanding what a class is all about. Then, Chapters 2 through 6 build on that concept incrementally.

Class templates are presented as soon as possible in Chapter 2 (even before constructors are presented). This order of presentation might surprise some, but if we are going to teach data structures with class templates, we have a choice: (1) to present bad data structure design first (without the class template) and then the more sophisticated design (with the class template), something I said earlier that I try to avoid, (2) to teach classes first for a good bit, then class templates, and then data structures, or (3) to teach classes, jump into class templates fairly quickly, let them sink in with more material, and then teach data structures. Choice (2) doesn't work out very well, because before the students even have a chance to get a good grip on class templates, they are beginning to struggle with data structures. But the arrangement in this textbook means that some extra time should be spent on Chapter 2.

All of the data structures presented in the book are made from class templates. Presenting class templates early gives students a chance to adjust to the idea while things are still simple. Then the templates won't be confusing at all when they are used in data structures. Overloaded operators are also presented in Chapter 2, because they tie in with class templates nicely. I think that the relationship between overloaded operators and class templates is often overlooked. For example, if we are searching through a linked list for an element, part of our code might look like this:

```
template <class DataType>
 bool LinkedList<DataType>::retrieve( const DataType & element )
{
// beginning code here is omitted
        while( ptr != NULL ) {
               if ( element == ptr->info )   {
                      element = ptr->info;
                      return true;
                      }
// other code here is omitted
```

If we want this code to be as general as possible, then *element* can be a simple type, such as an integer, or something more complex, like an object of a struct with a key value that has been set to something we want to look for. In the latter case, the == operator will need to be overloaded for the struct, written so that a comparison of key values can be made. Then the rest of the information is retrieved. So, overloaded operators fit in nicely with templated data structures.

If you're thinking that I talk about storing objects (records) as elements in data structures a lot, you're right. After all, most of the practical uses for data structures employ objects as elements. Students should get used to it. Now, keep in mind, the first six chapters are just on classes, so once we get around to talking about objects as elements, it won't be too confusing, especially since I introduce the use of objects in classes within the first six chapters.

The Stack data structure is also presented in Chapter 2, but we don't actually examine the contents of it in detail at that point. We just use the stack for a program in the exercises. This helps teach the importance of abstraction.

Chapter 3 gets into const specifiers and constructors, but also talks about something else that is important: how classes should be modified. There are two sections in Chapter 3 on modifying a class (with the client in mind, of course).

Chapter 4 is devoted to the use of pointers and dynamic arrays, assuming that students don't have much of a background in these subjects. In Chapter 4, we also talk about how dynamic arrays can be adjusted in size. Their size doesn't actually change, of course, but a new dynamic array is made with a different size, the elements are copied over, the old array is freed, and the pointer that was used as the "name" of the old dynamic array is reassigned the address of the new one. When we do this, an array never really gets filled up (unless we run out of heap memory). Later, I use this idea for array implementations of data structures, to conserve memory and so that arrays don't get filled up. In the stack, for example, when we push an element onto the array and there is no more space left, a function is called so that the array doubles in size before the element is pushed. Similarly, when only 25% of the stack array is being utilized after a pop, the array size is cut in half. A later chapter shows that, by using such an expansion–contraction strategy under the worst possible conditions, the average push or pop won't have any more than a couple of elements copied between the arrays.

Chapter 5 is on an Array class, which serves as a base to cover other important topics associated with classes: destructors, overloaded assignment operators, and copy constructors, and why they should be used for every class when the objects of that class will contain dynamically-allocated memory. By using the simple concept of an array, these important functions and how they work become very clear.

Chapter 6 has a section on composition, which should be required, since later chapters will use that idea. Chapter 6 also has optional sections on inheritance and polymorphism for those who would like to, or have to, teach these topics. Again, there are exercises throughout the text, marked with an asterisk, that require the use of inheritance.

With this background in classes under the students' belt, data structures can be presented in a way in which they are easily understood. In addition, it is possible to present niftier implementations without confusion, such as using adjustable arrays and using shift operators for greater speed when multiplying or dividing by a power of two.

Chapter 7 is all about the methods used for making data structures. It is here where we talk about the strategy for the expansion and contraction of dynamic arrays within the data structures. Also, linked lists are introduced in this chapter. The amount of memory wasted in overhead is discussed with respect to both arrays and linked lists, so that students can make an informed decision about whether or not an array or linked implementation should be used in a data structure. Code sections are shown (without using classes initially) that illustrate how to work with linked lists. In this discussion, it is emphasized that students need to think about addresses, not just arrows, in writing such code. In fact, I've gone through great lengths to show the thought processes that should take place as one solves problems with the use of linked lists.

Chapter 8 talks about stacks and queues, using both array and linked list implementations. The fixed-length array implementation is not discussed; if the array is too small, it is too easily filled, and it the array is too large, it may end up wasting a lot of memory. Instead, the array-based implementations of this chapter use dynamic arrays, which can adjust their size as the number of elements changes. Sometimes the fixed-length array implementation of a data structure is presented as a prelude to a more sophisticated data structure. However, as I stated earlier, many of the concepts needed to understand these implementations are presented in earlier chapters, using ordinary classes.

Chapter 9 is entirely devoted to time complexities. It sounds like it might get deep into them, but it really doesn't—it just makes sure the understanding is deep. Issues that affect choosing a data structure are looked at. Logarithms are explained in a way that can be easily understood. And a time complexity's effect on the speed of computation is carefully noted.

Chapter 10 takes a look at a linked list as a data structure itself. In Chapter 11, this linked list is used in a hash table with chaining. The HashTable class has the client write a hash function that is most appropriate for its application. The client then passes the hash function into the HashTable constructor, by using function pointers, so that the HashTable functions can call the hash function that the client wrote, no matter where the client wrote it. Chapter 11 also discusses an implementation of a doubly-linked list in which any element in the list can be randomly accessed or removed in $\Theta(1)$ time. This is done by using a hash table implementation.

Chapter 12 discusses priority queues and introduces trees and heaps. Implementation issues related to speeding up heap functions include the use of "one-assignment swaps" when reheaping upwards or downwards and the use of shift operators. There are two optional sections on a linked heap (which is actually embedded in a more sophisticated data structure, in order to keep the time complexities of the operations the same as in the array-based heap).

Recursion is examined in Chapter 13. A way of understanding recursion is presented by making copies of functions, which I have found greatly cuts down on confusion. There aren't numerous examples of recursion in this chapter, because, with the way it is explained, they are not needed.

Chapter 14 presents some important sorting algorithms, along with some minor algorithm analysis, that may help students make the transition to an algorithm analysis course. There is also a section on sorting a linked list.

Binary search trees and graphs are presented in an open-ended fashion in Chapter 15. The student is made aware that these subjects need to be covered in more depth in a more advanced course.

INSTRUCTOR'S RESOURCES

This textbook is accompanied with a complete set of resources, available from http://www.prenhall.com/childs, including the following:

- PowerPoint slides, including action slides, showing how code affects data structures; the slides should be given to the student as a learning resource.
- Answers to nonprogramming exercises.
- All complete program code and class code used in examples throughout the text; these were compiled and tested with Microsoft Visual Studio 2005 C++.
- A test bank of questions.

CONTACT ME

I welcome your comments, suggestions, and feedback. Feel free to contact me at jchilds7@windstream.net.

ACKNOWLEDGMENTS

I would like to thank Elizabeth (Liz) Wildes, for her invaluable assistance at nearly every phase in the publishing process. I would also like to thank the many reviewers involved for their useful comments and suggestions.

- Charles Dierbach; Ph.D.; Computer and Information Sciences, Towson University
- Stephanie Elzer; Assistant Professor; Computer Science, Millersville University
- Robert G. Eyer; MS Computer Science; Computer Science, Penn State University (York Campus)
- David Falconer; Ph.D.; Computer Science, California State University (Fullerton)
- John M. Gauch; Ph.D.; Electrical Engineering and Computer Science, University of Kansas
- Nancy Kinnersley; Ph.D.; Electrical Engineering and Computer Science, University of Kansas
- Frank Migacz; MS Computer Science; Computer Science, Northern Illinois University
- Mike Morris; MS ABD; Computer Science, Southeastern Oklahoma State University
- Taewan Ryu; Ph.D.; Computer Science, California State University (Fullerton)
- Alla Webb; Professor; Computer Science; Montgomery College
- Zhigang Zhu; Ph.D.; Computer Science, The City College of New York

I would also like to thank the people at Prentice Hall: Tracy Dunkelberger, Executive Editor of Computer Science; Carole Snyder, Christianna Lee and ReeAnne Davies, Assistant Editors of Computer Science; Camille Trentacoste and Scott Disanno, Managing Editors; and Robin O'Brien, Executive Marketing Manager.

Thanks also to the producer, Rose Kernan, the copy editor, and proofreader at RPK Editorial Services for their fine work during the production of this book. Thanks also to the compositor, Laserwords.

In addition, I would like to thank my department secretary, Nancy Harriger, who suggested (and finally convinced me) that I should try to get this book published.

Finally, I would like to thank the biggest sources of my inspiration, my wife Analisa (Lisa), and my two sons William and Edward.

JEFFREY CHILDS

Clarion University of Pennsylvnia

CHAPTER 1

Structs and Classes

Look around you. Data is everywhere. It's in your phone book. It's in a list of football scores and statistics. It's in a list of people who belong to an organization. It's in your cornflakes, for heaven's sake (23% sugar, 5% corn, etc.). Whenever we write practical programs for the real world instead of a classroom, our task typically involves processing, or at least working with, large amounts of data.

Data structures are structures that store data. They have important uses when it comes to handling data. Some data structures are used as a necessary part of an algorithm that deals with data. Some data structures are used for more efficient processing of data.

We can think of data structures as being a set of tools in a toolbox. We select the right data structure for a certain program, just as we would select any other tool from a toolbox to do a job around the house. When you want to drive a nail into a board, you do the job much better if you select the right tool. For example, use a hammer instead of a wrench. The same thing is true with data structures. Selecting the right data structure from your data structures toolbox can help you solve a difficult problem or speed up an algorithm. Selecting one data structure over another might save on the amount of memory (RAM) used in a program. In some cases, it may be in your program's best interest if you design your own data structure as a specialized tool. So a typical data structures course or textbook will familiarize you with the most common data structures that are available, as well as give you the knowledge you need to design data structures.

Like anything else in a computer program, a data structure has to be written with code. A *class* is a section of program code that is used, among other things, to make most of the objects that we call data structures. Up to this point, you have probably written C++ programs with functions, while loops, for loops, if statements, etc., but you have probably never written a class before, so it will be completely new to you. But it is essential to be able to write classes in this day and age.

A *struct* is a classlike structure, but is typically much simpler than a class. Therefore, we will start our discussion with structs and then lead up to classes.

1.1   STRUCTS

A struct is similar to an array, because it can be used to store more than one element of data. However, in an array, all of the elements have to be the same type. For example, in an array of integers, each element has to be an integer. In an array of floats, each element has to be a float. A struct is different because one of its elements can be a float, one can be an integer, one can be a character, etc. A struct is often used to store a record of information. For example, a record of information about a book can contain the ISBN number, the title, the author, the data of publication, the price, etc. A struct facilitates storing such a record in a nice little package, because all of its data members can be of different types. It is worthwhile to talk about structs, because records of information are often stored in data structures. In addition, a struct can be used to create building blocks for the data structure itself.

The following example shows a simple program using a struct:

```
1    #include <iostream>
2    #include <iomanip>
3    #include <string>
4
5    using namespace std;
6
7    struct CarType {
8         string maker;
9         int year;
10        float price;
11   };
12
13   void getYourCar( CarType & car );
14
15   int main( )
16   {
17       CarType myCar, yourCar;
18
19       myCar.maker = "Mercedes";   // I wish
20       myCar.year = 2005;
21       myCar.price = 45567.75;
22
23       getYourCar( yourCar );
24
25       cout << "Your car is a: " << yourCar.maker << endl;
26       cout << fixed << showpoint << setprecision( 2 ) <<
27            "I'll offer $" << yourCar.price - 100 << " for your car." << endl;
28
29       return 0;
30   }
31
32   void getYourCar( CarType & car )
33   {
```

```
34     cout << "Enter your maker: ";
35     cin >> car.maker;
36     cout << "Enter the year: ";
37     cin >> car.year;
38     cout << "Enter the price: $";
39     cin >> car.price;
40  }
```

In this program, the struct is defined in lines 7–11, above the main function, but it can be defined almost anywhere. Like a function prototype, where you define the struct will determine where it is recognized. In this case, it is recognized throughout all functions of the program.

When you make a struct definition, it always begins with the keyword struct. After the keyword struct, you may choose a name for the struct, similar to the way you choose variable names. By convention, the name is usually capitalized, but it does not need to be. Use a pair of braces around the elements of the struct. These elements are commonly called **data members** (or members, for short). Notice that the members are declared similarly to the way other variables are declared in a program. Be careful to use a semicolon at the end of the closing brace (line 11). Failing to do so is a common mistake, since we are not used to having semicolons after the closing braces in functions, if statements, while loops, etc.

You can't use the members of a struct right after you define it. This is because a definition is not the same thing as a declaration. A definition, such as the struct definition, is used just to make a data type. The type CarType is a user-defined type, as opposed to built-in types like int or float. (Here, the word *user* refers to the programmer.) A declaration is used to tell the compiler that a name of a variable (that has a particular data type) exists. So we must declare variables that are of CarType defined by the struct definition in order to use this struct. When variables are declared with the use of struct types (or class types, for that matter), they are called **objects**. You can make one or more **objects** from a struct; in the example presented, the objects are made on line 17.

Accessing members of a struct object is a little different from accessing elements of an array. To access an array element, we use the familiar [ ]'s after the array name. To access a struct member, we use a dot after the object name, followed by the name of the member we wish to access, as shown in lines 19–21, 25, 27, 35, 37, and 39. With this notation, you should feel free to use the member just as you would any other variable, as shown in the program.

Lines 23 and 32 show that an object of a struct can be passed into another function. In this case, it is passed by reference. Notice that the name of the object passed is yourCar, but it is renamed car in the getYourCar function. This is similar to the way any variables can be renamed when you are passing them into a function. Notice that the getYourCar function prompts the user to enter information about his or her car. All changes to the car object of this function will be reflected in the yourCar object in the main function, since the object was passed by reference. If it were passed by value instead, no changes would be reflected in the main function.

Notice that we have two objects in this program, but only one struct was defined, with one set of members. It is important to realize that a struct definition is actually just a blueprint for making an object. When you define a struct, none of its members actually exist yet. This is similar to other blueprints: You can make a blueprint for a house without making any houses. The struct blueprint tells us information about what the members would be in the actual object—if an object is ever declared. It tells us the type and the name of each member. When you declare an object of the struct, these members are created within that object. If you declare a second object, a separate set of members is created for that second object. All of these members can be set differently in the different objects. The maker in myCar was set to "Mercedes", but the maker in yourCar may have been set to "Toyota" (depending on what the user enters). You can make as many objects from a struct blueprint as you want; you can even make an array of objects:

```
CarType dealerCar[ 100 ];
```

To set the year at index 10 to 2004, you would use the code

```
dealerCar[ 10 ].year = 2004;
```

The members declared in a struct can be arrays. They can even be other structs. Let us expand the CarType struct a little. In the following example, an EngineType struct and a CarType struct are defined:

```
struct EngineType {
        int numCylinders;
        float numLiters;
        string countryMade;
};

struct CarType {
        string maker;
        int year;
        float price;
        string wheel[ 4 ];
        EngineType engine;
};
```

Then a data member called engine and made from the EngineType struct is declared in the CarType struct. Notice, however, that engine is not an object yet, and it won't be until an object of CarType is declared—engine is just part of a definition at this point. The order of definition of these structs is important; we use the EngineType struct in the CarType struct, so EngineType must be defined above CarType in order for it to be recognized in CarType. We may make objects of EngineType in the main function, but we probably would just want to make CarType objects (unless we're in the business of selling engines). We can declare CarType objects the same way as in the preceding program. Suppose we have myCar declared as a CarType object for this example. If we wanted to set numCylinders in the engine of myCar to 6, we would use the code

```
myCar.engine.numCylinders = 6;
```

where we use the engine declared in the CarType struct. If we wanted to set wheel 2 to Goodyear, we would use the code myCar.wheel[2] = "Goodyear";

One important and useful property of structs is that an object of a struct can be assigned to another object from the same struct. For example, the code

yourCar = myCar;

is completely acceptable. It would assign the value of each member of myCar to the corresponding member of yourCar, so that all their members are set to the same values. All the values in the wheel array of myCar would even be assigned to the wheel array of yourCar. This is interesting, since, if we normally try to assign one array to another array, we would get a compiler error. Figure 1.1 shows an example of struct object assignment.

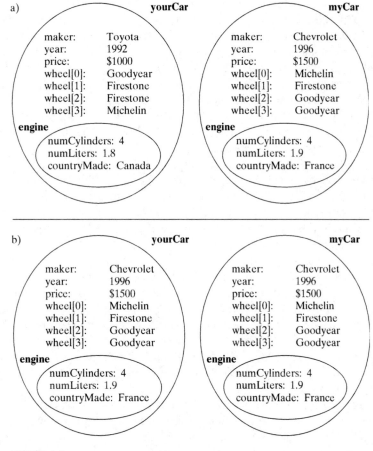

FIGURE 1.1

a) The yourCar and myCar struct objects before an assignment is made. b) The yourCar and myCar struct objects after the assignment "yourCar = myCar;" is performed.

Object assignment can be done only on objects made from the same struct. If we make an object myEngine from the EngineType struct and we try to assign myEngine to yourCar, we would get an error. However, we could use the code

yourCar.engine = myEngine;

1.2 BASIC CLASS CONCEPTS

Classes are very important, and they will be used for making nearly all of the data structures in this textbook. (We say *nearly all* because arrays and struct objects can be regarded as simple types of data structures.) We will first discuss the concept of a class before we attempt to look at the code.

Like a struct, a class is a blueprint for making an object, and more than one object can be made from the same class. Such objects form the basis of a very popular style of programming called ***object-oriented programming (OOP)***.

An object made from a class contains members, similar to the members of an object made from a struct. However, there are some important differences. First, it is common for an object of a class to contain members that are functions, in addition to the regular data members. Second, in a correctly written class, a program can access only the functions of an object made from it. The data members of a struct object can be easily accessed, as shown in lines 19–21 of the program in the previous section, but the data members of the object of a correctly written class cannot be accessed at all. The only thing that can access the data inside an object is the object itself. We call this characteristic ***encapsulation***, because the data is in a capsule, so to speak, inside the object and it is hidden from the rest of the program. For that reason, an object made from a class is thought of as being separate from the rest of the program. Encapsulation turns out to be an advantage of object-oriented programming, because if a class ever needs to be modified, we can change the types of data in a class without affecting the rest of the program (i.e., we won't have to make any changes to the rest of the program).

A typical real-world object-oriented program can use 25 or more different classes — sometimes even hundreds of different classes. The program makes one or more objects from each class, as appropriate. Usually, such programs are developed by a team of programmers. One programmer may be assigned just one class, which may involve an extensive amount of code in itself, since there may be a good number of functions as well as data members in each class. Another programmer might write the main program that uses all of the classes. Each of the objects made from the classes of such a large program is thought of as being separate from the rest of the program. However, the program can communicate with the objects, and communication is what makes everything work.

Figure 1.2 shows a program that has created three objects. The program uses the objects by communicating with them. The communication is carried out by functions. A program communicates with an object by calling one of its member functions. The object can also communicate with the program, through the return value from the function that was called by the program. A program can't use all of its objects at one time, so Figure 1.2 shows a possible sequence in which a program uses objects. Figure 1.3 shows what happens every time a program uses an object.

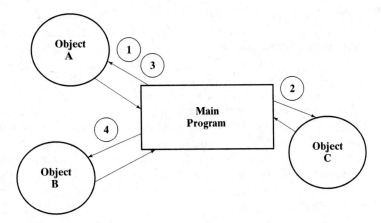

FIGURE 1.2

A program with three objects. The main program must use the objects one at a time. The numbered circles show the order in which the main program uses the objects in this example. The arrows show communication between the main program and the objects.

As shown in the figure, we can think of an object as being divided into sections. The *public* section of the object contains functions, and it is called public because it can be used by anything outside the object. The *private* section of the object contains data members; they can be accessed only by the object.

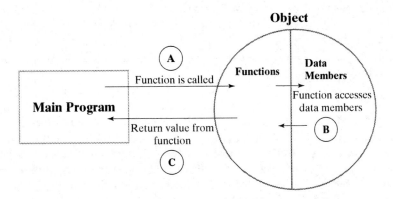

FIGURE 1.3

How the main program uses an object. The object is divided into two sections; the left section contains the functions of the object, and the right section contains the data members. The arrows between the main program and the object show communication between them. In step A, the main program calls a function in the object, possibly passing parameters. In step B, the function accesses and works with the data members of the object to help produce a result; the function may also call other functions within the object. In step C, the function that was called in step A returns a value (through its return type) to the main program if the return type of the function is not void. After returning, the main program picks up where it left off.

When a program calls a function in an object, the function may be designed specifically to change or set a value of one of the data members. For example, suppose the price of a car object needs to be adjusted for inflation. Then there may be a function in the object called adjustForInflation. The program would call this function, passing in the inflation rate as a parameter. The function then uses the inflation rate to change the price of the car. There may also be a function called setPrice, which sets the price to the parameter passed in. Sometimes a program calls an object's function that is specifically designed just to retrieve a data value, like the price of the car, and send it back as a return value. Such a function might be called getPrice. You can see that the public section of the object (the section containing the functions of an object) acts as an *interface* between the program and the object's data. So, in computer science lingo, the public section is often referred to as the *class interface*.

You may wonder at this point why classes are designed so that the main program cannot access data directly. Why must it use these functions to access data? The reason is that programs have to be continually updated in response to the changing needs of customers, and sometimes the changes involve data in class objects. It turns out that there is far less work involved in making the necessary changes if there is a class interface and far more work involved if the main program is allowed to access the data directly. As a simple example, let's suppose we store the price of a car as a float data member in a class. The program involving this class is sent to a customer who, a couple of years later, requests that we design class functions which perform extensive calculations involving the prices of cars. Because of the errors involved in floating-point operations, we realize that it would be better to store the price as an integer—the number of cents ($10000.69 = 1000069 cents)—within the class. The main program is rather lengthy (as most programs are) and sets the prices of about 25 cars in 25 places, scattered throughout its various functions. Let's consider two scenarios: (1) The main program is allowed to change the price directly, as if it were a data member of a struct object, and (2) the price is stored as private data, so that it cannot be accessed by the main program.

In the first scenario, we change "float price" to "int cents" within the car class, but now we have to search for and change the 25 accesses to price throughout the main program. We need to change the code for each of these accesses so that it stores the number of cents into the price, instead of a price in dollars and cents. In the second scenario, we change "float price" to "int cents" within the car class, and the main program passes a regular price into the setPrice function in the class; the main program then makes 25 calls to the setPrice function, with the calls scattered throughout the program. We rewrite the setPrice function to convert the price to cents before storing it. Notice that in the second scenario no changes need to be made at all to the main program! Thus, a class interface is an excellent technique for reducing the amount of work involved in updating a program, and such updates occur frequently.

No one can argue, however, that the program doesn't run a little slower because of these function calls; accessing data directly would be faster. This is apparently a price worth paying, as there are numerous benefits of a class. One point is worth making, however: Sometimes data structures are used to speed up the processing of data. All of this function calling affects the amount of speedup we actually get from the data structure, but the effect is negligible. (In other words, it is not worth considering.)

1.3 CLASS IMPLEMENTATION

Now, let's talk about the ***implementation*** of a class. *Implementation* is a word you should get used to. It just refers to coding, but it is used a lot in computer science lingo. So, when we talk about the implementation of a class, we are talking about how a class is put into code.

First of all, two files should be used for every class. This means that a program which uses three classes should have seven files altogether, six for the three classes and one (the file containing the main function and other functions) for the main program. Up to this point, you've probably written programs that use just one file of source code, containing the main function and several other functions. Those days are over, my friend.

The two files for a class are called the ***class specification file*** and the ***class implementation file*** (often called simply the specification file and the implementation file, for short). The specification file for a class contains only the definition of the class. The class definition looks similar to a struct definition, but it contains the function prototypes in addition to the data member declarations. The function prototypes are written exactly as they would appear in a one-file program. Since you now know the definition of implementation, you might guess that the implementation file contains a bunch of code. It does. It contains all the function definitions for the prototypes in the class definition.

I admire your patience. You've been dying to see what the code for a class looks like, but you've patiently read about classes first. Do me a favor: Read Section 1.2 over again and the beginning of this section again, and make sure that you understand everything. If you're sure you've got it down, let's take a look at a class and a program that uses it:

```
1   // checkbook.h – A class for a checkbook
2
3   class Checkbook
4   {
5   public:
6       void setBalance( float amount );
7       bool writeCheck( float amount );  // returns false if amount is greater than balance;
8                                         // otherwise returns true
9       void deposit( float amount );
10      float getBalance( );
11      float getLastCheck( );
12      float getLastDeposit( );
13  private:
14      float balance;
15      float lastCheck;
16      float lastDeposit;
17  };
```

The code you see is the class specification file, where the class definition is located. This is a class for a Checkbook object. I'm starting off simple, as a gesture of kindness to you, and excluding some things that you would normally see in a class. By convention, the name of the class specification file is the name of the class within it, followed by a .h extension. The name of the class is Checkbook, shown on line 3. Therefore, this file has been named checkbook.h. A file with a .h extension is called a **header** file.

Notice that the class definition is a lot like a struct definition. Instead of starting off with the keyword struct, it starts off with the keyword class on line 3. The keyword class is followed by the class name, which we choose, similarly to a struct. Also like a struct, there are members inside surrounded by braces, and the last brace is followed by a semicolon on line 17. Again, don't forget that semicolon when you make a class definition! It is an easy mistake to make, and a typical compiler won't complain that you forgot the semicolon; instead, it will give you a lot of errors that won't make much sense. The declaration of the data members in lines 14–16 is also similar to the way they are declared in a struct definition.

One difference from a typical struct is the inclusion of the keywords public and private, on lines 5 and 13, respectively. These keywords tell which section of the class is public (can be used by anything outside an object of the class) and which section is private (can be used only by an object of the class). By convention, in C++, the public section is placed first in the class and the private section is placed last. They can be placed in different orders, but you should follow conventions because it is what programmers expect when they examine your class. You can also put more than one type of the same section into a class. For example, you could use two public sections, one above the private section and one below it, but this isn't good practice either. I point it out only because you will sometimes see code written that way.

By convention, the function prototypes are placed into the public section, lines 5–12, and the data members are placed into the private section, lines 13–16. Notice that the function prototypes are similar to the way you have written them in other programs. A function prototype is sometimes placed into the private section, but only when the class designer does not want such a function to be called from outside the object. The class designer wants such a function to be called only from other functions within the object. It is considered extremely poor programming practice, however, to place data members in the public section.

The section of code presented next shows the class implementation file, where the function definitions for the function prototypes are found. By convention, the name of this file is the name of the class, followed by a .cpp extension. In the following code, the file has been named checkbook.cpp:

```
18   // checkbook.cpp – The functions for the Checkbook class
19
20   #include "checkbook.h"
21
22   void Checkbook::setBalance( float amount )
23   {
24       balance = amount;
25   }
26
27   bool Checkbook::writeCheck( float amount )
```

```
28  {
29      if ( amount > balance )
30              return false;
31      balance -= amount;
32      lastCheck = amount;
33      return true;
34  }
35
36  void Checkbook::deposit( float amount )
37  {
38      balance += amount;
39      lastDeposit = amount;
40  }
41
42  float Checkbook::getBalance( )
43  {
44      return balance;
45  }
46
47  float Checkbook::getLastCheck( )
48  {
49      return lastCheck;
50  }
51
52  float Checkbook::getLastDeposit( )
53  {
54      return lastDeposit;
55  }
```

We must include checkbook.h at the top of this file, as shown on line 20. The double quotes are used instead of the angle brackets that we normally use. The double quotes tell the compiler that the file we need to include is found in the same directory (or folder) as this .cpp file. Angle brackets tell the compiler that the file to be included is in the library of header files. In Microsoft Visual C++, these header files are located in the include folder of the compiler installation.

The function definitions in the implementation file are similar to function definitions that you have written before. There is one difference in notation, however. Notice, for example, on line 22, that the class name is inserted into the function heading, followed by a double colon (Checkbook::). If we took out this part of the code the function heading would be the same as any other function heading you have ever written. The Checkbook:: notation tells the compiler that the prototype of the function we are defining can be found inside the Checkbook class definition, something that may seem obvious at this point.

There is something else, however, that might seem peculiar. Take a look at the setBalance function on lines 22–25. This function is used to set the initial balance of the checkbook. The variable called amount was passed in as a parameter, but what about the variable called balance? It wasn't even declared in this function. Won't that give us a compiler error? The answer is a resounding *no*: The balance variable was declared in the class definition, on line 14. *Every function of a class "knows about" the data members in the class definition.* So there is no need to declare them, and in fact, we would be creating a new variable if we did (which would be used instead of the variable in the private section). By the way, if you left out the Checkbook:: part of the function heading in line 22, the compiler would probably tell you that the variable balance is undeclared. It is a common mistake to do this, so if you see this type of compiler message, you'll know what the problem is.

The setBalance function is a typical example of a function that would have to be called from a program in order to change the balance variable of a Checkbook object. (Remember that the program can't access the data members.) The amount to which to set the balance is passed in as a parameter, and then the balance is simply set to that amount on line 24. Sometimes beginners will make the mistake of naming the parameter in the function heading as balance, thinking that it will be set that way. It doesn't work. Think of the balance variable in the class definition as being a variable already declared within the function, because that is the way it acts *during the execution of the function*. You wouldn't pass in a variable called balance into a function and declare a variable called balance within the function at the same time.

Another question someone might ask is why the balance variable is put into the class definition. Why isn't it just declared in the setBalance function to begin with? We are allowed to declare variables within class functions, and sometimes we do. The reason we don't do it in this function is that there is an advantage to declaring a variable in the class definition. The object will always remember the value of that variable in the class definition, even when code of the object is no longer executing. So, when we return from the setBalance function, and execution resumes in some program outside the object, the object retains the value of its balance variable. Later on, the program might make a deposit, which will need to be added to the balance to produce the updated balance. But this can happen only if the object remembers what the last balance was. Therefore, the variable balance was declared within the class definition, giving us this important advantage.

This advantage doesn't occur with local variables (variables declared within the function). When you return from a function with a local variable, the local variable is destroyed along with its value. However, sometimes it is advantageous to declare variables within a class function. We would do so with a variable designed just for temporary use, such as the counting index *i* of a for loop. Here, we don't want the object to remember the last value of that variable. We use up RAM memory when we force objects to remember values that aren't that important. So a class definition loaded chock full of variables that don't need to be remembered is wasting a lot of memory.

The return type of setBalance is void, because there is no need for the object to communicate anything back to the program. The program calls this function to set an initial balance, and it assumes that that has been done.

The next function is the writeCheck function on lines 27–34. We have to watch that we don't write a check larger than the balance, so line 29 checks for that. If the amount is larger than the balance, writeCheck does nothing and returns false, a signal to the program that the check shouldn't be written for that amount. So here, the object communicates with the program. If the amount is less than or equal to the balance, lines 31–33 execute. Line 31 subtracts the amount of the check from the balance. Line 32 saves the check amount into lastCheck, which is declared in the class definition. Then, true is returned, which indicates to the program that the check was acceptable.

We can always make an acceptable deposit, so the deposit function in lines 38–39 just adds the deposit to the balance and then saves the amount of the deposit into last-Deposit, which is declared in the class definition.

The object will always remember the latest values of balance, lastCheck, and last-Deposit, since these variables are declared in the class definition. Therefore, whenever the program needs one of these values, it calls one of the next three functions: getBalance, getLastCheck, and getLastDeposit. These functions then communicate with the program by returning the value of the appropriate variable.

The code that follows is an example of a main program file that uses the Checkbook class. The name of the program file is useCheckbook.cpp.

```
1    // useCheckbook.cpp – A program for using the Checkbook class
2
3    #include <iostream>
4    #include <iomanip>
5    #include "checkbook.h"
6
7    using namespace std;
8
9    int menu( );
10
11   const int CHECK = 1, DEPOSIT = 2, BALANCE = 3, QUIT = 4;
12
13   int main( )
14   {
15       Checkbook cb;
16       float balance, amount;
17       int choice;
18       cout << "Enter the initial balance: $";
19       cin >> balance;
20       cb.setBalance( balance );
21
22       cout << fixed << showpoint << setprecision( 2 );
23       choice = menu( );
24       while ( choice != QUIT ) {
25           if ( choice == CHECK ) {
26               cout << "Enter check amount: $";
27               cin >> amount;
28               if ( cb.writeCheck( amount ) )
29                   cout << "Check accepted." << endl;
30               else {
31                   cout << "Your balance is not high ";
32                   cout << "enough for that check." << endl;
33               }
34           }
35           else if ( choice == DEPOSIT ) {
36               cout << "Enter deposit amount: $";
```

```
37                        cin >> amount;
38                        cb.deposit( amount );
39                        cout << "Deposit accepted." << endl;
40                        }
41            else  {  // must be a balance request
42                        amount = cb.getBalance( );
43                        cout << "Your balance is: $" << amount << endl;
44                        }
45
46            choice = menu( );
47            }
48
49      return 0;
50  }
51
52  int menu( )
53  {
54      int choice;
55
56      cout << endl;
57      cout << "1     Write a check" << endl;
58      cout << "2     Make a deposit" << endl;
59      cout << "3     Get the balance" << endl;
60      cout << "4     Quit" << endl << endl;
61      cout << "Enter a number between 1 and 4: ";
62      cin >> choice;
63      return choice;
64  }
```

Before we discuss this code specifically, a number of things must be pointed out in general. First, all of the lines of code we have presented thus far (the two class files plus the preceding program for using the Checkbook class) can be rewritten without using a class. Furthermore, if we wrote them without using a class, the code would be a lot shorter. Even more, without a class the code would be a little faster. I realize that I can't keep you from laughing, but I can talk about why we are doing this.

Well, let's get back on track. Nearly all data structures in C++ are made from classes. Data structures are a lot more complicated than the preceding example. You have to learn about the basics of classes before you can learn about data structures. All we are doing now is taking a look at a simple example, so that we can focus on the mechanics of how classes work and how classes are designed.

One of the important things to note is that we have to include the class specification file on line 5. Don't make the mistake of including the class *implementation* file here. The .cpp files are put together by the linker and they do not need to be included. Appendix A discusses the correct way to compile these files.

The main program has just a main function and a menu function. Let's talk about the menu function first, on lines 52–64. The menu function gives the user the option of whether to write a check, make a deposit, see the balance, or quit. Once the user enters the right number for an option, the menu function returns the number.

The main function first declares a Checkbook object on line 15. This is similar to the way an object from a struct is declared. A class is like a blueprint. You can't actually use it until you make an object of the class. Once an object of the class is declared, a set of data members (from the class) are made for that object, and any public functions within the object can be called from the main program.

As with structs, you can declare more than one Checkbook object for your program if you like. Each of them would have its own set of variables (declared in the class definition), as structs do. Remember, though, that the Checkbook object is thought of as being separate from the main program, which knows nothing about the existence of the variables declared in the class definition. The main program knows only about the functions of the class; it does not know the contents of the functions or any variables declared within the functions. It knows what it must pass into the functions, what the functions are supposed to accomplish, and what it receives from the functions, and that's it.

The main function declares a balance variable on line 16. This variable has the same name as the balance variable declared in the class definition. The two, however, are entirely separate variables with no link. In fact, if we tried to use the balance variable in the main program without declaring it, the compiler would claim that it is undeclared.

On lines 18–19, the main program asks the user to enter an initial balance. Then it sets the initial balance in the object by calling the setBalance function on line 20. Notice that it uses the object name, followed by the dot, followed by the function call. This notation is similar to that used by our first program to access the data members of a CarType object. It is a common mistake to leave off the object name and just make the function call. That should be done, because the compiler needs to know which object this function call is for (even if it is obvious that there is only one object).

After setting the initial balance, the main program gets a menu choice from the user. It processes the user's choice on lines 25–44 and then gets another menu choice on line 46. The while loop iterates until the user finally enters number 4 to quit the program.

If the user wants to write a check, lines 25–34 are executed. Remember that the writeCheck function returns true only if the balance is enough to cover the amount of the check. The writeCheck function returns false if the check cannot be written. Appropriate messages are displayed to the user for the return values. Requests for making deposits and for checking the balance are processed on lines 35–44.

Appendix A gives some guidelines for compiling programs with multiple files. If you feel uneasy about this, you should go through that appendix and compile the preceding sample program. It can be obtained from http://www.prenhall.com/childs (as well as any of the classes or programs written in this book).

Sometimes people get confused when writing and using classes. To avoid confusion, keep the following in mind:

1. No access can be made to the private data members of an object from outside the object. Only the object can access its private data members.
2. Upon returning from an object's function, the object will retain the current values of its data members. Thus, these values will still be the same when another function of the object is called.

3. All of the functions of a class can use any data members declared in the class definition. The main program cannot use the private data members of an object, nor does it know anything about them.

The main program in our sample program does not make use of the getLastCheck and getLastDeposit functions in the class definition. This was no mistake. In very large programs, the work is divided up among a team of programmers. Some people write classes, some the main program. Often, the person who writes a class writes it as if it may be used in a hundred or even a thousand different programs. When a class is written, it is intentionally made so that it may be reused without any alterations. So one main program may not use some of the functions of a class, but another main program may. To reuse the class in our example, we just need to write a new program that declares and uses an object of the class and then copy the two class files into the folder our new main program is in. Just compile and enjoy; reusing classes can save a lot of programming time.

When you've written programs in the past, you've written them with the user in mind. Hopefully, you always asked the questions "What can I do to make this program more user friendly?", "What can I do so that the person who uses my program knows what to do?" and "How can I make the output look a little neater for the user?" When you write a class, you have to change the way you think. You have the main programmer in mind. You don't think about the user. Your questions are always "What can I do to make this class easier for the main programmer to use?", "What functions can I put into this class that would be useful to a main programmer?" and "How can I give main programmers the greatest flexibility in the way they use my class?" In other words, you are thinking on an entirely different level. For these reasons, the main program is often called a *client program* and the main programmer is often called a *client*.

Some programmers may make the mistake of including a message to the user in the writeCheck function, such as "You can't write a check that is greater than the balance." If one did this, one would have to include the iostream file (along with "using namespace std;") at the top of the class implementation file. This would allow cout to be used in the class functions. But the entire approach is a mistaken one. One main programmer might like your messages and another might hate them. You should always let the main programmer decide what message is appropriate for his or her program, because sometimes the main programmer might not even want to give a message. So, in general, you should avoid thinking about the user when you write a class. This is a rule of thumb, but sometimes you can't help but disregard it. For example, you might be writing a function of a class that draws some wonderful rectangles on the screen, and obviously, the user is going to see those.

1.4 TESTING A CLASS

In object-oriented programming, when you make a class, you are supposed to test the class before you use it. The way to test a class is to write a main program that uses each function of the class and then make sure that each function does what it is supposed to do. When a main program is written just for testing purposes, it is called a ***test driver*** (or driver, for short). Once you are sure that the entire class works correctly, you can discard the driver you used to test it. This might seem like a lot of work: Write a driver, only to discard it later. Let's put it into perspective, however. Imagine writing a very large program—thousands of lines long—like a typical program in the real world. Let's say you use about 50 classes. Let's consider two approaches to compiling and debugging: In the first approach, we don't test each class as we make it; in the second approach, we do.

In the first approach, once you get rid of all the compiler errors, you are sure to have many runtime errors. Let's say we have 500 runtime errors in the classes, an average of 10 in each class. Remember that these classes will be considerably larger and more complex than the class in our example. How long would it take us to track down each runtime error? It would take quite a while, especially since the runtime errors are probably interacting with each other. It might take 2 hours to track down each runtime error. (I am actually being optimistic!) That would give us a total time of 1000 hours to knock down all the runtime errors in the classes.

In the second approach, we write a driver to test each class. Let's say that it takes about an hour to write the driver for each class, so we have 50 hours of time writing programs that we will discard. The good news is that it will take considerably less time to find a runtime error in the class. If we get a runtime error, we have already narrowed down where it has to be (it has to be in the class we are testing), and since there aren't that many runtime errors interacting with each other, if any, we will probably have a good idea about which function the runtime error is in. Let's say it now takes a half hour, on average, to knock down each runtime error this way. Then, since there are 500 runtime errors among the classes, this is 250 hours of time used to knock down the runtime errors. Add that onto the 50 hours of time spent writing drivers to test the classes, and we have a grand total of 300 hours of runtime debugging—a lot better than the 1000 hours in the first approach (and a lot less frustrating).

Get into the habit of testing each class as you make it, right now, as you are writing smaller programs. It is something you will have to do, and it will be good to get some experience at it. Keep it in mind. If you still feel uneasy about writing test drivers only to discard them later, it may help you to know that in the real world, the test drivers are saved. If the class needs to be updated, the same test drivers can be used (or updated if necessary).

1.5   PLACING FUNCTION DEFINITIONS IN THE CLASS DEFINITION (AND WHY WE SHOULDN'T DO IT)

There is another way of writing classes that makes it easier for the class programmer. But this method has its own advantages and disadvantages, and lately the disadvantages seem to outweigh the advantages. We present the method here because you will, no doubt, see classes written that way.

The method is to place the function definition with the function prototype in the class definition. With this technique, the function definition does not need to be placed in the class implementation file. However, the technique should be used only when the function definition does not contain more than a few simple lines of code. Certainly, there should not be any if statements or loops.

If we used this technique to rewrite our Checkbook class, it would look like this:

```
1   // checkbook.h – A class for a checkbook

2   class Checkbook
3   {
4   public:
5       void setBalance( float amount )  { balance = amount; }
6       bool writeCheck( float amount );  // returns false if amount is greater than balance;
7                                         // otherwise returns true
8       void deposit( float amount ) { balance += amount; lastDeposit = amount; }
9       float getBalance( ) { return balance; }
10      float getLastCheck( ) { return lastCheck; }
11      float getLastDeposit( ) { return lastDeposit; }
12  private:
13      float balance;
14      float lastCheck;
15      float lastDeposit;
16  };
```

Then, the class implementation file would look like this:

```
17  // checkbook.cpp – contains the function definitions for the Checkbook class
18
19  #include "checkbook.h"
20
21  bool Checkbook::writeCheck( float amount )
22  {
23      if ( amount > balance )
24              return false;
25      balance -= amount;
26      lastCheck = amount;
27      return true;
28  }
```

No changes are needed in the main program; its use of the class remains just the same as it was before.

First, let's take a look at line 5. It looks a little funny, but we can write it this way because the C++ compiler doesn't care if code is placed on different lines or not. We could have written the line like this:

```
void setBalance( float amount )
```

```
{
        balance = amount;
}
```

But that would take up more lines of code. What we have done is simply put all this code on the same line—in the same sequence, of course. When you use this technique, a common mistake is to place a semicolon at the end of the function heading. It is not a function prototype anymore, however; it is a function definition, and it needs to be written that way.

The only function that couldn't be placed in the class definition was the writeCheck function, since it has an if statement and is more than a few lines long. Placing function definitions in the class definition is considered to be poor programming practice if the definitions have more than a few lines of code or if the lines of code are anything more than simple assignments or returns. The reason is that the function definition then clutters up the class definition and makes it difficult to read.

In the past, class programmers used this technique all the time. Lately, there has been a movement away from it. One of the reasons for that movement is *maintenance*. Let's discuss why.

In the software engineering world, a customer of a software company requests that the company write a program that meets certain specifications, much as your instructor requests programs from you. After the program has been designed, tested, and debugged, it is shipped to the customer and the customer uses it; at this point, the program is considered to be in operation. *Maintenance* is any work that needs to be done on a program *after* it is in operation. Maintenance work needs to be done all the time, because the world and our understanding of the world keep changing. When the world changes, a program that was written for the way the world previously was can't always handle the changes. So the customer requests that the software company update the program to handle these changes. When our understanding of the world improves, a lot of programs that were written with poor understanding can't compete with the programs that were written with greater understanding. But they are still around, so maintenance needs to be done on them as well.

In the past, most of the work on a program was spent in designing, coding, and debugging it; little work was spent on maintenance. Today, only 20% of the work on a program is spent in designing, coding, and debugging; 80% of the work is spent on maintenance. Part of the reason for this is that today programs are a lot larger than they used to be. In the past, if a program became outdated, the easiest thing to do was to write a new program. Today, it might take a team of programmers a year or more to write a program. If it becomes outdated, we don't just want to scrap it; it is often more cost effective to maintain it. This is part of the reason for the popularity of object-oriented programming; the programs are easier to maintain. Maintenance has a big effect on the programming world. Today, we do everything we can to make programs easier to maintain.

When someone needs to maintain the code for a class, right away they look in the class implementation file. When they don't see it there, they know it is written in the class definition, in the class specification file. It can be a little frustrating guessing where the code is written. It is even more frustrating when the maintainer needs to add more complex code to the function, so that code needs to reside in the class implementation file. Today, the philosophy is to put everything in the class implementation file, because, for one thing, it is easier to maintain the code that way.

1.6   COMMENTING A CLASS

Finally, let's say some words about commenting a class. Every software company has its own way of commenting. A company will certainly let its employees know what its prescribed method of commenting is, if there is one. Sometimes, the commenting method is excessive and tends to clutter up programs unnecessarily, especially if it is obvious what the functions do. Sometimes, people don't comment enough, which makes it hard for maintainers to understand the program. If you name functions correctly, like setBalance, you are really commenting. This is called *self-documenting* code. If it is not obvious what the class is about, you should put a long comment at the top of the class header file to explain it. Also, remember that the main programmer might be looking at your class definition to see what functions he or she can use. If it is not obvious what a function does, what the purpose is of the parameters that get passed in, or what gets returned, you should put in a comment to explain these, as appropriate. The function writeCheck, for example, has a bool return type. It may not be obvious what this is all about, so a comment is placed next to the writeCheck function to explain it.

Nowadays, comments in a class definition that tell a client how to use a class are not as important as they used to be. Instead, clients generally read other documentation about how to use the classes that are available; sometimes this information is found under the Help menu of their programming environment. But it doesn't hurt to provide some good comments in a class for a client who may be looking directly at it.

When comments are used in the private section, they are for maintainers. The main programmer should have no interest in this section, as his or her program cannot access these data members. You should use comments here when it is not obvious what the data member is for simply by looking at its name.

Don't expect the main programmer to go through your class implementation file and look at that. Often, the class implementation file is available to the main programmer only in the form of object code. When you place comments here, you are basically placing them here for maintenance reasons. So put in comments that explain how code works if the code looks fairly difficult to understand. As with the class definition, if it is not obvious what a function does, what the purpose is of the parameters that get passed in, or what gets returned, you should put in a comment to explain these, as appropriate.

You will encounter people who have the philosophy that everything should be commented with the use of a consistent system of commenting, regardless of whether what they are commenting is obvious. The rationale is that what is obvious to one person may not be obvious to another. You have to make up your own mind about this, but in the end you should conform to the pattern of commenting that is used by the software company you work for if the people there think that it is important for you to do so.

1.7   THE DIFFERENCES BETWEEN A STRUCT AND A CLASS

Throughout this chapter, we have pointed out many similarities between structs and classes. Part of the reason was just to help you get a handle on classes. But another reason is that, in fact, they are very, very much the same. Like classes, structs can have function members. Like classes, structs can have a public and a private section. In fact, anything you can do with a class, including the more advanced tasks that we will cover later, you can also do with a struct. Also, classes don't need to have the keywords public and private written within them. So, you should now be convinced that structs and classes are about the same. There are, in fact, only two very small differences between a struct and a class. The first difference is obvious: One begins with the keyword struct and the other begins with the keyword class. The second difference is that if we leave the public and private sections out of each of them, everything in a struct is automatically public (i.e., by default), and everything in a class is automatically private. When everything in a class, including the functions, is private, the class is essentially useless, so we use public and private sections in the class.

By convention, we use a struct when we want all its members to be public. So it is rare to see the keywords public and private within a struct. We don't use functions in a struct unless we absolutely have to. So, just because of the convention, people generally think that there is a bigger difference between structs and classes than there actually is.

SUMMARY

This chapter has introduced structs, classes, and their implementation. Nearly all data structures in C++ are made from classes and often use structs within them, so it is important to understand all the basic concepts having to do with structs and classes presented in this chapter.

Large programs can be split up into pieces (classes), allowing each member of a team of programmers to work on his or her own piece of the program. Classes can also be easily reused by hundreds or even thousands of clients. Classes also make it easier to update (maintain) programs, because when we need to change the way the data in a class is represented, we can change it without having to rewrite any of the main programs that use the class.

When you create a class, you should have maintenance in mind, and you should focus on the client of the class, not the user of the program. The class should be commented appropriately. Keep all function definitions in the class implementation file. Avoid providing output to the user within a class function (if at all possible), and avoid getting input from a user in a class function. Let these jobs be handled by the client, as the client sees fit.

When you are creating classes for clients, it is important to test them thoroughly after they are done. Even when you are creating classes for your own program, each class should be tested individually as it is made. Doing this will save large amounts of time in debugging runtime errors.

EXERCISES

1. Answer the following questions about the structs shown:

```
struct Course
{
       string courseCode;
       string days;
       string time;
       int numCredits;
};

struct Student
{
       int age;
       Course c[ 6 ];
       int credits;
       float gpa;
};
```

   a. Suppose a student Jane is declared:
   Student Jane;
   Write a section of code that will set Jane's age to 24, set her GPA to 3.4, and then output her age.
   Write a line of code to set the time of her third course to "11:00 A.M."
   Write a line of code that multiplies the number of credits in Jane's second course by 4 and saves the result in a variable called quality.
   b. Suppose a classroom of students is declared:
   Student students[25];
   Suppose that the days variable for the second course of the 10th student has been set to "MWF". Change days to "MTF" without replacing the whole string. (Replace only the W with a T.)

2. Explain the difference between the public and private sections of a class.
3. What is implementation?
4. Name and describe the two files that are made for each class.
5. How many files would a program have if it has 10 classes? Do we know how many files a program has if it has 10 objects? Why or why not?
6. Explain the difference between a variable declared in the private section of a class and a variable declared locally within a class function. When should we use each one?
7. Explain how a main programmer would obtain the values of data members in the private section of a class. How would a main programmer change the values of data members in the private section of a class?

8. What is a class interface? Why is it called an interface?

9. What is a test driver?

10. Why should a class be tested thoroughly once it is created? Why not instead create all classes for a program and then test the whole program all at once?

11. What is maintenance? How would placing a class function definition within the class definition hinder maintenance?

12. What is a client?

13. Explain why we should avoid creating class functions that interact with the user of a program (i.e., class functions that provide output to the user or obtain input from the user).

14. Explain the differences between a struct and a class.

15. What is the advantage of keeping data members private in a class, as far as program maintenance is concerned?

16. This exercise will provide practice in working with structs and arrays. Although there might be many ways of doing the assignment, it must be done exactly as specified here (for purposes of practice). Write a program that will record information about employees and compute their paychecks. Each employee must be represented by a struct containing the last name of the employee, the hours worked each day of the week, the hourly rate, and the pay for that week. The "hours worked each day of the week" must be an array storing five values for the hours from Monday to Friday. (The company is not open on Saturday or Sunday.) Therefore, this array will be inside the struct. There will also be an array of all the employees (an array of structs). There must be at least four employees.

    The array of structs must be declared in the main function of the program. Then the entire array must be passed to a function called "initialize", which will ask the user to enter values for every part of every struct, except for the pay for that week (which will be computed in a different function).

    A loop for processing the array of employees must be set up in the main function. Inside the loop, a single employee will be passed into a function called "compute", which will calculate the paycheck for that employee. If the employee worked longer than 40 hours, overtime pay of 1.5 times the hourly rate is to be used for each hour worked over the 40 hours. For example, an employee who works a total of 50 hours for $10.00 an hour would make $550. *Do not* pass the entire array of employees into the "compute" function; the employees will be passed, one at a time, into the "compute" function until all of their paychecks have been calculated, at which time the loop will terminate. The employee will need to be passed by reference.

    A single employee must be passed into the "result" function, which will output the last name of the employee and the amount of the paycheck for that employee. *Do not* pass the entire array of employees into the "result" function. Each employee must be passed through call by value, one at a time, until all the paycheck amounts have been output, at which time the loop (in the main function) will terminate. Then the program will end.

17. Create a Road class. The class should have functions for setting the width of the road in feet and the length of the road in miles. It should also have functions for obtaining the width of the road and the length of the road. Remember that the class functions should not interact with the user of the program, either by providing output or by getting input. Create a function called asphalt that will accept a road thickness as an input parameter; then, on the basis of the thickness, it will compute and return the number of cubic feet of asphalt needed to pave the road (1 mile = 5280 feet). Test each function of the class thoroughly with a driver.

18. Make a Temperature class. The class should have a function for setting the temperature in Fahrenheit and a function for setting a temperature in Celsius. Keep only one data member

in the private section for storing the temperature. Create a function for obtaining the temperature in Fahrenheit and a function for obtaining the temperature in Celsius. Test each function thoroughly with a driver ($F = \frac{9}{5}C + 32$ and $C = \frac{5}{9}(F - 32)$).

19. Make a Time class. The class should have three variables, for hours, minutes, and seconds. Write three functions called setHours, setMinutes, and setSeconds for setting these variables. Write three functions called timeInHours, timeInMinutes, and timeInSeconds that return the appropriate amount of time. For example, if hours = 1, minutes = 40, and seconds = 30, then timeInSeconds should return 6030 and timeInMinutes should return 100.5. Test each function thoroughly with a driver.

CHAPTER 2

Overloaded Operators, Class Templates, and Abstraction

Data structures are frequently made from classes, and very often structs are used within data structures to store records of information. Also very often, there are special functions placed within a struct, or directly underneath a struct, called ***overloaded operator*** functions.

2.1 OVERLOADED OPERATORS

First of all, let's recall what an operator is. In programs that you've written in the past, an operator was usually some symbol that acts on one or more variables or constants to produce a result. The symbols +, <=, !, and && are all examples of operators. Sometimes the result is a calculated value. Sometimes the result is 'true' or 'false', as in a condition of an if statement. But there is always some type of result; otherwise, there would be no reason to use the operator. Now, however, you have to change the way you think about operators. You should now think of an operator as (usually) some symbol that acts on one or more variables, constants, *or objects* to produce a result.

The expression

```
z = x + y;
```

can call a function if the '+' is an overloaded operator. Repeat that to yourself 10 times and let it sink in, because I'm sure you're not used to the idea. That's right: This expression, as innocent as it looks, can call a function written by you, the programmer.

The if statement heading

```
if ( x > y )
```

can also call a function if the '>' sign is an overloaded operator. Again, if you are not used to that idea, keep repeating it to yourself and get used to it before you read on. You don't have to understand how the if statement heading calls the function at this point or what the ramifications are; you just need to realize that it can call a function.

In any function, we have to consider what gets passed in and what gets returned. You know from past experience that the return value replaces the function call. For example, if function foo returns an integer, say, 3, then the expression

```
x = foo( ) + 2;
```

is going to place the value 5 in x. This is because foo( ) gets replaced with its return value of 3, the 3 is added to 2 to get 5, and then 5 is stored in x.

In overloaded operator functions, the return value replaces the function call, too. It just may not be very clear, at this point, what the function call is. In an overloaded operator function, *the function call consists of the operator and any variables, constants, or objects it acts on*. Therefore, in the expression

```
z = x + y;
```

where the '+' is an overloaded operator, the expression x + y is the function call. The whole expression x + y will get replaced with the return value of the function. Then that value will be assigned to z. Similarly, in the expression

```
if ( x > y )
```

where the '>' is the overloaded operator, the expression x > y is the function call. So the whole expression x > y will get replaced with the return value of the function. In this case, the return value of the function would probably be a bool type, so the whole expression x > y would get replaced with either 'true' or 'false', whichever is returned from the function after it is done executing.

In these examples, if neither x nor y is an object, we cannot use an overloaded operator function. If they are both integers, for example, C++ already knows what to do; it will just add them together as it always does. If one or both of x and y are objects, then we can write an overloaded operator function for them. In fact, we would have to, or the compiler would give us an error; if they are objects, C++ has absolutely no idea of what to do with the operation. So, overloaded operator functions can be written only for objects and must be written for operators acting on objects.

Let's make this more clear with our familiar CarType struct:

```
struct CarType {
        string maker;
        int year;
        float price;
};
```

Suppose we were to declare myCar as an object of this struct. Then we fill in all of the data members with values. Afterwards, we write the lines of code:

```
if (myCar > 2000)
    cout << "My car is more than 2000!" << endl;
```

C++ has no idea what to do with this code. It doesn't know if it should compare the year in myCar with 2000 or compare the price in myCar with 2000. We have to tell C++ what to do with this condition by writing a function that it can execute. If the function returns 'true' after executing, it will replace the expression myCar > 2000 with 'true'. Then, since the condition is true, it will output the text shown. Whenever you use an operator on an object, if you do not write an overloaded operator function for it, you will get a compiler error.

But how *do* we write an overloaded operator function? Because of the wide variety of operators, there are many ways to write them. We will limit our discussion to **binary operators**—and, at that, only the ones used for calculations or comparisons. Binary operators act on exactly two variables, constants, or objects, which we will refer to as **operands**. So, in short, a binary operator acts on exactly two operands. There are overloadable unary operators that act on only one object, such as the '++' operator. There are also binary operators that are not used for calculations or comparisons, such as the "<<" operator that is commonly used with cout. However, these types of operators are not commonly used for data structures. To overload them, you should consult a C++ text on object-oriented programming. (Java does not have overloaded operators.)

In C++, there is often one operand to the left of the binary operator and one operand to the right of the binary operator. (This isn't always true in other computer languages; both operands can be on the left side of the operator or both on the right). Recall that at least one of the two operands must be an object in order for you to be able to write an overloaded operator function. If the left operand is an object of a struct, the entire function definition usually appears inside the struct definition. Then the operand on the right is passed into the function as a parameter. Following is a short program that illustrates such a function:

```
1   // A program that uses an overloaded operator in a struct
2
3   #include <iostream>
4   #include <string>
5
6   using namespace std;
7
8   struct CarType {
9       string maker;
10      int year;
11      float price;
12      bool operator >( int num ) { if ( price > num ) return true; return false; }
```

```
13  };
14
15  int main( )
16  {
17      CarType myCar;
18
19      myCar.maker = "Mercedes";   // I wish
20      myCar.year = 2005;
21      myCar.price = 45567.75;
22
23      if ( myCar > 2000 )
24          cout << "My car is more than 2000!" << endl;
25
26      return 0;
27  }
```

First, take a look at line 12. This is the function definition for the overloaded operator '>'. It is okay to place such function definitions within a struct, since a struct definition does not normally have a struct implementation file associated with it. Notice that the function definition on line 12 has a bool return type, as we would expect. The name of the function is unusual. You cannot name such functions using just any name. You must use the keyword operator followed by the symbol for the operator that is being overloaded. (The space between them is optional.) The parameter num is the right operand. The function definition is placed on one line, but it would normally look like this:

```
if ( price > num)
        return true;
return false;
```

The condition in the if statement is telling C++ to compare the price of myCar with the variable num. How do we know that it is the price of the myCar object? When the left operand is an object of a struct, the function is called for *that object*. So it is as if we called the function with the line of code

```
myCar.operator >( 2000 );
```

You can see that if the price of myCar is greater than num, the function will return true. Otherwise, it will return false.

The operator > function is called on line 23. Recall that the expression myCar > 2000 is the function call, and this function call will be replaced with the return value. The operator > function is called for the myCar object. If yourCar were an object and the expression yourCar > 3000 were used, the operator > would be called for the yourCar object. Since 2000 is the right operand in our example, it is passed into the parameter num. Then the price of myCar, which is 45567.75, is compared with 2000, and it is greater. Therefore, true is returned from the function and

(a)

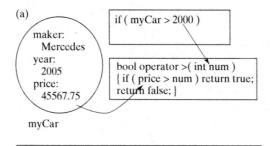

myCar

(b)

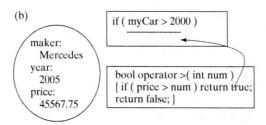

FIGURE 2.1

(a) The right operand is passed as a parameter into the overloaded operator function and is compared with the price in the myCar object. (b) The condition "price > num" is true, so "true" is returned; the value "true" will replace the function call (underlined), making the condition "myCar > 2000" true.

replaces the function call myCar > 2000. The condition on line 23 is now true, so the program outputs "My car is greater than 2000!". Figure 2.1 provides an illustration of this process.

Now, what if yourCar is an object in the program and we use the following lines of code:

```
if ( myCar > yourCar )
        cout << "My car is greater than your car!" << endl;
```

What will happen? The compiler will give an error because yourCar cannot be passed into parameter num. It is not an int type. We can, however, write another operator > function:

```
1   struct CarType {
2        string maker;
3        int year;
4        float price;
5        bool operator >( int num ) { if ( price > num ) return true; else return false; }
6        bool operator >( CarType car )
7                   { if ( price > car.price ) return true; else return false; }
8   };
```

Here, yourCar would be passed into parameter car. We have to remember to access the price of the car by using car.price. We don't need a myCar.price, because myCar was the left operand. Thus, any use of the data members named maker, year, or price will automatically be understood as the use of a myCar data member.

Now we have two operator > functions. The one that gets called will depend on what the right operand is. C++ will try to match it. If it can't, you will get a compiler error. We can write as many operator > functions as we need. One thing we can't do is write another one to compare the year of myCar with an integer. This is because we would then have two operator > functions that pass in an int parameter, and C++ would not know which one to use. If we decided to use the year for comparison, we could replace price with year on line 5. An alternative that makes sense would be to use float as the type of parameter to compare prices and then use int as the type of parameter in a different overloaded > function to compare years.

C++ doesn't require you to do anything special for overloaded operator functions, other than supply the correct name for the function and pass in one parameter (for binary operators). Inside the function, you can declare local variables, use for loops, and do anything you can do in any other function. By convention, however, the result of the function should have some relationship to the usual usage of the operator being overloaded.

Commonly overloaded operators for structs (records of information) in data structures include all the relational operators: >, <, >=, <=, ==, and !=. Although assigning one object to another object made by the same struct is permitted, testing structs for equality by using the operator '==' is not permitted unless the equality operator is overloaded.

Operators that produce calculations are sometimes used, so we should take a look at one of these next. Suppose we want the result of adding two CarType objects together to give the result of adding their prices. Then our code might look like this:

```
float totalPrice;
totalPrice = myCar + yourCar;
```

Try to write the function for this operator without looking at the struct that follows. If you are done writing the function, let's take a look:

```
struct CarType {
        string maker;
        int year;
        float price;
        bool operator >( int num )  { if ( price > num ) return true; else return false; }
        bool operator >( CarType car )
                { if ( price > car.price ) return true; else return false; }
        float operator +( CarType car )  { return price + car.price; }
};
```

The first thing you need to think about is the return type. That is, what is the data type of the result that you expect to get out of the operation? We've already said that we want to add the prices together, so the result should be a float. Therefore, we make the return type for operator + a float. The right operand is a CarType object, so the parameter for our function must be a CarType object. (The variable name doesn't matter.) Then we return the result of adding the prices together.

The resulting price that is returned will replace the function call myCar + yourCar. Then it will be assigned to totalPrice.

Now, let me throw you a curveball: What would happen if we write the following lines of code?

```
if ( 2000 < myCar )
        cout << "2000 is less than my car!" << endl;
```

What object's function is called by the if statement's condition? The answer is that no object's function is called, because the left operand is not an object. Can we write an overloaded operator function for this condition? It turns out that we can; we just can't put it inside the struct definition. When the left operand is not an object, but the right operand *is* an object, it is best to place the function definition directly underneath the struct definition. So the result would look like this:

```
struct CarType {
        string maker;
        int year;
        float price;
        bool operator >( int num )  { if ( price > num ) return true; else return false; }
        bool operator >( CarType car )
                { if ( price > car.price ) return true; else return false; }
        float operator +( CarType car )  { return price + car.price; }
};

bool operator <( int num, CarType car )
        { if ( num < car.price ) return true; else return false; }
```

This code works exactly the same as the function definition in the struct, except for two differences. The first is that this function definition doesn't belong to an object, so the left operand is passed into the left parameter of the function heading and the right operand is passed into the right parameter, as illustrated in Figure 2.2. The second

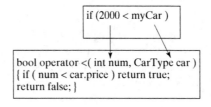

FIGURE 2.2

Illustration of the way parameters are passed when the left operand is not a struct object.

difference is that myCar isn't recognized as being the owner of the function, so we have to access its price with car.price instead of just price.

You can also create as many operator < functions as you need underneath the struct definition. You just need to make sure that the left parameter is different for each of them.

When overloaded operator functions are written for classes, they are written the same way. The only difference is that the function prototypes are placed into the class specification file and the function definitions are placed into the class implementation file, like any other function of the class. When the left operand is an object of the class, the function prototype is placed within the public section of the class definition. The function definition is written in the class implementation file similarly to the way other function definitions for the class are written.

When the left operand is not an object of the class, but the right operand is, the function prototype is placed directly beneath the class definition. The function definition is placed into the class specification file, but the class name is not used in the function heading. For example, if, in writing an overloaded operator >= function for our Checkbook class, we used an integer left operand, we would place the function prototype under the class definition, and the function heading in the class implementation file would look like

bool operator >=(int num, Checkbook cb)

instead of like

bool Checkbook::operator >=(int num, Checkbook cb)

Remember that the expression "Checkbook::" tells the compiler that the prototype for the function we are defining is found in the Checkbook class definition.

It is not common to overload operators for the classes of data structures, except for overloading the assignment operator, '='. We will discuss this feature in more depth later on. Pages and pages can be written about overloading operators. If more information about them is desired, consult a textbook on C++ object-oriented programming.

2.2   USING A CHECK STRUCT IN THE CHECKBOOK CLASS

Well, it's time to go one step further. If you haven't noticed by now, we are builders in this textbook. We lay in one chunk of knowledge, and then we build on top of it. Then we build on top of that. Then we build on top of that. Don't worry; we are not in an infinite loop. There is a back cover on the book. Just make sure you lay in a good foundation, or your house will crumble. In other words, do your best to get everything down.

Anyway, we are going to put a struct in our Checkbook class. We desire to have more information about the last check that we wrote. After all, there is more to a check than just its amount. There is the check number, the date the check was written, and the place or person we wrote the check to. We can put all of this information neatly into a Check struct:

```
struct Check {
        float checkAmount;
        int checkNum;
        string date;
        string receiver;
};
```

Our Checkbook class is re-created here (from Section 1.3):

```
// checkbook.h – A class for a checkbook

class Checkbook
{
public:
        void setBalance( float amount );
        bool writeCheck( float amount ); // returns false if amount is greater than balance;
                                         // otherwise returns true
        void deposit( float amount );
        float getBalance( );
        float getLastCheck( );
        float getLastDeposit( );
private:
        float balance;
        float lastCheck;
        float lastDeposit;
};
```

We really don't have to change too much in this class. We are going to pass a Check object, instead of a simple float, into the writeCheck function. We are going to return a Check object from the getLastCheck function, so that the main programmer will be so happy to get all this information. Instead of having a lastCheck float type variable in the private section, we are going to have a lastCheck Check object.

But there is one thing more we need to consider. The compiler needs to know what a Check is before it can compile the code in the class definition. Otherwise, it will give an error message when it sees Check. We could place the Check struct definition up above the class definition. If we do, then our new checkbook.h file looks like this (the changes to the class definition are shown in bold):

```
// checkbook.h – A class for a checkbook

struct Check {
        float checkAmount;
        int checkNum;
        string date;
```

```
            string receiver;
    };


    class Checkbook
    {
    public:
            void setBalance( float amount );
            bool writeCheck( Check amount );  // returns false if amount is greater than
                                    // balance; otherwise returns true
            void deposit( float amount );
            float getBalance( );
            Check getLastCheck( );
            float getLastDeposit( );
    private:
            float balance;
            Check lastCheck;
            float lastDeposit;
    };
```

There is something very important that I want you to notice: All we did was change the word "float" to "Check" in appropriate places in the class definition inside the class specification file. But there is a problem with this layout, namely, that we really ought to let the main programmer or the client determine what struct, if any, to use. It might be that some clients like the structs with the extra information. It might be that the struct is a thorn in the side to other clients, and just having a float type, as before, would be sufficient for them. Still other clients might have some unusual information that they need to put into the struct. We can't be omniscient about this and foresee everything they might need, but some things come to mind: Maybe a client has two checking accounts and wants to state which one is being used, or maybe a client has a joint checking account with someone else and would like to state who wrote the check. Would it be appropriate for a client to go into the class specification file and modify the struct as needed? Not really. Clients shouldn't have to touch the code in the class files; if they do, the class designer is making things inconvenient for them. It would be ideal for the clients to make their own structs inside the client file or the main program file.

Another improvement would be to allow client programs to create all different kinds of Checkbooks within the main program file if they like. For example, maybe they would like to create a Checkbook object that stores the check amount as a float and another Checkbook object that stores the check amount as a Check object. Maybe the client would like a dozen different kinds of Checkbooks in the same program.

Do all these improvements sound impossible? Well, take a deep breath. They are not impossible. A *class template* would be the answer to these improvements for the client. A class template would allow clients to store the check any way they want in the

Checkbook; they can store it as a Check object or as a float for just an amount, without having to touch any class code. A class template would keep the class programmers from making a dozen different types of Checkbook classes to satisfy the client. A class programmer would just have to create one class template.

2.3 CLASS TEMPLATES

A class template is a blueprint for making a class, just as a class is a blueprint for making an object. More than one class can be made from the same class template, just as more than one object can be made from the same class. All the C++ data structure classes in this textbook are made from class templates, so class templates definitely need to be covered.

A class template looks something like a class, and sometimes we talk about them as if they really are classes, but they really are not. In fact, when a class template is created, no class exists until the client would like to make one. It is very easy for the client to have a class created with a class template; all it takes is a simple line of code. The compiler makes the classes that the client wants out of the class template.

Remember when we changed the Checkbook class to accommodate a Check object? All we did was change the word "float" to "Check" in appropriate places. A class template works on the same principle, except that a class template will allow any type to be used in those appropriate places: A string, a char, an int, a float, a struct, and more can all be used for the data type. The compiler makes a class for each data type desired by the client. With this in mind, let's take a look at a class template for a Checkbook class:

```
1   // checkbook.h – a class template for a Checkbook, where the check is any data type
2
3   template <class DataType>
4   class Checkbook
5   {
6   public:
7       void setBalance( float amount );
8       bool writeCheck( DataType amount );  // returns false if amount is greater than
9                                            // balance; otherwise returns true
10      void deposit( float amount );
11      float getBalance( );
12      DataType getLastCheck( );
13      float getLastDeposit( );
14  private:
15      float balance;
16      DataType lastCheck;
```

```
17      float lastDeposit;
18  };
19
20  #include "checkbook.cpp"
```

The class template looks similar to a class. One nice advantage is that we no longer have to include a struct definition above it. The struct definition can be made in the main program. The main programmer requests that a class be made using the struct; the compiler sees the request and knows what the struct is from already seeing it in the main program; and the compiler makes the class.

A line of code needs to be added to let the compiler know that this is a class template. It is on line 3. The line is written starting with the keyword template; then, inside angle brackets, we have the keyword class, followed by a name that we choose. This is the name that will be used for the data type of the check. Sometimes people think of it as being a variable for a data type. By convention, the name is capitalized. We're going to be consistent throughout the text by using the same name, DataType, but any name like a variable name can be used here.

On lines 8, 12, and 16, the word "Check" used for the Check object is now replaced with the more general word "DataType" that we chose on line 3. DataType can be any data type: the float we used in the original class, or a Check we used recently. If it would be appropriate, it could even be some other data type, such as a string.

Finally, notice that on line 20 we include the class implementation file. This is not done when we just use a class, but we do it when we use a template.

The class implementation file for the class template is as follows:

```
21  // checkbook.cpp -- The function definitions of the class template for the Checkbook
22
23  template <class DataType>
24  void Checkbook<DataType>::setBalance( float amount )
25  {
26     balance = amount;
27  }
28
29  template <class DataType>
30  bool Checkbook<DataType>::writeCheck( DataType amount )
31  {
32     if ( amount > balance )
33          return false;
34     balance -= amount;
35     lastCheck = amount;
36     return true;
37  }
38
```

```
39   template <class DataType>
40   void Checkbook<DataType>::deposit( float amount )
41   {
42      balance += amount;
43      lastDeposit = amount;
44   }
45
46   template <class DataType>
47   float Checkbook<DataType>::getBalance( )
48   {
49      return balance;
50   }
51
52   template <class DataType>
53   DataType Checkbook<DataType>::getLastCheck( )
54   {
55      return lastCheck;
56   }
57
58   template <class DataType>
59   float Checkbook<DataType>::getLastDeposit( )
60   {
61      return lastDeposit;
62   }
```

Notice that checkbook.h is not included at the top of this file. Above each function, we must include the same template line that was written on line 3 for the class definition. Another difference is that <DataType> is added to the end of each class name in the function heading. Similarly to the way the class definition was turned into a template, wherever we had the word "Check" for a Check object in the class implementation file, it was replaced with the more general word "DataType" (lines 30 and 53).

What about the funny way we use #include for the files of a class template? At the bottom of the class specification file, we include checkbook.cpp, the class implementation file, but we don't include checkbook.h at the top of the implementation file. When we are writing just a class, we *don't* include the class implementation file at the bottom of the class specification file, but we include the specification file at the top of the implementation file. This is not always easy to remember, so let's explain the reason for this difference between a class and a class template, because there is a rule that students learn sooner or later: When you understand something, it is easier to remember it. (Interestingly, this rule itself isn't easy to remember, because it is difficult to understand why it works!)

The reason for this difference is that when we have a class template, the compiler cannot readily compile the implementation file; the class template must be made into a class first. So the implementation file is included at the bottom of the header file, essentially making a much longer header file. And if you are using Microsoft Visual C++, you don't include the implementation file in the project at all (see Appendix A), because if you did, the compiler would try to compile it right away, without making a class out of the class template first. When we are using just a class, the compiler needs to compile the implementation file, but it can't make sense out of it unless the header file is included at the top.

Some people combine the code for both the class specification file and the class implementation file into one long header file. The compiler won't complain about this, regardless of whether classes or class templates are used. When classes are used, however, the separate files have an advantage. The implementation file can be provided to the client as object code only, and the client will not be able to see how the code is written. This feature can be important for proprietary reasons, when software companies want to protect the ideas they use in their algorithms. When class templates are used, these ideas are not so easily protected. Someday, hopefully, compilers will advance to the point where they can compile the implementation file for a class template. When that happens, the existing class templates may need to be modified for such compilation. It will probably be easier to do the modification if the code is already in separate files.

Now, let's get into the nuts and the bolts of the function definitions in the template, particularly the writeCheck function:

```
29   template <class DataType>
30   bool Checkbook<DataType>::writeCheck( DataType amount )
31   {
32       if ( amount > balance )
33               return false;
34       balance -= amount;
35       lastCheck = amount;
36       return true;
37   }
```

On line 30, the client may be passing in a Check object for amount, or just a float amount, depending on what the client decides to use for DataType. Take a look at line 32, which compares the amount with the balance, because if the check is too large, the writeCheck function needs to return 'false'. But the way the operator > will work will depend on what type the client chooses for amount. If amount is a Check object, an overloaded operator > will need to be written for the client's Check struct. If amount is just a float, the > operator will work the way it normally does with floats. The same is true for the −= operator used on line 34. Whether or not it needs to have an overloaded operator function depends on what type the client decides to use for amount. This is the only function, however, in the Checkbook class in which such operators may need to have functions written for them.

The client needs to be told that these operators need to have functions written for them if the client decides to use a struct object for a check. Such comments should be placed above the class template in the class specification file, and they should look like this:

```
// to use a struct for the DataType, you must overload the following operators:
//    >        left operand: struct object      right operand: float
//             used to compare the amount of the check in the struct object with the
//             balance
//    -=       left operand: float              right operand: struct object
//             used to subtract the amount of the check in the struct object from the
//             balance
```

A description is provided about what operators need to be overloaded, what types the left and right operands are, and what the operation does. Your comments here should provide enough information for someone to write an overloaded operator. It is obvious from reading the description that there should be a data member for the amount of the check; otherwise the Checkbook class won't work for the client. It won't matter, though, what the name of the data member for the check amount is, because the client will write the overloaded operators, using the name of the data member there. No access needs to be made (or should be made) to the Check object's data members in the class.

Finally, let's take a look at a client program that uses the class template. We'll examine the first part of the client program first, which defines the struct together with overloaded operators:

```
1    #include <iostream>
2    #include <iomanip>
3    #include <string>
4    #include "checkbook.h"
5
6    using namespace std;
7
8    struct MyCheck {
9        float amt;
10       int checkNum;
11       string checkComment;
12       bool operator >( float bal )
13               { if ( amt > bal ) return true; else return false; }
14   };
15
16   void operator -=( float & bal, MyCheck ch ) { bal -= ch.amt; }
```

The $-=$ operator is a little different, so let's look at the function definition for the operator $-=$ and compare it with the line of code in the writeCheck function, where it is used:

```
balance -= amount;
```

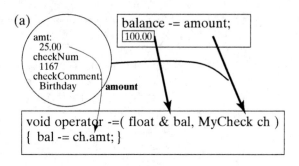

FIGURE 2.3

(a) Illustration of the way parameters are passed from the "balance −= amount;" statement in the writeCheck function. The amount object is shown on the left and is passed into the ch parameter. The balance (with a value of 100.00) is passed into the bal parameter by reference. The amt data member is set to 25, so it is subtracted from bal. (b) bal becomes 75.00, and since it was passed by reference, the 75.00 is reflected back to balance in the writeCheck function.

Recall that the returned value of a function replaces the function call—but the function call in this case is the whole line of code! A return value for the function call would have no use, so the return type for the overloaded −= function is void on line 16. We need to change the balance variable in the writeCheck function, because the check is subtracted from it. So, on line 16, we pass in the balance variable by reference, intending to change it within the operator −= function. The Check object is the right operand, so it is passed into the right parameter of the operator −= function. Then we change bal by subtracting ch.amt from it in the function body on line 16. Since bal was passed by reference from balance, the change to balance will be reflected back into the writeCheck function. This process is illustrated in Figure 2.3. The description of the −= operator in the comments above the class template give the client enough information to write such a function, but a little thought has to go into it.

Following is the rest of the client program:

```
17
18 int main( )
19   {
20     Checkbook<float> johnsCheckbook;
21     Checkbook<MyCheck> susansCheckbook;
```

```
22
23     MyCheck susansCheck;
24     float amount;
25     bool johnsCheckAccepted = false, susansCheckAccepted = false;
26
27     johnsCheckbook.setBalance( 1000 );
28     susansCheckbook.setBalance( 2000 );
29
30     cout << "John, your balance is $1000.00." << endl;
31     cout << "Susan, your balance is $2000.00." << endl;
32
33     cout << "John, enter your check amount: $";
34     cin >> amount;
35     if ( johnsCheckbook.writeCheck( amount ) ) {
36             cout << "Your check was accepted." << endl;
37             johnsCheckAccepted = true;
38             }
39     else
40             cout << "Your balance was not high enough to cover the check." << endl;
41
42     cout << "Susan, enter the check number for your check: ";
43     cin >> susansCheck.checkNum;
44     cin.ignore( );
45     cout << "Please also enter any comment you wish to make about the check: "
46             << endl;
47     getline( cin, susansCheck.checkComment );
48     cout << "Susan, enter your check amount: $";
49     cin >> susansCheck.amt;
50     if ( susansCheckbook.writeCheck( susansCheck ) ) {
51             cout << "Your check was accepted." << endl;
52             susansCheckAccepted = true;
53             }
54     else
55             cout << "Your balance was not high enough to cover the check." << endl;
56
57     cout << fixed << showpoint << setprecision( 2 );
58     cout << "John, your balance is: $"  << johnsCheckbook.getBalance( ) << endl;
59     if ( johnsCheckAccepted )
60             cout << "Your last check amount is: $" <<
61             johnsCheckbook.getLastCheck( ) << endl;
62     cout << "Susan, your balance is: $" << susansCheckbook.getBalance( ) << endl;
63     if ( susansCheckAccepted ) {
64             MyCheck testSusansCheck;
65             testSusansCheck = susansCheckbook.getLastCheck( );
```

```
66              cout << "Your last check amount was: $" << testSusansCheck.amt
67                  << endl;
68              cout << "for check number: " << testSusansCheck.checkNum << endl;
69              cout << "with check comment: " << testSusansCheck.checkComment
70                  << endl;
71          }
72
73      return 0;
74  }
```

This program doesn't do much except illustrate the mechanics of using a template, which are extremely easy. Some Checkbook objects are declared on lines 20 and 21. But these lines do more than declare Checkbook objects: They tell the compiler to make Checkbook classes from the Checkbook class template. They are similar to other declarations of objects that we have used before, but they include angle brackets after the class name, and inside the angle brackets the client includes the data type that he or she wants. That's the only difference. So when the compiler sees line 20, it makes a class out of the class template by substituting the word "float" for the word "DataType" throughout the class specification and class implementation files. The compiler makes exactly the same class that we had in Section 1.3. When the compiler sees line 21, it makes an additional class out of the class template by substituting the word "MyCheck" for the word "DataType" throughout the two class template files. This produces a class that has a struct almost similar to the one we had in Section 2.2 to except that the main programmer decided to put different information into the struct.

So John's checkbook just stores the check amount as a float, while Susan's checkbook stores the check as a MyCheck object. Notice that, for John's checkbook, all of the operators in the Checkbook object act just like regular operators. They act on two float operands, so the overloaded versions of the operators are not used. For Susan's checkbook, the overloaded operators *are* used, since, in those cases, one of the operands is a MyCheck object.

If you want, you can make more than one object from each of these classes—for example,

Checkbook<float> johnsCheckbook, samsCheckbook;

Other than on lines 20 and 21, the Checkbook object's functions are used exactly the way they were used before in our other examples. The only thing you have to keep in mind is which Checkbook stores what. On lines 33–40, we handle a check for John; on lines 42–55, we handle a check for Susan. The Checkbooks each have their own balance variables, so, finally, lines 58 and 62 show the balance for each person.

The getLastCheck function is used on lines 61 and 65, once for each checkbook. However, for John's checkbook, the function returns only a float. In Susan's checkbook, it returns a MyCheck object, from which information is obtained and printed out on lines 66–70.

Appendix A describes how to compile files when class templates are used. When you try to compile a class template as if it were a class, you will get numerous compilation errors.

As was stated earlier, all the C++ data structures in this textbook use templates, so be sure to understand the template example completely before we move on. When records of information are searched for values in data structures, the comparison operators have to be overloaded for the structs (records of information) in a similar fashion, so be sure to understand the use of the overloaded operator functions as well.

2.4   CLASSES AND ABSTRACTION

Even though you may not be ready to design a data structure yet, I think you are ready to try your hand at using one of them. Let's discuss a simple data structure called a *stack*. Think of a stack like a stack of plates, only in data structures, a stack is a stack of elements, all of the same type. Any type of element can be used for a stack: You can have a stack of strings, a stack of floats, a stack of objects, etc. You can see already how a class template comes in handy.

There are only a few things you can do with a stack. You can place an element on top of the stack; this operation is called a ***push***. You can take an element off the top of the stack, too; this operation is called a ***pop***. Get used to this terminology; it is common computer science lingo in discussions of stacks. Figure 2.4 shows a pop, while Figure 2.5 shows a push. By calling the peek function, you can get the element at the top of the stack without removing it. You can also check to see if a stack is empty. You should do this before you try to use pop or peek, unless the nature of the algorithm makes it impossible for the stack to be empty when these functions are used.

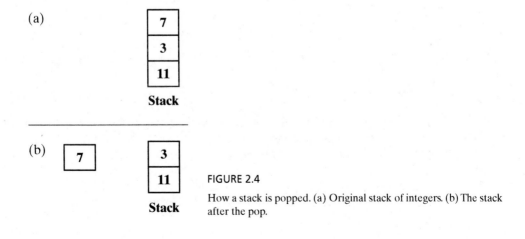

FIGURE 2.4

How a stack is popped. (a) Original stack of integers. (b) The stack after the pop.

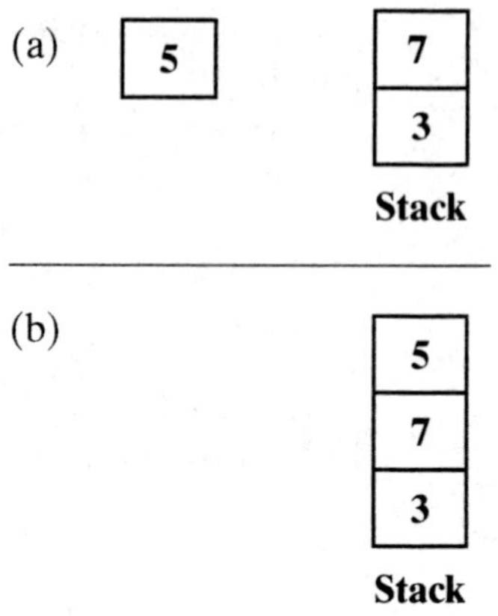

(a)

5

7
3

Stack

(b)

5
7
3

Stack

FIGURE 2.5

How an element is pushed onto a stack (a) Original stack of integers with an element 5 ready to push. (b) The stack after the push.

If you work with any elements in the middle or the bottom of a stack, you are not really working with a stack. You would have to call it something else. You wouldn't reach into the middle of a stack of plates to get a plate; you wouldn't do that with a stack of elements either.

Stacks are important for solving certain types of problems, as we shall see later. They are an important tool to have in your data structures toolbox. They are often called LIFO (last-in, first-out) data structures because the last element put into a stack is the first element to come out of it. (Think about it.) Stacks are also perhaps the simplest data structure. Accordingly, when you have a stack of objects, you don't need overloaded operator functions for those objects.

The class template for a stack is as follows:

```
1   // stack.h - the array implementation of a stack
2   #include "Array.h"
3
4   template <class DataType>
5   class Stack
6   {
7   public:
8       Stack( );
9       void push( DataType elementToPush );
10
11      // removes an element from the top of the stack and returns it in poppedElement;
12      // returns false if called on an empty stack; otherwise, returns true
13      bool pop( DataType & poppedElement );
14
15      // returns the top of the stack without removing the element
16      // returns false if called on an empty stack; otherwise, returns true
```

```
17      bool peek( DataType & poppedElement );
18      bool isEmpty( ) const;  // returns true if the stack is empty;
19                             // otherwise, returns false
20      void makeEmpty( );
21   private:
22      Array<DataType> elements;
23      int top;
24   };
25
26   #include "stack.cpp"
```

The class template has comments that explain how to use the functions (return values, etc.)

Using a stack is no harder than using the Checkbook class. For example, if we want to make a stack of floats, push a variable onto the stack, check to see if the stack is empty, and then pop a value from the stack, we would write a section of code that would look like this:

```
Stack<float> stk;
float x = 1.5, y;

stk.push(x);
if ( !stk.isEmpty( )  )
      stk.pop( y );
```

At this point, you may not be able to understand everything about how the stack class implementation works. But that won't keep you from using it. An exercise at the end of the chapter evaluates expressions by using the stack class template.

As you work on this expression evaluator, you might be glad that you don't have to think about how the stack works. You just use it. You'll have other things to think about. This is a benefit of classes called **abstraction**. For very large programs with thousands of lines of code, it would be difficult, if not impossible, to have to think about how every part of the program works every time you write a section of code. When such a large program is divided into, say, 50 classes, everything becomes a lot easier from the main programmer's perspective. The classes act like little black boxes. You have no idea of how they work, nor do you care. You just use them. You can concentrate on writing code to solve your problem, instead of diverting your attention to the code inside the classes. Abstraction occurs when you can ignore the details of how something works and just use it. It makes the development of large programs much easier, and it is a benefit of classes.

Abstraction is very important for the maintenance of our sanity in everyday life. Whenever we put our foot on the gas pedal of a car, we don't have to think about the details of what's taking place in the car's engine, such as the pistons moving faster. Instead, using the gas pedal is an abstraction; we just know that this is how to make the car go, and we do it. Without abstraction, our minds would be constantly cluttered with details that would make everyday life impossible. The same thing is true in programming: If we just use 50 or so classes without thinking about how they work, then writing large, complex programs becomes much easier.

Another example of abstraction is the use of the string data type. The string is actually a class. I'm sure you remember declaring a string such as:

string str;

and then later on using a function of the string class, such as

x = str.length( );

And the string also has an overloaded operator function: the [ ] function that you use to access elements of the string. But when you first learned about strings, you probably never knew there was a class involved; you just used them. The string is a data type, like int or float. But it is a special data type called an **abstract data type** (or **ADT**, for short). An abstract data type has functions as well as data. We don't know or think about the details of how the functions work (and sometimes we don't even know we are using functions), so that provides the abstraction.

As with the string, when a class is used for a data structure (like a stack, for example), the data structure is referred to as an abstact data type. The stack is thought of as a data type in itself (like the string), but it is abstract.

SUMMARY

Class templates are extremely important to understand. They enable the client to use any data type—objects or otherwise—for the data stored in a data structure. All of the data structures used in this textbook use class templates. Data structures wouldn't need a class template if they had a specialized use—that is, if it would only make sense to store a particular type of data within them. However, this situation is not really common.

Overloaded operators are also very important to understand, because they are commonly used for the records of information stored in C++ data structures. Data structures sometimes have to search for information, comparing values stored in their records with values that the client passes in as parameters. This comparison is done with operators like '==' and '!='. However, the records of information can be anything; therefore, these comparison operators need to have overloaded operator functions for the struct object that is being used for the records.

Classes provide a level of abstraction, making the development of large programs easier. When writing a main program, using the functions of a class, we do not need to think about the details of how the class functions work; we only need to know what they are supposed to do. Thus, when a large program is split up into 50 classes or so, the main program is considerably easier to write; our attention can be focused on solving the problem that the main program is supposed to solve, without worrying about the details of how the classes work.

EXERCISES

1. What does the function call for an overloaded operator look like?
2. Suppose that two objects of the same type are added together with the use of an overloaded operator +. Which object is the operator + function called for? How does the operator + function know about the other object?
3. Where is an overloaded operator function definition placed when the operand on the left is an object of a struct? Where is the overloaded operator function definition placed if the right operand is the object of the struct, but the left operand is not?
4. Explain how, when the right operand of an overloaded operator is the object of a struct, but the left operand is not, the parameters are passed into the overloaded operator function. Does such a function belong to the struct when the right operand is an object of the struct? Why or why not?
5. Is it possible to write two or more function definitions for the + operator and place them both in a struct definition? Why or why not?
6. What advantage(s) do we get from using a class template?
7. What causes the compiler to make a class from a class template?
8. Explain how classes are made from a class template.
9. When the client makes a struct for use in a class template, why is it that the struct definition can be placed in the main program instead of at the top of the header file for the class template?
10. What is abstraction? How do classes provide abstraction? What is an abstract data type?
11. Explain the push operation in the use of a stack. Explain the pop operation.
12. Create a Fraction struct that has a numerator and a denominator. Make an overloaded operator + for the struct that can add two Fractions and return a Fraction result. Make an overloaded * that can also multiply two Fractions together. Make an overloaded operator > that can compare two Fractions and determine whether the first one is greater than the second one. Make another overloaded operator * that has a Fraction as a first operand and an integer as a second operand, which together produce a Fraction result, and a third overloaded operator * which has an integer as a first operand and a Fraction as a second operand.
13. Create a Rectangle class template that can store the lengths of the sides (in the private section) as any DataType. Make class functions for setting the width and length of the rectangle. Make a function that will return 'true' if the length is greater than the width and 'false' otherwise. Make two other functions that will return the perimeter and area of the Rectangle. Test the Rectangle class template by using a float for DataType and a Fraction for DataType (from Exercise 12).
14. Write a program that uses a stack to evaluate postfix expressions. This is the first part of a larger program described in Exercise 15 that evaluates regular expressions. In a postfix expression, the two operands come first, followed by the operator. For example,

5 3 –

would evaluate to 2. Longer postfix expressions are evaluated by picking out any group of two operands followed by an operator, evaluating the result, and then substituting the result for the group. For example, in the postfix expression

3 4 * 8 7 3 - / / 4 +

we could pick out the group "73−" first (which one you pick first doesn't matter) and then substitute the result of 4:

3 4 * 8 4 / / 4 +

We'll take "8 4 /" next:

3 4 * 2 / 4 +

Now there is only one group that works, "3 4 *" (I told you it didn't matter):

12 2 / 4 +

Next, we can use only "12 2 /":

6 4 +

which evaluates to 10.

Two interesting things about postfix expressions are that (1) because of the way they are evaluated, you never need to consider operator precedence, and (2) since there is no consideration of operator precedence, you never need parentheses. We use parentheses only when we want to force an operation of lower precedence to be performed before an operation of higher precedence. For example, in the infix expression

2 + 3 * 4

we need to use parentheses to force the operation 2 + 3 to be done first:

(2 + 3) * 4

In postfix, the former expression would be

2 3 4 * +

while the latter expression would be

2 3 + 4 *

The order of the operands in the expression remains the same, while the positions of the operators change to determine what gets done first.

The algorithm to evaluate a postfix expression is as follows:

```
1    while the end of the postfix expression has not been reached
2            Read the next token from the postfix expression
3            if the token is a number
4                    Push the token onto the stack
5            else (the token must be an operator)
6                    Pop an element from the stack; call it operand2
7                    if operand2 is 0 and the token is a division or modulus operator
```

8   output error: Division by zero
9   stop
10   (end if)
11   Pop another element from the stack; call it operand1
12   Perform the operation: operand1 token operand2
13   Push the result of the operation onto the stack
14   (end else)
15   (end while)
16   Pop the stack (the popped element is the answer)

The algorithm starts at the beginning of the postfix expression. On line 2, if no token has been read thus far, the next token is assumed to be the first token. When the token read from the postfix expression is an operator, say, '−', it will be used for a calculation. Let's suppose that operand2 popped from the stack on line 6 is 8 and operand1 popped from the stack on line 11 is 10. If the token is the '−' operator, line 12 says that the operation 10 − 8 is to be performed, giving us a result of 2. Then, on line 13, the 2 is pushed onto the stack.

The algorithm could use a stack of int's or float's, depending on what is expected from the instructor. If you are reading numbers that have negative signs or numbers that have more than one digit, you will need to find a way to convert such strings to numbers. If each number is only one positive digit, you can easily convert the character digit to an integer to push onto the stack by using an expression such as:

int x = ch − '0';

where ch is the character for the digit read from the postfix string. This expression actually takes the ASCII value in ch and subtracts the ASCII value of character '0'. Since the ASCII values are sequential from '0' to '9', this subtraction works to give the right integer value.

The Stack class uses the Array class, which will be discussed in Chapter 5. All you need to know for now is that the Array.h and Array.cpp files must be in the same folder that you place the stack.h and stack.cpp files in and Array.h should be included in the project. For the main program, just include stack.h, not Array.h, at the top. The Stack class and Array class can be found in the ch8ex1 folder for Chapter 8.

15. Let's consider the following problem: We wish to have the user enter an expression that contains numbers, operators, and parentheses into the computer. Our program will then evaluate the result. There are two challenges, however. One is that our program must account for operator precedence. That is, if the user enters

2 + 3 * 5

the 3 must be multiplied by the 5 before the 2 is added, because multiplication takes precedence over addition. The second challenge is that there is no limit to the number of nested parentheses that may be used. Two levels of parentheses would look like this:

5 * ((2 + 4 * 5) / 2 + 9)

Parentheses can be nested inside each other with as many levels as the user wishes.

Writing such a program would ordinarily be a horrible experience. However, there is an algorithm involving stacks that solves the problem nicely. The preceding expressions are called *infix* expressions. In an infix expression, the binary operator has one operand on the left and one operand on the right. Our algorithm will first convert such infix expressions to *postfix* expressions.

The algorithm to turn an infix expression into a postfix expression is as follows:

```
1    Push a '(' onto the stack
2    Add a ')' to the end of the infix expression
3    while the stack is not empty
4            Read the next token from the infix expression.
5            if the token is a '('
6                    Push the token onto the stack
7            else if the token is a number
8                    Add the number to the end of the postfix expression
9            else if the token is a ')'
10                   Pop the element c from the stack
11                   while c is not a '('
12                           Place c at the end of the postfix expression
13                           Pop another element c from the stack
14                   (end while)
15           else (the token must be an operator)
16                   while the top of the stack is an operator with precedence greater than or
17                   equal to the token
18                           Pop the element c from the stack
19                           Put c at the end of the postfix expression
20                   (end while)
21                   Push the token onto the stack.
22           (end else)
23   (end while)
```

This algorithm assumes that the infix expression is written correctly. On line 4, the token is either a number, an operator, a '(', or a ')'. If no token has been read from the infix expression thus far, it is assumed that "next token" refers to the first token. Likewise, on line 8, if the postfix expression is empty thus far, adding to the end of the postfix expression means just placing it into the postfix expression.

Lines 10–14 keep popping elements from the stack until a '(' is encountered. One must be encountered, because one was pushed on line 1. Therefore, it is not necessary to check whether the stack is empty before popping. (Ordinarily, it might be.) Take note that when a '(' is finally popped from the stack, nothing is done with it. Remember that the '(' and ')' aren't used in postfix expressions.

When the while loop on lines 16–20 executes, the token is an operator. This loop continues popping elements from the stack until the top of the stack either (1) is not an operator or (2) has a precedence less than the token operator. After the while loop terminates, the token is pushed onto the stack on line 21.

Once the infix expression has been converted to a postfix expression, the result of Exercise 14 can be used to evaluate the postfix expression. You would be expected to use stacks of two different data types to solve this problem, one for the current exercise and one for Exercise 14. In the algorithm of the current exercise, you can use a stack of char's.

Make sure that you can go through a fairly long example by hand before you try to put the algorithms into code. The first step in coding the solution to a problem is to understand the solution.

CHAPTER 3

More about Classes

Our Checkbook class that we've been looking at was a little better at the end of Chapter 2 than it was at the beginning of Chapter 1. It is still missing some important ingredients, however. In this chapter, we will cover more basics about classes that are essential to data structures and apply them to the familiar Checkbook class so that they can be easily understood.

3.1   THE CONST SPECIFIER

One ingredient that is considered to be good programming practice is the use of const in the function heading. If you look back at the Stack template in Section 2.4, you will see const used at the end of the isEmpty function prototype on line 18. When const is used in this manner, it tells the compiler that when the function executes, no changes will be made to the data members of the class. At first blush, that doesn't seem to be so important. But it is a good tool to help debug classes when classes are being implemented. Let's examine why.

Suppose we have a variable called numDependents in the private section of a Tax class. In a class function called threeDependents, we would like to compare numDependents to see if it is equal to 3. However, suppose we make a mistake when we write the if heading:

if (numDependents = 3)

Instead of using the equality operator '==', we accidentally use the assignment operator '='. Has this happened to you? Do you know what will happen next? Normally, the compiler won't think that anything is wrong with this if heading. That's because the assignment operator produces a result which is substituted for the expression "numDependents = 3". That's right: It doesn't just assign 3 to numDependents; it produces a result, just as 3 + 4 produces the result 7. The result of an assignment happens to be whatever is assigned to the left side. So, when the if statement is executed, it does two things: It assigns 3 to numDependents and then it evaluates to

if (3)

In C++, any nonzero number is regarded as true, so the compiler thinks that the if statement is fine and the condition will always be true when written with this mistake. Thus, the mistake becomes a runtime error.

Let's suppose that the threeDependents function is supposed to return true if numDependents is 3 and is supposed to return false otherwise. Obviously, that function does not intend to change any data members in the private section. But it does change one accidentally with the incorrectly written if condition. If we use const at the end of the function heading, we are telling the compiler that no changes should be made to the data members of the class. If there are changes that take place by mistakes in code, the compiler will catch them and give a compiler error. That way, our mistaken if heading produces a compiler error instead of a runtime error. You know from experience that it is a lot easier to fix a compiler error than it is to fix a runtime error. Therefore, using const at the end of function headings is considered good programming practice when the function should not change any data members in the private section. The const specifier should be at the end of the function prototype in the class definition and also at the end of the function heading in the class implementation file.

When the const specifier is used on a function heading, nothing changes about the way the function is called. The main program continues to call the function without using const in the function call.

There is another use of const that is noteworthy. When we pass objects as parameters (whether they are struct objects or class objects), a common practice is to pass them by reference whenever possible. The reason for passing by reference (when passing by value would suffice) is that objects can be quite large, full of data members. When the object is passed by value, a copy of it is made, which means that each and every data member is copied over. For large objects, this can be a bit time consuming, so we get a little performance boost when we pass by reference. (Only the address of the object is copied over.)

This said, if the object does not need to change inside the function, the parameter should be preceded by const in the function heading. If it is not preceded by const and the object changes, the change will be reflected back to the calling function (since it was passed by reference), and the mistake will turn into a runtime error. By contrast, if the object parameter is preceded by const and we inadvertently change the object in the function, the mistake will be a compiler error instead of a runtime error. This type of parameter passing is often called passing by **const reference**.

To summarize,

- *Pass by reference* if the object needs to change inside the function and such changes should be reflected back to the calling function.

- *Pass by value* if the object needs to change inside the function and such changes should *not* be reflected back to the calling function.
- *Pass by const reference* if the object does not need to change inside the function. (This approach will give a performance boost and turn a possible runtime error into a compiler error.)

Using const, the class specification file for the Checkbook class is as follows, with changes in bold:

```
1    // checkbook.h – a class template for a Checkbook, where the check is any data type
2
3    // to use a struct for the DataType, you must overload the following operators:
4    //      >       left operand:  struct object    right operand:  float
5    //              used to compare the amount of the check in the struct object with the
6    //              balance
7    //      -=      left operand:  float            right operand:  struct object
8    //              used to subtract the amount of the check in the struct object from the
9    //              balance
10
11   template <class DataType>
12   class Checkbook
13   {
14   public:
15       void setBalance( float amount );
16       bool writeCheck( const DataType & amount );  // returns false if amount is greater than
17                                          // balance; otherwise returns true
18       void deposit( float amount );
19       float getBalance( ) const;
20       DataType getLastCheck( ) const;
21       float getLastDeposit( ) const;
22   private:
23       float balance;
24       DataType lastCheck;
25       float lastDeposit;
26   };
27
28   #include "checkbook.cpp"
```

On line 16, we are passing in amount by const reference, since it could be a large object (depending on what the client uses for DataType) and it does not need to change inside the writeCheck function. The const specifier is used at the end of the function prototypes on lines 19–21 to indicate that these functions should not change any data members of the class. If they do, compiler errors will result. The class implementation file is not shown, but all function headings will match the function prototypes in their use of const.

3.2 CONSTRUCTORS

Another important ingredient of a class is something called a *constructor*. Every class has to have at least one constructor. If one is not written by the programmer, then a constructor that does nothing is supplied by the compiler automatically.

A constructor is a function of a class, but it is an unusual function, for a number of reasons. For one thing, it doesn't have a return type, not even void. If a return type is put in by the programmer, a compiler error will promptly result. For another thing, the name of the constructor *must be* the name of the class; you have no choice. The third quality of a constructor that makes it unusual is the way it is called. It is called only when an object of the class is declared. So, if we have an object declared with a statement such as

Checkbook cbook;

then the statement will automatically call the constructor function for the cbook object (in the Checkbook class). So now you know that such a line of code does two things: It declares an object, and it calls the constructor of the cbook object. There is no other way to call a constructor besides declaring an object of a class.

A constructor is always called when you declare an object of a class. If you don't write a constructor into a class (we didn't in Chapters 1 and 2), a constructor that does nothing will automatically be supplied by the compiler. Then this supplied constructor will be called when an object of the class is declared. If you want a constructor that does nothing, it is considered good programming practice to write the constructor in yourself instead of leaving it out. (It was left out initially because I was being kind in my introduction to classes.) The reason a constructor should always be written (even one that does nothing) is that it becomes clear that you intended to write the constructor that way; you didn't just forget to write one. The prototype for a constructor that does nothing would look like this in the Checkbook class:

Checkbook( );

In the class implementation file, the function definition for a constructor that does nothing would look like this:

```
Checkbook::Checkbook( )
{
}
```

Notice that the return type is absent, as it should be with constructors. However, the function heading is the same as other class function headings: It consists of the class name, followed by two colons, followed by the function name. In this case, however, the constructor name must be the same as the class name—hence the repetition.

You can write almost any code in the constructor that you would in any other function, and you should feel free to do so. The innocent-looking declaration of an object can end up executing hundreds of lines if the constructor is that long. Most often, however, constructors are rather short. They are commonly used just to initialize the data members of the private class if it is appropriate to do so.

Let's put this constructor idea into our Checkbook class:

```
1   // checkbook.h – a class template for a Checkbook, where the check is any data type
2
3   // to use a struct for the DataType, you must overload the following operators:
4   //   >          left operand:  struct object    right operand:  float
5   //              used to compare the amount of the check in the struct object with the
6   //              balance
7   //   -=         left operand:  float          right operand:  struct object
8   //              used to subtract the amount of the check in the struct object from the
9   //              balance
10
11  template <class DataType>
12  class Checkbook
13  {
14  public:
15      Checkbook( );
16      Checkbook( float initBalance );
17      void setBalance( float amount );
18      bool writeCheck( const DataType & amount );  // returns false if amount is greater than
19                                    // balance; otherwise returns true
20      void deposit( float amount );
21      float getBalance( ) const;
22      DataType getLastCheck( ) const;
23      float getLastDeposit( ) const;
24  private:
25      float balance;
26      DataType lastCheck;
27      float lastDeposit;
28  };
29
30  #include "checkbook.cpp"
```

Line 15 shows the function prototype for the constructor, which is typically placed first in the public section. Parameters can be passed into constructors as well. A second constructor was written for this class on line 16 that passes in an initial value for the balance. This is an alternative to calling the setBalance function, and it provides a benefit for the main programmer, who can then set the initial balance with one less line of code. (There is no need to use the setBalance function.)

More than one constructor can be made for a class, as long as either (1) the number of parameters passed in is different or (2) at least one of the parameters has a different data type. In other words, the function prototypes for the constructors have to be different.

It may seem surprising that a parameter can be passed into a constructor, since a constructor can be called only by the declaration of an object. The notation for passing the parameter is added to the declaration, and it is rather simple, although strange looking:

Checkbook<float> cbook(1000);

It looks strange because cbook looks like the name of a function instead of the name of an object. However, it only looks that way. This is just the way the notation is for passing a parameter into a constructor. If we need to pass more than one parameter into a constructor, the parameters are separated by commas, just as they are with any other function call. We can also declare two or more objects on the same line:

Checkbook<float> cbook1(150), cbook2(346);

A constructor does not always need to have parameters passed into it in order to initialize data members in the private section. For example, suppose we have a data member called count that counts the number of times a certain class function is called. We can increment count at the beginning of this function. We would want to set it to 0 in the constructor; such a constructor need not have parameters. A constructor with no parameters is called a ***default constructor***, whether or not it initializes any data members. The default constructor for our Checkbook class would be called like this:

Checkbook<float> cbook;

The part of the class implementation file that contains the function definitions for the constructors is as follows:

```
1    // checkbook.cpp — The function definitions of the class template for the Checkbook
2
3    template <class DataType>
4    Checkbook<DataType>::Checkbook( )
5    {
6    }
7
8    template <class DataType>
9    Checkbook<DataType>::Checkbook( float initBalance )
10   {
11        balance = initBalance;
12   }
```

The function definition for the constructor that accepts no parameters is on lines 3–6. It does nothing. The function definition for the constructor that accepts an initial balance parameter is shown on lines 8–12. It looks the way you would expect it to look, setting the balance in the private section of the class.

Following is a simple program that uses the second constructor:

```
1   #include <iostream>
2   #include <iomanip>
3   #include "checkbook.h"
4
5   using namespace std;
6
7   int main( )
8   {
9    float bal;
10   cout << "Enter your initial balance: ";
11   cin >> bal;
12
13   Checkbook<float> cbook( bal );
14
15   cbook.deposit( 500.00 );
16   cbook.writeCheck( 25.00 );
17
18   cout << fixed << showpoint << setprecision( 2 );
19   cout << "The balance is now: $" << cbook.getBalance( ) << endl;
20
21   return 0;
22  }
```

Lines 10–11 ask the user to enter an initial balance named bal. Then bal is passed into the constructor on line 13, where the cbook object is declared.

3.3   CLASS MODIFICATION

Since we are setting the initial balance with the use of a constructor, should we remove the setBalance function from the class definition? And why do we have a constructor that does nothing? Should we eliminate this constructor as well? Well, we are just playing a learning game here, but when you modify a class, you should avoid removing functions. In modifying a class, your goal is to improve the class while providing backwards compatibility with the (potentially) hundreds of client programs that are still using the old class. So a client program that is using your old class should still be able to compile and run correctly with your new class.

Consider that your old Checkbook class may be placed into a library. Hundreds of clients write programs using the old class. Then, an updated, improved library that happens to include your new Checkbook class replaces the old library. In your new Checkbook class, you've decided to remove the setBalance function and the constructor that does nothing. A client decides to make some small change to his or her old main program, maybe asking the user for an extra piece of information. The client recompiles the old program with the new library, only to get errors in the program. The errors come about because the client has a couple of lines of code that look like this:

```
Checkbook<float> cbook;
```

.

.

.

```
cbook.setBalance( bal );
```

This is very frustrating; it didn't even have anything to do with what the client was changing in the main program. Accordingly, when you modify a class, make sure that the old client code will still work. It worked before; let it keep working.

Here is one thing you have to watch out for in keeping your class backward compatible with old client code: If you switch from a class to a class template, everyone's client code will have to change, because the declaration of objects is different. You need to decide early on whether to make a class or a class template, and be careful with your decision.

3.4 MODIFYING THE CHECKBOOK CLASS TO KEEP A HISTORY OF CHECKS

Let's consider making another improvement to our Checkbook class. This time, we want to keep a history of checks that were written. After all, what kind of checkbook is it if we can get information only about the last check? Well, we could handle the change by replacing lastCheck with an array declared in the private section and that looks like this:

```
DataType checks[ 5 ];
```

The old client programs can't access the data in the private section, so we won't need to worry about our clients modifying their code on account of this change. Recall from Chapter 1 that this is the very reason for using the private section: It allows us to change the way our data is represented without affecting clients.

The new class template for Checkbook is as follows:

```
1   // checkbook.h – a class template for a Checkbook, where the check is any data type
2
3   // to use a struct for the DataType, you must overload the following operators:
4   //  >        left operand: struct object   right operand: float
5   //           used to compare the amount of the check in the struct object with the
6   //           balance
7   //  -=       left operand: float           right operand: struct object
8   //           used to subtract the amount of the check in the struct object from the
9   //           balance
10
11  const int CAPACITY = 5;
```

```
12
13  // The templates for an associated CheckInfo and Checkbook must match in
14  // DataType
15  template <class DataType>
16  struct CheckInfo {
17      int numChecks;
18      DataType checks[ CAPACITY ];
19  };
20
21  template <class DataType>
22  class Checkbook
23  {
24  public:
25    Checkbook( );
26    Checkbook( float initBalance );
27    void setBalance( float amount );
28    bool writeCheck( const DataType & amount );  // returns false if amount is greater than
29                               // balance; otherwise returns true
30    void deposit( float amount );
31    float getBalance( ) const;
32    DataType getLastCheck( ) const;
33    // getLastChecks returns up to CAPACITY checks in a CheckInfo struct
34    // the number of checks is also in the CheckInfo struct
35    // checks in the checks array are stored in order, with the latest check first
36    CheckInfo<DataType> getLastChecks( ) const;
37    float getLastDeposit( ) const;
38  private:
39    float balance;
40    int numChecks;  // the number of checks stored in the array
41    int lastIndex;  // the index of the last check that was written
42    DataType lastChecks[ CAPACITY ];  // saves up to CAPACITY checks
43    float lastDeposit;
44  };
45
46  #include "checkbook.cpp"
```

A CheckInfo struct has been defined before the class template on lines 15–19. When the client wants information about his or her checks, the information stored in the Checkbook object will be placed into an object of the CheckInfo struct and returned. Notice that the checks array on line 42 is of type DataType, whatever the client chooses for the class template. Therefore, the CheckInfo struct has to be templated as well, as shown on line 15. This means that more than one struct can be made from the struct template, similarly to the way more than one class can be made from a class template. There is a comment on lines 13–14 that tells the client to use the same DataType for an associated CheckInfo struct and Checkbook class in the client program.

The client is still free to make more than one type of class from the class template. However, for each class that he or she makes by using a certain type, the same type must be utilized to make a CheckInfo struct that is to be used with that class. The use of the template in the declarations of struct objects and class objects is the same.

A new function called getLastChecks is added on line 36. This function returns all the checks that have been written, up to the number defined by CAPACITY on line 11. The getLastChecks function will place the information about checks into a CheckInfo object and return it. Notice that the return type is CheckInfo<DataType>, which means that the CheckInfo object is made from a struct with the same DataType that the class is made from.

The getLastCheck function is still there on line 32, for clients that would like to use it (or clients that already are using it in older programs).

In the private section, an array has replaced the lastCheck variable that used to be there. There is an extra variable called numChecks that keeps track of the number of checks stored in the array and an extra variable called lastIndex that keeps track of the lastIndex of the lastChecks array, which has been filled with a check. So if only three checks have been written, lastIndex will be 2. It may seem redundant to have both of these variables, but the capacity of the checks array is only 5. If more than five checks are written, we will start writing at the beginning of the array again, so we can store the last five checks that were written. The highest value that numChecks can be, therefore, is 5. So if seven checks are written, numChecks will be 5, but lastIndex will be 1. This is called a *circular array*, and it is illustrated in Figure 3.1.

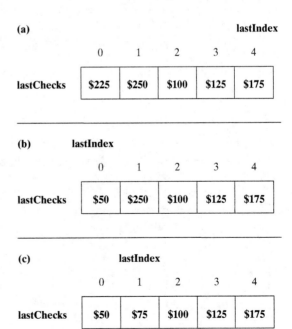

FIGURE 3.1

A circular array in which the last five checks will be stored into the lastChecks array. (a) The array is full of checks, and lastIndex has been set to 4. (b) A new check of $50 has to be written, so lastIndex becomes 0 and the new check amount overwrites the oldest check amount in the array. c) Another check of $75 is written, so lastIndex is incremented, and this check amount overwrites the oldest check amount in the array.

The new class implementation file for Checkbook will now be examined, beginning with the top section that includes the constructors:

```
47   // checkbook.cpp — The function definitions of the class template for the Checkbook
48
49   template <class DataType>
50   Checkbook<DataType>::Checkbook( )
51   {
52      lastIndex = -1;
53      numChecks = 0;
54   }
55
56   template <class DataType>
57   Checkbook<DataType>::Checkbook( float initBalance )
58   {
59      balance = initBalance;
60      lastIndex = -1;
61      numChecks = 0;
62   }
```

The constructors are the same, except that we now set lastIndex to −1 and numChecks to 0 in both. The reason for the −1 setting in lastIndex is that when we write a new check, we are going to increment lastIndex first and then use lastIndex as the index for the lastChecks array. So the first check that is written will be placed in array position 0.

The setBalance function remains unchanged:

```
63   template <class DataType>
64   void Checkbook<DataType>::setBalance( float amount )
65   {
66      balance = amount;
67   }
```

But some changes were made to the writeCheck function:

```
68   template <class DataType>
69   bool Checkbook<DataType>::writeCheck( const DataType & amount )
70   {
71      if ( amount > balance )
72            return false;
73      balance -= amount;
74
75      lastIndex++;
76      if ( lastIndex == CAPACITY )
77            lastIndex = 0;
78      lastChecks[ lastIndex ] = amount;
79      if ( numChecks != CAPACITY )
80            numChecks++;
```

```
81
82      return true;
83  }
```

Lines 68–74 are the same. But now, instead of saving amount to lastCheck, we must place it in the array. On line 75 we increment lastIndex first, as we said we were going to. If lastIndex is equal to CAPACITY, then we need to start writing checks at the beginning of the array again, so lastIndex is set to 0 on line 77. The amount is placed into the array on line 78. (Notice that this could be a struct assignment, which is valid: Each element of the array could be a struct object.) Finally, since numChecks is the number of checks stored in the array, we increment it on line 80 only if it has not exceeded CAPACITY.

The deposit and getBalance functions remain unchanged:

```
84   template <class DataType>
85   void Checkbook<DataType>::deposit( float amount )
86   {
87           balance += amount;
88           lastDeposit = amount;
89   }
90
91   template <class DataType>
92   float Checkbook<DataType>::getBalance( ) const
93   {
94           return balance;
95   }
```

But we need to write the getLastCheck function a little differently:

```
96   template <class DataType>
97   DataType Checkbook<DataType>::getLastCheck( ) const
98   {
99           return lastChecks[ lastIndex ];
100  }
```

Now the last check is stored at the position lastIndex, so this position is the one we return.

The getLastChecks function is a new function:

```
101  // getLastChecks returns up to CAPACITY checks
102  // checks in the info.checks array are stored in order, with the latest check first
103  // info.numChecks is the number of checks that are returned
104  template <class DataType>
105  CheckInfo<DataType> Checkbook<DataType>::getLastChecks( ) const
106  {
107      CheckInfo<DataType> info;
108      info.numChecks = numChecks;
```

```
109
110    for ( int i = 0, j = lastIndex; i < numChecks; i++, j— — ) {
111            if ( j == -1 )
112                    j = CAPACITY - 1;
113            info.checks[ i ] = lastChecks[ j ];
114    }
115
116    return info;
117 }
```

The checks are placed into the client's array (in the CheckInfo<DataType> object) in order, with the latest check first. This is opposite to the way they are saved. We save them in such a way that it makes it easy for us to update the array when a new check is written. When we return them to the client, we return them in the order that the client would be most interested in, with the latest check first. The interface (functions in the public section) is often involved in this kind of *data translation*. That is another purpose of the interface: to translate data between the form that is most useful for the client and the form that is most useful for the class designer. Let's take a look at the getLastChecks function to see how it works.

First, on line 108, the number of checks is provided (as a convenience to the client). Then, on line 110, the for loop initializes i to 0 for the client's array (info.checks), and initializes j to lastIndex, which is the latest check in our array (lastChecks). In the first iteration of the for loop, we write the latest check into the first position of the client's array on line 113. Then, in the heading of the for loop, we increment i to go to the next position in the client's array and we decrement j so that j will be the next-to-the-latest check in our array. Because we are using a circular array, it is possible that, when we decrement j, it becomes −1; then the next check that we need to save to the client's array is at the end of our lastChecks array. Therefore, on line 112, we start index j at the back of our lastChecks array. We keep iterating through the for loop until the number of checks stored (numChecks) has been written into the client's array. Figure 3.2 gives an example of how the for loop saves the client's checks.

Finally, the getLastDeposit function remains unchanged:

```
118   template <class DataType>
119   float Checkbook<DataType>::getLastDeposit( ) const
120   {
121           return lastDeposit;
122   }
```

Notice that in the class specification file on line 11 we set a constant integer called CAPACITY to 5, which sets the size of the array. This is a useful technique, since the size of an array, in addition to the declaration of the arrays on lines 18 and 42, can be used throughout the code. We use CAPACITY, for example, in the

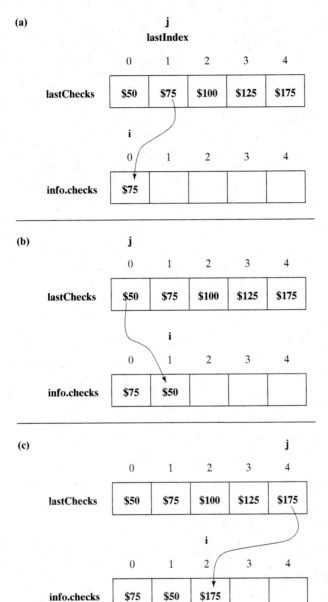

FIGURE 3.2

(a) The lastChecks array from Figure 3.1c with lastIndex set to 1 and numChecks == 5. The checks need to be supplied to the client from the latest check to the oldest check, so they are to be placed into the client's array (info.checks) in the order $75, $50, $175, $125, and $100. The index j will be used for the lastChecks array and is set to lastIndex, while the index i will be used for the info.checks array and is set to 0. The $75 amount is copied from the lastChecks array (at index j) to the info.checks array (at index i). (b) Index j is decremented, while index i is incremented. The $50 amount is copied over. (c) Index j is decremented, but this time it becomes −1. So index j is reset to CAPACITY −1 (or 4) inside the for loop. Index i has been incremented, so the $175 amount is copied over.

writeCheck function on lines 76 and 79. We also use CAPACITY in the get-LastChecks function on line 112. Finally, we use CAPACITY in the comments on lines 33, 42, and 101. If we did not use the CAPACITY constant and used numbers instead, then it would be inconvenient to make a change to the size of the array. We would have to go throughout the code and the comments, making changes. By using

(d)

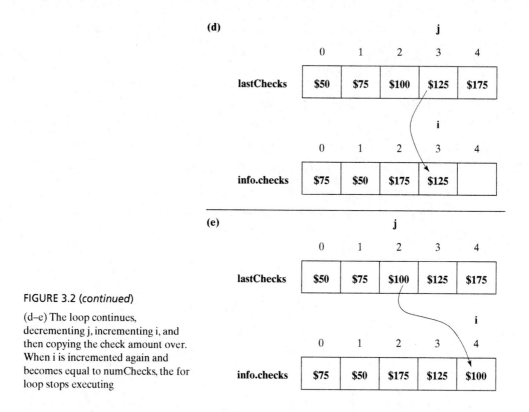

FIGURE 3.2 (*continued*)

(d–e) The loop continues, decrementing j, incrementing i, and then copying the check amount over. When i is incremented again and becomes equal to numChecks, the for loop stops executing

the CAPACITY constant, we need to make only one change in order to change the array size. That change occurs on line 11 of the class specification file.

Following is an example of a main program that uses the new class:

```
123    // useCheckbook.cpp – A program for using the Checkbook class
124
125    #include <iostream>
126    #include <iomanip>
127    #include "checkbook.h"
128
129    using namespace std;
130
131    int menu( );
132
133    const int CHECK = 1, DEPOSIT = 2, BALANCE = 3, QUIT = 4;
134
135    int main( )
136    {
137       float balance;
138       cout << "Enter the initial balance: $";
```

```
139    cin >> balance;
140    Checkbook<float> cb( balance );
141    float amount;
142    int choice;
143    bool checkAccepted = false;
144
145    cout << fixed << showpoint << setprecision( 2 );
146    choice = menu( );
147    while ( choice != QUIT ) {
148        if ( choice == CHECK ) {
149                cout << "Enter check amount: $";
150                cin >> amount;
151                if ( cb.writeCheck( amount ) ) {
152                        cout << "Check accepted." << endl;
153                        checkAccepted = true;
154                        }
155                else {
156                        cout << "Your balance is not high ";
157                        cout << "enough for that check." << endl;
158                        }
159                }
160        else if ( choice == DEPOSIT ) {
161                cout << "Enter deposit amount: $";
162                cin >> amount;
163                cb.deposit( amount );
164                cout << "Deposit accepted." << endl;
165                }
166        else {   // must be a balance request
167                amount = cb.getBalance( );
168                cout << "Your balance is: $" << amount << endl;
169                }
170
171        choice = menu( );
172        }
173
174    if (  checkAccepted ) {
175        cout << "Your last check was: $" << cb.getLastCheck( ) << endl;
176        CheckInfo<float> ci;
177        ci = cb.getLastChecks( );
178        if ( ci.numChecks > 1 ) {
179                cout << "Your last checks are:" << endl;
180                for ( int i = 0; i < ci.numChecks; i++ )
181                        cout << "$" << ci.checks[ i ] << endl;
182                }
183        }
```

```
184
185      return 0;
186   }
187
188   int menu( )
189   {
190      int choice;
191
192      cout << endl;
193      cout << "1     Write a check" << endl;
194      cout << "2     Make a deposit" << endl;
195      cout << "3     Get the balance" << endl;
196      cout << "4     Quit" << endl << endl;
197      cout << "Enter a number between 1 and 4: ";
198      cin >> choice;
199      return choice;
200   }
```

This main program is similar to one written in Section 1.3. The user chooses the same options from the menu and the program carries them out. There are a couple of differences, however. We make use of the second constructor on line 140, after getting the balance from the user. Then, after the user selects the QUIT option, some information about the checks is provided on lines 175–181. The last check is printed out on line 175. Then a CheckInfo object is declared, with CheckInfo<float> used to make a struct with a float array. Since there is only one type of Checkbook class, the client must make the CheckInfo struct with the same type (float in this case) or get a compilation error. A CheckInfo object is returned from the getLastChecks function on line 116, and it is assigned to the ci object. The CheckInfo object contains the number of checks (numChecks), as well as an array of the checks. The number of checks is made use of in the condition of the for loop on line 180. This is, in fact, the reason it was supplied: It makes looping easier for the client. The body of the for loop prints out each check in the check array.

Now, consider all of the client programs that may have been made with the older version of our class. Notice that all of the old programs of our clients will still compile with our new class, *because we have been careful not to change the function prototypes of the functions that they have been using.* If we make a change to a prototype, such as adding another parameter, then clients' code will not compile because the compiler will complain that they need another parameter. We've carefully left the getLastCheck function in for our client's old programs, on line 32. We've had to change the function definition of getLastCheck, but our clients' programs know nothing about that change. They just make the function call and they get the right result. That's all they want. A client might make a small change to his or her main program and then recompile it. If they recompile it with the latest version of a library that has the latest version of our class, and if our class has not been carefully written, the client's program will have compilation errors that weren't there before.

At this point it is appropriate to ask the question "What changes can we make to the interface (i.e., the public section) of a class?" The interface is a delicate part of the program. It communicates between the main program and an object of the class. The changes that can be made are really not that many. We can change the void return type of a function to some other type, because no compiler errors will be incurred if the client neither uses the value that is returned from a function nor assigns it to anything. We can remove or add the const specifier on a function heading if needed. We can change a parameter that was passed by value so that it is passed by const reference. We can always add new function prototypes to an interface. Functions do not need to be used; if they are not used, they don't become a part of the machine code of the program. Beyond this, you must be very careful with any changes you make. If you absolutely must make changes to an interface that would prevent old client programs from compiling, it may be best just to make a new class and leave the old class in the library. If clients would like to make use of your new function or your new class, that is one thing; they can rewrite their code to do it. If clients are already happy with the way their program works, that is something else.

SUMMARY

In this chapter we've examined important ingredients of classes, such as const specifiers and constructors. These weren't provided in the classes of the first two chapters, just to make things simpler at the beginning. However, every class should use const specifiers (when appropriate), and every class should have one or more constructors.

We've also looked at what is involved when we want to change a class. We should always try to keep the class backwards compatible for our clients. We should not eliminate functions or make any changes to the public section that will cause compilation problems with old client code. The main modifications to a class should be the addition of new functions, changes in the private section, and/or changes in the function bodies.

EXERCISES

1. Explain how const specifiers aid in debugging.
2. What is passing by const reference? Why should we use it?
3. How is a constructor called? Is a constructor called when the class programmer doesn't write a constructor? Why or why not?
4. In what ways does a constructor differ from other functions?
5. Can more than one constructor be made for a class? If so, how must the constructors differ?
6. What is the purpose of a constructor? (What is it used for?)
7. Suppose a class Foo is written with just one constructor. The constructor just passes in two integer parameters. Declare an object called f, of the Foo class, that passes the integer parameters 5 and 7 into the constructor.
8. In modifying a class, what can we change about the class (including the interface) in order to keep it backwards compatible with old client code?

9. If you need to make a change to a class that would affect old clients' code, what would be a reasonable alternative?

10. Add const specifiers and a constructor to the Road class of Chapter 1, Exercise 17. Have the constructor pass in two parameters, for the width and length of the road. Why should you not remove the functions for setting the width and the length of the road?

11. Add const specifiers and a constructor to the Temperature class of Chapter 1, Exercise 18. The constructor should pass in two parameters; the first parameter is the temperature, and the second parameter is a flag that indicates whether the first parameter is in Fahrenheit or Celsius.

12. Add const specifiers and two constructors to the Time class of Chapter 1, Exercise 19. One constructor passes in no parameters and does nothing. The second constructor should pass in three parameters, for hours, minutes, and seconds.

13. Add const specifiers and two constructors to the Rectangle class template of Chapter 2, Exercise 13. The first constructor passes in no parameters and does nothing. The second constructor passes in the width and the length of the rectangle.

CHAPTER 4

Pointers and Dynamic Arrays

Let's talk about a problem that exists with the last class presented in Section 3.4. Once we set CAPACITY, we should not set it to something different for a new library. It may prevent old client programs from working correctly if they are recompiled. But what should we set the array size to? Would all the clients be happy with an array size of 10? Would they all be happy with an array size of 100? Maybe we should set the array size to 10,000. Well, . . . that might satisfy a lot of clients, but probably most clients would use only a small part of that array—and that array sure could waste a lot of memory space, especially if each element is a Check object.

What would be ideal is an array that can adjust its size—that is, an array that gets larger with the more checks that are written. Such an array can get filled only if you run out of RAM memory that can be used for the array's capacity. Now, if you've learned anything about arrays, you are probably shaking your head. But don't shake it too much; you should be nodding it instead, because this kind of array is possible. In fact, adjustable arrays are often used in data structures and can even be used in main programs. It just requires a little "magic." The magic comes about by two things: a *pointer* and *dynamically allocated memory*. Welcome to the wonderful world of pointers!

4.1 POINTERS

It would do no good to discuss dynamically allocated memory without first discussing a pointer. So what *is* a pointer? Well, a pointer is a variable. (Are you breathing a sigh of relief?) As you know from past experience, a variable can store a data type if it is declared with that data type. An int variable can store integers, a char variable can store characters, etc. So what does a pointer store? A pointer stores an *address*—a binary number that the operating system uses to identify a memory cell of RAM, just as a person's address identifies where he or she lives. Every memory cell has an address. Memory is *byte addressable*, meaning that every byte of memory has an address (but every bit does not).

A pointer is used to store the address of a variable or an object whose data type is used to declare the pointer. For example, the declaration of a pointer that can store the address of an integer looks like this:

```
int *ptr;
```

And the declaration of a pointer that can store the address of a char looks like this:

```
char *chptr;
```

The first part of the declaration is the data type of the variable or object whose address can be stored by the pointer. Then there must be an asterisk in front of the pointer. Finally, there is the pointer name that you choose, as you would choose any other variable name.

Often, programmers will declare a pointer like this:

```
int* ptr;
```

They put the asterisk next to the data type, as if the data type and the asterisk were collectively a pointer data type. This code is accepted by the compiler, but I personally prefer not to use such notation because it is misleading. To declare more than one pointer on the same line, you have to use more than one asterisk:

```
int *ptr, *ptr2;
```

You can also mix the declarations of pointers and other variables on the same line:

```
int *ptr, x, y, *ptr2, z;
```

In this code, x, y, and z are integer variables, and ptr and ptr2 are integer pointers.

Now let's talk about how an address can be assigned to a pointer. The address-of operator, &, can be used to assign the address of a variable to a pointer. For example, &x is an operation that results in the address of x. Remember from your first course in programming that a variable was defined as a location in memory whose value can be changed by the programmer? Back then, you probably didn't think that it was important for a variable to be thought of as a location. You may have even ignored the definition. If so, get ready to change the way you think. When we use the address-of operator on x, &x, it really refers to the *address* of that location in memory which is reserved for x. Therefore, with the preceding declaration, the address of x can be stored in ptr by using the code

```
ptr = &x;
```

We say that ptr *points to* x when it holds the address of that memory location which is reserved for x (computer science lingo, again). In figures, pointers are drawn with an arrow. The result of the previous line of code is shown in Figure 4.1a, while Figure 4.1b shows what really happens in RAM.

In talking about pointers, it is important to distinguish between a variable name, a location, a value at a location, and the address of a location. Figure 4.2 illustrates the differences among them.

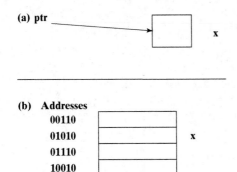

(a) ptr

x

(b) Addresses

Addresses		
00110		
01010		x
01110		
10010		
10110	01010	**ptr**

FIGURE 4.1

(a) How pointers are usually drawn. In such a drawing, ptr is understood as containing the address of the location of memory reserved for x. (b) How x and ptr are actually placed into RAM. The pointer ptr contains the address of the location reserved for x. The variable x has not been assigned anything. Memory is byte addressable, but each cell is shown as a 4-byte chunk. An address on today's computers is 32 bits long and would be impractical to show in the drawing.

Keep in mind that a variable is a location. When locations are used in code, their behavior depends on where in the code they appear. If they appear to the left of an = assignment operator, they behave differently than if they appear anywhere else. If they

(a) Addresses

Addresses		
00110		
01010	15	x
01110		
10010		
10110		

(b) Addresses

Addresses		
00110		
01010	15	x
01110		
10010		
10110		

(c) Addresses

Addresses		
00110		
01010	**15**	x
01110		
10010		
10110		

(d) Addresses

Addresses		
00110		
01010	15	x
01110		
10010		
10110		

FIGURE 4.2

(a) A chunk of RAM memory broken up into 4-byte pieces (locations). The name of a variable is shown in bold on the right. (b) The location, or actual variable itself, is shown in bold. (c) The value at the location (value of the variable) is shown in bold. (d) The address of the location is shown in bold.

don't appear to the left of the assignment operator, then the location gets replaced with the value at that location. For example, if x is 3, then in the expression

y = x + 5;

x gets replaced with the value at its location (or memory cell), which is 3, and then 8 gets assigned to y. However, if a location appears to the left of the assignment operator, it is *not* replaced with the value at that location. If y were 10, for example, the expression

y = x + 5;

would not be replaced with

10 = x + 5;

If it were, we would be in trouble! Instead, the behavior is different: When locations are used on the left of the assignment, they simply act as locations (not *values at* locations). So the location gets assigned the resulting value to the right of the assignment.

The dereference operator, *, can be applied to pointers (or, indeed, to any expression that yields an address). The result of the operation is a location. (Most operations have a result that is some sort of value.) The resulting location is the location at the address that is being dereferenced. So, if ptr were assigned the address of x, as in

ptr = &x;

then *ptr would give the location reserved for x.

The dereference operator, *, looks like it is also used in the declaration of a pointer. However, no operator is used in the declaration. It is just the notation that is necessary to declare a pointer.

Since the use of the dereference operator, *, gives a location as a result, the way it behaves depends on where it appears in the code, as we have said. Let's look at an example:

int x, *ptr;
x = 3;
ptr = &x;

After this code, if we don't use *ptr to the left of the assignment operator, it will act just like a variable (location), giving the value stored at the resulting location. In the expression

y = *ptr + 5;

the operation *ptr results in the location reserved for x. Hence, the operation *ptr will be replaced with the value 3 (assigned to x before). If *ptr appears to the left of the assignment operator, as in

*ptr = 10 + z;

then it acts just as a variable (location) does on the left of the assignment: It will be used simply as a location, and the result of adding 10 + z will be stored in the location reserved for x. Take note, however: With pointers, the value of x can change by the preceding line of code. If z is 5, for example, the value of x changes to 15, and if the line of code

```
cout << x << endl;
```

executes, the value of 15 will be output. Figure 4.3 illustrates what happens when this code is used.

You should keep the following in mind when working with pointers:

- A variable is a location.
- When the dereference operator is used on an address, the result is the location of that address; dereference operators may be used on pointers (since they store

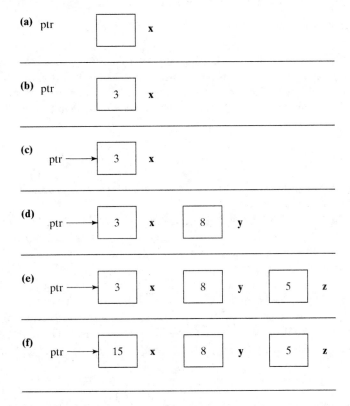

FIGURE 4.3

Effects of dereferencing.

    (a) int x, *ptr;
    (b) x = 3;
    (c) ptr = &x;
    (d) int y = *ptr + 5;
    (e) int z = 5;
    (f) *ptr = 10 + z; // changes the value of x without using x

addresses), and also may be used on expressions that produce an address as a result.

- A location (whether from a variable name or the result of a dereference) behaves differently, depending on whether it appears on the left side of an assignment or somewhere else in the code. If a location appears on the left of an assignment, it behaves as a location. If it appears anywhere else in code, the *value* at that location is used.

If we use the dereference operator, *, on a pointer that does *not* store the address of a location, the compiler will not catch the error; it will be a runtime error. Therefore, to avoid the frustration of incurring runtime errors, always make sure that when you use the dereference operator, the pointer you are using it on has been assigned an address.

Sometimes, when we write code, we initialize a pointer to NULL, as in the code:

float *ptr = NULL;

NULL is defined to be 0 in the iostream header file, an address of a location that cannot be assigned a value. If the pointer is set to NULL, then executing a line of code that uses the dereference operator on the pointer will give a runtime error. Later in the code, if we are not sure whether a pointer has been assigned an address, we can test for it:

if (ptr != NULL)
        *ptr = 3.14;

Using code like this helps to prevent runtime errors that result from not having a valid address stored in a pointer.

The fact that NULL is defined in the iostream header file should be kept in mind when you are writing the word NULL in class functions. You should #include iostream at the top of the class implementation file, so that the use of NULL will be recognized, along with "using namespace std;".

In data structures, pointers are almost always used to hold either the address of an array or the address of an object. We will discuss arrays first and objects much later. To declare a pointer that will be used to hold the address of an array, we need only declare it with the data type of the array. For example, to declare a pointer that will hold the address of an array of integers, we need to declare the pointer with the code

int *ptrToArray;

This is exactly the same notation that was used earlier. The reason is that the pointer will be used to store the address of the *first element* of the array, which in this case *is* an integer. In storing the address of the first element of the array, the pointer is, in effect, storing the address of the entire array.

We should discuss arrays a little further than you are probably used to at this point. First of all, the name of the array, when used by itself, stores the address of the array (i.e., the address of the first element of the array). So, if we have an array of integers given by

```
int num[ 5 ];
```

we can assign num to this pointer with the code

```
ptrToArray = num;
```

Since num stores the address of the array, the address is now assigned to ptrToArray, so ptrToArray stores the address of the array, too. When ptrToArray holds the address of an array, we say that ptrToArray *points to* the array.

So is num a pointer? It stores an address, but it is important to realize that an array name is *not* a pointer. The reason num is not a pointer is that a pointer is defined as a variable that stores an address. The name "variable" implies that its value can be changed. But we can't store a different address in num; if we try to, we will get a compiler error. We can store a different address in ptrToArray a little later in the code if we like, so it *is* a pointer.

4.2   THE [ ] OPERATOR

There is another thing about the use of arrays that you may not be fully aware of, but it is important for adjustable arrays: When [ ]'s are used to access an element, as in num[3], the [ ]'s constitute an operator. It may seem strange, because it is an operator made up of two symbols that are separated from each other in the code. But still, [ ] is an operator. We can even write an overloaded operator function for it, but we won't discuss that until the next chapter. In the example num[3], the operands are num and 3. The result of the operation, as you might expect, is a location. So, [ ] acts the way that locations act, depending on where they appear in the code. But you already know this through experience.

How the operator [ ] arrives at producing a resulting location is interesting. The best way to describe it is that, in the example num[3], the result of the operation is *(num + 3), which we will need to explain. The expression num + 3 produces an address as a result, so we can dereference that address and get its location. The way that C++ calculates the resulting address is by first looking at the data type of the address used in the expression (stored in num). Then, it multiplies the integer by the number of bytes in the size of that data type. If each element is 4 bytes, for example, then 3 * 4 = 12 bytes will be added to num to get the address. Finally, the location at that address is produced by using the dereference operator, *. Figure 4.4 shows why the resulting address, in this case, is the correct address for num[3].

All of this might be hard to swallow, and I would really like it to sink in, so let's look at a different example. Get the following program, compile it, and run it to make sure that it works. All it does is add a bunch of numbers in an array.

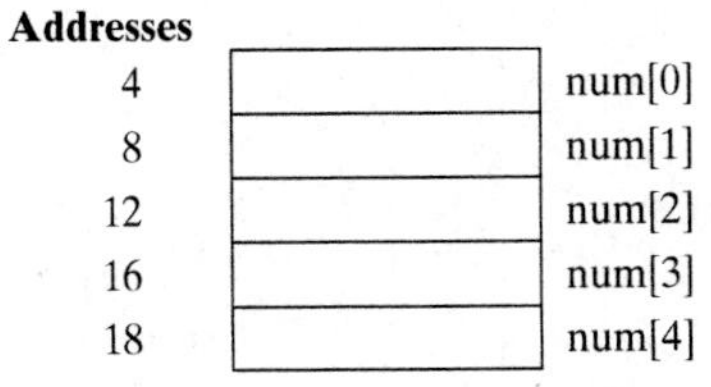

Addresses

4	num[0]
8	num[1]
12	num[2]
16	num[3]
18	num[4]

FIGURE 4.4

The num array is shown. It is an array of integers, so each element occupies 4 bytes. The addresses of the elements are shown in decimal for clarity. The expression num[3] is the same as *(num + 3). Note that num stores the beginning address of the array, 4. Therefore, (num + 3) yields the address 4 + 3(4) = 16, which is the correct address of num[3].

```
1   #include <iostream>
2
3   using namespace std;
4
5   int main( )
6   {
7       int num[ 5 ];
8       int sum = 0;
9
10      for ( int i = 0; i < 5; i++ ) {
11              cout << "Enter element " << i << ": ";
12              cin >> num[ i ];
13              }
14
15      for ( int i = 0; i < 5; i++ )
16              sum = sum + num[ i ] ;
17
18      cout << "The resulting sum is: " << sum << endl;
19
20      return 0;
21  }
```

Yes, we could just use one loop, but it is more interesting if we don't. Now, we're going to change the program a little bit on line 16. The resulting program, with the change shown in bold, is as follows:

```
1   #include <iostream>
2
3   using namespace std;
4
5   int main( )
6   {
7       int num[ 5 ];
8       int sum = 0;
9
10      for ( int i = 0; i < 5; i++ ) {
11              cout << "Enter element " << i << ": ";
12              cin >> num[ i ];
13              }
14
15      for ( int i = 0; i < 5; i++ ) {
16              sum = sum + **i[ num ]** ;
17
18      cout << "The resulting sum is: " << sum << endl;
19
20      return 0;
21  }
```

On line 16, the variable i was put to the left of the [ ] operator, and the name of the array was placed inside the operator. Line 12 of the program stays the same. Go ahead and compile the new program. You won't get a compiler error. You won't even get a compiler warning. Go ahead and run it. Works perfectly, right? That's because addition is commutative.

Are you thoroughly convinced now that [ ] is an operator? If you are not, then all I have to say is, you're a hard case. I'd rather teach my lizard to do backflips than try to convince you any further. By the way, when you write programs, don't write code like this. You'll drive everybody crazy.

I've gone through great lengths to convince you that [ ] is an operator and to explain exactly what it does. The reason is that we are going to build on this idea shortly. But first, we need to discuss *dynamically allocated memory*.

4.3   DYNAMICALLY ALLOCATED MEMORY

Dynamically allocated memory comes from using the *heap*, a special part of RAM set aside for program usage. Chances are that you've never written a program that used the heap before, at least not in your own code. (The library code that you've included in your program may have used the heap.) The only way to access memory in the heap is to use the *new* operator, an unusual operator because it is written in English. Most operators, such as '+', '/', '&&', and '%', come from symbols that aren't in the alphabet. Most people have trouble thinking of *new* as an operator, but it is. We can even write an overloaded operator function for it. It is a unary operator that takes only one operand on its right. The operand, interestingly enough, is a data type instead of the value of a data type.

The result of the *new* operation is also quite interesting. It is an address of a chunk of memory in the heap that is large enough to hold the data type operand. Since the result of the *new* operation is an address, the result is almost always assigned to a pointer. All of this takes a while to get used to, so let's look at an example:

```
float *ptr;
ptr = new float;
```

In this simple example, we declare a pointer that can hold the address of a float. On the second line, the new operator is used. It accesses an arbitrary chunk of memory in the heap that is large enough to hold a float—say, 4 bytes. The address of this 4-byte chunk of memory is the result of the operation "new float", so that address replaces the operation. The address is then assigned to ptr, which is fine, since ptr holds the address of a float. The 4-byte chunk of memory is called *dynamically allocated memory*. Figure 4.5 illustrates the result of the execution of the two lines of code shown.

When memory is dynamically allocated, the usage of RAM results from an instruction rather than from a declaration. When the usage of memory results from a declaration, the compiler must know the exact size, in bytes, of whatever is being declared. When memory is dynamically allocated, the compiler does not need to know the size of what is being declared. However, the size must be known at the time of execution of the line of code containing the *new* operator.

Notice that when memory is dynamically allocated with the *new* operator, it doesn't have a variable name. The only way for a programmer to use dynamically allocated memory is with a pointer. So, in the example,

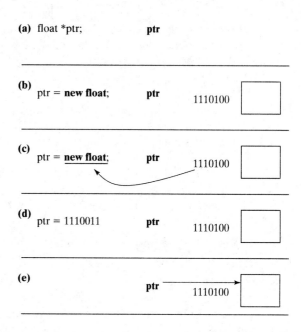

FIGURE 4.5

How the *new* operation works. (a) A pointer is declared, but like any other variable that is declared, it does not have an initial value. (b) The pointer is assigned a value, which will be the result of the "new float" operation. A chunk of memory is found in the heap that is big enough to store a float type. (c) How the result of the new operation is obtained. The address of the location becomes the result of the operation "new float". (d) The actual replacement is made (just the way an operation 3 + 4 is replaced with 7). This address is assigned to the pointer ptr. (e) Since ptr has the address of the heap memory location, it points to it.

```
float *ptr;
ptr = new float;
```

if we want to assign 1.5 to the dynamically allocated memory, we have to do it this way:

```
*ptr = 1.5;
```

If we want to print out the value of the dynamically allocated memory, we use the following line of code:

```
cout << *ptr << endl;
```

That is, the dynamically allocated memory acts like a float variable, but it doesn't have a name.

4.4   DYNAMIC ARRAYS

If we want to dynamically allocate an array, we use the same notation as we do for a declared array, but we leave the name of the array out (since a name is not associated with dynamic memory). An example is the code

```
int *ptr;
ptr = new int [5];
```

In the second line, the *new* operator finds a spot in the heap big enough to hold an array of five integers and then produces the array's address, which is stored in ptr. Since you are starting to get used to pointers now, we can combine the preceding two lines of code as

```
int *ptr = new int [5];
```

This line of code produces the result shown in Figure 4.6. Now, with what code would we access the element of the array with index 3? I know you can answer this question because you know that [ ] is an operator. (Don't you?) So, to assign 25 to the element with index 3, we use the line of code

```
ptr[ 3 ] = 25;
```

The pointer to the array acts like the name of the array for all practical purposes. The name of the array would store the address of the array, but so does the pointer. This array is called a ***dynamic array***. By contrast, when an array is declared, it is called a ***static array***.

The nice thing about dynamic arrays is that the size does *not* need to be known when the code is compiled. For example, we could write code like this:

```
int numElements;
cout << "How many elements would you like the array to have? ";
cin >> numElements;
float *ptrArr = new float [ numElements ];
```

In the fourth line, numElements is used to determine the size of the array to find in the heap. In a static array, a variable such as numElements cannot be used to declare its size. We must use either an integer or a const int. For example, we could use numElements if it is declared as follows:

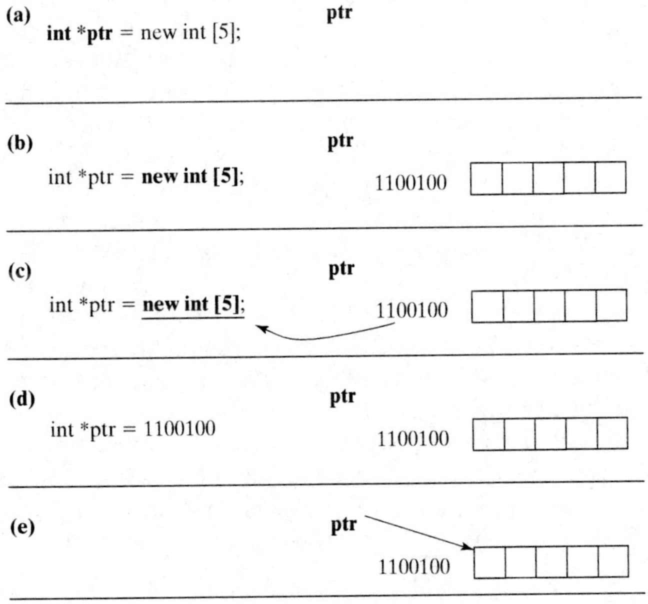

(a) **int *ptr** = new int [5];   ptr

(b) int *ptr = **new int [5];**   ptr   1100100

(c) int *ptr = **new int [5];**   ptr   1100100

(d) int *ptr = 1100100   ptr   1100100

(e)   ptr   1100100

FIGURE 4.6

How the *new* operation works with a dynamic array. (a) A pointer is declared. (b) The pointer is assigned a value on the same line. The value will be the result of the "new int [5]" operation. A chunk of memory is found in the heap big enough to store an array of five integers. (c) How the result of the *new* operation is obtained. The address of the location (the address of the first element of the array) becomes the result of the operation "new int [5]". (d) The actual replacement is made. This address is assigned to the pointer ptr. (e) Since ptr has the address of the dynamic array, it points to it.

```
const int numElements = 25;
float nums[ numElements ];
```

In a static array, a compiler must know the exact size of the array when it is declared. Otherwise, a compiler error will result.

4.5   THE DELETE OPERATOR

Suppose a function uses a dynamic array, processes the array, and provides some output to the user. Such a function might look like this:

```
1   void foo( )
2   {
3        int numElements;
4        cout << "How many elements would you like the array to have? ";
5        cin >> numElements;
6        float *ptrArr = new float [ numElements ];
7
8        // the array is processed here
9        // output to the user is provided here
10  }
```

The code preceding this function was copied into the function. Then, the array is used for its intended purpose, and output is provided to the user. (Comments are shown here on lines 8–9, whereas code would ordinarily be there.) As you know, when the program returns from a function, all local variables are destroyed along with the values they contain. In this function, numElements and ptrArr would be destroyed. When ptrArr is destroyed, the address of the dynamic array is lost. But what does this mean? Is the dynamic array destroyed, too? The answer is no, but there is no longer any way to access it: Its address has been lost, and there is no way to determine what the address is (at least, not from the program). The memory used for the array is no longer accessible; it will be ignored when the *new* operator is used the next time. Such a situation is called ***memory leak***. Figure 4.7 shows what happens in this example.

Before you panic, this memory is not permanently unavailable; it will become available again when you stop the program and then restart it. But allowing memory leak to occur is poor programming practice, because it is often a simple matter to prevent it from happening, as will be shown shortly. A large program that constantly uses the *new* operator and continually allows memory leak may eventually run out of heap memory space to use for the rest of the program.

To prevent memory leak from occurring, we use the *delete* operator, which acts on a pointer operand to its right. The *delete* operator frees the dynamically allocated memory pointed to by the pointer; that is, it makes this memory available for reuse in the heap. Using the *delete* operator, we would rewrite the function as follows:

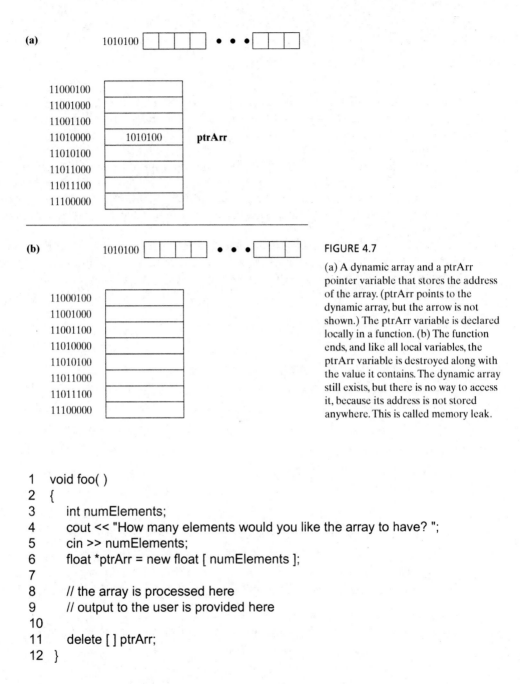

FIGURE 4.7

(a) A dynamic array and a ptrArr pointer variable that stores the address of the array. (ptrArr points to the dynamic array, but the arrow is not shown.) The ptrArr variable is declared locally in a function. (b) The function ends, and like all local variables, the ptrArr variable is destroyed along with the value it contains. The dynamic array still exists, but there is no way to access it, because its address is not stored anywhere. This is called memory leak.

```
1   void foo( )
2   {
3       int numElements;
4       cout << "How many elements would you like the array to have? ";
5       cin >> numElements;
6       float *ptrArr = new float [ numElements ];
7
8       // the array is processed here
9       // output to the user is provided here
10
11      delete [ ] ptrArr;
12  }
```

On line 11, we use [ ] only when we are freeing an array of elements. If we want to free a single space, we would omit the [ ]'s. For example, we would write float *ptr = new float;

.

. // other code

.

delete ptr;

If we use "delete ptrArr" to free an array, no compiler error message will be given. However, only the first element of the array will be freed; there will be memory leak for the rest of the elements in the array.

Sometimes people make the mistake of thinking that the *delete* operator deletes the pointer that follows it. This is not so. The *delete* operator only frees the memory that is pointed to by the pointer. You may continue to use the pointer for other purposes after using *delete* on it. But you must assign an address to it first, because once *delete* is used on a pointer, the pointer is no longer considered to have a usable address stored in it.

Another common cause of memory leak occurs when a pointer contains the address of dynamically allocated memory and we decide to assign a different address to the pointer without freeing the dynamic memory it points to. The address of the dynamically allocated memory is then lost. Figure 4.8 shows an example of this situation.

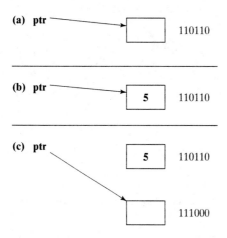

FIGURE 4.8

Another common cause of memory leak:

(a).ptr = new int; // ptr contains address 110110.

(b).*ptr = 5;   // 5 is placed into the dynamically allocated block.

         // Some other code is executed that uses the block

(c).ptr = new int; // A new address (111000) is assigned to ptr, creating

         // memory leak. The address 110110 is not saved anywhere else,

         // so this block can no longer be accessed or reused by the new

         // operator. To solve this problem, use

         // delete ptr;

         // before line c executes.

To prevent memory leak, the *delete* operator can be used on a pointer before assigning a different address to it. There is no need, however, to use the *delete* operator on a pointer that does not have the address of dynamically allocated memory.

4.6 POINTERS TO OBJECTS

Pointers may be declared for objects, too. In that case, they would hold the address of the object. For example, to declare a pointer that holds the address of a Check object, we would use the declaration

Check *chkptr;

If we like, we can dynamically allocate a Check in heap memory and assign this address to the pointer:

Check *chkptr = new Check;

We can even make an array of checks and assign it to a pointer:

Check *chkptrArray = new Check [10];

To free such dynamic memory, we use the *delete* operator the same way. To free the dynamic Check object pointed to by chkptr, we would use the code

delete chkptr;

To free the dynamic array pointed to by chkptrArray, we would use the code

delete [ ] chkptrArray;

4.7 RUNNING OUT OF HEAP MEMORY

For large programs that use the heap extensively, the *new* operator may not be able to find enough free space in the heap for the size of the *new* operator's operand. For example, suppose there are only 10 bytes of free heap space left and the *new* operator needs to find space for a float array of size 20. With large programs, we can run out of heap memory even if we don't have memory leak, simply by using a lot of dynamically allocated memory. If the *new* operator cannot find a space in the heap large enough, and nothing special is done to handle this case, the program will crash. However, in such a case C++ throws an **exception**. You may not have encountered exceptions before, so let's talk about what they are and how they can be handled.

An exception allows a programmer to write code to handle a problem that, if left unhandled, would cause the program to crash. Here is a simple program that illustrates the way we could write exception code to handle the exception gracefully so that the program doesn't crash:

```
1       #include <iostream>
2
3       using namespace std;
```

```
4
5        int main()
6        {
7           char *ptr;
8
9           try {
10                 ptr = new char[ 1000000000 ];
11          }
12
13          catch( ... ) {
14             cout << "Too many elements" << endl;
15          }
16
17          return 0;
18       }
```

Line 7 just declares a pointer to a character, and then the exception code begins. There are two parts to the exception code written here: the try clause, on lines 9–11, and the catch clause, on lines 13–15. The try clause has just a single statement within its block—in this case, on line 10—but it could include many statements. When the program is executing and a try clause is encountered, nothing special occurs in the execution at this point; the code in the try clause is executed as if the try keyword wasn't even there. The only importance a try clause has is if a problem that causes an exception occurs within the block of the clause. (In computer science lingo, we say that an *exception is thrown*.) If an exception occurs within a try clause, C++ looks for a following catch clause that can handle the exception. If it finds one, the code in the catch clause is executed. If it doesn't find one, the program crashes.

In this case, during the execution of line 10, if we don't have 1 GB of heap memory available, an exception is thrown and the catch heading on line 13 will catch it. The code in the catch clause then executes. We say that the catch clause *catches the exception*. On line 14, a message is given that there are too many elements. The ending brace for the catch block is on line 15. After leaving the catch block, the program will continue execution with the statements after the catch block, as if nothing happened. Of course, in this program, the only statement we have when the catch clause ends is "return 0;".

When a try block that has more than one statement executes, and a statement within the block causes an exception, the rest of the statements in the try block will not be executed. Instead, execution begins immediately in the catch clause.

The only way a catch clause is executed is if the code in the try clause causes an exception. Otherwise, the entire catch clause is ignored as if it isn't even there.

If the try clause contains a function call, then an exception that is thrown between the function call and the return from the called function can be caught by the catch clause that follows. The following program shows an example of this situation:

```
1        #include <iostream>
2        #include "Foo.h"
3
4        using namespace std;
5
```

```
6      int main( )
7      {
8              Foo foo;
9
10             try {
11                     foo.bar1( 35 );
12                     foo.bar2( 10 );
13                     foo.bar3( );
14             }
15
16             catch ( ... ) {
17                     cout << "Out of memory" << endl;
18             }
19
20     return 0;
21     }
```

This program declares an object of some Foo class on line 8. Then, on lines 11–13, some functions in the foo object are used. If any of these functions should happen to throw an exception (or any functions called by them throw one), the catch clause on lines 16–18 can catch the exception. We say *can* catch it, because if the Foo class programmer decides to write try and catch clauses in these functions, the exception will be caught and handled there instead. So there may be many catch clauses written at various levels that can handle an exception, but the one that is encountered first will be used, and the other catch clauses will be ignored.

Well, we've probably gone into far more technical detail than is necessary, but we've only scratched the surface of the technical detail involved in writing exceptions. When we write data structures, we don't have to worry about the exception too much, because the client is the one who handles it the way he or she sees fit. If the Foo class in the preceding program is a data structure class, the client can handle exceptions in the manner shown. Some clients don't even bother to handle exceptions, since (1) it is unusual to run out of heap memory, given the plentiful amounts of memory in today's computers, and (2) if an exception *is* thrown, most of the time the program is doomed to failure anyway—whether it crashes or throws an out-of-memory message on the screen before it aborts can sometimes be a moot point. The knowledge about why the program failed may or may not do a computer user much good. However, there are a few interesting situations in which the program can continue running even if there is not enough heap memory for a new operation. In these few cases, we will use try and catch clauses in our class functions. Also, it is good practice to warn the client with comments or other documentation about the possibility (however remote) that use of the class functions can (1) exhaust heap memory and (2) throw an exception (if your functions use the *new* operator). Then the client at least has the option of handling the exception in the client code.

4.8 ADJUSTABLE ARRAYS

Finally, we are ready to start talking about adjustable arrays. Remember, we got on this rocket trip in the first place by talking about adjustable arrays at the beginning of the chapter. We want to store all the checks that were written in an array, but we want the size of the array to grow with the number of checks that are written. On the one hand, we don't want to start off with a large array, because that might waste a lot of memory space if there aren't that many checks. On the other hand, we don't want a small array either, because it might get filled before all the checks are written. So the answer is an array that can adjust its size—that is, start off small and then grow. This can be done only with a dynamic array.

The first issue is how often we should change the size of the array. Should we increase the size by one every time a check is written? This approach turns out to be largely inefficient. As we will see later on in the book, an efficient way to handle the problem is to double the size of the array when it becomes full.

We keep adding checks to the dynamic array pointed to by checks until it becomes filled. Figure 4.9 illustrates how to double the size of the array when it is full. It

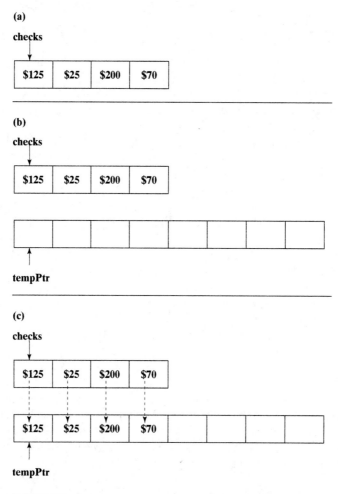

FIGURE 4.9

(a) The checks array is full. (b) A new dynamic array is created that is twice the size of the checks array; tempPtr points to it. (c) The values of the elements are copied, one by one, from the checks array to the tempPtr array with the use of a loop.

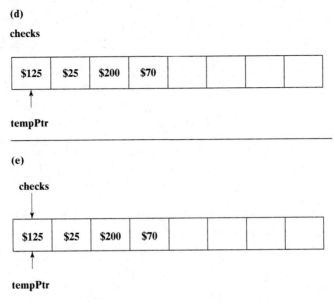

(d)

checks

| $125 | $25 | $200 | $70 | | | | |

tempPtr

(e)

checks

| $125 | $25 | $200 | $70 | | | | |

tempPtr

FIGURE 4.9 (*continued*)

(d) The dynamic array pointed to by checks is freed. (e) The checks pointer is assigned the same address that is stored in tempPtr.

is important that the checks pointer be assigned the address of the larger array, because it is acting like the name of the array (even though it is only a pointer). When used like the name of an array throughout the code, it needs to be used like the name of the new array. When the new array gets filled up, the process repeats.

Thus, to double the size of the array, we need to do the following:

- Make a new array that is twice the size in the heap.
- Copy the elements from the old, smaller array into the new, larger array.
- Free the dynamic memory used by the smaller array.
- Reassign the pointer, used as the "name" of the array, to the larger array.
- Keep the current capacity of the array as a variable and double it

Let's look at the section of code that shows how to double the size of the array, where the variable capacity is the current capacity of the checks array. We will use the Check object as the data type of the array, keeping in mind that this should be templated in the class specification. The code is as follows:

```
1   Check *tempPtr = new Check [capacity * 2];
2
3   for ( int i = 0; i < capacity; i++ )
4       tempPtr[ i ] = checks[ i ];
5
```

```
6   delete [ ] checks;
7   checks = tempPtr;
8   capacity *= 2;
```

On line 1, the *new* operator finds a Check array in the heap that is large enough to hold capacity * 2 elements. This will create an array twice as large as the checks array. The *new* operator produces the address of this larger array, and the address is assigned to tempPtr. In the for loop, all of the Checks in the checks array are copied to the array pointed to by tempPtr. Notice that, within the for loop, we are assigning one Check object to another Check object. (Each element is a Check.) On line 6, the old checks array is freed. On line 7, the address stored in tempPtr is assigned to the checks pointer. This means that the checks pointer now points to the new array. Then, on line 8, the capacity value is doubled to reflect the capacity of the new array. It is important to keep capacity updated for the next time when this code must be executed (i.e., when the checks array becomes full again). The implementation of the Checkbook class by using the adjustable array is left as an exercise.

SUMMARY

This chapter has introduced pointers and dynamic arrays. Data structures make extensive use of pointers and addresses, so it is essential to understand them completely. Many data structures are made from dynamic arrays. When a pointer is declared in the private section of a class in order to point to a dynamic array, it is important to be able to change the size of the array that it points to. This makes it appear as if the size of the same array used in the data structure has changed, but it really hasn't, of course; rather, a different dynamic array has been created, and the old one is freed. As we will see later on, both expanding and shrinking the array that such a pointer points to is important for memory conservation.

Linked structures are also common in data structures and use a lot of dynamically allocated memory. These structures will be introduced in Chapter 7. It is important to understand the use of the *new* and *delete* operators for we shall work with them in dealing with dynamically allocated memory in later chapters of the book.

EXERCISES

1. What is a pointer? What does it store?
2. Declare an integer called num. Then, without using num on the left side of an assignment, assign 10 to num.
3. Recall that a variable is a location. When a location is on the left side of the assignment operator in a particular statement, how is its behavior different (in the statement) than when it is on the right side?
4. How do you get a location from a pointer?
5. What is stored in the name of a static array?
6. Why isn't a static array name a pointer?
7. Describe how the [ ] operator arrives at a result when given two operands.

8. What is dynamically allocated memory? What is the heap? Once memory has been dynamically allocated, it has no name, so how can it be accessed?

9. When the *new* operator is used, what happens? What happens when you use the *new* operator and there is no more space in the heap?

10. What is the difference between a dynamic array and a static array? What advantage does a dynamic array have over a static array? What advantage does a static array have over a dynamic array?

11. What is memory leak and how can it be prevented?

12. When the *delete* operator is used on a pointer, does it delete the pointer? Does it delete anything? What happens?

13. How would we use the *delete* operator to free a dynamic array?

14. When the size of a dynamic array is adjusted, the size of the same array doesn't actually change. Why? What gives us the perception that the size of the same array has changed?

15. Is the dynamic array at the same location in memory after its size is adjusted? Why or why not?

16. This exercise gives some programming practice with dynamic arrays, but is part of a larger project, continued in Chapters 5 and 8. Write a class called ServerGroup, which will be a simple custom-made data structure. It will be a special-purpose class, so it will be untemplated. Recall that you must #include files differently for untemplated classes. This is the first of three programs that will be combined to form a larger project. You can think of the Server-Group as a class that will serve people waiting in line.

The private section of the ServerGroup class will have a pointer to a dynamic integer array called servers, an integer variable called spServer (a special-purpose server), and an integer variable called freeServer. It will also be useful to have a variable called size, for the number of elements in the dynamic array. Then write the following functions for the class:

   a. The constructor will pass in an integer parameter that will be used to set the number of elements in the dynamic integer array. (This number is actually the number of general-purpose servers.) The constructor will also set all elements of the array to 0 and spServer to 0.

   b. Write a function called spServerFree that will return true if spServer is 0 and return false otherwise. (The integer value is the number of clock ticks until the special-purpose server is free; if the integer value is 0, the special-purpose server is already free.)

   c. Write a function called serverFree that will return true if it finds a 0 in the array and false otherwise. (These integers also represent the number of clock ticks until the corresponding servers are free.) If the function finds a 0 in the array, it will set freeServer to the index of that element. (freeServer has the index of one of the servers that are free.)

   d. Write a function called useServer that will pass in an integer parameter, avTransTime, and set servers[freeServer] to avTransTime. (avTransTime is the average transaction time, in clock ticks, to serve a person in line.)

   e. Write a function called usespServer that will pass in an integer parameter, avTransTime, and set spServer to avTransTime. (This is the same function as in (d), except that it is for the special-purpose server whereas (d) is for the general-purpose servers.)

   f. Write a function called decServers that will decrement spServer by 1, unless spServer is already 0. (If it is 0, it stays the same.) The decServers function will also decrement each element in the array by 1, unless the element is already 0. For example, if the array is 0 5 6 0 0 10, then after decServers is called, the array will be 0 4 5 0 0 9. (You guessed it, this function is called when a clock tick of time elapses.)

To test your class, you might want to write a temporary print function in the class to print out the values of the array and the other private variables. Once you are sure that everything works, delete the print function.

17. Write a new Checkbook class that uses a dynamic array. Call the class a different name, since it will be different from the latest version that uses a static array. Start off with a dynamic array size of 2, made by the constructor. Every time the dynamic array becomes full and a new check has to be written, double the current size of the array. Write a doubleArray function for the class to do this, but place the function prototype in the private section, since you don't want the client to call the function. Keep a pointer to the dynamic array in the private section. Write a getChecks function that will return a pointer to DataType (which is going to be the address of a dynamic array). Create a dynamic array in the getChecks function, copy the checks to it, and return the pointer to this dynamic array (so that you return its address). Do not return the pointer in the private section, because you don't want the client to access (or possibly change) the saved array. Note that the dynamic array created in the getChecks function will not be destroyed at the end of the function; only the local pointer that points to it will. The client will receive the address of this dynamic array created in the getChecks function, however, and will be able to use the array. Write a comment which makes it clear that the client must free the dynamic array when the client is done with it (to prevent memory leak). Use a Check struct of your own design to test the class template.

CHAPTER 5

An Array Class

In this chapter, we present an Array class that can be used for an adjustable array in client programs. This class will be your first taste of the design of a data structure made from a class. The Array class will make it a lot easier and convenient to work with arrays. We will also introduce three important functions that should be written whenever a class contains a pointer as a data member: the destructor, the copy constructor, and the overloaded assignment operator.

The Array class can be used in data structures that contain arrays. With the use of the Array class, the adjustable array will become an abstraction. We don't have to think about the details of how to change its size. We just call a function in the Array class that does it. When we use the Array class for a data structure, we simply declare an object of the Array class in the private section.

5.1   ARRAY CLASS TEMPLATE

Let's take a look at the Array class template:

```
1   // Array.h -- class template for an adjustable array
2   // When debugging, use #define DEBUG_ARRAY above your #include Array line.
3   // When done debugging, comment out #define DEBUG_ARRAY for better performance.
4   // The constructor and the changeSize function can cause an exception to be thrown if out of
5   // heap memory.
6
7   #include <string>
8
9   using namespace std;
10
11  template <class DataType>
```

```
12  class Array
13  {
14  public:
15      Array( int size );
16      inline DataType & operator [ ]( int index );
17      void changeSize( int newSize );  // will not alter values unless newSize is smaller
18                                       // than current capacity; in this case, the values
19                                       // from 0 to newSize - 1 will not be altered
20      inline int length( ) const;      // returns the current capacity of the array
21      string err( ) const;             // returns error message from errorCode
22  private:
23      DataType *elements;              // points to the dynamic array
24      int capacity;
25      DataType dud;                    // returned from operator [ ] if index error occurs
26      int errorCode;                   // contains code for error if array misuse occurs
27  };
28
29  #include "Array.cpp"
```

In the private section, on line 23, we have a pointer called elements that will point to the dynamic array. The capacity of the array is declared on line 24.

The constructor for the Array is on line 15. The client passes in a size for the array as a parameter. There is no default constructor (a constructor that has no parameters).

We are also overloading operator [ ] on line 16, so that we can use [ ]'s on the Array object to access and change elements, the same way we would do so in a static or dynamic array. This makes the Array class more intuitive to use.

Notice that the first keyword on line 16 is "inline". Let's first explain what this is all about. Function calls generally involve some overhead, as you will learn later in your computer science education. It takes quite a few instructions in the machine code to set up parameters, pass them in, change functions, get return values, etc. These instructions are all invisible to us as C++ programmers, but machine-language instructions are inserted by the compiler to take care of all of these tasks. The problem, though, is that they slow down execution of the program: They are extra instructions that need to be executed. When we use the keyword "inline", it speeds things up a little. The code of the function is actually inserted by the compiler into the place where the function is called, so in the machine language, no function is actually called. This is a great place to use inline, since we would expect the operator [ ] function to be called rather intensely during the use of the Array class.

So why not use inline with every function, for the sake of program speed? Well, let's say you call a function from 10 different places in the code. Without inline, there is only one copy of the function body in machine language. However, with inline, there are 10 copies of the function body in machine language, since one copy is substituted for each function call. So, if we use inline with everything in sight, the program size is expected to be much larger than it normally would be. If the program cannot fit in RAM, along with everything else that happens to be hanging around in there, increased use of the hard disk can result, actually slowing down program execution. (The use of the hard disk for software that is executing is called *virtual memory*.) So we should be judicious when using inline. However, if the main use of a function is expected to be inside of loops, as it is with the [ ] function, then inline can be a worthwhile tool.

By the way, if you try to use inline for a function in a class (instead of a class template), the whole function definition needs to be placed within the class specification (in the header file). The compiler needs to see the code right away, so that it can do this code substitution into the function call. In a class template, it doesn't really matter: We include the class implementation file at the end of the header file, essentially making one long header file.

Notice on line 16 that the return value of operator [ ] is DataType &. This is something unusual that you may have never seen before: Its return type is a reference type. The reason is that it allows the location to be returned instead of the value. For example, if the name of the Array object is arr, we can use a line of code like this:

```
arr[ 5 ] = 10;
```

The left side of the assignment is a function call to the overloaded operator [ ] function, which returns the location, so that 10 can be assigned to the fifth index of the elements array. If the return type is a reference type, we can also use the code

```
x = arr[ 5 ];
```

In this case, the location is still returned, but since it is on the right side of the assignment, the *value* at that location is used.

There is another advantage to overloading an operator [ ] for an Array class, however. For example, if the client uses a variable for an index, and the result of the variable was arrived at by calculation, then errors in the client's code may cause the index to be negative or greater than the capacity of the array. We can write code in the operator [ ] function to check whether the index used is valid. If the index is invalid, we won't access the elements array, because that will give us a runtime error. Instead, we will have a dud of type DataType (the same type an element is made from) and return that instead. We could return a position of the elements array, such as index 0, but the elements array should probably not be altered if the index is not valid. The dud is declared on line 25 of the private section.

The changeSize function, provided on line 17, passes in a new size to set the array to. The current size of the array will change to that size. If the new size is greater than or equal to the current size, none of the values of the elements will be destroyed. If the new size is smaller than the current size, then the values in the range from 0 to newSize − 1 will be intact. Thus, the client can use changeSize without worrying about losing the values of the elements, unless he or she wants them lost.

The length function on line 20 will return the capacity of the array. When an Array object is passed into a function, its capacity does not need to be passed in as a second parameter, contrary to what is often done with normal arrays. Only the Array object needs to be passed in; its capacity can now be determined by calling the length function. We use inline with this function also, since it will usually be used in the condition of a loop.

The err function, declared on line 21, returns an error message as a string to the client. Note that lines 7 and 9 were put in because of the string return type. If the client made any mistakes in the way the Array object was used, such as using an invalid index, the mistake is recorded in the errorCode variable declared on line 26. The mistake is not saved as a string, because strings take up a lot of space. Instead, the err function interprets the error code and provides a client with a message about what went wrong, making it easier for the client to debug the program. When a program is written that uses an Array object, it would probably be best to call the err function in various places for debugging purposes. For example,

```
cout << "function foo: " << arr.err( );
```

can tell the programmer that, regardless of how everything looks, something went wrong during program execution. If the results of a program are wrong, such a use can make a program easier to debug, by enabling us to know *why* the results are wrong. If no mistake was detected, the err function will return "No error". Once the program has been debugged, such lines should be commented out or removed from the client code, of course.

A number of things can go wrong during the use of the Array object. In the constructor, for example, the initial size of the parameter passed in might be a negative value. We shouldn't ordinarily expect that the client would do something like this, but suppose that the client is calculating the size of the array to make. There may be a mistake in the formula the client uses, providing a negative result. The client might also try to use an index less than zero (for the same reason) or an index greater than or equal to the capacity of the array. Another problem can occur if the client passes a negative number into the changeSize function (as the new size to set the array to). We can use different numbers to represent each of these types of errors and set errorCode (in the private section) to the appropriate number should a mistake occur.

However, it would be a little nicer if, when two or more different kinds of errors occur, we inform the client of all of these errors in the string returned from the err function. Now, we might start thinking that if both an invalid size were used in the constructor and an invalid index were used, we should invent a new number for that case. But if we continue to assign random numbers to every possible combination of error conditions, it would severely complicate things, especially if there are a lot of

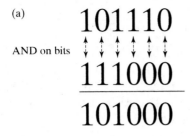

(a)

AND on bits

$$101110$$
$$111000$$
$$101000$$

(b)

OR on bits

$$101010$$
$$100100$$
$$101110$$

FIGURE 5.1

(a) The bitwise AND operation 46 & 56. The binary representation of 46 is 101110, and the binary representation of 56 is 111000. The & operator works on each bit, where 1 is regarded as true and 0 is regarded as false, to produce the binary representation result 101000, which is decimal number 40. (b) Shows the bitwise OR operation 42|36. The binary result is 101110, which is decimal 46.

different types of errors. A technique that makes it much easier to handle such situations is to use the bitwise operators OR and AND, represented by the symbols '|' and '&', respectively. In case you haven't seen these operators before, Figure 5.1 describes how they work.

To apply these operators to the problem at hand, we would associate a number with an error, where the number of bits set to 1 in the binary representation of the number is exactly 1. Figure 5.2 shows an example of such an association for the three types of errors we have been discussing. It turns out that a number associated with an error is an exact power of 2. The no-error condition can be represented by 0, which has no 1-bits.

We can store combinations of errors now simply by using the bitwise OR operator. For example, if we wanted to add the index-out-of-range error to the errorCode, we would use

000000   no error

000001   size passed into constructor isn't valid

000010   index used was out of range

000100   new size for changeSize isn't valid

FIGURE 5.2

Binary representations of the types of errors that can occur during the use of the array. The no-error condition can be represented by a decimal 0. Any other error, when it occurs, can have a binary representation with exactly one bit set to 1. The representation 000001 is decimal 1, 000010 is decimal 2, and 000100 is decimal 4. Such a representation gives us an exact power of 2.

errorCode = errorCode | 2;

or

errorCode |= 2;

for short. If the errorCode were initially 0, this would give us a binary 000010 for the error code. If we needed to add the nonpositive-new-size error (in the changeSize function) to the error code later on, we would use the line

errorCode |= 4;

which would now give us a binary 000110 for the error code. Thus, for a particular error, the appropriate 1-bit gets set in the error code. Notice that if a particular error occurs more than once, the bitwise OR won't affect the binary representation. A 32-bit integer errorCode can allow us to store quite a few different kinds of errors, and combinations thereof, very easily.

So much for storing errors. Now, what about retrieving them? We can test the errorCode for an index-out-of-range error by using the expression

if (errorCode & 2)

If the 1-bit for index-out-of-range has not been set, this expression will yield 0 (false in C++) as shown in Figure 5.3a. Otherwise, the expression will yield 2, as shown in Figure 5.3b, and any nonzero number is regarded as true in C++. Thus, any type of error can be tested in errorCode by using the number associated with it (from Figure 5.2) in a bitwise AND with the errorCode.

The error codes are provided, for maintenance reasons, at the top of the class implementation file:

```
1    // Array.cpp – – function definitions for an array
2
3    // Error codes – – use powers of 2
4    // 0         No error.
5    // 1         Nonpositive size passed into constructor.
6    // 2         Invalid index was used.
7    // 4         Nonpositive new size passed into changeSize function
```

If we ever needed to modify this class in the future to deal with other possible errors, the maintainer would add an error code 8 here for the next code, along with a description. No error code is necessary for the situation in which we run out of heap memory (for example, in resizing an array). In this case, the new operator will throw an exception, which the client may choose to catch.

The constructor is shown next:

```
8    template <class DataType>
9    Array<DataType>::Array( int size )
10   {
11       if ( size < 1 ) {
12           capacity = 1;
```

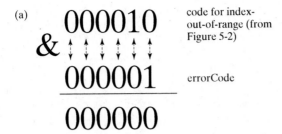

(a)

000010   code for index-
          out-of-range (from
          Figure 5-2)

000001   errorCode

000000

FIGURE 5.3

(b)

000010   code for index-
          out-of-range (from
          Figure 5-2)

000110   errorCode

000010

(a) The bit for the index-out-of-range has not been set in the errorCode, so such an error did not occur. When a bitwise AND is performed with the code for index-out-of-range, a 0 result is obtained, which represents false in C++. (b) The bit for index-out-of-range *has* been set for the errorCode, so such an error did occur. When a bitwise AND is performed with the code for index-out-of-range, we obtain a nonzero result, representing true in C++.

```
13                     errorCode = 1; // nonpositive size
14          }
15          else {
16                     capacity = size;
17                     errorCode = 0; // no error
18          }
19
20          elements = new DataType [capacity];
21  }
```

If the client passes in an invalid array size on line 9, it is checked on line 11. We don't want the program to crash, so we will create an array of size 1, setting capacity to 1 on line 12. The errorCode can then start off as 1 on line 13. If, however, size is valid, we use size for the capacity on line 16 and start errorCode off at 0 on line 17. Either way, the capacity is set to something we can use, and the dynamic array is created with the use of capacity on line 20.

Next, the overloaded operator [ ] is written:

```
22  template <class DataType>
23  inline DataType & Array<DataType>::operator [ ]( int index )
24  {
25  #ifdef DEBUG_ARRAY
26      if ( index < 0 || index >= capacity ) {
27              errorCode |= 2;  // invalid index
28              return dud;
29                  }
```

```
30  #endif
31      return elements[ index ];
32  }
```

For now, pretend that lines 25 and 30 aren't there. The index is checked on line 26 to see if it is valid. If it is not valid, line 27 performs a bitwise OR with errorCode and code 2, as described earlier. Then we return the dud element. (Something has to be returned, since the return type is DataType &.) Thus, lines 26–29 are for error checking. If it weren't for this, all we would need is line 31, which returns the array element at the *index* position, where index is passed in as a parameter. The return type is a reference type, so the location of this array element actually is returned; that way, the client can assign something to it, as in the statement

arr[5] = 10;

for example, where the name of the Array object is arr and index is 5. This line of code would assign 10 to elements[5]. When the location returned is used on the right side of an assignment (or anywhere else other than the left side of an assignment), the value at that location is used. Thus, with a reference return type, the overloaded operator [ ] can be used just like the array operators. We just have the added benefit of error checking, to prevent a program crash.

But without lines 25 and 30, we run into a performance problem. We would expect the operator [ ] function to be used intensely within the main program, and every time it is used, we would check for the index being out of range. As you can imagine, all this checking would slow down program execution. After all the bugs have been worked out of a program, we would like to remove the index checking, which would just waste time. Lines 25 and 30 allow what we call ***conditional compilation***. The client, in effect, chooses whether or not to compile lines 26–29 with the program. As an example, let's say the client has problems with his or her program and would like to debug it. If you look back in the Array header file, line 2 tells the client to use the lines of code

```
#define DEBUG_ARRAY
#include "Array.h"
```

in the client file in that order, for debugging purposes. The first of these lines sets up a preprocessor definition DEBUG_ARRAY. Then, on line 25 of the overloaded [ ] function, a preprocessor directive is used to test for the definition DEBUG_ARRAY (ifdef is short for "if defined"). If it has been defined, lines 26–29 are included in the compilation, helping the client debug the program. The #endif preprocessor directive on line 30 marks the end of the preprocessor "if" section. Notice that a program crash will occur if the client uses an invalid index and does not define DEBUG_ARRAY. Once the client has worked out all of the bugs in the program, line 3 (back in the Array header file) tells the client to comment out the definition of DEBUG_ARRAY for improved performance. Thus, the client would change these two lines to

```
// #define DEBUG_ARRAY
#include "Array.h"
```

and then recompile the program. This time, lines 26–29 of the overloaded [ ] function would be cut out of the compilation, improving performance.

The changeSize function is shown now:

```
33  // will not alter values unless newSize is smaller than current capacity;
34  // in this case, the values from 0 to newSize - 1 will not be altered
35  template <class DataType>
36  void Array<DataType>::changeSize( int newSize )
37  {
38      if ( newSize < 1 )
39      {
40              errorCode |= 4; // nonpositive new size
41              return;
42      }
43
44      DataType *newArray = new DataType [newSize];
45
46      int limit = (newSize > capacity)? capacity : newSize;
47
48      for ( int i = 0; i < limit; i++ )
49              newArray[ i ] = elements[ i ];
50
51      delete [ ] elements;
52
53      elements = newArray;
54
55      capacity = newSize;
56  }
```

This function is reminiscent of the doubleArray function used in Section 4.8, except that the new size of the array may be smaller if the client sees fit. On line 38, we check to see if newSize is less than 1. If so, we won't change the size of the array, the error-Code is updated on line 40, and we return on line 41. Otherwise, we create a new dynamic array with the new size, pointed to by newArray, on line 44.

Next, we use the ternary operator on line 46 to set a limit variable to either capacity or newSize. You may never have seen the ternary operator before, as it is sometimes not taught in lower level programming courses. The ternary operator, ?:, is an unusual operator, because it takes three operands; the first operand is placed to the left of the question mark, the second operand is placed between the question mark and the colon, and the third operand is placed after the colon. The first operand is a condition that evaluates to true or false. The second operand is the result of the operation if the condition is true. The third operand is the result of the operation if the condition is false.

For example, on line 46, we want limit to be the number of elements we actually need to copy over from the old array to the new array. If newSize > capacity, the client wants to create a larger array, so we will need to copy all elements over. Therefore, we want to set limit to the current capacity. The condition (newSize > capacity) is true, so the result of the operation is the second operand, capacity. Therefore, the result of the operation, capacity, replaces the entire operation (newSize > capacity)? capacity : newSize.

When capacity replaces the result of the entire operation, it is assigned to limit, which is what we want. If newSize is less than capacity, the client is making a smaller array, and we only need to copy newSize elements from the old array to the new array. The condition will be false and the result of the operation will be newSize, which is assigned to limit.

The condition can be written without using parentheses. I personally prefer parentheses because it makes it look more like an if condition. Line 46 could have been written as four lines:

```
if ( newSize > capacity )
        limit = capacity;
else
        limit = newSize;
```

Verify that these four lines do exactly the same thing as the one line with the ternary operator. Sometimes the ternary operator is used so that the program code is terser.

Finally, limit is used in the for loop on line 48, so that the minimum number of elements are copied from the old array pointed to by elements to the new array pointed to by newArray.

Once all of the values in the old array have been copied, the old array is freed on line 51. Then, since the elements pointer is in the private section, it is given the address of the new array on line 53. Finally, the new capacity of the array is set on line 55.

The length function is shown next:

```
57  template <class DataType>
58  inline int Array<DataType>::length( ) const
59  {
60     return capacity;
61  }
```

This function just returns the capacity. Such a function is called an ***accessor***.

Finally, the err function is shown:

```
62  template <class DataType>
63  string Array<DataType>::err( ) const
64  {
65
66     if ( errorCode == 0 )
67            return "No error.\n";
68
69     string errorMessage = "";
70     if ( errorCode & 1 ) { // nonpositive size
71            errorMessage += "Nonpositive size passed into constructor, so\n";
72            errorMessage += "the capacity was set to 1 by default.\n";
73     }
74     if ( errorCode & 2 )  // invalid index
```

```
75              errorMessage += "Index out of range.\n";
76      if ( errorCode & 4 ) { // nonpositive new size in changeSize
77              errorMessage += "Nonpositive size passed into changeSize, so\n";
78              errorMessage += "the size of the array was not changed.\n";
79      }
80
81      return errorMessage;
82 }
```

This function converts the errorCode into a useful string message for the client and returns it. On line 66, if there is no error, we return the appropriate message on line 67. On line 67, the '\n' character, called the newline character, will produce the same visual effect as endl if the string is printed to the screen. (This feature is provided as a convenience to the client.) If there is an error, the errorMessage string variable is first declared on line 69 and is set to the empty string. The bitwise AND is used on lines 70, 74, and 76 to test for the various errors. If these errors are found, appropriate messages are concatenated to the errorMessage string, with newline characters as appropriate. (This can make for a long message!) Then, errorMessage is returned on line 81.

It is unusual for data structure classes to contain error codes and conditional compilation. They were used in this class because (1) arrays are widely used in code and (2) arrays are commonly misused, causing quite a few problems.

5.2   USING THE ARRAY CLASS

Next, we'll look at a program that uses the Array class:

```
1   // useArray.cpp – – a program that demonstrates the use of the Array class
2
3   #include <iostream>
4   #define DEBUG_ARRAY
5   #include "Array.h"
6
7   using namespace std;
8
9   void getElements( Array<int> & numbers );
10
11  float calcAverage( Array<int> avnums );
12
13  int main( )
14  {
15      Array<int> nums( 2 );
16
17      getElements( nums );
18      float average = calcAverage( nums );
19
```

```
20      cout << "The average is: " << average << endl;
21
22      return 0;
23  }
24
25  void getElements( Array<int> & numbers )
26  {
27      int i = 0;
28
29      cout << "Enter a positive integer: ";
30      cin >> numbers[ i ];
31      while ( numbers[ i ] != -1 ) {
32              i++;
33              if ( i == numbers.length( ) )
34                      numbers.changeSize( i * 2 );
35              cout << "Enter a positive integer (enter -1 to stop): ";
36              cin >> numbers[ i ];
37              }
38
39      numbers.changeSize( i );
40
41      cout << "getElements: " << numbers.err( );
42  }
43
44  float calcAverage( Array<int> avnums )
45  {
46      int sum = 0;
47      for ( int i = 0; i <= avnums.length( ); i++ )
48              sum += avnums[ i ];
49
50      cout << "calcAverage: " << avnums.err( );
51      return sum / float( avnums.length( ) );
52  }
```

This program isn't so well written, but it does demonstrate some of the capabilities of the Array class. It contains an error that will be found during debugging. The program gets a series of positive integers from the user, who enters −1 when done entering positive integers. Then the program calculates the average of all the integers.

There are two functions, other than main. The getElements function gets all of the integers from the user. The calcAverage function calculates the average of all the numbers. This program could be written without using an array, of course, but then the Array object would not have a demonstration program, and everybody would be wondering what in the world a program that has nothing to do with arrays is doing here.

The file "Array.h" is included on line 5, and DEBUG_ARRAY is defined on line 4. On line 15, an array of two integers called nums is declared. Then the client calls the getElements function, passing in the nums object. This technique is similar to the way an array is passed by using the name of the array.

The getElements function begins on line 25. We start by setting an index i to 0 on line 27, as we would with any other array. We also read a value into the array on lines 30 and 36, as we would with any other array. We are using the overloaded operator [ ] on lines 30 and 36, but the client doesn't have to think about this. (Isn't abstraction wonderful?) The while loop on line 31 stops when the user enters a −1; otherwise the user can enter as many values as desired. However, in this program, the client assumes that the user won't enter so many values that the program runs out of heap memory.

The index i is incremented on line 32. At this point, the array may be filled, so we check i against the length function of the Array object. If the array is full, we double the size of the array on line 34. Then the user enters another positive integer (or −1) on line 36. When the user finally enters a −1, the last line of the function, line 39, sets the array size to the number of positive values entered by the user, because the array may not have been filled up to whatever the capacity happens to be at that time. Thus, we don't need to have a count of the number of elements as a reference parameter in the function either. Line 41 is used for debugging purposes.

Since the array was passed by reference, the changes to it have been reflected back up to the main function on line 17. Then the calcAverage function is called, passing in the nums array. The calcAverage function starts by setting a sum variable to 0 on line 46. Next, a for loop is written on lines 47–48 that adds all of the elements of the array. We use the length function of the Array object to stop the for loop on line 47. Line 50 is used for debugging purposes. Then the average is returned on line 51 by dividing the sum by the float type-casted length of the array, so a float result is calculated.

The main function gets the result on line 18 and then prints out the result on line 20. After the client runs the program and enters a series of positive values, the output of the program will be

getElements: No error.
calcAverage: Index out of range.
The average is: [some wrong result]

The client has a mistake on line 47: '<=' should be '<'. After the client is sure that everything is working, line 4 can be commented out for improved performance:

// #define DEBUG_ARRAY

Lines 41 and 50 can be commented out in a similar manner. It may be best to comment them out instead of remove them, so that they can easily be put back in if updates need to be made to the program.

Our Array class template is not really complete yet. This is because, when a data member in the class definition is a pointer and has been assigned an address of dynamic memory, there should always be three functions included in the public section: the destructor, the copy constructor, and the overloaded assignment operator. We will discuss the destructor first, since it is the easiest to understand.

5.3   DESTRUCTORS

A destructor is a special function of a class that is called automatically whenever an object is destroyed. That is, the client does not call this function explicitly. Let's suppose that we declare an Array object in a function called foo of the client program. Then when the foo function is done executing, the Array object will be destroyed, since it was declared within that function. However, the dynamic memory of the Array object will not be destroyed. The dynamic memory will be lost, causing memory leak—unless we write a destructor for the Array class. The destructor is called automatically whenever an object is destroyed, so, within the destructor, we can write a line of code that frees the dynamic array. Then, when the function foo is done executing, the Array object is destroyed, the destructor is called automatically (the client does not call it explicitly), and the dynamic array is freed. In that case, there is no memory leak.

The prototype for a destructor of the Array class should be in the public section of the class and is as follows:

```
~Array( );
```

The name of the destructor must be the name of the class, preceded by a tilde. Destructors take no parameters, because they are not called explicitly by the client. For the same reason, they have no return type (not even void). The function definition for the destructor (placed in the class implementation file) is shown next:

```
template <class DataType>
Array<Datatype>::~Array( )
{
        delete [ ] elements;
}
```

Its heading is similar to headings of other functions, except that it does not have a return type. Within the destructor, we use *delete* on all the pointers that exist as data members in the class. In this case, there is only one: a pointer to a dynamic array called elements. We would not need to use *delete* on any pointers that do not point to dynamic memory, of course. These types of pointers, however, are extremely rare, and we often do not even consider them.

Any code can be written in a destructor, just as it can in any other function. However, writing code that has nothing to do with the destruction of the object is usually not advised.

Objects can be destroyed in a number of different situations, each of which would call a destructor if one were written. As mentioned earlier, an object is eventually destroyed if it is declared locally within a function or within some other block of code, such as a while loop.

Objects are also destroyed when they are declared dynamically, and then *delete* is used to free them. For example,

```
Array<float> *ptr = new Array<float>(10);
.
. // other code
.
delete ptr;
```

In this case, the heap is searched for a chunk of memory large enough to hold an Array object with a float DataType. The address of the object is assigned to ptr. Later, we use *delete* to free this space. But we are actually destroying the object, so the destructor of the object is called automatically (if one is written).

At the time the program ends, if any objects are still in existence, their destructors will be called automatically (if they are written).

It is not always necessary to write a destructor for a class. They should always be written when there is a data member that is a pointer. Otherwise, there may be no purpose for a destructor.

5.4   THE COPY CONSTRUCTOR

If we wish to pass an Array object by value (instead of by reference) into a function, we need to write a special constructor called a copy constructor for the Array class. Let's examine why.

The parameter in the function call is called the ***actual parameter***, while the parameter in the function heading is called the ***formal parameter***, as illustrated in Figure 5.4. A good way to remember this is that the 'a' in actual comes before the 'f' in formal alphabetically and the function call comes before the execution of the function. Observe that if we pass a struct object by value into a function, the formal parameter becomes a copy of the actual parameter. This means that the value of each data member is copied from the actual parameter to the formal parameter, as Figure 5.5 shows. We can also pass an object of a class by value into a function, and the same effect occurs: The value of each data member in the actual parameter (the class object) is copied over into the formal parameter.

However, if we don't use a copy constructor and we have a data member that is a pointer, then the *address* stored in the pointer is copied from the actual parameter into the formal parameter. After all, the address is the value of the pointer variable. But we get an unexpected effect from this action: The pointers in both objects now point to the

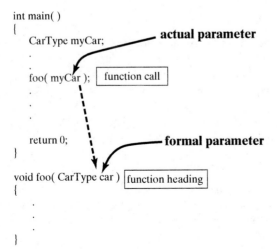

FIGURE 5.4

The actual parameter (myCar) and the formal parameter (car) when a function is used.

(a)

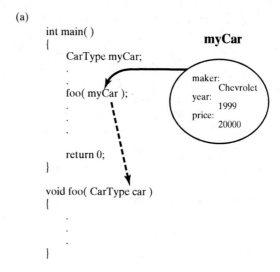

(b)

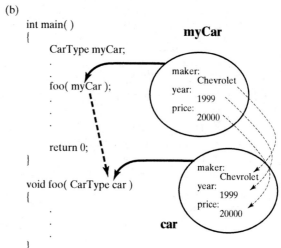

FIGURE 5.5

(a) The data members in the myCar object at the time the function call is made. (b) Since the function call is made by value instead of by reference, the car object is created (in the foo function heading) and the values of the data members are copied from myCar (the actual parameter) to car (the formal parameter).

same place in memory, because they both have that same address. Therefore, if we use the pointer of one object to change what it points to, it essentially changes the other object. This situation is illustrated in Figure 5.6 for the Array object. It is not what we want in pass by value: We don't want changes in the formal parameter to be reflected back to the actual parameter.

It gets worse. The formal parameter will be destroyed at the end of the function, being a local object, and the destructor will be called for it. For Array objects, this will free the array that elements points to. But now, the actual parameter won't have an array any more! When that happens, the elements pointer in the actual parameter is called a ***dangling pointer*** or a ***dangling reference***. Since a client doesn't expect this effect from passing by value, it can wreak havoc with clients' programs, especially because the client does not know or care whether or not we are even using pointers in the class.

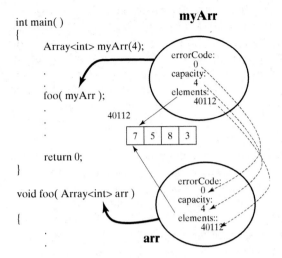

FIGURE 5.6

The elements pointer in the myArr object stores the address of the array shown, so elements points to it. When function foo is called, passing in the Array object myArr by value, the values of the data members in the myArr object (the actual parameter) are copied into the arr object (the formal parameter). The address stored in the elements pointer is also a value that is copied over. So now, the elements pointer in the arr object points to the same array. Any change made to the array in function foo will be reflected back into the main function. (The myArr object will have the same change made to its array.)

We can use a copy constructor to get rid of this problem. In fact, one should be written whenever there is a data member that is a pointer in a class whenever the pointer will point to dynamic memory. The copy constructor usually allocates new dynamic memory for the formal parameter's pointer. The values in the dynamic memory of the actual parameter are copied into the dynamic memory of the formal parameter. Then the actual parameter and the formal parameter are no longer pointing to the same thing (their pointers will store different addresses), but what they point to will contain the same values. Figure 5.7 shows the effect that would be produced from using a copy constructor.

When a copy constructor function is written for a class, the normal copying of data members from the actual parameter to the formal parameter isn't done anymore.

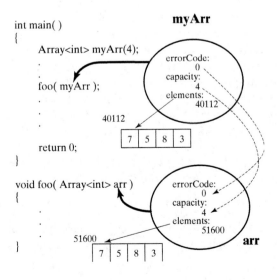

FIGURE 5.7

Effect that a copy constructor would achieve when an Array object is passed by value. The values of the data members that are not pointers would be copied over. However, for the elements pointer in arr (the formal parameter), a new array is created in the heap and the address is assigned to elements. All values, however, from the array in myArr (the actual parameter) are copied into the array in arr (the formal parameter).

Instead, the code in the copy constructor is followed to do the copying. A copy constructor is a special function that is called automatically when an object of the class it belongs to is passed by value. The programmer does not call the copy constructor explicitly. If a copy constructor is not written by the programmer, a copy constructor is supplied automatically by the compiler. But such a copy constructor will copy the address of pointer data members from the actual parameter to the formal parameter, which is not what we want.

Let's look at the prototype for the copy constructor of the Array class template:

Array(const Array<DataType> & ap);

As you might expect, it has no return type. Its name must be the name of the class, as with other constructors. Let's suppose that a client passes an Array object by value into a function called foo. The copy constructor heading passes in one parameter, which is the foo actual parameter object. The copy constructor function is called for the foo *formal* parameter object. The parameter of the copy constructor is passed by const reference, so the foo actual parameter cannot be changed within the copy constructor function. The parameter of the copy constructor is never passed by value. If it were, the pass by value would call the copy constructor again automatically, and then call it again and again, creating an infinite loop. The name of the parameter has been designated ap, short for *actual parameter*. It is easy to recognize a copy constructor when you look at any class definition; it has the name of the class, and it passes in an object of the class as a parameter.

So, let's be clear what happens with copy constructors at this point. The client passes an Array object by value into one of his or her functions, say, function foo. The copy constructor is called automatically for the foo formal parameter object. The copy constructor creates a copy of the foo actual parameter object for the foo formal parameter object, as we saw in Figure 5.7, so the pointer problem doesn't occur. Then, after the copy constructor has completed execution, function foo begins execution.

When only the address of a pointer in one object is copied into a pointer of another object, the copy is said to be a ***shallow copy***. This kind of copy often leads to confusion, such as inadvertently changing the original object when changes to a copied object are made; or it leads to other problems, like dangling pointers. In order to avoid these problems, we make a ***deep copy*** in the copy constructor. In a deep copy, all variables and objects that don't use heap memory are copied normally. When it comes to pointers, however, the way to avoid copying addresses is to dynamically allocate more memory for the formal parameter, so that the structure being copied matches that of the actual parameter. A deep copy also means that we must copy all of the *data* in the dynamically allocated memory of the original into the dynamically allocated memory of the copy. Thus, in a deep copy, the *structure* and the *data* are the same in the copy, but the addresses of the used heap memory are necessarily different, to avoid having the pointers in the two objects point to the same thing.

Deep copies also need to be made when the programmer uses the assignment operator = to assign one Array object to another Array object, as in the code

arr1 = arr2;

where arr1 and arr2 are both Array objects. This statement copies the data members of Array objects just as if it were a struct object assignment. If we don't use an overloaded assignment operator function written for the Array class, however, and we have a data member that is a pointer, then a shallow copy is made: The address stored in the pointer in the object on the right of the assignment is stored in the corresponding pointer in the object on the left side of the assignment. This action, however, creates the same type of pointer problem that we saw earlier: A change in what the object on the left points to will cause the same change in the object on the right as a side effect, and vice versa. Therefore, an overloaded assignment operator function is written to do a deep copy as well. Since the copy constructor and the overloaded assignment operator function both make a deep copy, it will benefit us to make a function called deep-Copy that will be called from the copy constructor and overloaded assignment operator functions. We shall do so throughout this book whenever we need to make copy constructors and overloaded assignment operator functions. The deepCopy function prototype should be placed in the private section, since we do not want the client to call that function. For example, the private section of the Array now looks like this:

```
private:
        DataType *elements;        // points to the dynamic array
        int capacity;
        DataType dud;           // returned from operator [ ] if index error occurs
        int errorCode;               // contains code for error if array misuse occurs
        inline void deepCopy( const Array<DataType> & original );
```

The copy constructor can simply be written in the implementation file, then, to call the deepCopy function:

```
template <class DataType>
Array<DataType>::Array( const Array<DataType> & ap )
{
        deepCopy( ap );
}
```

Recall that when the client passes an Array by value into a function, say, foo, the copy constructor is called for the foo formal parameter object in the function foo heading and the ap parameter shown is the foo actual parameter object from the function call for foo. The use of the copy constructor is illustrated in Figure 5.8. This copy constructor is passing the foo actual parameter Array object to the deepCopy function. The deepCopy function will now make the deep copy:

```
1   template <class DataType>
2   inline void Array<DataType>::deepCopy( const Array<DataType> & original )
3   {
4      capacity = original.capacity;
5      errorCode = original.errorCode;
6      elements = new DataType [capacity];
7      for ( int i = 0; i < capacity; i++ )
8              elements[ i ] = original.elements[ i ];
9   }
```

FIGURE 5.8

How the copy constructor is used. The numbers in circles indicate the steps that take place, in the order shown. In step 1, the function call is made, which is pass by value. This automatically calls the copy constructor for the arr object (the formal parameter). In step 2, the myArr object (the actual parameter) is passed into the ap parameter of the copy constructor. The deepCopy function is then called, to make the kind of copy that was shown in Figure 5.7, using the myArr object as the original. After the copy constructor is done executing, step 3 executes the foo function.

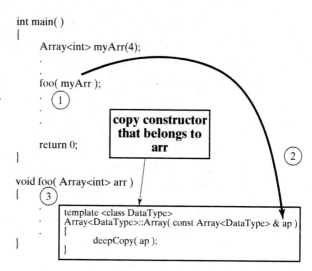

```
int main( )
{
    Array<int> myArr(4);
    .
    .
    foo( myArr );
    ①
    .
    .
    .
    return 0;
}

void foo( Array<int> arr )
{  ③
    .
    .
    .
}
```

copy constructor that belongs to arr

②

```
template <class DataType>
Array<DataType>::Array( const Array<DataType> & ap )
{
    deepCopy( ap );
}
```

We can use inline on the deepCopy function, since it is called only from the copy constructor and the overloaded assignment operator functions. The assigning of normal data members takes place on lines 4–5. On line 4, the variable capacity is for the formal parameter (in the foo function heading in this example). So we are simply assigning the capacity of the formal parameter the same value as the capacity of the actual parameter, *original.capacity*, from the foo function call. This is the same type of copying that would take place in passing an Array object by value if a copy constructor were never written. The errorCode is copied the same way on line 5. We could make a copy of the dud data member here as well, but since it is not really useful to do so, we do not.

Handling the assignment of the pointer (for the deep copy) is done on line 6. We create a new array and assign its address to the elements pointer on the left side of the assignment. Then, using the for loop on lines 7–8, we copy all the elements stored in the dynamic array of the actual foo parameter into the separate dynamic array of the formal foo parameter. In our example, then, the deep copy function finishes and returns to the copy constructor. The copy constructor is done, too, at this point (it just called deepCopy), so function foo executes with its Array object parameter fully formed and without any interference to the actual Array parameter.

It is important to realize that a copy constructor is called automatically in a couple of other situations, other than just passing an object by value. A copy constructor is also called when an object is returned by value from a function if a copy constructor is written. This is because the object is actually copied back to the calling function.

Finally, a third situation that will call a copy constructor is when an object is initialized in its declaration, as in the code.

Array<float> arr = arr2;

Many people make the mistake of thinking that this statement will call the overloaded assignment operator function for the Array class if such an operator function is written. But it doesn't; if the object is initialized in its declaration by an assignment, the copy constructor for that object is called (if a copy constructor is written). In this case, the regular constructor is not called for the arr object. Instead, the *copy* constructor for arr is called, passing in arr2 as its parameter. The overloaded assignment operator would be called when the object on the left of the assignment is not being declared.

When you make a copy constructor for any class, it will only need to make a call to a deepCopy function, declared in the private section of the class. When you write your own deepCopy function, you can follow these guidelines:

- Copy all data members directly that are not pointers; copy static arrays element by element, using loops.
- Do a deep copy for all data members that are pointers; that is, allocate dynamic memory from the heap for them, and then copy all of the values over into the dynamic memory.
- The deepCopy function can throw an exception if there is not enough heap memory. Write comments in the class specification file to let a client know that object assignment and passing by value can throw an exception.

5.5   THE OVERLOADED ASSIGNMENT OPERATOR FUNCTION

If we wish to assign one Array object to another Array object, so that all the elements are copied over with a simple assignment, we need to do this by overloading the assignment operator for the Array class.

Recall that it is permitted to assign an object of a struct to another object of the same struct—for example,

yourCar = myCar;

where yourCar and myCar are objects made from the same CarType struct. Recall that the effect of such an assignment would be to set the value of each data member in yourCar to the same value in the corresponding data member of myCar. We may also assign the object of a class to another object of the same class without using the overloaded assignment operator. The result of the assignment is the same as it is for structs: Each data member of the object on the left of the assignment is assigned the value of the corresponding data member of the object on the right of the assignment.

However, if we don't use an overloaded assignment operator, and we have a data member that is a pointer, then the address stored in the pointer in the object on the right of the assignment is stored in the corresponding pointer in the object on the left side of the assignment. As in the problem with passing objects by value, the pointers in both objects now point to the same place in memory, because they both have that same address. A possible side effect of this problem is illustrated in Figure 5.9. Another problem is that when we change the array for one object, it will affect the other object also.

We can use an overloaded assignment operator function to get rid of this problem, the same way we use a copy constructor to get rid of the problem of passing objects by value. In fact, such a function should be written whenever a data member that is a pointer in a class will point to dynamic memory.

(a)   Array Object
arr1

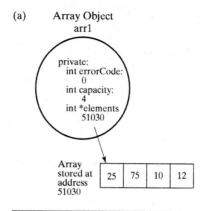

FIGURE 5.9

(a) An Array object called arr1. Consider
the code section:

```
Array<int> arr1(4);
// other code
if ( a > b ) {
    Array<int> arr2(4);
    arr2 = arr1;
    .
    . // other code
    .
}
```

(b) Result of the assignment of arr1 to arr2:
All values of all data members are copied
over, including the address stored in
elements. (c) Array arr2 was declared inside
the body of the if statement, so it no longer
exists when the body of the if statement is
done executing; the destructor for arr2 is
called, freeing the dynamic array. But now,
the elements pointer in arr1 is a dangling
reference.

(b)   Array Object   Array Object
arr1   arr2

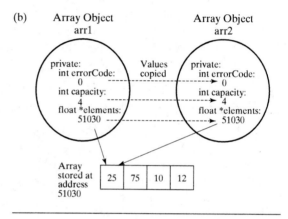

(c)   Array Object
arr1

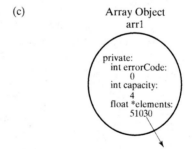

The overloaded assignment operator function will call the deepCopy function to
make the deep copy, but it has to do a little more than just that: We must account for
some situations that make assignment different from passing parameters. One such situation that is sometimes overlooked is the use of the result of the assignment operation. Recall that the assignment operation produces a result, other than just assigning,
in much the same way as an addition operation produces a result. The result of the assignment operation happens to be the value assigned to the variable on the left. If that
didn't happen, then code like this wouldn't work:

x = y = 1;

The assignment operation is right associative, so y = 1 is performed first. It produces a result of 1. This 1 gets substituted for y = 1, just as the value resulting from an addition gets substituted for the addition. After the substitution, the expression x = 1 is evaluated. Its result is not used, and only the assignment is performed. So now, both x and y are assigned the value 1.

When an Array assignment is made, such as

arr1 = arr2 = arr3;

the result of the Array assignment should be an Array object for the same reason: so that a string of array assignments can be made. Therefore, our overloaded assignment operator will have an Array object as a return type. However, recall from the last section that the copy constructor is called if an object is returned by value. To be more efficient and avoid a call to the copy constructor, we can return an Array object by reference. Hence, the function prototype for the overloaded assignment operator of the Array will look like this:

Array<DataType> & operator =(const Array<DataType> & right);

The return type of the function is Array$<$DataType$>$ &. Thus, if we declare an array such as

Array<int> arr1(4);

the return type of operator = will be Array$<$int$>$ &. (Recall that when a class template is involved, the type of the object must include the angle brackets with the type used to make the class.) So the return type looks intimidating, but there is nothing to it. After that, we have the name of the function, "operator =". Finally, we have the parameter. Recall that for a binary overloaded operator, the operator function will be called for the object on the left and the object on the right is passed in as a parameter. Hence, the parameter is the Array object on the right side of the assignment. Notice that it is appropriately passed in by const reference. Its name is "right", short for "right array," a reminder that it is the object on the right of the assignment.

Let's take a look at the function definition for the overloaded assignment operator, as written in the class implementation file for the Array:

```
1   template <class DataType>
2   Array<DataType> & Array<DataType>::operator =( const Array<DataType> & right )
3   {
4       if ( this == &right )
5               return *this;
6       delete [ ] elements;
7       deepCopy( right );
8
9       return *this;
10  }
```

We'll discuss lines 4–5 last. Notice that the deepCopy function is called on line 7. Recall that in the deepCopy function, a new dynamic array is created. (In the assignment situation, it would be for the Array object on the left side of the assignment.) Without line 6, the creation of the array will give us memory leak. Now, consider

arr1 = arr2;

where arr1 already has a dynamic array, which would be created when its constructor was called. The elements pointer has the address of this array. This address would be lost when a new address is assigned to elements (on line 6 of the deepCopy function). Therefore, we must be very careful to free the memory that is pointed to by the elements pointer on line 6 of the overloaded assignment function before we call the deepCopy function on line 7.

On line 9, we return *this. You might conclude from the notation that *this* is a pointer, and you would be right. But you won't see it declared anywhere, because it is a keyword. It is recognized by the compiler as a pointer to the object that owns the function that is being executed. Therefore, in this case, it is a pointer to the object on the left side of the assignment operator. The *this* keyword can be used in any class or struct function. If we use *this* by itself, it gives the address of the object that owns the function. If we dereference *this*, as on line 9, we are getting the actual object that owns the function. We are returning that object, which means that it is the result of the assignment operation. It can then be assigned to another Array object if it is in a multiple assignment statement, such as

arr1 = arr2 = arr3;

Finally, let's discuss lines 4–5. We are comparing *this* with the address of the object on the right of the assignment. This condition will only be true if the addresses are the same, and the addresses will be the same only if they are exactly the same object. In other words, the condition is true if the client writes code like this:

arr1 = arr1;

This example is impractical, but we will explain lines 4–5 by looking at this example first and then a more practical example. If the client writes the preceding code, and we don't include lines 4–5, then the dynamic array is freed on line 6! If it is freed, forget about copying it in this situation. We certainly don't want this to happen, so if the client writes such code, operator = returns *this, the left object, right away on line 5. Although the assignment shown would not normally be written by a client, the client might be writing some complicated code and might be assigning the same object to itself without even knowing it. For example, consider an array of Array objects. The client might assign

arrOfArray[i] = arrOfArray[j];

Since each element is an Array object, if i and j are calculated to store the same value, this would give us precisely the situation where we need lines 4–5. I have noticed that some algorithms (particularly sorting algorithms, discussed in a later chapter) can assign an element of an array to itself during the algorithm in some situations. So we are just being safe here on lines 4–5, and it is good to be safe.

Again, we return the left Array object by reference to avoid a call to the copy constructor, which would be called if the Array object were returned by value. When we write other types of functions, we cannot always return an object by reference when we need to return an object. This would give us problems, for example, if the object were declared locally in the function. The object would be destroyed, and the function would try to return its location (which is what is returned by reference). We *can* return by reference in the case of the overloaded assignment operator function because the object on the left of the assignment will not be destroyed when the function completes execution. An object can always be returned by value from a function, even if it is declared locally, because the copy constructor will make a copy of it for the calling function before it is destroyed.

When a class has a data member which is a pointer that will point to dynamic memory, you should always write an overloaded assignment operator, even if it seems highly unlikely that such object assignments will take place in the client program. We can never completely foresee the multitude of ways in which clients will use our classes. If, however, a class does not have a data member that is a pointer, it is usually not necessary to write an overloaded assignment operator.

When you write your own overloaded assignment operator, you can follow these guidelines:

- Check for the same object (as on line 4), and return *this if the objects are the same.
- Free the dynamic memory pointed to by all pointers in the left object.
- Call the deepCopy function.
- Return *this at the end.

5.6   AN EXAMPLE

To summarize, when a class includes data members that are pointers which will point to dynamic memory, if the class is well designed, it will include (1) a destructor, (2) a copy constructor, and (3) an overloaded assignment operator. Let's look at an example which caps off most of the things that were written about here. First of all, we will output a line in each of these three functions. When we enter the function, we will print out that fact. For example, let's write the destructor as

```
template <class DataType>
Array<DataType>::~Array( )
{
        cout << "Destructor called" << endl;
        delete [ ] elements;
}
```

We will also do this for the copy constructor and the overloaded assignment operator. But we should never write any of these functions with the output statements shown; they are being used for demonstration purposes only.

We will use the main program that appears in Section 5.2, with some changes:

```
1    // useArray.cpp – – a program that demonstrates the use of the Array class
2
3    #include <iostream>
4    #include "Array.h"
5
6    using namespace std;
7
8    Array<int> getElements( );
9
10   float calcAverage( Array<int> avnums );
11
12   int main( )
13   {
14       Array<int> nums(2);
15
16       nums = getElements( );
17
18       Array<int> nums2 = nums;
19
20       float average = calcAverage( nums2 );
21
22       cout << "The average is: " << average << endl;
23
24       return 0;
25   }
26
27   Array<int> getElements( )
28   {
29       cout << "getElements called." << endl;
30
31       Array<int> numbers( 2 );
32       int i = 0;
33
34       cout << "Enter a positive integer: ";
35       cin >> numbers[ i ];
36       while ( numbers[ i ] != -1 ) {
37           i++;
38           if ( i == numbers.length( ) )
39               numbers.changeSize( i * 2 );
40           cout << "Enter a positive integer (enter -1 to stop): ";
41           cin >> numbers[ i ];
42           }
43
```

```
44       numbers.changeSize( i );
45
46       return numbers;
47  }
48
49  float calcAverage( Array<int> avnums )
50  {
51       cout << "calcAverage called." << endl;
52       int sum = 0;
53       for ( int i = 0; i < avnums.length( ); i++ )
54               sum += avnums[ i ];
55
56       return sum / float( avnums.length( ) );
57  }
```

This program's getElements function now declares an Array object locally, gets all the values from the user, and then returns the Array object by value. Line 18 is an extra line that is thrown in, and the program calculates the average of the nums2 Array on line 20. This average will be the same as that for the nums Array. Also, at the beginning of the getElements and calcAverage functions, we print out a line showing that these functions were called.

This program ran, and the following input values were typed in: 9 8 7 6. After a −1 (the sentinel value) was entered, the following output was displayed:

```
58   getElements called.
59   Enter a positive integer: 9
60   Enter a positive integer (enter -1 to stop): 8
61   Enter a positive integer (enter -1 to stop): 7
62   Enter a positive integer (enter -1 to stop): 6
63   Enter a positive integer (enter -1 to stop): -1
64   Copy constructor called
65   Destructor called
66   Overloaded assignment operator called
67   Destructor called
68   Copy constructor called
69   Copy constructor called
70   calcAverage called
71   Destructor called
72   The average is:  7.5
73   Destructor called
74   Destructor called
```

As an exercise, try to follow the code and see how the output was created. If you get stuck, look at the explanation in the next paragraph.

First, the getElements function is called, as shown on line 58. Afterwards, some values were entered on lines 59–63, with −1 being the sentinel value. The copy constructor is called next, as shown on line 64. (The copy constructor is called to return the Array object by value.) The destructor is called on line 65 for the numbers Array declared locally in the getElements function. Then the overloaded assignment operator is called, as shown on line 66, to carry out the assignment on line 16. There is no more use for the Array object that was returned by value (copied by the copy constructor), so C++ wisely destroys it, as shown on line 67. (This Array object conceptually replaced the getElements function call.) On line 68, the copy constructor is called to perform the assignment on line 18. Then, nums2 is passed by value into calcAverage, so the copy constructor is called again, as shown on line 69. After the copy constructor is done executing, the calcAverage function starts, as shown on line 70. When the calcAverage function finishes executing, the avnums Array (line 49) needs to be destroyed, as shown on line 71. Execution resumed in the main function, so the average is shown on line 72. After the program is done executing, there are two Array objects that remain—nums and nums2—so they are destroyed, as shown on lines 73–74. (The order of destruction is not known.)

You should go through the last example again and make sure that you understand everything perfectly before we move on. There shouldn't be any mysteries; after all, you need a good foundation when you're in the building business.

5.7   ADVANTAGES AND DISADVANTAGES OF AN ARRAY CLASS

The Array class has both advantages and disadvantages. The first disadvantage is that we can run out of heap memory (although that is very unlikely). The changeSize function, for example, can throw an exception if there is no more heap memory. The client can check for this exception by using try...catch clauses if the client thinks that running out of heap memory is possible, but a static array doesn't have that problem. A second disadvantage is that one has to remember to include "Array.h", something that doesn't have to be done with regular arrays.

The Array class has a number of advantages over regular arrays:

1. Whenever an array needs to be passed into a function, it can be passed as a single parameter. A class programmer can rest assured that the length function truly returns the capacity of the array. If the size is passed as a parameter, the size can be faulty; consequently, a class function may try to access an array position that doesn't exist, causing the program to crash.

2. The Array class is easier to use in a data structure or in any client program that needs adjustable arrays. There is no need to write lengthy doubleArray or cutArray functions; all that is required is a simple call to the changeSize function.

3. Programs will no longer crash when the client uses an invalid index in an array and defines DEBUG_ARRAY. Instead, there will be no effect on the array. This makes debugging less frustrating, and the client can use the err function to identify any errors.

4. The err function makes debugging easier. In regular arrays, when an invalid index is accessed, the program crashes, but the client may have no idea why. The program won't crash because of an invalid index in an Array object when DEBUG_ARRAY is defined, but the program still won't work; the err function tells the client why the program doesn't work.

5. The length function makes it easier to set up loops for processing arrays. When the length is equal to the count of the number of elements used, there is no need to create an extra variable to store the count of the number of elements.

6. The client has a choice of whether to pass an array by reference or by value; regular arrays can be passed only by reference.

7. The client can assign one array to another array with the assignment operator, which would copy all of the elements over in a single statement (because we have a written overloaded assignment operator). In regular arrays, a client would have to set up a loop and copy the array element by element.

8. When an Array object is declared in the private section of a class, instead of a pointer for a dynamic array, there may not be any pointers in the private section. If not, there will be no need to write a copy constructor, an overloaded assignment operator, and a destructor for that class. In assigning one object of the class to another object of the same type, for example, each data member is assigned individually. In such a case, the overloaded assignment operator of the Array class will be called automatically.

5.8   THE STANDARD TEMPLATE LIBRARY

This is a good place to mention the *Standard Template Library (STL)* provided with C++. The STL is a nice package of commonly used templates that clients often want to use in their programs. For example, there is a class template called *vector* that is similar to the Array class template. To use it, one would put

#include <vector>

at the top of the file in which one intends to use it (instead of including Array.h). The vector class template has both an overloaded [ ] operator and a function similar to changeSize called resize. It also has more than one constructor, and one of them is similar to the Array class template's constructor, passing in the size of the initial array.

Some people are going to wonder why on earth I made an Array class template instead of using the vector class template. Well, I might have to hang some garlic around my neck after I explain why, but the operator [ ] function in the vector class can crash the program if the client supplies the wrong index. This can be frustrating for the client, who won't know why the program doesn't work. If the client defines DEBUG_ARRAY and supplies the wrong index, the program won't crash; it won't work either, but the client may easily find the cause of the problem by using the err function.

That being said, the STL contains some useful class templates that have been well designed, and I don't blame people at all for using them. (Maybe I won't need the garlic after all!). The STL contains templates for some of the data structures we will be discussing later. The reason that you will see these data structures designed from scratch is that you really need to see how they are designed. Throughout your career, you'll encounter many situations in which you will need to make a custom data structure that doesn't exist in the STL (or anywhere else, for that matter). So we won't be using the STL in the remainder of the book. But it is still good to know that it is there, and you can see what is available in the STL from the Help section of your compiler or by consulting one of the many texts that are written on the STL.

SUMMARY

In this chapter, an Array class has been presented, which will make it easier to write data structures that use a dynamic array. The Array class is rather convenient, and many clients may choose to use it as well. We may not want to use the Array class in every single situation in which an array is used, because there are some disadvantages, which were disclosed in Section 5.7. However, there are many advantages that were listed in that section, too, which make the Array an attractive choice.

We will use the Array class for several data structures, including stacks, hash tables, priority queues, and graphs. As we shall see, we will not have to write copy constructors, destructors, or overloaded assignment operators for these classes, even though they have a dynamic array, because the use of the Array class will free the dynamic array in the Array destructor and deep copies of the Array object will be made automatically with the copy constructor and overloaded assignment operator of the Array class.

Whenever a pointer in the private section of a class will be used to point to dynamic memory, you should always have a destructor, an overloaded assignment operator, and a copy constructor. If you do not have the overloaded assignment operator and the copy constructor in such a case, you will not get a deep copy in assignments and parameter passing. In all of the classes of this textbook, when a pointer in the private section points to dynamic memory, these three functions have been provided. It is enlightening to go through the last example in Section 5.6 and see exactly how those functions are called.

EXERCISES

1. What is a destructor? Why is it necessary to have one when there is a pointer in the private section of a class?
2. What are the three situations in which a destructor is called?
3. Why is it necessary to have an overloaded assignment operator when there is a pointer in the private section of a class?
4. What is the difference between a shallow copy and a deep copy?
5. What does the *this* keyword stand for?
6. In the overloaded assignment operator, why is a parameter passed by const reference?
7. Why is a copy constructor necessary when there is a pointer in the private section of a class?
8. What is an actual parameter and what is a formal parameter?
9. In what three situations is a copy constructor called?
10. Write a destructor, an overloaded assignment operator, and a copy constructor for the ServerGroup class of Exercise 16 in Chapter 4. Make sure to test the overloaded assignment operator and the copy constructor by using them in a main program.
11. Explain what return by reference means and why it was used in the return type for operator [ ] of the Array class.
12. The shift operator $<<$ can sometimes come in handy when a scheme similar to the error-Code is used in the Array class template. The shift operation $1 << n$ is equal to 2^n for some nonnegative integer n, but is performed a lot faster. Suppose that an organization has 20 people, identified from 0 to 19. When a meeting is held, it is unlikely that all 20 people will attend. Devise a way to store a list of all people who attended a meeting by storing them into

a single integer. How would you find out if a person with a particular identification number attended the meeting?

13. Why is it possible for the following line of code to be valid, given that foo is an object of the Foo class and bar is a function within the Foo class?

```
foo.bar( ) = 3;
```

14. If an Array object is passed as a parameter into a class function and DEBUG_ARRAY is defined, how do we know that the class function won't crash the program by accessing an invalid index of the array?

15. Describe the disadvantages and advantages of using the Array class.

CHAPTER 6

Introduction to Object-Oriented Programming

At the beginning of Chapter 4, we talked about setting the size of the checks array and stated that setting a fixed size could end up to be a problem. If the size is set too small, it will be a problem for some clients who would like to store more checks. If the size is too large, it will waste a lot of memory for many other clients, who will only use a small number of checks. Setting a fixed size for data in a data structure presents a similar problem. We talked about using an adjustable array, where the size increases with the number of checks that are written. With our Array class in hand, let's use it now in the Checkbook class, to achieve this goal. When one class object is a member of another class object, as the Array will be a member of the Checkbook, we call this a **composition** relationship between the classes.

6.1   COMPOSITION

Our new class for the Checkbook is as follows:

```
1   // CheckBook.h – a class template for a CheckBook, where the check is any data type
2   // The constructor and the writeCheck function can throw exceptions if out of heap
3   // memory.
4
5   // to use a struct for the DataType, you must overload the following operators:
6   //    >       left operand:  struct object     right operand:  float
7   //            used to compare the amount of the check in the struct object with the
8   //            balance
9   //    -=      left operand:  float                    right operand:  struct object
```

```
10  //          used to subtract the amount of the check in the struct object from the
11  //          balance
12
13  #include "Array.h"
14
15  template <class DataType>
16  class CheckBook
17  {
18  public:
19      CheckBook( float initBalance );
20      bool writeCheck( const DataType & amount );  // returns false if amount is greater
21                                      // than balance; otherwise returns true
22      void deposit( float amount );
23      float getBalance( ) const;
24      Array<DataType> getChecks( );
25      float getLastDeposit( ) const;
26  private:
27      float balance;
28      int lastIndex;  // the index of the last check that was written
29      Array<DataType> checks;
30      float lastDeposit;
31  };
32
33  #include "CheckBook.cpp"
```

A number of changes have been made. Let's look at line 24 first. This function used to be called getLastChecks, but is now called getChecks. And it is now returning an Array<DataType> type instead of returning a CheckInfo<DataType> type. Recall that the CheckInfo struct included the array and also the number of elements in the array as members, to make things convenient for the client. But in the Array class, we have a length function already, so all we really need to do is return the Array object.

So what happened to the backward compatibility that we kept harping on in the earlier chapters? Won't our changes create a problem? Well, we could have added new functions with different names and kept the old ones in, but the class would become more cluttered. This sometimes happens when continuous modifications are made to a class in the maintenance cycle of the software. Sometimes when a class becomes too cluttered, it is best just to design a new class, possibly for a library, and keep the old class in the library for backward compatibility. If you haven't noticed, we've really made a new class: CheckBook with a capital B. (It used to be Checkbook.) Keeping the old class in the library allows backward compatibility, and the clients can start using the new CheckBook class if they so desire.

In the new CheckBook class, we've eliminated the code for the default constructor and the setBalance function as well. We also no longer have a getLastCheck function. So our CheckBook class is a little leaner and meaner.

On line 29, we are using an Array as a private member, and we've included Array.h on line 13. However, line 29 does not call the constructor. When an object of one class is declared as a data member of another class, the constructor for it is not called until the constructor of the containing class (in this case CheckBook) is called. Notice, however, that there is no pointer in the private section. Therefore, we do not need the copy constructor, the destructor, and the overloaded assignment operator.

Yet, if we pass a CheckBook by value into a function, won't the copy constructor of the Array class need to be called? The answer is yes, and it is called automatically. C++ actually has an implicit copy constructor for passing data members from one object into another. But when it comes time to pass the Array object, the copy constructor for the Array object is called. The same thing happens with assignment: An overloaded assignment operator is not necessary in order for an assignment to take place; C++ has an implicit assignment operator that copies the data members from the right side of the assignment to the left side. When the Array object has to be copied, the overloaded assignment operator for it will be called automatically. No destructor is written here either. Whenever an object is destroyed, the destructors of all objects that it contains as data members are called, even if no destructor is written for the containing object. So the destructor for the Array object will be called whenever the Check-Book is destroyed. Nice, huh?

One important thing you have to keep in mind about an object in the private section is that the private data members of this object cannot be directly accessed by the containing object. For example, we cannot directly access the errorCode variable in the Array class when we write the class functions for the CheckBook class. When data members are private, they really *are* private.

Let's turn our attention now to the implementation file, beginning with the constructor:

```
1    template <class DataType>
2    CheckBook<DataType>::CheckBook( float initBalance )
3    : balance( initBalance ), lastIndex( - 1 ), checks( 2 )
4    {
5    }
```

This constructor has something you've probably never seen before, called an *initializer list*, on line 3. An initializer list has to be used when an object in the private section is a data member that has no default constructor (a constructor with no parameters). In this case, that object is the Array object called checks, which must pass a size. At the end of the initializer list on line 3, the constructor for the Array object is called, passing in a size of 2 with the expression "checks(2)". Think about how this expression would relate to an Array declaration that would call its constructor:

```
Array<float> checks( 2 );
```

In the initializer list, values can be assigned to any data members of the class (not just object data members). The value assignment for non-object data members is a little different, however. No assignment operator is used. Instead, parentheses are used around the value that is being assigned. Take a look at the expression balance(init-Balance) on line 3, for example. It assigns initBalance to balance. The constructor could have been written like this:

```
template <class DataType>
CheckBook<DataType>::CheckBook( float initBalance )
: checks( 2 )
{
        balance = initBalance;
        lastIndex = -1;
}
```

But then you wouldn't have another example of how other data members can be assigned in an initializer list.

The index lastIndex is set to -1. The initial value of lastIndex cannot be 0, because it would mean that there is one check in the checks array at index 0. Since we are going to increment lastIndex when we add a check, and we want lastIndex to be 0 when the first element is added, the initial value of -1 makes perfect sense. The lastIndex is initialized in the initializer list on line 3 also.

We set the Array object with an initial capacity of 2 on line 3, but we will double the capacity of the array whenever it is filled. As you will see later, doubling the capacity of an array when it is filled is a good strategy for efficiency. Doubling the capacity of the Array takes place in the writeCheck function, shown next:

```
1    // returns false if amount is greater than balance; otherwise, returns true
2    template <class DataType>
3    bool CheckBook<DataType>::writeCheck( const DataType & amount )
4    {
5            if ( amount > balance )
6                    return false;
7            balance -= amount;
8
9            if ( lastIndex == checks.length() - 1 )
10                   checks.changeSize( 2 * checks.length( ) );
11
12           lastIndex++;
13           checks[ lastIndex ] = amount;
14
15           return true;
16   }
```

Lines 1–7 haven't changed. If the Array is filled with checks on line 9, then the capacity of the array is doubled on line 10. Then, on line 12, lastIndex is incremented before the new check is added on line 13.

The deposit, getBalance, and getLastDeposit functions are the same and are not shown. Next, we'll take a look at the getChecks function:

```
1    template <class DataType>
2    Array<DataType> CheckBook<DataType>::getChecks( )
3    {
4            Array<DataType> info( lastIndex + 1 );
5            for ( int i = 0, j = lastIndex; j >= 0; i++, j– – )
6                    info[ i ] = checks[ j ];
7
8            return info;
9    }
```

We still need to do the same kind of data translation that we did before in Chapter 3. The checks are stored in the checks Array from oldest to newest, not in an order the client would like. So an Array object to store the desired order is declared locally on line 4, set to a capacity that is equal to the actual number of checks. The data translation takes place on lines 5–6, the same way it did in Chapter 3, and then the Array object is returned on line 8.

This section has illustrated the composition relationship that can occur between classes, but that is not the only type of relationship between classes that we employ in object-oriented programming. The next type of relationship we will discuss is the inheritance relationship.

*6.2   INHERITANCE

Suppose a checkbook for YBNice Bank would have to account for fees charged if the balance should drop below a certain minimum balance. In YBNice Bank, there are two fees: a check fee for each check written when the balance is under the minimum and a service charge that is periodically applied when the balance is under the minimum. In YBNice Bank, these fees are allowed to make the balance go into the negative realm.

There are a number of approaches we can take to implement such a checkbook. One approach would be to update the CheckBook class with data members for the minimum balance, check fee, and service fee. We can pass the additional values needed into a new constructor for setting the additional data members. Then we rewrite the writeCheck function to include a possible subtraction of the check fee, and we add in another function called deductServiceFee. If the CheckBook is being used for a free checking account, the client can just use the original constructor, which would be rewritten to set these additional data members to zero. While that would work, it would be wasting memory for these clients, since the minimum balance and the fees are being stored in the CheckBook object, but really aren't being used. Another disadvantage would be that it would make the CheckBook class a little more complicated. Indeed, if we had to account for the practice of every single bank in our CheckBook class, the class would probably be too difficult to maintain.

A second approach is to make a different CheckBook class and give it another name, say, YBNiceCheckBook. We could start by just copying the CheckBook class into another file and then change each occurrence of CheckBook to YBNiceCheck-Book. After that, we make the necessary modifications. This would work, too, and it is simple enough to do. However, such an approach does not allow the CheckBook and the YBNiceCheckBook classes to have compatible types. For example, we cannot have a parameter of a function that would accept both a CheckBook object and a YB-NiceCheckBook object (the same way that a float parameter of a function heading can accept both an int and a float). Also, if we made a different type of checkbook class for each different type of bank, we would have a mass of unorganized classes and finding the right class for the right job might be very cumbersome.

Our third approach, using **_inheritance_**, would allow all of these checkbook classes to have a degree of type compatibility. We could even make an array in which each element refers to a different type of checkbook object. It will take a little while to work our way up to how that is done, because we can have inheritance without type compatibility. But this is one of the main reasons for using inheritance. Using inheritance would also allow us to organize all of our checkbook classes into a hierarchy (much as the folders on your computer are organized into a hierarchy), so we can find the right class for the right job more easily.

So what exactly is inheritance anyway? To put it simply, it is a mechanism that allows one class to "inherit" the members of another class, or to obtain these members automatically. For example, consider the deposit, getChecks, getLastDeposit, and getBalance functions. If we used the second approach described, these functions would be written the same way in both checkbook classes. But by using inheritance, we wouldn't have to write them in the YBNice CheckBook; instead, they would be automatically included from the CheckBook class through inheritance.

Let's give our new class a more general name: MinBalCheckBook. If we are not using class templates, we can specify that MinBalCheckBook inherits from the Check-Book class at the top of the class definition by using the following line of code:

```
class MinBalCheckBook : public CheckBook
```

Underneath this line, we can write the public and private sections of the Min-BalCheckBook class as we did with other classes. But this time, we don't need to put in function prototypes (or definitions) for deposit, getChecks, getLastDeposit, and getBalance; they will be automatically included from the CheckBook class. So clients who declare a MinBalCheckBook object can use these functions and get the result they want. The MinBalCheckBook object can also contain additional functions that the client can use. In addition, the simple line of code just presented will make it possible for us to give these two classes the type compatibility that we talked about earlier, but we will discuss how that is done in the next section.

In an inheritance relationship, the class we inherit from is called the ***base*** class and the class that does the inheriting is referred to as the ***derived*** class. Therefore, in our example, CheckBook is the base class and MinBalCheckBook is the derived class. When a client uses a derived class, it appears from the client's perspective as though one class is being used. In other words, the client may not even be aware that there is a base class or object. But what actually happens when a client declares a derived object is that both a base object and a derived object are made. The base object is a part of the derived object, something like the composition relationship that we talked about earlier. The difference, however, is that we don't have an object name for the base object. For example, when the client uses the inherited getBalance function, he or she will be using the name of the derived object. Similarly, if the functions of a derived object call the inherited functions, no object name preceding these inherited function calls is used; it is as if the functions exist in the public section of the derived object. Almost anything that is public in the base object can be used by the derived object; a derived class inherits all public functions from the base class, except for any constructors (including the copy constructor), the destructor, and the overloaded operator = function. Private functions, if any, are not inherited. Private data members are also not inherited. "Private" really means private.

However, if we would like to inherit data members or private functions from a base class, yet not make them public, we can use a third type of section for the base class, called a ***protected*** section. (The first two types of sections are public and private.) The protected section acts like a private section as far as the client program is concerned; however, it acts like a public section to the derived class, so that the derived class can inherit any such data members included in the protected section.

A derived class can use a different function definition for a function it would normally inherit. Consider, for example, the writeCheck function. If our balance is below the minimum balance, YBNice Bank charges a fee for each check written, so we should deduct this fee (if applicable) in the writeCheck function. As such, we don't really want to inherit the writeCheck function from the base class CheckBook. We need to write this function a little differently. To write it differently for the Min-BalCheckBook, we would include its function prototype in the public section and write its new definition normally in the implementation file for MinBalCheckBook. Now, when a MinBalCheckBook object is declared and the writeCheck function is called, the program will use the writeCheck function written specifically for this class, instead of the writeCheck function for the CheckBook class. This is called function ***overriding***.

Inheritance can be used for both classes and class templates. The following class template for MinBalCheckBook is an example of a specification file using inheritance from the CheckBook class template:

```
1   // MinBalCheckBook.h – a class template derived from the CheckBook class template.
2   // The constructor and the writeCheck function can throw exceptions if
3   // out of heap memory.
4
5   // to use a struct for the DataType, you must overload the following operators:
```

```
6  //    >        left operand:  struct object      right operand:  float
7  //             used to compare the amount of the check in the struct object with the
8  //             balance
9  //    -=       left operand:  float              right operand:  struct object
10 //             used to subtract the amount of the check in the struct object from the
11 //             balance
12
13 #include "CheckBook.h"
14
15 template <class DataType>
16 class MinBalCheckBook : public CheckBook<DataType>
17 {
18 public:
19     MinBalCheckBook( float initBalance, float minBalance, float sfee, float cfee );
20     bool writeCheck( const DataType & amount );  // returns false if amount is greater
21                                                  // than balance; otherwise returns true
22     void deductServiceFee( );
23 private:
24     float minBalance;
25     float serviceFee;
26     float checkFee;
27 };
28
29 #include "MinBalCheckBook.cpp"
```

Notice that we have included comments about the roles of operators on lines 5–11. All comments about overloaded operators that are used in inherited functions, as well as those used for additional functions of the derived class, should be included. That way, the client does not need to consult the base class specification file for additional overloaded operator functions that may be needed.

Notice on line 13 that we must include CheckBook.h, so that the compiler knows about the class template we will be inheriting from. There are seven files that need to be in the folder for this file to make everything work: CheckBook.h, CheckBook.cpp, MinBalCheckBook.h, MinBalCheck.cpp, Array.h, Array.cpp, and the main program.

Line 16 shows the line of code we use for specifying inheritance when class templates are involved. When an object of the derived class is declared, a type will need to be specified for DataType so that a class can be made as usual. However, a base class also needs to be made from the base class template before a base object can be made. Therefore, it is necessary to set a type for the base class template, as shown on line 16. This type will be set to whatever type is used for DataType in the derived class.

Some additional data members are made for this class on lines 24–26. They are for the minimum balance, the service fee that is periodically charged, and the fee for each check that is written when the balance is under the minimum balance. These data members need to be initialized by the constructor, so the constructor on line 19 passes in values for them, in addition to the first parameter, which is used for the initial balance.

The writeCheck function has to be written a little differently, as we discussed before, so we want it to override the writeCheck function of the CheckBook class. Therefore, a function prototype for it is declared on line 20. (It must have the same number of parameters and types of parameters as the original writeCheck function in order to be an overriding function.) An additional deductServiceFee function is supplied on line 22. The other public functions of CheckBook are inherited. Figure 6.1 shows a conceptual picture of a MinBalCheckBook object.

When we write the writeCheck function, we may want to work with the balance data member directly so that we can deduct the check fee, if applicable, from the balance. If so, we need to make a protected section for the base class and transfer the balance data member into it, as shown in the following code:

```
1   #include "Array.h"
2
3   template <class DataType>
4   class CheckBook
5   {
6   public:
7       CheckBook( float initBalance );
```

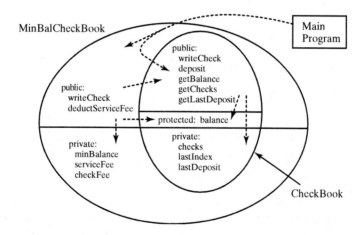

FIGURE 6.1

A conceptual layout of the MinBalCheckBook object and its CheckBook component, showing public, protected, and private sections. A dashed arrow indicates accessibility. For example, the main program in the upper right corner can access the public section of MinBalCheckBook and the public section of CheckBook. (Both would appear to be a part of the MinBalCheckBook object from the perspective of the main program.)

```
8       bool writeCheck( const DataType & amount );  // returns false if amount is greater
9                                             // than balance; otherwise returns true
10      void deposit( float amount );
11      float getBalance( ) const;
12      Array<DataType> getChecks( );
13      float getLastDeposit( ) const;
14  protected:
15      float balance;
16  private:
17      Array<DataType> checks;
18      int lastIndex;  // the index of the last check that was written
19      float lastDeposit;
20  };
21
22  #include "CheckBook.cpp"
```

The comments about overloaded operators should be included here as well, but are omitted in the text for brevity. (Clients may still want to use the basic CheckBook class.) The protected section is shown on lines 14–15. This section will keep the balance data member private from the client's perspective (and the perspective of any other object that might be using this class), but the balance can now be inherited (and used) by functions of the derived class.

The implementation file for MinBalCheckBook is shown next, starting with the constructor:

```
1   // MinBalCheckBook.cpp  – –  The function definitions of the class template for
2   // MinBalCheckBook
3
4   template <class DataType>
5   MinBalCheckBook<DataType>::MinBalCheckBook( float initBalance, float minBal,
6        float sFee, float cFee )
7   : CheckBook<DataType>( initBalance ), minBalance( minBal ), serviceFee( sFee ),
8        checkFee( cFee )
9   {
10  }
```

The initializer list for the constructor is shown on lines 7–8. When the constructor for the derived class is called, the constructor for the base class must also be called, so that a derived object is made complete with a base object. The only way a constructor can be called is in the declaration of an object, so the constructor for the base object must be called with the use of the derived class constructor. Line 7 shows how the base class constructor is invoked if it has parameters. Recall that the base object has no name, so init-Balance (passed in on line 5) is passed on to the base class constructor with only the use of the class type. When inheritance is used, this method for invoking constructors is quite common: The parameters needed for the base class constructor are passed into the derived class constructor and then are passed on through the base class constructor (in this case, the initBalance parameter). Some additional parameters passed into the derived class constructor are often used to set members of the derived class, as the rest of line 7 and line 8 show. If a default constructor exists for the base class and one wants to use it, then it is typically left out of the initializer list and will be invoked automatically. But a constructor for a base class *must* be invoked when there is inheritance. If no constructor at all is written for the base class, one will be supplied automatically by the compiler.

Recall that we needed to write the writeCheck function a little differently, to subtract the check fee if the balance is less than the minimum balance. Following is the overriding writeCheck function:

```
11    // returns false if amount is greater than balance; otherwise returns true
12    template <class DataType>
13    bool MinBalCheckBook<DataType>::writeCheck( const DataType & amount )
14    {
15        bool success = CheckBook<DataType>::writeCheck( amount );
16
17        if ( success && balance < minBalance )
18                balance -= checkFee;
19
20        return success;
21    }
```

This writeCheck function calls the writeCheck function of the base object (CheckBook object) on line 15. You must first use the type of the base class, followed by two colons, followed by the function call. The variable amount, passed in on line 13, is passed on to writeCheck on line 15. Recall that the writeCheck function compares the amount with the balance to see if the check can be written. If it can't be, the function returns false. It also subtracts the check from the balance if the check can be written. Furthermore, it increases the size of the checks array, if necessary, before storing the new check amount. We want all of this to take place in our overriding writeCheck function, so the wise thing to do is just to call the writeCheck function of the base class. We save the truth value it returns in a bool success variable on line 15.

On line 17, if the check was successfully written and the balance is less than the required minimum balance, a check fee is deducted from the balance on line 18. We pass on the result of the writeCheck function in the base object back to the client on line 20.

Finally, we have a deductServiceFee, which the client can use periodically, to deduct the service fee if the balance is less than the minimum balance:

```
22    template <class DataType>
23    void MinBalCheckBook<DataType>::deductServiceFee( )
24    {
25        if ( balance < minBalance )
26                balance -= serviceFee;
27    }
```

Should we want to make a derived class from the MinBalCheckBook class, we can also do that. Such a derived class would inherit from both the CheckBook class and the MinBalCheckBook class. And we can go on and on. All public and protected members (other than constructors, copy constructors, destructors, and the overloaded = operator) are available to successively derived classes. We can also make more than one derived class from a particular base class if we so desire. So by now, you can see how hierarchies of classes can be established with inheritance.

One may be tempted, when making a class, to make all data members protected instead of private. After all, they still act as if they are private with respect to the client. And if we should inherit, they will all be available to the derived class(es), the way that balance was available for use in the writeCheck function of the derived MinBalCheck-Book. This approach is, however, a temptation to be avoided. If we need to change the way the data is represented in a base class, and the data is protected, we will now have to think about rewriting all of the derived classes. In a sense, this was the purpose of the private section from the client's perspective.

In fact, it may have been better in the overloaded writeCheck to keep the balance variable as a private data member and just call the getBalance function. The balance needed to be updated on line 18, but we could always write a setBalance function (like the one we had before) to update the base class with the new balance. So now we've gone from "Let's make all private members protected" to "Why make any data members protected at all?" Well, the point is, we should be judicious. If we are really not expecting to use much inheritance, it is more efficient to access data directly than to use function calls. It is also possible that we know that the data representation has very little chance of changing. One way or the other, just give it some thought.

If destructors are written for classes in an inheritance relationship, then the destructors for all base objects will be called at the time the derived object is destroyed. After these destructors are executed, then the destructor for the derived object (if one is written) is executed.

A class can inherit from more than one class of otherwise unrelated classes in an inheritance hierarchy, but such inheritance is usually ill-advised. We will not be discussing it in this textbook.

Sometimes students know that two classes should have either a composition relationship or an inheritance relationship, but they are not really sure which one to use. A good rule of thumb is to think of the relationships between such classes as being IS_A or HAS_A relationships. If a relationship is an IS_A relationship, use inheritance. If it is a HAS_A relationship, use composition. For example, a Car HAS_A Wheel, so a Wheel object should be a data member of a Car class. A Bear, by contrast, IS_A Mammal, so the Bear class should inherit from the Mammal class. In our previous examples, a Check-Book HAS_A record of written checks, so the checks Array is a data member of Check-Book. And a MinBalCheckBook IS_A CheckBook, so it inherited from CheckBook.

In making drawings of the relationships between classes in a large project, **Unified Modeling Language** (**UML**) notation is often used. UML includes, among other things, a standard way of drawing the relationships between classes so that software engineers can easily communicate their ideas about project design through drawings. The composition relationship between classes is shown in Figure 6.2. Sometimes, more than one object of a certain class is a data member in another class, and in that

FIGURE 6.2

UML diagram which shows that an object of Class B is used as a data member of Class A.

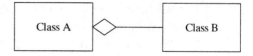

case, the number of objects may be specified as in Figure 6.3, or it may be specified as one or more objects (with the use of an asterisk) as shown in Figure 6.4. An asterisk may be used, for example, when a dynamic array of objects of a class is a data member in another class.

The inheritance relationship is shown in Figure 6.5. It is not always easy for students to remember which way the arrow points. Since a child inherits features from its parents, we sometimes refer to the base class as the parent class and the derived class as a child class. Then, since the arrow points to the parent, we might want to think of it as a form of "ancestor worship" to remember it. Figure 6.6 shows the combined relationships between the classes that we have been talking about in this chapter. There are other relationships between classes that you will see in a software engineering course. It is not uncommon to see a picture of 10 or more classes related to each other in various ways with UML notation.

The inheritance relationship lays some important groundwork for achieving a degree of type compatibility between classes that have such a relationship. This type

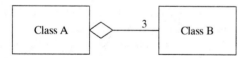

FIGURE 6.3

UML diagram which shows that three objects of Class B are all data members of Class A.

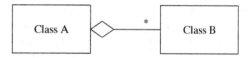

FIGURE 6.4

UML diagram which shows that one or more objects of class B are used as data members of Class A (possibly a dynamic array of class B objects).

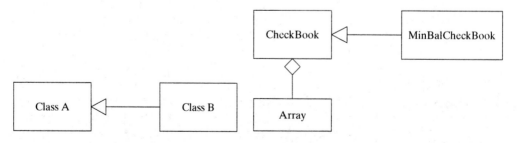

FIGURE 6.5

UML diagram which shows that class B inherits from class A. (That is, an object of class B is the derived object, whereas an object of class A is the base object.)

FIGURE 6.6

UML diagram that shows relationships among the CheckBook, Array, and MinBalCheckBook classes.

compatibility, in turn, can be used to create polymorphism, described in the next section.

*6.3 POLYMORPHISM

Suppose we have a program that uses both CheckBook objects and MinBalCheck-Book objects. Then the declaration of objects in this program might look something like this:

```
CheckBook<float> cbook1( 500 );
MinBalCheckBook<float> cbook2( 1000, 200, 10, 0.5F );
```

Furthermore, suppose we have a function called foo that passes in a checkbook as a parameter, and suppose the function foo calls the writeCheck function. We would like to be able to pass in cbook1 as the parameter to foo and have the writeCheck function work the way it does in the CheckBook class. But we would also like to be able to pass in cbook2 as a parameter, even though it is a different type of object, and have the writeCheck function work the way it does in the MinBalCheckBook class, subtracting a check fee from the balance if applicable.

Even though cbook1 and cbook2 are different kinds of objects, the fact that they are related by inheritance makes them type compatible to some extent. It is valid in C++, in fact, to assign the address of an object of a derived class to a pointer of an object of a base class, as long as the derived class has the base class as an "ancestor" somewhere in the derivation hierarchy. So, given the earlier declaration of cbook2, the statement

```
CheckBook<float> *ptr = &cbook2;
```

is a valid statement. However, the reverse situation is not valid: We cannot assign the address of an object of a base class to a pointer of an object of a derived class. In the assignment, note that the type used for the template (if templated) has to be consistent, because otherwise the two classes would not be related by inheritance. (For example, MinBalCheckBook<MyCheck> is not a derived class of CheckBook<float>.)

This level of type compatibility makes it possible to pass both cbook1 and cbook2 as parameters into function foo, even though they are different types of objects. We simply use the base class type in the formal parameter. For example, if they are passed by reference, we are really passing the address, which achieves the same result as the assignment shown. We can also make the formal parameter a pointer to a base class object and use the address-of operator (&) to pass the address of either a CheckBook or a MinBalCheckBook object into the formal parameter. Using the former method, we might code the foo function like this:

```
1   void foo( CheckBook<float> & cbook )
2   {
3   // other code
```

```
4     cbook.writeCheck( checkAmount );
5     // other code
6     }
```

Now the function calls

```
foo( cbook1 );
foo( cbook2 );
```

are both valid. Sometimes students will get confused and forget about which way assignments or parameter passing can be done between base and derived objects (from base to derived or from derived to base). It is not intuitive at all, but the C++ language design decision to have it done from derived to base is not arbitrary. It is done that way for maintenance reasons. As hierarchies of classes evolve over time, new classes are derived from old ones. Allowing us to use a base class type in a formal parameter means that whatever classes are derived, and regardless of how long the hierarchy is, the objects of the derived classes can always be passed into the function. This makes the function reusable for future classes that will be descendants of the base class that is being used in the formal parameter type. If you remember this explanation, it will help keep you from being confused as to which way parameters are passed and consequently, which way assignments are done.

However, this level of type compatibility is not sufficient, in itself, to make the writeCheck function call behave differently in the foo function. We want the function call to invoke a CheckBook writeCheck function if cbook1 is passed in, but we want it to invoke a MinBalCheckBook writeCheck function if cbook2 is passed in. Recall that the difference is that the MinBalCheckBook writeCheck function will subtract a check fee if the balance is below a minimum balance.

We can cause this type of behavior by using the keyword "virtual" in the function prototype of the writeCheck function in the base class. This will not change the interface of the base class as far as clients of the base class are concerned. So the writeCheck function prototype in the CheckBook class template now looks like this:

```
virtual bool writeCheck( const DataType & amount );
```

Now, with this small change, the writeCheck function call in foo will invoke the CheckBook writeCheck function if a CheckBook object is passed into foo, and it will invoke the MinBalCheckBook writeCheck function if a MinBalCheckBook object is passed into foo.

Note that it makes sense to use "virtual" only on functions in which overriding is done by derived classes. If the keyword virtual is not used, the compiler will decide which writeCheck function to use on the basis of the type that it sees, which in this case is CheckBook in the foo function heading. So the compiler will use the CheckBook writeCheck function, regardless of which type of object is passed in, if the keyword virtual is not used. This behavior is called ***static binding***. The object name cbook, used in function foo, is statically bound to the CheckBook<float> type at compile time. ("Static" means that it cannot change.) By contrast, when the compiler encounters the keyword virtual at compile time, it will not make the decision about which writeCheck function to use. Instead, that decision is made at runtime, and it will be based on the actual object that is passed into the foo function during execution. This behavior is called **dynamic binding**, because the object name cbook can change its binding to different types (related by inheritance) and the writeCheck function that will execute will be based on the type that cbook is bound to.

When the keyword virtual is used to enforce dynamic binding on overriding functions, it is used only on the function prototype. Including it also in the function definition in the implementation file is an error. Further, dynamic binding is forced on the corresponding overriding functions of all descendants of the class in question, regardless of whether the keyword virtual is or is not used on the prototypes of the overriding functions. Still, for readability, it is good practice to use the keyword virtual on the prototypes of overriding functions in such descendant classes; if the keyword is not written in, one would have to look through the class hierarchy to see if dynamic binding is taking place.

When we have dynamic binding between an object name and a type, we refer to the resulting behavior as being an instance of **polymorphism**. In Greek, polymorphism means "many forms". In C++, polymorphism comes about by having one object name, but many possible types for that name. Often, polymorphism is viewed in terms of function calls, because that is where the difference in execution behavior shows up. In our example, it is the writeCheck function that behaves differently, depending on what is passed into the cbook formal parameter.

Another flavor of polymorphism can come about by making an array of different types of elements. This can be done, as you might guess, by creating an array of pointers to base class objects. Then, an address of a derived object can be assigned to a pointer element. If there are many different kinds of derived classes, the array can essentially be made of many different objects.

Let's consider an example in which an array contains many different types of shapes. Suppose that the shapes are organized into the derivation hierarchy shown in Figure 6.7. Then we can make an array of pointers to Shape, the base class at the top of the hierarchy:

Shape *shp[20];

One way of initializing the elements of this array is by using the *new* operator. For example,

```
1    shp[0] = new Circle( 5.4F );
2    shp[1] = new Rectangle( 8.7F, 3.2F );
3    etc.
```

On line 1, we are using the Circle constructor, which accepts a radius. On line 2, we are using a Rectangle constructor, which accepts a length and a width. Note that we are still using the principle that an address of a derived object is being assigned to a pointer of a base object. (Each element is such a pointer.) So the array can include all types of different shapes. We can do some interesting things with this array, such as sort it based upon the perimeter of each shape, or perhaps we can find the average area of all the shapes. Each shape will have its own way of calculating its area with an area function. So, in the base class called Shape we will have a virtual area function, and

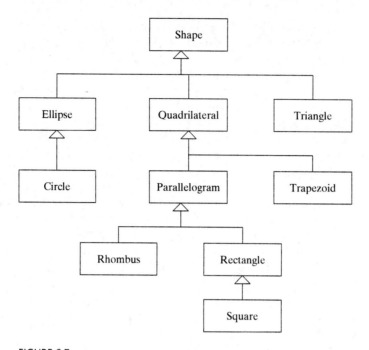

FIGURE 6.7

UML diagram showing the inheritance relationships among various shape classes.

each derived shape class will override it, using its own formula to calculate its area. We can now set up a loop to calculate the average area of all the shapes as follows:

```
1    float sum = 0.0F;
2    for ( int i = 0; i < 20; i++ )
3            sum += (*shp[ i ]).area( );
4    cout << "Average area is: " << sum / 20 << endl;
```

Note that the area function will work differently for each shape, using its own formula for calculating the area, as long as virtual is used for the area function prototype in the base class Shape. Note also that on line 3 the pointer shp[i] must be dereferenced before its area function is accessed. The parentheses are needed because the dot operator (member access operator) takes precedence over the dereference operator.

  It is important to realize that we don't form a hierarchy of shape classes for the purpose of setting up a single for loop like this; doing that would be a lot of effort for just a little benefit. Instead, such a hierarchy would come about because we are making some software system that uses a lot of geometry; we may never need to use for loops or arrays at all in the current software system, but we just need a bunch of classes that can store shapes of different kinds for our geometric software. Realizing that we may benefit later on from type compatibility among the shapes, we form an inheritance hierarchy. We may not even have any idea at this point of how such type compatibility may come in handy; we just know that it often does. Then, situations naturally arise in programs that we develop later on whereby we can take advantage of our built-in type compatibility. (Remember that classes are designed for reusability among many different programs.)

Each derivation in an inheritance hierarchy represents an IS_A relationship, so that it makes sense to inherit the characteristics of the base class. For example, a circle IS_AN ellipse (in which the radius of the major axis is equal to the radius of the minor axis), and a square IS_A rectangle (in which the length is equal to the width). Inheritance hierarchies can similarly be formed for other objects that are related by definitions. For example, you can have an inheritance hierarchy for reptiles or motor vehicles.

The inheritance hierarchy of shapes is interesting, because we have a situation that sometimes doesn't occur with other inheritance hierarchies, namely, how should we write the area function for the Shape class? Remember, we need to put that function into the Shape class and make it virtual. Is there any general area formula that can be used for an arbitrary shape? Well, I'm not a mathematician, but I'm not so sure there is one. When we get in this situation (as we sometimes do), we can write the function prototype for area and make it virtual without defining it. To do so, we would "assign it 0," so that the function prototype for area in the Shape class (in the public section) would look like this:

virtual float area( ) = 0;

This statement tells the compiler that there is no definition for the area function in this class. Such a function is called a ***pure virtual function***, and a class that contains one or more pure virtual functions is called an ***abstract base class***.

No object can be made from an abstract base class, which may exist just for type compatibility among the other classes that are derived from it. An example is our array of pointers to Shape objects, so that the address of any shape class object can be assigned to an element. As another example, we might want to pass any shape as a parameter into a function. Even though we cannot make an object from an abstract base class, it is perfectly legitimate to declare a pointer to a Shape object (or an array of pointers to Shape objects), as long as you don't actually try to assign the address of a Shape object to the pointer(s)!

An abstract base class may contain definitions for some functions, but at least one or more functions are pure virtual functions. A derived class of an abstract base class must define all pure virtual functions in the abstract base class (by overriding), or it will itself be an abstract base class. In Figure 6.7, we may not be able to write an area function for the Quadrilateral class, and if not, we will need to "assign 0" to its area function as well.

Another situation that often comes up in inheritance hierarchies is the inclusion of a file more than once. For example, our Ellipse class inherits from the Shape class, so it would be written like this:

```
1    #include "Shape.h"
2
3    class Ellipse : public Shape
4    {
5    public:
6            Ellipse( float min, float maj );
7            // other functions
8            virtual float area( );
```

```
9     protected:
10           // other data members
11           float min_axis;
12           float maj_axis;
13    private:
14           // other data members
15    };
```

Our triangle class also inherits directly from the Shape class, so it might look like this:

```
1     #include "Shape.h"
2
3     class Triangle : public Shape
4     {
5     public:
6           Triangle( float b, float h  );
7           // other functions
8           virtual float area( );
9     protected:
10           // other data members
11           float base;
12           float height;
13    private:
14           // other data members
15    };
```

Note that on line 1 of each class we include Shape.h, a necessary inclusion since we are inheriting from it. The consequence, though, is that if we include both Ellipse.h and Triangle.h in another file, such as a client program, the Shape.h file will be included twice. The compiler will then complain that there is a redefinition of the Shape class. This problem can be circumvented by using preprocessing directives around the Shape class definition as follows:

```
1     #ifndef SHAPE_H
2     #define SHAPE_H
3
4     class Shape
5     {
6     public:
7           Shape( );
8           // other functions
8           virtual float area( ) = 0;
9     protected:
10           // data members
11    private:
12           // data members
```

```
13   };
14
15   #endif
```

The meaning is that if SHAPE_H is not defined (ifndef on line 1 is short for "if not defined"), then process lines 2–15. Line 2 defines SHAPE_H and lines 4–13 are included for the compiler. Line 15 ends the preprocessing "if" statement. Thus, on the first inclusion of Shape.h, SHAPE_H has not yet been defined, so the compiler will get lines 4–13. But on the second inclusion of Shape.h (or any subsequent inclusions thereof), SHAPE_H has been defined, line 1 will be false, lines 2–15 will not be processed, and the compiler does not see a subsequent definition of Shape.

It is common practice for #ifndef and #define to use the name of the file in capital letters, with an underscore replacing the dot, as shown on lines 1–2. With this convention, it is extremely unlikely that these preprocessing definitions will get mixed up with others in the software project.

SUMMARY

In this chapter, we have briefly covered some important topics in object-oriented programming, namely, composition, inheritance, and polymorphism. The chapter will help you make the transition to a more advanced course in object-oriented programming. Although we won't be discussing these concepts any further in the text (except for composition), you will see exercises throughout the rest of the book that make use of such concepts.

It is important to realize that one object can be a data member of another, different type of object (composition) and to understand what the implications of this relationship are, especially in designing constructors. Always remember that "private" really means private. We will be using Array objects in some of the data structures throughout this text.

Inheritance and polymorphism are important topics in object-oriented programming. Inheritance allows different types of objects to have a degree of type compatibility and allows us to organize classes into a derivation hierarchy. Polymorphism allows one line of source code, particularly an object function call, to behave in many different ways, depending upon the type the object name is bound to.

EXERCISES

1. The implementation of CheckBook in this chapter uses a dynamic array within the Array class. Yet, there was no need to have a destructor, an overloaded assignment operator, and a copy constructor for the CheckBook class. Explain why.
2. In the implementation of the CheckBook class in this chapter, an Array object is declared in the private section. Can the functions of the CheckBook class directly access the data member of the Array class called capacity? Why or why not?
3. What is an initializer list, and why did it need to be used in the CheckBook class of this chapter? How would you set an int variable called num to 10 in the initializer list?
4. What is inheritance and what benefits do we get from it?
5. If two classes should be related by either composition or inheritance, how should you decide what the relationship should be?

6. Explain the purpose of the protected section. When would it be wise to avoid placing a data member into a protected section?

7. What is function overriding and why would we want to use it? How can the function that is overridden be called from the overriding function?

8. What is polymorphism? How can polymorphism be achieved through classes that have inheritance relationships?

9. What is a pure virtual function? Why would we ever want to make a pure virtual function?

10. What is an abstract base class? Would it ever make sense to make an abstract base class and never use it as a base class? Why or why not?

11. If a header file is included more than once in a program, how can we avoid getting a redefinition error from a compiler?

12. A bank which uses a minimum balance decides to charge a periodic service fee that depends on how far the balance is under the minimum balance. The formula the bank wishes to use is

$$\text{service fee} = \text{maximum\_fee} * (\text{minimum balance} - \text{balance}) / \text{minimum balance}$$

This bank wishes to charge a flat check fee for each check written when the balance is under the minimum balance, but the bank also wants to charge a flat deposit fee for each deposit, which might be a fee different from the one for the check. Write a ScaledMinBalCheckBook class that inherits from the MinBalCheckBook class to accommodate the bank's wishes.

13. Can the address of a ScaledMinBalCheckBook object (in Exercise 12) be assigned to a pointer of a CheckBook object? Why or why not?

14. Construct the Shape, Quadrilateral, Parallelogram, Trapezoid, and Triangle classes discussed in this chapter. Have the user fill an array with Parallelograms, Trapezoids, and Triangles. The user should select the type of shape that gets entered into each position and the parameters for the shape. The user should then write a function that will find the element with the largest area. (The area of a parallelogram is base * height, the area of a trapezoid is $\frac{1}{2}$ * (base1 + base2) * height, and the area of a triangle is $\frac{1}{2}$ * base * height.)

15. Extend Exercise 14 and make a function that will get the average area of all of the trapezoids in the array. Do not pass anything into the function except for the array of pointers to Shape objects. Use a technique that will allow the function to test for any particular shape in any particular array position. (*Hint*: Consider adding a virtual method that will return the class name as a string.)

CHAPTER 7

Methods for Making Data Structures

Although arrays and structs can be regarded as simple data structures, when we refer to data structures in this textbook, we will be regarding them as abstract data types. Recall from Chapter 2 that an abstract data type is a data type that includes a set of data and a set of operations that act upon the data. In C++, a class facilitates the making of an abstract data type, since its private section is used to store data and its public section contains a set of operations (functions) that act upon the data.

Within the private section of a data structure, however, is some type of structure that is used to contain the data. This isn't said very often in a textbook on data structures, but there are really only two methods for making such a structure. (That might change in the future; who knows?) One method is to use an array, and the other method is to use a linked structure. You are already familiar with the former method, but we need to elaborate on it somewhat in this chapter. As far as linked structures go, you are probably not familiar with them at all, so we will introduce them in considerable detail in this chapter. Sometimes the two methods—arrays and linked structures—are combined in the same data structure.

In almost any data structure, some of the functions you will need are a function to add an element to the data structure and a function to remove an element from the data structure. Recall that in the Stack class used in Section 2.4, these were done by pushing and popping, respectively. As we shall see, the fact that such functions are needed in almost any data structure has a profound effect on the methods used to make a data structure.

7.1 USING ARRAYS IN DATA STRUCTURES

You are already familiar with using an array. The Stack class in Section 2.4 uses an array to store its elements. In a data structure, a dynamic array is often used so that it can expand as the number of elements in the data structure grows and shrink as elements are removed. In this manner, dynamic memory is conserved. Static arrays are sometimes used for simplicity, but they have a couple of disadvantages. If they are small, they can get filled and become a death sentence for the program. If they are large, then very often the program will use only a small portion of an array, wasting a lot of memory. Dynamic arrays that expand or contract are a reasonable solution. When dynamic arrays are used in a data structure and the data structure runs out of heap memory, the program that is using the data structure is generally doomed to failure. Therefore, it is very important to conserve dynamic memory as much as possible.

Sometimes a dynamic array is used, but is not made expandable or shrinkable. When it is used in such a fashion, the main programmer generally passes the desired size of the array into the constructor, and then the constructor makes a dynamic array of that size, but the size stays fixed throughout the life of the data structure. This method should be used if the number of elements in the array is not expected to change. However, if the number of elements can change, there are advantages and disadvantages. One advantage of this method is that the code for classes is simpler: We do not have to make function calls to expand or shrink the array. The method is also somewhat faster, since copying is involved in expanding or shrinking arrays. (Elements are copied from one dynamic array into the new dynamic array.) A disadvantage of the method is that it forces the main programmer to think about the size of the array needed, a task that goes against the idea of classes and abstraction, which relieves the main programmer from having to think about the details of the class. Another disadvantage is that the main programmer may misjudge how much space is needed in the array. The main programmer is writing code for a multitude of users, just as the class designer writes a class for a multitude of main programmers. The main programmer might pass the responsibility for the size of the array on to the user, but then the user gets saddled with the same problems.

Throughout the text, we will use dynamic arrays that can expand or shrink as needed, since our goal is to make things as easy for the main programmer as possible. In Chapter 8, we will see that the class for a data structure won't be any more difficult to write with these adjustable arrays and, in fact, will be simpler. There is time involved in copying the elements of an old dynamic array over to a new dynamic array, as we do in expansion and contraction, but it does not significantly increase the *average* amount of time that it takes to add or remove elements, as long as a reasonable technique is used for the expansion or contraction.

If the array expands or contracts every time an element is inserted or removed, respectively, then the technique is not reasonable. Too much time will be spent in copying, and the average time required to insert or remove an element will be too high. Instead, we should double the size of the array when it becomes full, and we should shrink the size when the number of elements used drops to 25% of the capacity. In the latter case, we should cut the capacity of the array in half, so that it is about half full after we cut it. Section 9.8 shows that such a technique does not significantly increase the average amount of time required to insert or remove an element.

The Stack class that you used in Section 2.4 to evaluate expressions is an example of a data structure that uses an object of the Array class, which encapsulates a dynamic array, as discussed in Chapter 5. The elements of the stack are stored in the dynamic array, and the array expands or contracts as needed. The top of the stack is actually the

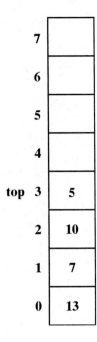

FIGURE 7.1

How an array is used for a stack. Currently, there are only four elements in the stack, so top has been set to 3, the index of the top of the stack. When an element is added, top is incremented, and when an element is popped, top is decremented.

index of the last element used in the array, as shown in Figure 7.1. When an element is popped, the top index gets decremented, and when an element is pushed, the top index is incremented. When we pop, we are going to check whether or not we should contract the array, and when we push, we are going to check whether or not we should expand the array. It's really that simple.

On occasion, you may want a two-dimensional dynamic array or even a higher dimensional dynamic array within a data structure. These can also be made, but they require a little more work than a one-dimensional dynamic array. To make a two-dimensional array, the idea is to make an array of arrays, but that is what a two-dimensional static array is anyway. The only difference is that, in the dynamic version, the main array is an array of pointers, where each pointer points to another array, as shown in Figure 7.2.

The pointer to the horizontal pointer array in Figure 7.2 must be a pointer to a pointer, which means that it stores the address of a pointer. So, for a two-dimensional dynamic array of integers, the pointer would be declared like this:

int **twoDarray;

The two-dimensional dynamic array is then created as follows: First, the array of pointers is created. Then, for each pointer in the pointer array, a dynamic array is created for it to point to. The following code is illustrative:

```
int xdim = 25;    // used for x dimension
int ydim = 30;    // used for y dimension
twoDarray = new int * [xdim];
for ( int i = 0; i < xdim; i++ )
        twoDarray[ i ] = new int [ydim];
```

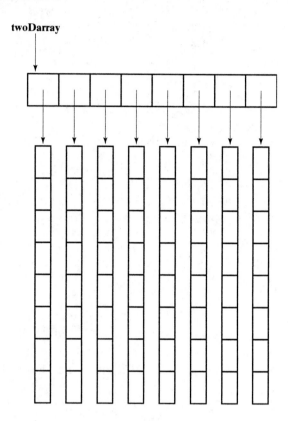

FIGURE 7.2

A dynamic two-dimensional array. The horizontal top array is an array of pointers. The pointer twoDarray points to the horizontal top array. Each pointer in the top array points to a vertical array.

Once the two-dimensional dynamic array has been created, it is used just as a static array is used:

```
for ( i = 0; i < xdim; i++ )
     for ( j = 0; j < ydim; j++ )
            twoDarray[ i ][ j ] = i * j;
```

Each array within a two-dimensional dynamic array is individually adjustable, which may be the reason for using it instead of a two-dimensional static array.

When it comes time to free the dynamic memory used by the array, first each of the arrays in the y dimension is freed and then the array of pointers is freed, as in the following code:

```
for ( i = 0; i < xdim; i++ )
      delete [ ] twoDarray[ i ];
delete [ ] twoDarray;
```

Higher dimensional arrays use the same technique. For instance, if a three-dimensional dynamic array is desired, then the pointer used for the array name would be declared, for example, as

```
Check ***threeDarray;
```

to create a three-dimensional array of Check objects. This is actually a pointer to an array of pointers. This time, however, each pointer in the array will point to a two-dimensional dynamic array, such as the pointer twoDarray in the earlier example. So techniques used to create higher dimensional arrays are just an extension of the techniques used to create lower dimensional arrays.

Next, we will consider linked data structures, a topic that you are probably unfamiliar with. Linking is an alternative to using an array for a data structure. Both arrays and linking have advantages and disadvantages, but you need to know both methods to decide when one is better than the other.

7.2   INTRODUCTION TO LINKED STRUCTURES

In a linked structure, each element is generally stored in an object of a struct. That is, there are a bunch of objects, and each object stores its own element. The objects, however, are not put into an array as you are accustomed to thinking. The struct for making these objects is generally declared above the class template for the data structure in the class specification file and often looks like this:

```
template <class DataType>
struct Node {
        DataType info;
        Node<DataType> *next;
};
```

When each object holds its own element in a linked structure, the objects are referred to as **nodes**. Therefore, the struct has been named "Node". The nodes are linked together, as will be shown later.

The struct only has two members. One is the info member, the member that is used for the element. The element can be anything: a float, a char, or, very often, an object of another struct. The DataType of the element is chosen by the main programmer, just as the DataType of the checks array was chosen as a float or a Check object by the main programmer. The same DataType is used as the type for the class template of the data structure.

Although the main programmer has access to the Node struct to make Node objects in the main program, it is extremely rare to do so. Rather, the main programmer just works with the elements, which are much easier to work with. When the main programmer needs to add an element to the data structure, the node isn't passed in as a parameter; rather, the element is passed in. Then the function to add the element stores it into its own node. The node is made by means of dynamic memory. When a function of a data structure needs to return an element to the client, the node is not returned; instead, the element stored in the node is returned. So, in short, the main program generally has nothing to do with nodes. This may seem surprising, since you may have thought that the main programmer is the only one that makes classes or structs from templates. But in the case of a linked structure, the functions of the data structure class template will make a struct from the struct template.

The second member of the Node struct is a pointer. However, there is something peculiar about this pointer: Its data type shows that it points to another object made from the same struct! This, then, is the glue that links these nodes together.

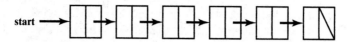

FIGURE 7.3

A linked structure. Nodes are illustrated by divided squares. Each node
is divided into two sections, representing the two data members of the
Node struct. The left section is the info member, and the right side is
the pointer called next.

Figure 7.3 shows a linked structure. Every block represents a node and is divided
into two halves, representing its two members. The member on the left is the info member, where the element is stored. The member on the right is the pointer member,
which points to another node. That is, the member on the right contains the address of
the node that it points to. It doesn't take much imagination to see that this is an alternative to an array for storing elements.

Sometimes data structure designers use a class, instead of a struct, for a node.
Then the info and the next data members are made public in the class. In this textbook,
we will only use structs for public data members and classes for private data members,
since that is traditionally the way structs and classes are used.

The linked structure in Figure 7.3 is often referred to as a ***linked list***. Although it
might be difficult to see right now, we can access any element in the linked list, we can
add any element to any position of the linked list, and we can remove any element
from the linked list (we can shorten the linked list).

One advantage that linked lists have over arrays is in conserving memory when
large objects (such as records of information) are used as elements. Figure 7.4 illustrates this conservation of memory.

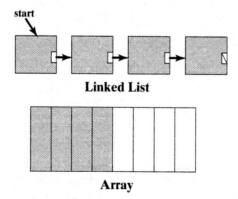

FIGURE 7.4

Memory conservation in a linked list versus an array for large element sizes. In this example, we are using a
record of information for an element (a struct), which is about 80 bytes. In the linked list, the element (stored in
info) is shaded. The pointer next (shown in white) is only 4 bytes, so it is small in comparison. Arrays, by
contrast, are hardly ever full. The one shown is half full. (The shaded section is the used section.) The white half
still uses memory for the struct members of the elements, but they have not been set to anything. The linked list
does a better job at conserving memory for this element size; the shaded areas, used for the elements, are of the
same area. However, the part of the linked list not used for elements is only 16 bytes total, whereas in the array
it is $4*80 = 320$ bytes total. The larger the array and linked list are, the more memory is conserved.

7.3   WRITING CODE FOR LINKED LISTS

Let's consider how to write code for linked lists. Working with linked structures requires a totally different way of programming that you just have to get used to. I will warn you that the programming involved is a major stumbling block for students of data structures, but it doesn't need to be. I firmly believe that the stumbling block exists because of the way students would *like* to think about linked structures. Nobody likes to think about addresses and how pointers store them. Instead, one looks at the drawing in Figure 7.3 and says, "What a nice way to think about linked structures — no addresses involved, just a lot of arrows." Then one tries to think of rules that can be used to translate arrows into code without thinking about addresses. It doesn't work, my friend: Many a student has stumbled and fallen on this rocky road. You must think about the arrows, *but you must also think about the addresses stored in the pointers*. And I will keep reminding you about this. When you think about addresses long enough, believe me, they will become second nature to you. In reality, the objects that belong to this linked structure are not really tied together in a physical sense, but are scattered throughout heap memory. The pointer of one just happens to contain the address of another.

7.3.1   Basics about Linked-List Code

One important aspect of using a linked list is that there must at least be a pointer to the first node of the list. This pointer is placed in the private section, so the address is remembered by the data structure. The reason is that each node of a linked list is created in heap memory with the use of the *new* operator. So if there is no way to access the first node, then there is memory leak. Often (but not always), the pointer to the first node is the only pointer to the linked list that is placed in the private section. So, if you accidentally change the address stored in this pointer, then all the nodes of the linked list are lost; that is, there is a massive memory leak. A pointer called start that points into the linked list is shown in Figure 7.3. If the linked list is empty (i.e., if it has no elements), then the pointer to the beginning of the linked list is set to NULL.

Remember that the member of the left half of a block is called info, in the struct template that was given previously:

```
template <class DataType>
struct Node {
      DataType info;
      Node<DataType> *next;
};
```

How would we write code to access info in the first node by using the start pointer? Recall that a pointer stores an address, not an object, so we dereference the pointer first and then use the dot operator:

```
(*start).info
```

However, there is another notation that is often used instead and that *means exactly the same thing*. This notation uses the arrow operator:

```
start->info
```

The arrow operator is typed on the keyboard with the minus sign followed by the "greater than" sign. The arrow operator is a much easier alternative, but it is important to understand that it uses both dereferencing and member access in one shot. Make sure you understand the difference between the dot and the arrow: Use the dot to access a member when the name on the left is an object; use the arrow to access a member when the name on the left is a pointer. If we have a pointer to an object of a class, we can call a function of the object by using the arrow operator, too, as in the following code:

```
ptr->foo( );
```

If we wanted to access the info member in the second node of the linked list by using the start pointer, we can do it like this:

```
start->next->info
```

Here, the start pointer is used first, to access the *next* member of the struct given a bit earlier. However, the *next* member is also a pointer that has the address of the second node. Therefore, we can access any member of the second node with this *next* pointer. We use the arrow operator again to access info in the second node.

It is true that we can access any node in the linked list simply by using a long chain of next->'s. But this approach is extremely rare, for a number of reasons, chief among them being that we often do not even know how many nodes are in the linked list. We can, instead, write a loop to access nodes of a linked list, as we will see shortly.

Another important aspect of the use of a linked list is that the pointer of the last node in the list is set to NULL. In a drawing, this is indicated by a slash drawn through the block half that is the pointer, as shown in the last node of Figure 7.3. No other node in the linked list has its pointer set to NULL, so during the execution of code, if a node is being examined and we find that its pointer is set to NULL, we know that it is the last node in the linked list.

7.3.2   Searching for a Value That Is Definitely in a Linked List

Let's take a look at an example of searching for a value in a list. We will use Figure 7.5. The three dots in the figure indicate that we do not know how many nodes are in the linked list; there could be a million, for all we know.

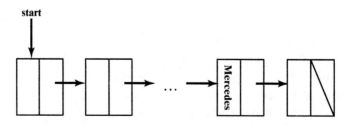

FIGURE 7.5

A linked list that contains Mercedes. A CarType object is stored at each node, but only the maker (Mercedes) is shown. The three dots represent an unknown number of nodes.

The struct for the nodes is made from the struct template given earlier. Let's suppose that DataType is a CarType object, so that we have a linked list of cars. Then each node object shown in Figure 7.5 is made from a Node<CarType> struct. Are you with me? One of the members of the CarType struct is maker—a string that holds the maker of the car. (By the way, string is a class in the C++ library, so maker is actually an object of the string class, but we don't have to think about that—I told you abstraction was nice.) We wish to search for Mercedes in the linked list. That is all we need to know, believe it or not, to write the code section to perform the search, making use of Figure 7.5. In the figure, there is a CarType object stored at each node, but only the maker (Mercedes) is shown. First, we will write code for a situation in which we know that there is a Mercedes in the linked list, but we just don't know where it is. The section of code to find that Mercedes looks like this:

```
1   CarType item;
2   item.maker = "Mercedes";
3
4   Node<CarType> *ptr = start;
5   while ( ptr->info != item )
6       ptr = ptr->next;
```

The code is rather short, but there is a lot to say about it. On line 1, we declare the item that we wish to find in the linked list. On line 2, we set the maker of the item to Mercedes. Then, on line 4, we declare a pointer called ptr that can point to a Node<CarType> object. We want it to point to the first node in the linked list. Realizing that start contains the address of the first node, we assign that address to ptr on line 4. Now ptr has the address of the first node, so ptr points to that node, as shown in Figure 7.6a.

Now we want to access the info member to see if it has a Mercedes. The while loop condition checks for this. The != operator in the while loop is an overloaded operator in the CarType struct. It is called for the info object, which is a CarType object. Therefore, the != operator is written inside the struct definition for CarType. It passes in item, which is another CarType object. Then it checks whether or not the maker in info is equal to the maker in item. The reason this is done the way it is will be explained shortly.

If info does not have a Mercedes, then the condition in the while loop is true, so line 6 executes. Let's look at the right half of the assignment. We know that next is a pointer that stores an address, so the result of the right half of the assignment is an address. But what address is it? The first time through the loop, on the right half of the assignment, ptr points to the first node, so the address is the one stored in pointer *next* of the first node. Since this is the address of the second node, the right half of the assignment is the address of the second node. This address is assigned to ptr, so now ptr points to the second node, as shown in Figure 7.6b. Whenever you see code for a pointer written the way it is on line 6, it moves the pointer to the next node in the linked list. This is one of the few rules that you can use in writing code for linked lists without thinking about addresses. Whenever you get a rule like this, latch on to it; it is like water in a desert.

The while loop condition is checked again to see if the info in the current node has a Mercedes. If not, we set ptr to the next node after that on line 6. We keep executing the while loop until we finally find the node that has the Mercedes. (Remember, we

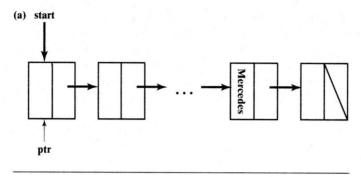

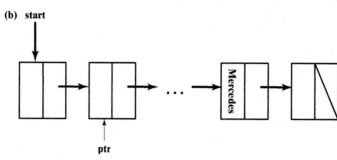

FIGURE 7.6

(a) The pointer ptr points to the first node in the linked list. (b) The pointer ptr points to the second node in the linked list.

know that some node in the linked list has the Mercedes.) When that node is found, the while loop condition becomes false, and we exit the loop. We can then examine the other information in the node we found, if we like, because ptr now points to it. We can look at the price, the year, and so forth.

Now, why on earth did we use an overloaded operator on line 5? Well, I'm trying to get you to think about the way this would be written in a class template function. You see, in a class template function, we would be using DataType instead of CarType, where DataType can be anything. The client would write lines 1–2 in the main program, and then item would be passed into a parameter of the function, using DataType as the type. The pointer ptr would be declared as a Node<DataType> pointer. Then the code in the function could be used for any objects, not just a CarType. The client determines what element of his or her struct should be searched for by writing the code for the operator !=. The item object would contain the value to search for, because the client set it that way before passing it into the function. Once the function finds the right node in the linked list, it will return an object of DataType back to the client, by returning ptr->info. (Notice that info is declared as a DataType in the Node struct.) If the client is using a CarType struct for the DataType, he or she can then look at the object returned to see its price, year, and so forth.

There is one more point to make about this code: What would happen if we didn't declare ptr and just moved through the list, using the start pointer? That is, in the body of the while loop, we use start = start->next. I hope you know the answer. We would get memory leak, because once we change the address stored in start, we don't know what the address of the first node is any more. (All nodes are created by the *new* operator and are in the heap memory.)

Once you have gotten used to working with pointers and addresses, searching through a linked list for a Mercedes won't be much more difficult than searching through an array for a Mercedes. It is just a different way of programming that you have to get used to. But you should go over the example and the explanation until it makes perfect sense. There shouldn't be any mysteries. If you are feeling comfortable at this point, get the cement ready: We're going to do some more building.

7.3.3   Searching for a Value That May Not Be in a Linked List

In the next example, we are going to search for a Mercedes in a linked list, but we don't know if there is one in there, and we don't even know whether the linked list is empty. The previous code won't work if the Mercedes is not in the linked list; we will get a run-time error. The reason is that eventually ptr will be pointing to the last node. Then, since the pointer of the last node is set to NULL, the line of code

```
ptr = ptr->next;
```

inside the while loop will access the pointer that is set to NULL on the right side of the assignment. Therefore, NULL will be assigned to ptr. When the condition in the while loop is checked, we are dereferencing ptr, which is set to NULL. (Recall that the arrow operator dereferences a pointer and accesses a member in one shot.) When we deref-erence a pointer that is set to NULL, it causes a runtime error. We didn't have to worry about this in the first example, because we knew that there was a Mercedes in the linked list. Let's take a look at some code that will handle the situation in which we don't know that:

```
1    // item is passed in as a parameter
2
3    Node<DataType> *ptr = start;
4    bool found = false;
5
6    while (ptr != NULL && !found ) {
7        if ( ptr->info == item )
8                found = true;
9        if ( !found )
10               ptr = ptr->next;
11   }
```

The code is more general this time, using a template and declaring a Node<DataType> pointer instead of a Node<CarType> pointer. Notice how a struct is made from the struct template. First, the client makes a class out of the class template, perhaps by using <CarType>. Then, each occurrence of DataType throughout the class template is replaced by CarType, making a class. One replacement occurs on line 3. This replacement has an added effect: It causes a struct to be created from the Node struct template. In this manner, the main programmer doesn't have to worry about whether the types match in the Node struct and in the class.

If the linked list is empty, start will be set to NULL. Then, on line 3, ptr is set to NULL. Since ptr == NULL, the condition in the while loop is immediately false and we do not enter the while loop. Notice that it is very important for the pointer called start to be initialized to NULL inside a constructor, to avoid a runtime error. If start is not initialized to NULL, it will not contain a valid address. Then ptr will be set to the invalid address. The condition in the while loop will be true, but a runtime error will occur on line 7 when the pointer ptr is dereferenced and the program attempts to access info member.

Now, let's consider what happens when the linked list is not empty, but it doesn't contain a Mercedes. The condition on line 7 contains an == operator, which must be written as an overloaded operator by the client. The condition here will never be true, because the Mercedes isn't in the list. But the only way found is set to true is if the condition is true, so found will always be false. Since found will always be false, the condition on line 9 will always be true. This will cause the pointer ptr to be advanced on line 10. Therefore, the only effect in the body of the while loop is to advance the pointer, similarly to the first example. Eventually, we will reach the last node in the linked list, where ptr is set to NULL on line 10. Then the condition in the while loop becomes false and we break out of the loop. You can see why it is very important for the pointer of the last node to be set to NULL: If it were not, we would keep trying to advance the pointer beyond the end of the linked list, which would create a runtime error.

If the Mercedes is in the linked list, then the condition on line 7 will eventually be true, which will set found to true. The condition on line 9 is now false, so the pointer is not advanced. Then the condition in the while loop heading is false because found was set to true, causing us to exit the while loop. In this case, we exit the while loop with found set to true and ptr pointing to the node containing Mercedes. If the Mercedes is not found and we exit from the while loop, we can determine that the Mercedes was not found, because the found variable will be set to false.

7.3.4   Inserting a Node into the Beginning of a Linked List

Thus far, we have discussed how any node of interest can be accessed in a linked list. We'll now turn our attention to the task of inserting a node into the beginning of a linked list. You should not try to memorize how to do all these tasks associated with linked lists; it is just too much to memorize. Besides, when you design your own data structure, you may run into situations that your memorized material doesn't handle. In short, you need to understand what you are doing, and this is going to require thinking about addresses, not just arrows. When you design your own data structure that involves a linked list, it is good to draw pictures of linked lists and of what is happening in your code, until you really become an expert.

Let's suppose that we want to insert a node at the beginning of the linked list shown in Figure 7.7.

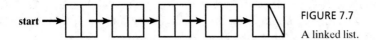

start →

FIGURE 7.7

A linked list.

The templated code to accomplish this task is as follows:

```
1   Node<DataType> *ptr = new Node<DataType>;
2   ptr->info = element;   // element is passed in as a parameter
3   ptr->next = start;
4   start = ptr;
```

On line 1, we create the node we wish to insert in heap memory and assign its address to pointer ptr. (Remember, all nodes are created in heap memory.) The next step is to assign data to the members of this node. We are assuming that a DataType called element is passed in from the client, to insert into the linked list. The info section of the node is set to element on line 2. Since we are inserting this node into the beginning of the linked list, we want the pointer *next* of the node to point to the first node that is already in the list. To figure out how to do this on your own, your thought processes should be something like the following:

1. I want this new node to point to the first node that is already in the list.
2. In order to get it to point to that node, I must find a way to get the address of that first node (so that I can store that address in the pointer *next* of my new node).
3. If I can find a pointer which points to that node already, then the address is stored in that pointer.
4. I notice from the drawing that the start pointer points to the first node that is already in the list, so the start pointer must contain the address of that node.
5. I therefore assign the address stored in start to ptr->next, using the following line of code:

    ptr->next = start;

6. Now, since ptr->next contains the address of the first node, it points to that node. I have inserted the node at the beginning of the linked list.

As hard as it is to force yourself to think this way, you truly have to in order to understand how to write code for linked lists. You should go over this list again and again until it is engraved into your psyche. Once you get used to it, your thought processes will instantly go through these steps in less than a second (as long as you understand them, that is). After line 3 executes, the resulting figure looks like Figure 7.8.

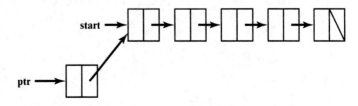

start →

ptr →

FIGURE 7.8

The pointer ptr->next is set to point at the beginning of the linked list.

Now we want start to point to the beginning of the new linked list. At this moment, it is pointing to the second node in the list. To figure out how to do this on your own, your thought processes should mirror the following:

1. I want start to point to the first node in the linked list.
2. In order to get it to point to that node, I must find a way to get the address of the first node (so that I can store that address in start).
3. If I can find a pointer that points to the first node already, then the address is stored in that pointer.
4. I notice in Figure 7.8 that ptr points to this node, so ptr must contain the address of that node.
5. I therefore assign the address stored in ptr to start by using the following line of code:

```
start = ptr;
```

6. Now start has the address of the first node, so it must point to it. I have made start point to the beginning of the linked list.

Figure 7.9 is the result of executing line 4. Well, I hope my brainwashing campaign is working. If you look closely at the brainwashing that is going on in your mind, you will notice that writing code for linked lists involves, first, translating from arrows to addresses, then accomplishing what you need to accomplish with address assignment, and, finally, translating back into a figure to reassure yourself that you have succeeded (even if the figure is only in your mind.)

The interesting thing about the preceding code is that it will work even if the linked list starts off empty. In that case, nothing changes in the execution of lines 1–2. On line 3, start is NULL because the linked list is empty. So, NULL is assigned to ptr->next. This is exactly what we want if this node is the only node in the linked list: NULL *should* be assigned to the pointer of the last node in the list. Then, on line 4, start is assigned the address of the only node in the linked list, which is what should happen, too. Once you design code for the general case, you should check to see if it handles special cases as well, like working on an empty list. Sometimes you have to add a few special touches to the code in order to get it to handle special cases.

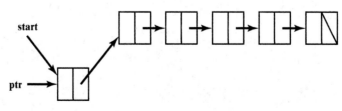

FIGURE 7.9

The pointer start is set to the beginning of the new linked list.

7.3.5   Inserting a Node into the Middle of a Linked List

Let's consider the more difficult problem of inserting a node into the middle of a linked list. Suppose we know that there definitely is a Mercedes stored in the list and we would like to insert a node containing Honda immediately after the first node in the list that stores Mercedes. We will assume that Honda is stored in elementToInsert, passed in from the client. Here is the templated code to accomplish our task:

```
1   Node<DataType> *ptr = start;
2
3   while ( ptr->info != element )  // element is a parameter; contains Mercedes
4       ptr = ptr->next;
5
6   Node<DataType> *newNode = new Node<DataType>;
7   newNode->info = elementToInsert;  // elementToInsert is from client, contains Honda
8   newNode->next = ptr->next;
9   ptr->next = newNode;
```

Lines 1–4 should be no surprise. We are just looking for the Mercedes, as we did before. Once we find it, we have the situation shown in Figure 7.10. Line 6 creates the new node to insert, while line 7 puts the Honda into it. Now, we have two goals: In the figure, (1) we want our new node to point to the dashed node, and (2) we want the Mercedes node to point to our new node. Then our new node will be inserted into the linked list. To accomplish the first goal, your thought processes should be as follows:

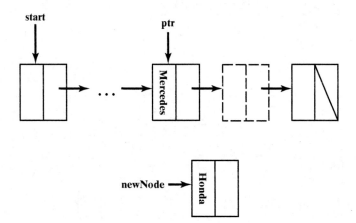

FIGURE 7.10

The pointer ptr points to the node that contains Mercedes. The pointer newNode points to the new node that contains Honda. We need to insert the new node between the Mercedes node and the dashed node.

1. I want my new node to point to the dashed node.

2. In order to get it to point to that node, I must find a way to get the address of the dashed node (so that I can store that address in the pointer *next* of my new node).

3. If I can find a pointer that points to that dashed node already, then the address is stored in that pointer.

4. I notice in Figure 7.10 that the pointer *next* of the Mercedes node points to the dashed node, so it must contain the address of that node.

5. I must find a way to access the pointer *next* of the node, in order to get its address.

6. If I can find a pointer that points to this Mercedes node, then I will be able to access the pointer *next* of the Mercedes node.

7. I notice in the figure that ptr points to the Mercedes node. Therefore, I will be able to use ptr to access the pointer *next* of the Mercedes node.

8. I therefore assign the address stored in ptr->next to newNode->next, using the following line of code:

```
newNode->next = ptr->next;
```

9. Now the pointer *next* of my new node has the address of the dashed node, so it must point to it. I have succeeded in getting my new node to point to the dashed node.

The result of this address assignment produces a linked list like that illustrated in Figure 7.11. Try to use your newly acquired, brainwashed thought processes to figure out, without looking at the code, how to get the Mercedes node to point to the new node. If you were unable do so, don't feel bad; it just means that your psyche is more resilient than others, and you need some more brainwashing:

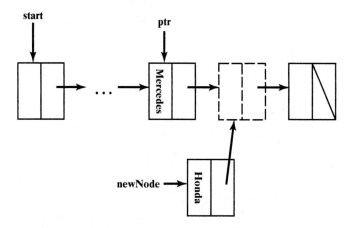

FIGURE 7.11

Step 1 for the insertion of a new node. The next pointer of the new node now points to the dashed node.

1. I want the Mercedes node to point to my new node.

2. In order to get it to point to my new node, I must find a way to get the address of my new node (so that I can store that address in the pointer *next* of the Mercedes node).

3. If I can find a pointer that points to my new node already, then the address is stored in that pointer.

4. I notice in Figure 7.11 that the newNode pointer points to my new node, so it must contain the address of my new node.

5. Now I must find a way to access the pointer *next* of the Mercedes node, so that I can store the address from newNode into it.

6. If I can find a pointer to the Mercedes node, then I will be able to access the pointer *next* of the Mercedes node.

7. I notice in the figure that ptr points to the Mercedes node. Therefore, I will be able to use ptr to access the pointer *next* of the Mercedes node.

8. I therefore assign the address stored in newNode to ptr->next, using the following line of code:

```
ptr->next = newNode;
```

9. Now, the *next* pointer of the Mercedes node contains the address of my new node, so it must point to it. I have succeeded in getting the Mercedes node to point to my new node.

The execution of this line of code produces the result shown in Figure 7.12. Again, you have to keep in mind that these thought processes will become rather fast the more you use them.

As good designers, let's make sure that our code works if the Mercedes happens to be stored in the last node of the linked list. We'll still find it by using lines 1–4, and

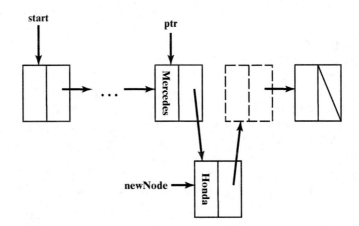

FIGURE 7.12

Step 2 for the insertion of a new node. The Mercedes node is made to point to the new node. The insertion of the new node into the linked list has been completed.

ptr will still point to it. The new node is still created and initialized on lines 6–7. The pointer ptr->next will be NULL this time, since ptr points to the last node in the linked list. So NULL will be assigned to newNode->next. This is what we want, because our new node will become the last node in the linked list, being inserted after the node that contains Mercedes. On line 9, ptr->next, which is now NULL, is assigned the address of the new node, effectively placing the new node last in the linked list. Does the code work in this special case? If your answer is yes, you're right.

7.3.6   Removing a Node Containing a Value That Is in a Linked List

Now, suppose that we know that there is a Mercedes in the linked list and we want to remove the first node that contains it from the linked list. The templated code to accomplish this task is as follows:

```
1    Node<DataType> *ptr = start;
2    if ( ptr->info == element ) {        // element is a parameter, contains Mercedes
3        start = start->next;
4        delete ptr;
5        }
6    else {
7        while ( ptr->next->info != element )
8                ptr = ptr->next;
9        Node<DataType> *ptr2 = ptr->next;
10       ptr->next = ptr2->next;
11       delete ptr2;
12       }
```

Lines 2–4 handle the special case where the Mercedes is in the first node of the linked list. If it is, ptr already points to it, because of line 1. We just slide the start pointer to the next node in the list in line 3, since this will be the new beginning of the linked list. Then, on line 4, we free the memory space used by the first node. Notice that this special case works even when there is only one node in the linked list. The pointer start will be assigned NULL on line 3.

On line 7, we check the next node for Mercedes *without moving the pointer ptr to that node*. We need to have the pointer one node behind the node that has Mercedes when we find it, as we will see later. On line 8, we keep sliding the pointer ptr to the next node, until we find Mercedes in the node that comes after the node that ptr is pointing to. When the Mercedes is found and the while loop stops, we have the situation shown in Figure 7.13a.

The dotted node must now point to the dashed node. We can accomplish this task by using

```
ptr->next = ptr->next->next;
```

but if we do, we will lose the address of the node that we need to free and we will have memory leak. Therefore, on line 9, a pointer ptr2 is created which points to the node that

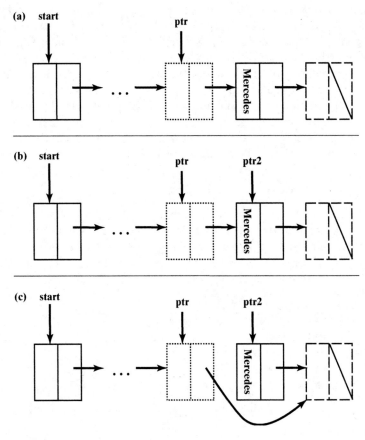

FIGURE 7.13

Deletion of the Mercedes node. (a) The pointer ptr is pointing to the node
before the node that has Mercedes. We would like to free the node that has
Mercedes and link the dotted node to the dashed node. (b) A new pointer
called ptr2 points to the node that has Mercedes. (c) The next pointer of the
dotted node now points to the dashed node, allowing us to free the node
pointed to by ptr2.

must be deleted, as shown in Figure 7.13b. Line 10 causes the dotted node to point to the
dashed node, as illustrated in Figure 7.13c. Then, line 11 frees the node pointed to by ptr2.

You can see why we need to have ptr pointing to the node to the left of the one
that contains Mercedes. If we did not, we would have no way of accessing the pointer
next in the dotted node. Sometimes, people write code using two pointers that walk
through the linked list, with one pointer following the other. This technique of walking
two pointers through a list accomplishes the same thing, but may be slightly slower.

Designing this code on your own requires you to think about addresses, too. If
you think about it, any time you need to change the way a pointer points, you really
need to assign a new address to the pointer. You find that address by looking at other
pointers and realizing that they store addresses. Then, you can figure out what address

assignment you need to do. Sometimes you can't find a pointer that contains the address you need. This would happen, for example, if we allowed ptr to point to the node that contains Mercedes in the previous example. If you can't find a pointer that contains the address you need, then you need to redesign the code so that you have one.

We should think about the special case where the only node containing Mercedes is the last node of the linked list and there is more than one node. In this case, ptr still stops at the previous node. The pointer ptr2 will point to the last node. Then, line 10 will assign NULL to ptr->next, which is what we want, when the last node is deleted. So, the code handles this case. When you write code to handle nodes in the middle of a list, will it always handle the last node correctly? It would be safe to assume not.

7.3.7   Using Header Nodes to Simplify Code

A **header** node is sometimes used in linked lists to simplify code. A header node is a node at the beginning of the linked list, which is like any other node except that no data has been assigned to it. We can have a pointer to the header node called start, as we did before. But the first node of the linked list that actually contains data will follow the start node. With this technique, the code in Section 7.3.6 can be simplified to

```
1   Node<DataType> *ptr = start;
2   while ( ptr->next->info != element )
3       ptr = ptr->next;
4   Node<DataType> *ptr2 = ptr->next;
5   ptr->next = ptr2->next;
6   delete ptr2;
```

We don't have a special case this time, because we never have to move the start pointer. Thus, we have shortened 12 lines to 6 lines.

Remember, this code always works if we know that there is a Mercedes in the linked list. If there isn't one, we would get a runtime error after reaching the end of the list. In writing code like this, you have to be very careful that you don't dereference a pointer which contains NULL.

7.3.8   Removing a Node if We Find One That Contains a Value

Let's look at another example now, one in which we are more cautious because we are not certain whether there is a node that contains Mercedes to delete or whether the linked list is empty or not. If a linked list is empty and we are using a header node, then start->next will be NULL, instead of start being NULL. The following code using a header node is illustrative:

```
1   Node<DataType> *ptr = start;
2   bool found = false;
3   while ( ptr->next != NULL && !found ) {
4       if ( ptr->next->info == element ) {
5           Node<DataType> *ptr2 = ptr->next;
6           ptr->next = ptr2->next;
```

```
7              delete ptr2;
8              found = true;
9              }
10     if ( !found )
11             ptr = ptr->next;
12     }
```

If the linked list is empty to begin with, the condition on line 3 will be false, and we won't bother trying to delete the Mercedes. Notice that if we did not check for this case, line 4 would give us a runtime error on an empty linked list.

The code on lines 5–8 will delete the node with Mercedes, as before, and will set found to true so that the program will exit the while loop.

The code inside the body of the while loop would be dangerous if ptr could be set to NULL. Then we would get a runtime error when the condition in the while loop heading is checked. So when we change the address stored in ptr on line 11, we have to make sure that ptr can't be set to NULL. We know that ptr->next is not NULL; otherwise we would have exited the while loop. So on line 11, we will be assigning an address of a node to ptr at all times.

When we don't know whether something we are searching for is in a linked list, a rule of thumb is to check for NULL in the heading of a while loop. Generally, we would use the condition ptr != NULL, but in this case, where we want the pointer to be one node to the left of the node that is found, we use ptr->next != NULL. Notice that if ptr->next is equal to NULL, ptr cannot be pointing to a node that contains Mercedes. If it were, it would already have been found on line 4 in the previous iteration of the while loop. Then it would have been removed on lines 5–8.

7.4   ARRAYS VS. LINKED LISTS

7.4.1   Comparing Arrays and Linked Lists for Speed

In deciding to use an array or a linked list for a data structure, the primary consideration is usually the amount of time that they take to achieve results. An array is faster in a situation where an index i is calculated and then the value at the index must be accessed. In a linked list, we would normally need to set up a loop to travel to node i before the value can be accessed. However, a linked list is faster in a situation where an element must be removed from the middle or inserted into the middle. As we saw in Section 7.3, all we have to do is a couple of simple operations with pointers. In an array, if we want to insert or remove an element from the middle, then we have to set up a loop to slide a group of elements appropriately (either to make room or to fill the gap). Figure 7.14 shows the case where we need to remove an element from the middle of an array.

In a great many other situations, the time may not differ significantly between an array and a linked list. For example, we may need a loop for both to search for an element. Or we may need to change each element in an array or a linked list, perhaps incrementing a certain value in the element by 1; in such a case, we would need to use a loop for both an array and a linked list, marching through them and changing values.

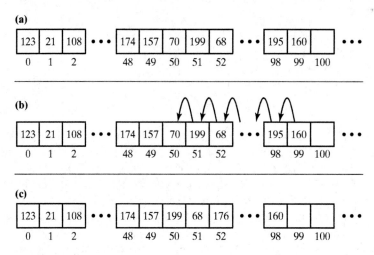

FIGURE 7.14

(a) Element 70 needs to be removed from the middle of an array with 100 elements. (b) Each element to the right of 70 needs to be slid to the left so that the elements are next to each other. A loop must be used to copy the elements one at a time. (c) The array with element 70 removed and with all elements next to each other.

7.4.2 Comparing Arrays and Linked Lists for Wasted Memory

Another consideration in comparing arrays and linked lists is how much memory is wasted by each method. For the purposes of this discussion, wasted memory is memory used by the data structure and that doesn't have anything to do with elements. We usually ignore the housekeeping variables used in the private section for flags, counts, header nodes, etc., and restrict ourselves to considering the memory wasted within the array or those linked nodes of the linked list that store data. The memory wasted in an array is the space of the array that is not being used; arrays are hardly ever completely filled with elements, and that part of the array which stores no elements is wasted. In a linked list, each pointer of each node is wasted memory.

Let's start by considering the percentage of wasted space in the linked list. The percentage of memory wasted depends on the size of the element. To determine the amount of wasted memory, we can use the formula

$$w_l = 100\% \times \frac{h}{h + e} \qquad (7.1)$$

where w_l is the percentage of wasted memory in the linked list, h is the "housekeeping space size per node" and e is the size of the element. The "housekeeping space size per node" is the space used by all pointers in the node, as well as by anything else that doesn't have to do with the actual info section (the element size). In this chapter, the housekeeping space size has been just the one pointer we have inside each node, but you can have more than one inside each node. So what the formula does is take the amount of wasted memory of a node, in bytes, and divide it by the total memory space of a node, in bytes. Once you get the percentage of wasted space in a node, it is also the percentage of wasted space in the linked list (ignoring housekeeping members of the private section of the linked list, such as the start pointer). This is because every node in the linked list wastes the same percentage of memory space. So if the element size is large, the percentage of wasted memory is small. By contrast, if the element size is small, the percentage of wasted memory will be large.

As an example, suppose the size of an element is 32 bytes and there is one pointer per node. The percentage of wasted memory would then be

$$w_l = 100\% \times \frac{h}{h + e} = 100\% \times \frac{4}{4 + 32} = 11.1\%$$

Now consider the case where we are just storing a character in the info section of a linked list and there is one pointer per node. Since each character is a byte, we would then have

$$w_l = 100\% \times \frac{h}{h + e} = 100\% \times \frac{4}{4 + 1} = 80\%$$

Thus, we waste a considerable amount of space in a linked list when the element size is small. These examples are illustrated in Figure 7.15.

When using this linked-list formula, one may have to estimate the average element size, because the element might be a struct object having one or more strings as data members. The amount of memory a string takes up can vary. If the string is long, it will use a lot of memory; if short, it will use less memory.

Speaking of strings, here is an eye-opener for you: An empty string object (that has not been initialized to a string) uses 32 bytes in Visual Studio 2005 C++. (For Visual Studio .NET 2003 C++, it was 28 bytes.) This fact can be ascertained by using the sizeof operator on the string type. We know that 4 bytes of storage are for the pointer that points to the dynamic character array used for the string. (Who knows what the other 28 bytes are for?) Take this information into account when you are figuring out your element size for the linked-list wasted-memory formula: Add the average (expected) length of the string (in dynamic memory) to the 32 bytes that an empty string would use.

As far as arrays are concerned, they are a little more difficult to analyze in terms of the percentage of wasted memory. The first thing to think about is whether the number

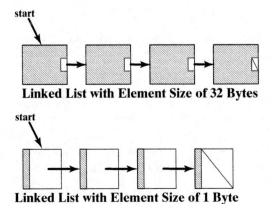

Linked List with Element Size of 32 Bytes

Linked List with Element Size of 1 Byte

FIGURE 7.15

Linked list with an element size of 32 bytes versus linked list with an element size of 1 byte. The shaded areas indicate the space taken up by the element; the white areas show the proportional size of the "next" pointer (which occupies 4 bytes). The size of the white area relative to the shaded area shows the amount of wasted memory.

of elements is going to change. If not, a dynamic array can be set to the number of elements without wasting any memory at all. This is, however, an unusual situation.

For other situations, we first have to consider that a used element size may be different from an unused element size. For example, if a string is part of an element in C++, the unused element includes only the empty string object, whereas the used element includes the empty string object as well as the dynamic character array. So the difference between used and unused sizes of elements can come from dynamic space, if any, in the element. In an array, there are actually three different types of elements to consider: a used element, a never-used element (which will contain no dynamic space), and a previously used element that is no longer accessible. An example of the last type occurs when an element is popped from the stack array; it can't just disappear from the array, but it is made inaccessible. This type of element takes up as much space as a used element, regardless of whether dynamic space is or is not used in the element, but it counts as wasted memory.

We may have a scenario, however, in which there are only used elements and never-used elements at any particular time in an array. Consider, for example, an array in which we are only adding elements and never removing them. Thus, we never end up with a "previously used" element.

Let s represent the static space in an element (that space which is not dynamic), and let h and e be defined as before. Then, using the technique for expansion and contraction of arrays discussed in Section 7.1, we have the following three cases:

- Case I. If there is only static space (and no dynamic space) within array elements, then

  1. If the element size e is less than h, the array is expected to waste less memory than the linked list.
  2. If the element size e is more than $3h$, the linked list is expected to waste less memory than the array.
  3. If the element size e is between h and $3h$, there may not be a significant difference in wasting memory between the array and linked list.

- Case II. If we only add elements to the data structure and never remove them (so that we never have previously used elements), and if dynamic space may be used in elements, then

  1. If $h < s/3$, the linked list is expected to waste less memory than the array.
  2. If $h > s/3$, the array is expected to waste less memory than the linked list.
  3. If $h = s/3$, then there may not be a significant difference in wasting memory between the array and the linked list.

- Case III. If all three types of elements mentioned are present during the use of the array, and if dynamic space is used in elements, then

  1. If $h < s/3$, the linked list is expected to waste less memory than the array.
  2. if $h > e$, the array is expected to waste less memory than the linked list.

3. if $s/3 \leq h \leq e$, then there may not be a significant difference in wasting memory between the array and the linked list.

Note that in C++ (using Visual Studio 2005), case III implies that if the only dynamic space in an element comes from string objects and 8 bytes or less are used for the housekeeping space h (a common situation), then we would expect to waste less memory in the linked list.

In all cases for these formulas, the true sizes of the objects involved should be checked by using the sizeof operator. Sometimes, a small amount of extra space is added onto an object to manage memory better. This characteristic is called ***boundary alignment***.

The next (optional) section provides an analysis of wasted memory for the three cases just set forth, for those who love algebra.

*7.4.3   Analysis of Wasted Memory

Consider the fraction of space that the three types of elements in an array use on average. For example, suppose an array contains 50% used elements, on average; we'll represent that percentage as the fraction $u = 0.5$. The fraction of previously used elements that are no longer accessible will be represented by p, and the fraction of never-used elements will be represented by n. Note that $u + p + n = 1$. The formula for computing the actual percentage of wasted memory in the array is then

$$w_a = 100\% \times \frac{ns + pe}{e - nd} \tag{7.2}$$

where s and e are defined as in Section 7.4.2 and d is the estimated (average) amount of dynamic space within an element. To understand this formula, note that the numerator gives us the amount of wasted space proportionally: ns is the fraction of never-used elements, which have only static space, while pe is the fraction of previously used elements that are no longer accessible, and these have the full element size. The denominator gives us the total space in the array proportionally: e is not preceded by a fraction and represents all elements in the array as full size; however, the never-used elements have no dynamic space and are subtracted off as nd. Thus, we are taking the amount of wasted memory in the array and dividing it by the total memory in the array (proportionally).

As an example, suppose an element of an array is a struct consisting of a character, an integer, and a string. In Visual Studio 2005 C++, the static space s would be $1 + 4 + 32 = 37$ (not accounting for boundary alignment). Suppose that the average length of the string is expected to be about 20 characters, so the dynamic space d would be 20. The element size e would be $37 + 20 = 57$. During the use of this array, on average, 50% of the array had used elements, 25% of the array had previously used elements, and 25% of the array had never-used elements. So $u = 0.5, p = 0.25$, and $n = 0.25$. Notice that the size of the array can expand and contract during the use of the array; we are just talking about the average percentage regardless of size. The percentage of wasted space in the array, on average, is then

$$w_a = 100\% \times \frac{(0.25)(37) + (0.25)(57)}{57 - (0.25)(20)} = 45.2\%$$

Note that if the elements consisted only of static space (and no dynamic space), then the fact that the array was, on average, 50% full would mean that it wasted 50% of its memory, on average. (The formula would reduce to just $n + p$, which would equal 0.5.) The fact that there are 25% of never-used elements, on average, and that a fraction of the element space is dynamic provides a little more benefit than the 50%.

To compare the linked list with the array, we'll equate their wasted-memory formulas and solve for h:

$$\frac{h}{h + e} = \frac{ns + pe}{e - nd}$$

$$h = \frac{ens + pe^2}{e - nd - ns - pe}$$

Since $-nd - ns = -ne$, we can factor out e, yielding

$$h = \frac{ns + pe}{1 - n - p} = \frac{ns + pe}{u} = \frac{ns + ps + pd}{u} = \frac{(n + p)s + pd}{u} = \frac{(1 - u)s + pd}{u}$$

Finally, splitting the result into two terms gives

$$h = \left(\frac{1 - u}{u}\right)s + \left(\frac{p}{u}\right)d \tag{7.3}$$

These are the conditions that produce the same amount of wasted memory, on average, between the linked list and the array. If h is greater than the right side of the equation, then the array would be better at wasting less memory, and if h is less than the right side, the linked list would be better.

But to make this equation meaningful, we need to be able to estimate the average u and p for a particular array. We will focus our attention on estimating u as a percentage—the percentage of used elements within an array, on average. Another way of looking at u is as the average *fullness* of the array.

First, we will consider how full a particular array can be. Unless an array is empty or we are out of heap memory, it must be between 25% and 100% full, given the technique that we talked about in Section 7.1. The reason it won't be less than 25% (unless empty or out of heap memory), is because, once it reaches this level of utilization, it is cut in half, so that it is 50% full. If we are out of heap memory, we cannot cut the size of the array in half. (A new, smaller array has to be made first.) In that case, we would normally want the program to continue, even though the level of utilization of the array would have dropped below 25%. If we are out of heap memory, therefore, the fullness of the array could drop to near 0%. (If it is at 0%, we could just free the array.)

In some situations, we can estimate the average fullness for a particular array, depending on how it is used. For example, suppose we have an array from which we never remove elements; we just keep adding elements. Then this array would stay between 50% and 100% full, giving us an average utilization of 75%. In another scenario, we might start a data structure with a large array, and from that point on, we just keep removing elements. When the first half of the elements is removed, the average is 75%. When the second half of the elements is removed, the array would stay between 25% and 50% full from that point on, giving an average of 37.5%. The overall average for this scenario would be 56.25%.

In other situations, we may not be able to calculate how full the array will be, on average. For example, the fullness of the array may depend on how the computer user uses the program. In these situations, we would want to try to get an average for *all* such arrays, to be able to compare arrays with linked lists. We will ignore the out-of-heap-memory situation, since this is unusual and would have little effect on an actual average. We will also start by assuming equal probabilities for insertions and deletions, and we will assume that insertions and deletions are performed independently of each other. Any expansion or contraction of the array will cause it to be 50% full. Therefore, we would expect that equally probable insertions and deletions would cause the average to hover near 50%. A string of operations that is heavier in insertions or deletions can occur, however, and a heavier string of insertions would have to occur for an expansion (at 100%) than a string of deletions for a contraction (at 25%). The midpoint of the range from 25% full to 100% full is 62.5%. Therefore, under all such conditions described, we would expect that the average fullness for an array would lie between 50% and 62.5%.

This range assumes that the probability of an insertion is equal to the probability of a deletion. If we want to take into account different probabilities for insertions and deletions, we can extend the range further. The extreme cases were described earlier. In one, we insert elements, but never remove them. (This gives us a 100% chance of insertion and a 0% chance of deletion.) In this case, the average fullness is 75%. In the other case, we start off with a full array and delete elements, but never insert them. In this case, the average fullness is 56.25%. So our range can extend from 50% to 75% if we want to take into account different probabilities for insertions and deletions.

One thing should be made clear, however: The average fullness for a particular array does not necessarily lie within the 50–75% range; we just expect it to. On the one hand, we can have very good luck and have an alternation between an insertion and a deletion at near the 100% full mark for a long time. This could end up giving us an average near 100% for a particular array. On the other hand, we can have very bad luck and have the same alternation at slightly above the 25% full mark for a long time, giving us an average near 25%. But when we talk about an average range, it doesn't include these good-luck and bad-luck cases; it is just a range within which we *expect* the average fullness of an array to be.

Now that we've estimated a range for the average fullness of an array (given that we don't know anything about how the array will be used), it is worth considering the case where there is no dynamic space within an element. In such a case, the range we calculated actually provides us with the range we can expect to have for wasted memory in the array. The range for wasted memory would be between 25% and 50%. This may seem like a large range, but not when compared with the range for a linked list. A linked list with one pointer in each node, for example, would waste 50% of its memory if the element size were 4 bytes. The same linked list would waste

25% of its memory if the element size were 12 bytes. A range from 4 to 12 bytes for element size is not that large of a range at all when it is possible to use a record of information for an element.

Another case is worth considering, because of the simplification of analysis. In this case, there are no previously used elements, and such a situation would occur only if we added elements to the array and never removed them. In such a case, $p = 0$ and equation 7.3 simplifies to

$$h = \left(\frac{1 - u}{u} \right) s$$

Since u is estimated to be 0.75, the formula reduces to

$$h = \frac{s}{3} \tag{7.4}$$

If h is larger than $s/3$, then the array would probably be better at conserving memory; if h is less than $s/3$, the linked list would probably be better.

If we don't know anything about how the array will be used, then the range for an expected u is between 0.5 and 0.75, which means that we can estimate a range for an expected p, namely, $0 \le p \le (1 - u)$. So in our next case, in which there is dynamic space in an element and there are previously used elements that are no longer accessible, the smaller h (from equation 7.3) would be found if we use $p = 0$ and $u = 0.75$. Therefore, in this case,

$$h < \frac{s}{3} \tag{7.5}$$

means that the linked list would probably be better at conserving memory. Setting $u = 0.5$ and $p = 1 - u = 0.5$, we have

$$h > s + d$$

which reduces to

$$h > e \tag{7.6}$$

and the array would probably be better at conserving memory. Again, anything in between indicates that there may not be a significant difference between the two.

SUMMARY

This chapter presented some general techniques that are used to make data structures. Although data structures are always made from classes, the methods used to make them can be different. Sometimes the structures take the form of dynamic arrays, and sometimes they take the form of linked lists. Sometimes arrays and linked lists will be combined into one structure, such as the hash tables in Chapter 11 and the graphs in Chapter 15.

Dynamic arrays can be made one dimensional or multidimensional. There won't be much of a need for creating multidimensional dynamic arrays in this textbook, but that doesn't mean you won't encounter them or need to use them in a data structure eventually.

It is quite common to use linked structures when making a data structure. Linked lists tend to waste little memory (percentagewise) for large objects. Arrays can waste less memory, however, for small elements. A decision about which structure to use might be based (at least in part) on both speed and the amount of memory wasted; often there is a trade-off between the two. The formulas presented in this chapter can be used to help make an informed decision about which structure to use.

Throughout the textbook, when dynamic arrays are used, they will expand when filled and contract when scarcely used, for the purpose of conserving memory. The technique we will employ is that when the array is filled, its capacity will double; when the number of elements used in the array shrinks to 25% of the capacity, the capacity will be cut in half (so that the array is about half full after it is cut in half). In actuality, what happens is that a new array is created with the new capacity and the elements from the old array are copied into it. Then the old array is freed and the pointer is made to point to the new array. All of this copying uses some time, but it will be shown in Chapter 9 that the average amount of time taken to insert and remove elements is not significantly affected.

You must use care when thinking about code for linked lists. Memorizing sections of code to perform specific actions on a linked list will only lead to low-quality programming. You must understand what you are doing and consider both the arrows in the drawings and the addresses stored in pointers to write code successfully. Anytime you need to change the way a pointer points, you really need to assign a new address to the pointer. You find that address by looking at other pointers and realizing that they store addresses. Then you can figure out what address assignment you need to make. Therefore, one of the first things you need to do is think about and draw a figure and then think about the addresses stored in the pointers of the figure. Also, think about how you need to change the pointers and about how you will find the addresses you need to assign to the pointers (in order to make them point to something else). Once you complete these assignments, draw and/or think about the resulting figure with arrows, to reassure yourself that you have been successful.

EXERCISES

1. Explain the strategy used in this textbook for the expansion and contraction of dynamic arrays.
2. Why not use the following strategy for expansion and contraction? When an element is added to an array, expand the array by 1, and when an element is removed from the array, contract the array by 1.
3. Suppose a full element size is typically 36 bytes and the element has no dynamic memory. Which would be better for conserving memory, a linked list with one pointer per node or an array? How did you arrive at your decision?
4. Suppose a struct having only two characters for members is to be used as an element. Which would be better for conserving memory, a linked list with one pointer per node or an array? Use the sizeof operator if you are not sure about the boundary alignment. How did you arrive at your decision as to which would be better?
5. Suppose that an array is significantly faster than a linked list for an application. Suppose also that we make the linked list faster by adding more housekeeping information per node in a complex data structure design. The linked list now has 24 bytes of housekeeping information

per node. The element size for the application is 128 bytes, of which 40 bytes will typically be used for characters in strings. The array may, at times, have previously used elements that are no longer accessible. Which one, the array or the modified linked list, would be better at conserving memory?

6. Write a class using a two-dimensional dynamic array. The constructor passes in the dimensions of the array. The constructor also initializes all values in the dynamic array to the row index multiplied by the column index.

Referring to Figure 7.2, create functions to
   a. Swap two columns of the two-dimensional array, where the column indexes are passed in as parameters. Do this just by copying addresses, not values of column elements.
   b. Delete a column of the two-dimensional array, where the column index is passed in as a parameter. Do not just use the delete operator on the column array and set the horizontal array element to NULL. Shrink the size of the horizontal array by 1.

Create a print function for the class to print out the values of the two-dimensional, array and make sure that your functions are working correctly. After you know that they are working correctly, delete the print function.

7. Describe the parts of a node.

8. In a linked list, what makes the first node different from the rest of the nodes (other than the fact that no other nodes point to it)? What makes the last node different than the rest of the nodes (other than the fact that it doesn't point to any other node)?

9. Write a function that will find a Mercedes in a linked list and then insert a node containing Honda before and after the node that contains Mercedes. (Be sure that both nodes that you insert are in different locations of memory; in other words, don't use the same node.) There may not be a node containing Mercedes in the linked list. If not, the function returns false. If there is, the function returns true.

10. Write a function that will remove all nodes that contain Mercedes from a linked list. Note that one Mercedes might follow another one. Consider the case where the entire linked list may be filled with nodes that contain nothing but Mercedeses, and consider the case where the linked list might be empty to begin with.

11. Write a section of code that will create a three-dimensional dynamic array. Then write another section of code that will free the dynamic memory used in the three-dimensional dynamic array.

CHAPTER 8

Stacks and Queues

In this chapter, we will examine data structure design for some of the simplest data structures: stacks and queues. You already had a taste of data structure design in Chapter 5 when the Array class was discussed. Here, we will explore further ideas in data structure design, which may be useful when you write your own data structures.

From this chapter on, we will be discussing a data structure as an abstract data type (ADT), before looking at the code used to implement them. Data structures can be implemented in many different types of computer programming languages, not just C++. Therefore, it is important to understand what a particular data structure is all about, without looking at the code used to implement it. Then, if you work with another programming language, you can use your code-independent understanding of the data structure to implement it.

8.1   THE STACK ADT

Back in Chapter 2, you were introduced to the idea of a stack, and it really was an abstraction for you. You didn't know how it worked, C++-wise, but you may have used it anyway to evaluate expressions in the exercises. Recall from Chapter 2 that an abstract data type includes a set of data and a set of operations that act upon the data. As you know, a stack is a stack of elements, and this is the set of data in the abstract data type that is operated on. Sometimes people describe the elements of a stack as being *homogeneous*, which is just a fancy way of saying that the elements are all of the same type. This description is really language dependent, though, and it is not hard to conceive of a stack whose elements can be of different types. Housekeeping data is also sometimes described as part of the abstract data type (such as a count of the number of elements), but this can change from language to language, so in this textbook we will not describe housekeeping data as part of the abstract data type. The most common operations that act upon the set of data in a stack are the following:

- push: places an element onto the top of a stack
- pop: removes an element from the top of the stack

- peek: retrieves (copies) a value from the top of the stack without removing it
- an operation to determine whether or not the stack is empty
- an operation to empty out a stack

A stack is regarded as a last-in, first-out (LIFO) data structure, because the last element to go in is the first element to come out.

8.2   ARRAY IMPLEMENTATION OF A STACK

Sometimes a stack is implemented with a fixed-length array for the elements. Although such an implementation is a little (but not much) easier than a dynamic-array implementation, we choose not to do it because (1) a fixed-length array might waste too much memory if only a tiny fraction of the array is used and (2) a fixed-length array might get filled, so that there is no more room to put in another element. A dynamic array can adjust its size to the number of elements, thus conserving memory, never getting filled, and making for a better implementation.

You used an array implementation of a stack if you wrote the code for evaluating expressions in Chapter 2, Exercises 14–15. Let's take a look at the implementation of that stack now. The class template is as follows:

```
1   // stack.h - the array implementation of a stack
2   // note:  the constructor, the (default) copy constructor, the (default) assignment operator, and
3   // the push function can cause an exception to be thrown if heap memory is exhausted
4
5   #include "Array.h"
6
7   template <class DataType>
8   class Stack
9   {
10  public:
11      Stack( );
12      void push( DataType elementToPush );
13
14      // removes an element from the top of the stack and returns it in poppedElement;
15      // returns false if called on an empty stack; otherwise, returns true
16      bool pop( DataType & poppedElement );
17
18      // returns the element at the top of the stack in topElement without removing it
19      // returns false if called on an empty stack; otherwise, returns true
20      bool peek( DataType & topElement );
21      bool isEmpty( ) const;  // returns true if the stack is empty;
22                              // otherwise, returns false
23      void makeEmpty( );
```

```
24  private:
25    Array<DataType> elements;
26    int top;
27  };
28
29  #include "stack.cpp"
```

This implementation uses an Array object, discussed in Chapter 5, that grows and shrinks as elements are pushed and popped, respectively. The same strategy for array expansion and contraction is used as was discussed in Section 7.1. The name of the Array object, elements, is given on line 25. This is a composition relationship, and it is similar to the example in Section 6.1, which you may want to review to familiarize yourself with the composition relationship and what its implications are.

The top member in the private section, line 26, is used as an index into the Array object. We maintain the top member so that it is always the index of the array element which represents the top of the stack. As elements are pushed onto the stack, they are actually just placed into the next position of the array and the top index is incremented. When elements are popped off the stack, they are not actually deleted as they would be in a linked list. Instead, the top index is just decremented. The value of the element is still there, but there is no way to access it anymore. The next time an element is pushed, it will be written over the value that was there before. Figure 8.1 gives

(a) elements

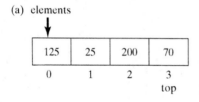

(b) elements

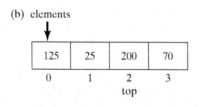

(c) elements

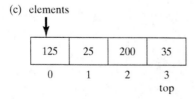

FIGURE 8.1

(a) A stack with top index set at 3. (b) An element is popped. The top index moves to 2. The value of 70 remains at index 3, but can no longer be accessed by stack functions. (c) A subsequent push of a value of 35 overwrites the value of 70 and sets the top index to 3.

an example of this implementation. The top index also provides the current number of elements in the array by adding 1 to it. For example, when there is only one element on the stack, top will be 0, the first index of the array. We can always get the number of elements by adding 1 to top.

The constructor in the implementation file is shown next:

```
1   // stack.cpp -- the function definitions for the array implementation of a stack
2
3   template <class DataType>
4   Stack<DataType>::Stack( )
5       : elements( 2 ), top( -1 )
6   {
7   }
```

The initializer list (which was first described in Section 6.1) sets elements (an Array object) to a capacity of 2, using the Array constructor; this is initially a small array, but we will double its capacity whenever it is filled. The initializer list also sets top (an index) to −1; the initial value of top cannot be 0 because that would mean that there is one element in the stack at index 0. Since we are going to increment top when we add an element, and we want top to be 0 when the first element is added, the initial value of −1 makes perfect sense. When top is set to −1, the stack is empty.

The push function of the stack is given next:

```
8    template <class DataType>
9    void Stack<DataType>::push( DataType elementToPush )
10   {
11       if ( ++top == elements.length( ) )
12               elements.changeSize( elements.length( ) << 1 );
13       elements[ top ] = elementToPush;
14   }
```

The parameter is not passed in by const reference, because, as the discussion in Chapter 7 shows, an array would normally be used for small element sizes. (The linked-list implementation of a stack is discussed in the next section.) Using a const reference would not allow us to pass in literal values, such as push('*').

The first thing to check is whether or not the array is already filled to capacity, because if it is, we can't push an element yet. In this case, when we increment top (which we need to do before pushing), it will equal the capacity of the array, so the condition on line 11 will be true. The shift operation

elements.length( ) << 1

means the same thing as

elements.length( ) * 2

but executes faster.

Then we are ready to push the elementToPush that was passed in from the client. We use the updated top index and assign elementToPush to that array position on line 13.

Now let's talk about the shift operator $\ll$ used on line 12. As stated earlier, the expression using the shift shown accomplishes the same thing as multiplying by 2, but is faster. In general, operations using integer addition and subtraction are fairly fast, while multiplication is slower and division is generally the slowest. Floating-point multiplication is slower than integer multiplication, and floating-point division should be avoided if at all possible. This may not seem like a big deal, but it can be for larger programs that take a long time to execute. Sometimes we can find a faster way to perform operations that is not too inconvenient.

A slightly different slant is taken here than was taken in previous chapters. We can use the shift operator, which is much faster than multiplication or division. There are two different shift operators that we can use. When we use

num << n

num is actually multiplied by 2^n (but the result is not saved to num—it can be saved by an assignment if needed). When we use

num >> n

num is actually divided by 2^n. (This is integer division—no float result.) Both operators are called shift operators because what actually happens is that the bits which make up the value of num are shifted to the left ($\ll$) or to the right ($\gg$) in the register that num is stored in. This operation is much faster than multiplying or dividing. Since the capacity is either doubled or cut in half, we are multiplying or dividing by 2, respectively, so we can use the shift operator.

In the expression elements.length( ) $\ll$ 1, we are taking the current capacity of the Array object and multiplying it by 2^1—that is, by 2. Thus, we are changing the capacity of the array to a capacity twice the size of the current length( ).

The pop function is now given:

```
15   // removes an element from the top of the stack and returns it in poppedElement;
16   // returns false if called on an empty stack; otherwise, returns true
17   template <class DataType>
18   bool Stack<DataType>::pop( DataType & poppedElement )
19   {
20      if ( top == -1  )
21              return false;
22
23      poppedElement = elements[ top ];
24      top--;
25
26      int trysize = elements.length( );
27      while ( ( top + 1 <= trysize >> 2 ) && trysize > 2 )
28              trysize >>= 1;
```

```
29
30      if ( trysize < elements.length( ) ) {
31              try {
32                      elements.changeSize( trysize  );
33              }
34          catch( … ) { }
35      }
36
37      return true;
38  }
```

Lines 20–21 handle the case where the stack is empty. If the stack is not empty, the element at the top index of the array is the current top of the stack, so it is assigned to poppedElement (passed in by reference) on line 23. Then, top is decremented on line 24 because that element is now the current top of the stack.

At this point, since an element has been removed, we should check to see if we can cut the array in half and conserve heap memory. It seems contrary to intuition, but before we free memory by calling the changeSize function of the Array object, we have to use more heap memory. The reason is that, while the current array is still in existence, the changeSize function creates a dynamic array that is half the capacity of the current array. Then, after the elements are copied over, changeSize frees the old, larger array. Therefore, it is possible to run out of heap memory when the changeSize function is called to reduce the size of the array.

However, if we run out of memory here, it should not cause the program to fail. We would like to cut the array, but we don't actually have to in order to keep the stack from functioning properly. For that reason, we don't return false after we reach this point in the pop function.

Another interesting situation can develop: If we are out of heap memory when the changeSize function is called, we may still be able to call it later to cut the size of the array. Sometimes the client uses another object that frees *its* dynamic memory, creating more heap memory for the changeSize function. Sometimes the number of elements in the stack is reduced to the point where the capacity needed is small enough that sufficient heap memory exists to create the dynamic array. To account for these situations, we will try to create a dynamic array with the *smallest* capacity that is still at least twice the number of elements (and is at least a capacity of 2). This is the purpose of the loop on line 27.

Before using the loop, we set trysize to the current capacity of the Array object on line 26. As we stated earlier, the expression top +1 gives the number of elements. We want to cut the array in half if top +1 is 25% of trysize. The expression trysize $\gg$ 2 divides trysize by 2^2, which gives us 25% of trysize. But if the capacity becomes as small as 2, we would like to exit the loop. Therefore, the right condition on line 27 is also checked. If the combined condition is true, line 28 tries a smaller trysize. Line 28 divides trysize by 2 and then saves the result to trysize by using the $\gg=$ operator. We want trysize to be the new capacity of the array, but as long as it is still too big, we keep dividing it by 2. Eventually, we get to the point where the number of elements is *greater than* 25% of trysize. We know that trysize is at least twice the number of elements here, because it was at least four times the number of elements on the last iteration, before it was divided by 2. Therefore, this is a suitable trysize to use. It is possible, however, that we exit the loop because the right side of the condition is false when trysize becomes equal to 2. In either case, we want to exit the loop and stick with the most recent value of trysize.

We check to see if trysize has changed on line 30 before we call the changeSize function; if it hasn't, we don't want to copy an array to a new array of the same size! If the changeSize function on line 32 is unsuccessful because of a lack of heap memory, we don't want the exception to be thrown to the client. In this case, the Array object won't change, and it will still function properly for the rest of the program. We would just *like* to reduce the capacity of the array, to conserve memory, if we can. Therefore, a try clause is used around the changeSize function, and if an exception is thrown, a catch clause (which does nothing) catches it in the pop function. Finally, true is returned on line 37, because we have successfully popped an element.

The peek function is shown next:

```
39   // returns the element at the top of the stack in topElement without removing it
40   // returns false if called on an empty stack; otherwise, returns true
41   template <class DataType>
42   bool Stack<DataType>::peek( DataType & topElement )
43   {
44       if ( top == -1  )
45               return false;
46       topElement = elements[ top ];
47       return true;
48   }
```

As in the pop function, we check for an empty stack on line 44, and if the stack is empty, false is returned on line 45. On line 46, topElement, passed in by reference from the client, is set to the element at the top of the stack. Then true is returned on line 47, indicating success.

The isEmpty function is as follows:

```
49   template <class DataType>
50   bool Stack<DataType>::isEmpty( ) const
51   {
52       return top == -1;
53   }
```

It just returns the result of the condition top $==-1$, which will be true or false.

The makeEmpty function is

```
54   template <class DataType>
55   void Stack<DataType>::makeEmpty( )
56   {
57       top = -1;
```

```
58    try {
59              elements.changeSize( 2 );
60    }
61    catch( ... ) { }
62  }
```

The top is set to −1 on line 57. We then change the capacity of the stack to size 2 on line 59. This could free a lot of dynamic memory. However, there is a chance that we are right on the edge of using all the heap memory, in which case the changeSize function cannot create a new array of two elements. We catch the exception that is thrown and do nothing. We can keep the old Array object. If dynamic memory is freed elsewhere in the program, then when the stack is used again and the next pop is made, the change-Size function may be called, setting the capacity appropriately.

8.3   LINKED-LIST IMPLEMENTATION OF A STACK

Stacks can also be implemented with a linked list. In such an implementation, the front of the linked list is the top of the stack. Thus, any elements pushed onto the stack are inserted at the front of the linked list. Any elements popped from the stack are removed from the front of the linked list. The linked-list implementation of a stack is left as an exercise, but you probably shouldn't attempt it until you read the rest of this chapter.

8.4   THE QUEUE ADT

A queue is like a line of people, except that it is a line of elements, and the line is the set of data that the queue operations act upon. The set of operations for a queue are as follows:

- enqueue: add an element to the end of the line
- dequeue: take an element from the front of the line
- peek: retrieve (copy) the element at the front of the line without removing it
- an operation to determine whether or not the queue is empty
- an operation that will empty out the queue

Like push and pop in stack terminology, a queue has its own set of terminology, namely enqueue and dequeue. A queue is regarded as a first-in, first-out (FIFO) data structure, because the first element to go into the queue is the first one to come out. (Think about it!) Another way to think of a queue is that it works by the first-come, first-serve principle, like a line of people waiting to be served. When a person joins the line, he or she goes to the end of the line. The person at the front of the line is served and taken off the line.

Queues are often used as parts of algorithms to solve problems, similarly to the way the stack was used in the expression evaluation algorithm in the exercises in Chapter 2. Sometimes queues are used for simulations, because there are so many situations in the real world that work by the first-come, first-serve principle. In other cases, they are used just to handle problems fairly and effectively. For example, if a bunch of people on a network all want to use a single printer, the print customers are placed into a queue by the operating system. The first person who requested a print gets the first spot in the queue. The second person who requested a print gets the next spot in the queue, but must wait for the first one to finish. When the printer is free to serve another customer, the customer at the front of the queue is removed. If another customer requests a print and there are still print customers in the queue, then the new request is placed at the end of the queue.

8.5   THE LINKED-LIST IMPLEMENTATION OF A QUEUE

In the linked-list implementation of a queue, the linked list becomes the line that we were talking about. There are two pointers into the linked list instead of just one start pointer. We call the pointer to the first node *front* and the pointer to the last node *back*. The back pointer makes it much faster to enqueue an element, since we don't have to walk a pointer all the way through the linked list to get to the last node. In the code for the queue, however, we must make sure that we maintain both the front and back pointers correctly. We have always made sure that start points to the first node of a linked list in the examples of Section 7.3, no matter how we changed the list. We have also made sure that start was set to NULL for an empty linked list. Now, in addition to doing the same thing for the front pointer of the queue, we must make sure that the back pointer is always set correctly too. To avoid handling special cases, we'll use a header node in the queue (described in Section 7.3.7). The queue is empty when the front and back pointers both point to the header node (i.e., when their addresses are equal). The fact that there is a back pointer to the last node gives the linked-list implementation of the queue a special twist: We do not need to set the last node's pointer to NULL, because the address of back can always be checked to see if we are at the last node. Figure 8.2 shows the enqueuing and dequeuing of nodes in the linked-list implementation of a queue, using a header node.

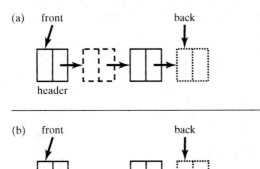

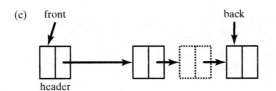

FIGURE 8.2

(a) A queue. The header node doesn't count as part of the line. The front of the line is the dashed node, while the end of the line is the dotted node. (b) The dashed node at the front of the line is dequeued. (c) A node is enqueued.

Following is the class template for the linked-list implementation of a queue:

```
1   // queue.h -- class template for the linked list implementation of a queue
2   // note:  use of the copy constructor, overloaded assignment operator, or enqueue function
3   // can cause an exception to be thrown when heap memory is exhausted
4
5   template <class DataType>
6   struct Node {
7       DataType info;
8       Node<DataType> *next;
9   };
10
11   template <class DataType>
12   class Queue
13   {
14   public:
15      Queue( );
16      Queue( const Queue<DataType> & apqueue );
17      ~Queue( );
18      Queue<DataType> & operator =( const Queue<DataType> & rqueue );
19      void enqueue( const DataType & element );
20
21      // dequeues element and returns it in deqElement
22      // returns false if called on an empty queue; otherwise returns true
23      bool dequeue( DataType & deqElement );
24
25      // returns element at the front of the queue into frontElement without removing it
26      // returns false if called on an empty queue; otherwise returns true
27      bool peek( DataType & frontElement );
28      bool isEmpty( ) const;      // returns true if queue is empty
29                                  // otherwise returns false
30      void makeEmpty( );
31   private:
32      Node<DataType> *front;
33      Node<DataType> *back;
34      Node<DataType> header;
35      inline void deepCopy( const Queue<DataType> & original );
36   };
37
38   #include "queue.cpp"
```

Lines 5–9 show the struct template for Node that we are already used to using. Since there are front and back pointers in the private section of the class (lines 32–33), it is necessary for good class design to have a copy constructor, a destructor, and an overloaded operator =, supplied on lines 16–18. The copy constructor and overloaded operator = will call the deepCopy function (line 35), as we said we would do in Chapter 5. The header node is supplied on line 34; it is not a pointer, but an actual node.

The enqueue function prototype is shown on line 19. Since elements used with linked lists are likely to be large, enqueue passes an element struct quickly by const reference. The dequeue function prototype is shown on line 23. It returns the element at the front of the queue in the parameter deqElement that is passed by reference. Dequeue will return false if the client tries to dequeue an empty queue and will return true otherwise.

Next, we'll take a look at the class implementation file for the queue, starting with the constructor:

```
1  // queue.cpp -- function definitions for the linked-list implementation of a queue
2
3  template <class DataType>
4  Queue<DataType>::Queue( )
5  {
6      front = back = &header;
7  }
```

Line 6 assigns the address of the header node (in the private section) to both the front and the back pointers. Thus, the queue is empty when front and back have the same address (the header node).

The copy constructor for the queue just calls the deepCopy function:

```
8  template <class DataType>
9  Queue<DataType>::Queue( const Queue<DataType> & apqueue )
10 {
11     deepCopy( apqueue );
12 }
```

The destructor is

```
13  template <class DataType>
14  Queue<DataType>::~Queue( )
15  {
16      makeEmpty( );
17  }
```

The makeEmpty function of the queue frees all the nodes in the linked list, so we make use of it.

The overloaded operator = function is written next:

```
18  template <class DataType>
19  Queue<DataType> & Queue<DataType>::operator =(
20                                      const Queue<DataType> & rqueue )
```

```
21  {
22    if ( this == &rqueue )
23          return *this;
24    makeEmpty( );
25    deepCopy( rqueue );
26    return *this;
27  }
```

On line 22, we check to see if the same queue is on both sides of the assignment; recall that, without this line, the queue on the left of the assignment would be destroyed when its memory is freed. The keyword *this* is a pointer to the left queue in this case, so the left queue is returned by returning *this. Recall that *this is returned in case there is more than one assignment on the same line, as in the code

q1 = q2 = q3;

When the overloaded assignment operator is called from the function call q2 = q3, *this will replace the function call and then be assigned to q1 in another call of the overloaded assignment operator.

If the queues are not the same, then the dynamic memory of the left queue is freed before we make a deep copy of the queue on the right. (The queue on the left might be initially empty, but it might not be.) On line 24, the makeEmpty function is used to free the memory of the left queue.

Line 25 makes a call to the deepCopy function, to make a deep copy of the queue on the right side of the assignment. Then line 26 returns the left-queue object.

Figure 8.3 shows how the following enqueue function works:

```
28  template <class DataType>
29  void Queue<DataType>::enqueue( const DataType & element )
30  {
31    Node<DataType> *ptr = new Node<DataType>;
32    ptr->info = element;
33    back->next = ptr;
34    back = ptr;
35  }
```

Note that lines 33 and 34 also work if the linked list is empty (i.e., if back is pointing to the header node).

The dequeue function is illustrated in Figure 8.4:

```
36  // dequeues element and returns it in deqElement
37  // returns false if called on an empty queue; otherwise returns true
38  template <class DataType>
39  bool Queue<DataType>::dequeue( DataType & deqElement )
40  {
41    if ( front == back )
```

(a) **Node\<DataType\> *ptr = new Node\<DataType\>;**

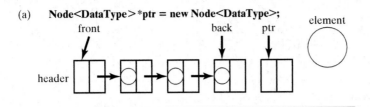

(b) **ptr-\>info = element;**

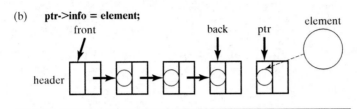

(c) **back-\>next = ptr;**

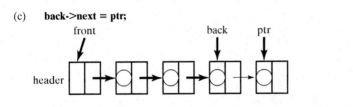

(d) **back = ptr;**

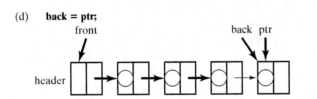

FIGURE 8.3

How the enqueue function works for the linked-list implementation of a queue. The line of code involved is shown at the top of each part. Elements are shown abstractly as circles.

```
42              return false;
43
44      Node<DataType> *ptr = front->next;
45      deqElement = ptr->info;
46      front->next = ptr->next;
47      if ( back == ptr )
48              back = front;
49      delete ptr;
50
51      return true;
52  }
```

If there is only one node in the queue, back will be pointing to that node. In this case, after the node is removed, the queue will be empty. So back is tested on line 47 to see if it is pointing to the node that needs to be removed; if it is, then back is set to the address of the header node on line 48.

(a)

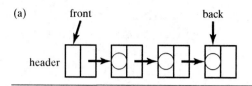

(b)   **Node<DataType> *ptr = front->next;**

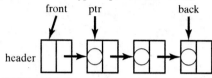

(c)   **deqElement = ptr->info;**

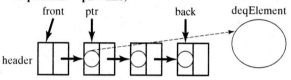

(d)   **front->next = ptr->next;**

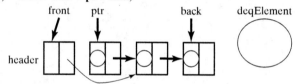

(e)   **delete ptr;**

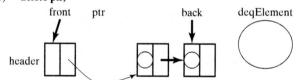

FIGURE 8.4

How the dequeue function works for the linked-list implementation of a queue.

The peek and isEmpty functions are simple:

```
53  // returns element at the front of the queue into frontElement without removing it
54  // returns false if called on an empty queue; otherwise returns true
55  template <class DataType>
56  bool Queue<DataType>::peek( DataType & frontElement )
57  {
58      if ( front == back )
```

```
59            return false;
60        frontElement = front->next->info;
61        return true;
62 }
63
64 template <class DataType>
65 bool Queue<DataType>::isEmpty( ) const
66 {
67        return front == back;
68 }
```

The last public function of the queue, the makeEmpty function, is as follows:

```
69 template <class DataType>
70 void Queue<DataType>::makeEmpty( )
71 {
72    DataType temp;
73    while ( dequeue( temp ) );
74 }
```

We make use of the dequeue function here. You may not have seen a while loop written the way it is written on line 73. When there is a semicolon following the while loop heading, the loop will keep executing as long as the condition is true. The dequeue function will return false when we try to dequeue an empty queue, so at that point, the while loop is exited. We keep dequeuing the queue on line 73 until it is finally empty. When the dequeue function dequeues the last node, it sets the back pointer to the header node, as shown in the dequeue function.

The deepCopy function, a private function that serves the copy constructor and overloaded assignment operator function, is presented next:

```
75    template <class DataType>
76    inline void Queue<DataType>::deepCopy( const Queue<DataType> & original )
77    {
78      Node<DataType> *copyptr = front = &header;
79      Node<DataType> *originalptr = original.front;
80      while ( originalptr != original.back ) {
81              originalptr = originalptr->next;
82              copyptr->next = new Node<DataType>;
83              copyptr = copyptr->next;
84              copyptr->info = originalptr->info;
85              }
86      back = copyptr;
87    }
```

Recall that the deep copy is being made for the queue that owns this function, while the original (passed in as a parameter on line 76) supplies the queue that needs to be copied. To make a deep copy of the linked list, we will need to set up two pointers, each of which will walk through its own linked list. These pointers are set up on lines 78 and 79 and are named so that we know which one is for the copy and which one is for the original. The address of the header node is assigned to both the front pointer and the copyptr on line 78. On line 79, the address of the header node of the original is assigned to originalptr.

If the original is an empty queue, originalptr will have the same address as original.back, since original.back will point to the header node. The while loop will not be entered, and back (for the copy) will be set to the header node of the copy on line 86.

If the original is not an empty queue, the while loop is entered. Figure 8.5 illustrates what happens within the body of the while loop. When the while loop is exited, copyptr will be pointing to the last node in its queue. Accordingly, we need to set the back pointer, which is done on line 86.

You should go over the deepCopy function again and make sure you understand it very well. Deep copies of linked lists need to be done this way when you make your own data structure. It may help to draw pictures as the code is executed. You will also need to remember to think about the addresses that are stored in pointers.

8.6   OTHER LINKED-LIST IMPLEMENTATIONS OF QUEUES

It is possible to implement the queue in Section 8.5 without using a front pointer, and it would not be that inconvenient to do so. One can use the header instead of the front pointer. However, if one wanted to access the first node in the queue, one would have to use the notation "header.next" instead of "header->next", which might be confusing to some. By using the front pointer, one can achieve the same result with "front->next". Linked-list implementations of queues sometimes do not even have a header node. However, the code is a little simpler if one is used.

It would be nice to be able to return a dequeued element by the return type of the function, rather than by a reference-type parameter. If we did this, the return type of the dequeue function would be DataType. However, if the client tries to dequeue an empty queue, it creates a problem. We can't just return; we must return something of type DataType. We also can't ignore the problem: We should always avoid writing a class function that can crash. If the client tries to dequeue an empty queue, and we don't check for it, our dequeue function will crash. Therefore, returning the dequeued element in a reference-type parameter turns out to be the easiest solution.

Sometimes the implementation of a queue (or any other data structure) will involve a function such as isFull, a complement of the isEmpty function. The isFull function, if written, would often check to see whether or not another node can be created in heap memory. If there is not enough heap memory, it catches the exception and returns true. If there is enough heap memory, it frees the node that was created and returns false. Thus, if no more nodes can be put on the queue, because of a lack of heap memory, the queue is

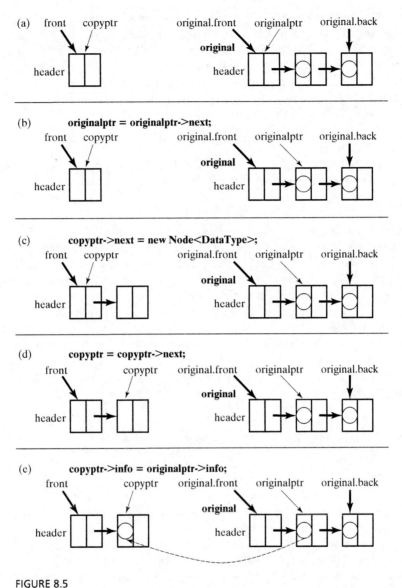

FIGURE 8.5

What transpires in the body of the while loop of the deepCopy function in the linked-list implementation of a queue.

considered to be full. The implementation of the isFull function isn't given here for a number of reasons, including the fact that the queue itself is never really full, but this might be more of a philosophical issue. It is like blowing up a balloon inside a jar. You reach a point where you can't put any more air into it, but, in the absence of the jar, the balloon could still hold more air.

A more important reason for not having an isFull function (at least, not one implemented this way) is that it can be misleading for a client. Suppose the client checks whether the queue is full and the isFull function returns false, but heap memory is close to being exhausted. Then, given that the queue is not full, the client's code executes some code that prepares an element for enqueuing. However, this preparation exhausts the remaining heap memory, and an error occurs during the attempt to enqueue, as illustrated in the following code:

```
if ( !q.isFull( ) ) {
    MyStruct *newElement = new MyStruct;  // exhausts heap memory
    q.enqueue( *newElement );  // error – no more heap memory
    }
```

This problem sort of ties into the philosophical idea that the queue's fullness has nothing to do with heap memory. The problem here is really that such an isFull implementation assumes that the client will immediately enqueue an element after checking that the queue is not full. In reality, however, the client's code might execute everything except the kitchen sink between the isFull function call and the enqueue function call. Another reason for not providing the client with an isFull function is that if you really need to put another node on a queue and you can't do it because there isn't enough heap memory, your goose is sort of cooked anyway. When heap memory has been extensively used up, further uses of the *new* operator will cause the program's performance to degrade (to the point of being impractical), even if there is enough heap memory left.

*8.7   ARRAY IMPLEMENTATION OF A QUEUE

Another way to implement a queue is to use an array to store the queue's elements. Sometimes a fixed-length array implementation is used, but it suffers from the drawbacks of not conserving memory well or being full when another element needs to be enqueued. Therefore, the fixed implementation is not covered here, and we focus on the dynamic-array implementation.

In this implementation, front and back are still used, but they are indexes into the array instead of pointers. We increment the back index when we enqueue, and we increment the front index when we dequeue. We can double the size of the dynamic array when the back index reaches the last index. However, we run into an interesting problem here: As elements are dequeued and the front index increases, all of the elements whose index is less than the front index result in much wasted memory.

This problem is remedied by having the back index restart at index 0 when it reaches the end of the array (if index 0 is not being used by the front). So, as the front and back indexes increase further (i.e., as elements are dequeued and enqueued, respectively), the back part of the queue might be the first part of the array and the front part of the queue might be the last part of the array! This phenomenon is illustrated in Figure 8.6. It may still be necessary to double the size of the array if the back index catches up with the front index.

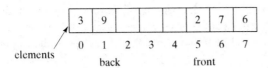

FIGURE 8.6

A queue that wraps around inside the array. The elements, in order from the front of the line to the back of the line, are 2, 7, 6, 3, and 9.

This is kind of an unnatural way to think of a queue, but that is no reason not to use it. As was pointed out in Section 7.4, one important consideration in making a data structure from an array or a linked list comes from the size of the data element. If the size is very small, this implementation would do much to conserve memory.

Let's first take a look at the class specification file for the Array implementation of a queue:

```
1    // queue.h -- class template for the Array implementation of a Queue
2    // The constructor, the (default) copy constructor, the (default) assignment operator, and the
3    // enqueue function can throw exceptions if there is no more heap memory.
4
5    #include "Array.h"
6
7    template <class DataType>
8    class Queue
9    {
10   public:
11       Queue( );
12       void enqueue( DataType element );
13
14       // dequeues element and returns it in deqElement
15       // returns false if called on an empty queue; otherwise returns true
16       bool dequeue( DataType & deqElement );
17
18       // returns the front element in frontElement without removing it
19       // returns false if called on an empty queue; otherwise returns true
20       bool peek( DataType & frontElement );
21       bool isEmpty( ) const;          // returns true if queue is empty
22                                       // otherwise returns false
23       void makeEmpty( );
24   private:
25       Array<DataType> elements;
26       int front;
27       int back;
28   };
29
30   #include "queue.cpp"
```

As one might expect, the function prototypes look exactly the way they do in the linked-list implementation of a queue. An Array object is used on line 25 to store the data in the queue. Since there is no pointer in the private section, we do not need a destructor, a copy constructor, or an overloaded assignment operator, as was the case with the Array implementation of a stack. The front and back indexes of the queue are provided on lines 26–27.

The implementation file is shown next, starting with the constructor:

```
1   // queue.cpp -- function definitions for the Array implementation of a Queue
2
3   template <class DataType>
4   Queue<DataType>::Queue( )
5   : elements( 2 ), front( -1 ), back( -1 )
6   {
7   }
```

The constructor uses the same initialization of the Array object that was used in the array implementation of the stack. An empty queue is indicated by setting both the front and back indexes to -1. If they were both set to 0, it would indicate that there is one element in the queue at index 0.

Next, we will examine the enqueue function:

```
8    template <class DataType>
9    void Queue<DataType>::enqueue( DataType element )
10   {
11     if ( back + 1 == front || ( back == elements.length( ) - 1 && !front ) ) {
12            elements.changeSize( elements.length( ) << 1 );
13
14            // if front end was last part of array, readjust
15            if ( back < front ) {
16                    int i = elements.length( ) - 1;
17                    for ( int j = ((i + 1) >> 1) - 1; j >= front; i--, j-- )
18                            elements[ i ] = elements[ j ];
19                    front = i + 1;
20                    }
21       }
22
23     if ( back == -1 ) // queue is empty
24            front = 0;
25     back = (back == elements.length( ) - 1)? 0 : back + 1;
26     elements[ back ] = element;
27   }
```

Since arrays are expected to contain small element sizes (as we learned in Section 7.4), the parameter is passed by value into the enqueue function on line 9, instead of by const reference. This makes it possible to pass in literals (e.g., q.enqueue(0);).

Line 11 checks to see if the Array if full. It will be if the back has caught up with the front. If the back index is not the last index, then the back catches up with the front when back +1 equals the front. If we tried to enqueue here, we would write the

(a) **back < front**

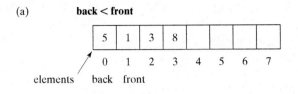

(b)
int i = elements.length( ) - 1;
int j = ((i + 1) >> 1) - 1;

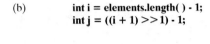

(c)
for (int j = ((i + 1) >> 1) - 1; j >= front; i--, j--)
elements[i] = elements[j];

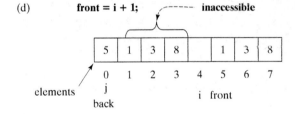

(d)
front = i + 1; ------- **inaccessible**

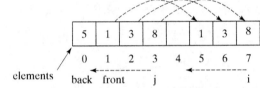

FIGURE 8.7

The readjustment when the array doubles in size and back < front.

element over the top of the front of the queue. The back can also catch up with the front when the back is the last index and the front is index 0. Since the enqueue would wrap around to the beginning of the array again, the enqueue would overwrite the front. If front is 0, then !front is true. If the queue is full, then we double the size of the array on line 12. Figure 8.7 shows the purpose and function of lines 15–21.

Lines 23–26 take care of adding the new element to the queue. If the queue is initially empty, the new front of the queue will be at index 0, so it is set on line 24. Ordinarily, we would only need to increment the back index, using back++. But if the back index is the last index of the array, it needs to wrap around to index 0. The modified incrementation is taken care of on line 25. The element passed into the enqueue function is written into the position at the new back index on line 26.

Now, we'll turn our attention to the dequeue function:

```
28   // dequeues element and returns it in deqElement
29   // returns false if called on an empty queue; otherwise returns true
30   template <class DataType>
31   bool Queue<DataType>::dequeue( DataType & deqElement )
32   {
33       if (front == -1 )
34            return false;
35
36       deqElement = elements[ front ];
37       if ( front == back ) // only one element was in queue
38            front = back = -1;
39       else
40            front = (front == elements.length( ) - 1)? 0 : front + 1;
41
42       // try to reduce the size of the array
43       int trysize = elements.length( );
44       int numElements = (front <= back)? back - front + 1 : back + trysize - front + 1;
45       while ( ( numElements <= trysize >> 2 ) && trysize > 2 )
46            trysize >>= 1;
47
48       if ( trysize < elements.length( ) ) {
49            // readjust so we won't lose elements when shrinking the array size
50            int i, j;
51            if ( front > back ) {
52                 for ( i = trysize - 1, j = elements.length( ) - 1; j >= front; i--, j-- )
53                      elements[ i ] = elements[ j ];
54                 front = i + 1;
55                 try {
56                      elements.changeSize( trysize );
57                 }
58                 catch( ... ) {
59                      for ( i = elements.length( ) - 1, j = trysize - 1; j >= front; i--, j-- )
60                           elements[ i ] = elements[ j ];
61                      front = i + 1;
62                 }
63                 return true;
64            }
65            else if ( front <= back && back >= trysize ) {
66                 for ( i = 0, j = front; j <= back; i++, j++ )
67                      elements[ i ] = elements[ j ];
68                 front = 0;
69                 back = i - 1;
70            }
```

```
71          try {
72                  elements.changeSize( trysize );
73              }
74          catch( ... ) { }
75          }
76
77      return true;
78  }
```

Lines 33–34 handle the problem of trying to dequeue an empty queue. Line 36 saves the dequeued element at the front of the queue to deqElement, passed in by reference. Here, we would ordinarily just increment the front of the queue, using front++. However, there may only be one element left to dequeue, which is the case if back is equal to front (line 37). Then we would need to set front and back to −1 as on line 38, to indicate an empty queue. The front index might also wrap around from the last index to index 0, so we can't just increment it if there are more elements left in the queue. Line 40 handles the modified incrementation.

Afterwards, we try to decrease the size of the array, similarly to the way we tried to do so in the stack earlier in the chapter. We must be able to get the number of elements in the queue, however, before we can see if the number of elements has fallen to 25% of the capacity. This task is handled on line 44. If the front index is less than or equal to the back index, the elements aren't wrapping around, and we simply use the formula back − front +1. Otherwise, we total the number of elements in two parts:(back − 0 + 1) + (trysize − front). This expression simplifies to back + trysize − front + 1. An alternative to using these formulas is to keep a count of the number of elements in the queue (in the private section). Then, every time we enqueue, we increment the count, and every time we dequeue, we decrement the count.

Lines 45–46 are similar to lines 27–28 of the stack implementation, and they have the same explanation. Recall that we got the number of elements in the stack by using top +1.

If trySize ends up being smaller than the current capacity (line 48), we don't want to decrease the capacity of the array just yet. One reason is that the queue might be wrapping around the array. If we cut some elements off the back of the array, we would be losing elements in the queue! Figure 8.8 on p.198 shows how lines 51–57 handle this case. If we cannot cut the size of the array in half because of a lack of heap memory, then we reverse what we've done on lines 51–54 in the catch clause.

Figure 8.9 on page 199 shows how lines 65–70 handle another case, in which the queue isn't wrapping around, but the elements can still be lost. The only other case, where we don't do anything, is when front is less than back and back is less than trySize. This is the easiest case, since we don't need to shift anything. We won't lose queue elements by cutting the size of the array.

The capacity of the array is cut for the last two cases on line 72. If the cut does not succeed because of a lack of heap memory, we can continue using the array the way it is, so the catch clause doesn't do anything. Then true is returned on line 77 for the last two cases, indicating a successful dequeue.

(a) **front > back**

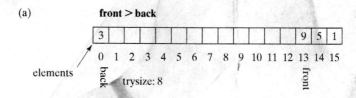

(b) for **(i = trysize - 1, j = elements.length( ) - 1**; j >= front; i--, j--)
    elements[i] = elements[j];

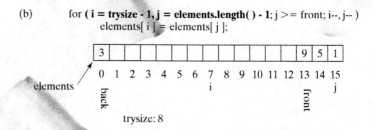

(c) for (i = trysize - 1, j = elements.length( ) - 1; **j >= front; i--, j--)**
    elements[i] = elements[j];

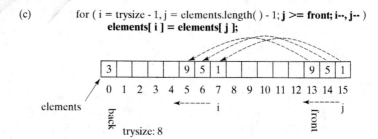

(d) **front = i + 1;**

FIGURE 8.8

The preparation for cutting the array in half when the queue wraps around the array.

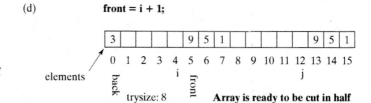

The peek, isEmpty, and makeEmpty functions are rather pleasant in their simplicity:

```
79  // returns the front element in frontElement without removing it
80  // returns false if called on an empty queue; otherwise returns true
81  template <class DataType>
82  bool Queue<DataType>::peek( DataType & frontElement )
83  {
84      if (front == -1 )
85              return false;
86      frontElement = elements[ front ];
87      return true;
88  }
89
90  template <class DataType>
```

```
91  bool Queue<DataType>::isEmpty( ) const
92  {
93      return front == -1;
94  }
95
96  template <class DataType>
97  void Queue<DataType>::makeEmpty( )
98  {
99      front = back = -1;
100     try {
101             elements.changeSize( 2 );
102     }
103     catch( ... ) { }
104 }
```

(a)   **front <= back && back >= trysize**

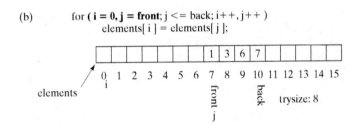

(b)   for (**i = 0, j = front**; j <= back; i++, j++)
                  elements[i] = elements[j];

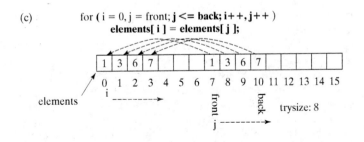

(c)   for (i = 0, j = front; **j <= back; i++, j++**)
                  elements[i] = elements[j];

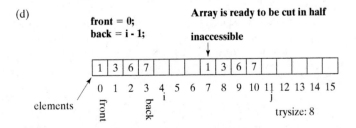

(d)   **front = 0;**   **Array is ready to be cut in half**
             back = i - 1;

FIGURE 8.9

The preparation for cutting the array in half when the queue doesn't wrap around the array, but elements can still be lost.

SUMMARY

This chapter has presented the array and linked-list implementations of stacks and queues, although the linked-list implementation of the stack was just described and left as an exercise. Stacks and queues are the most basic types of data structures. The decision on whether or not to use an array or a linked-list implementation of a stack or a queue can be based on the ideas presented in Chapter 7.

Stacks are used in evaluating expressions, as in Chapter 2, Exercises 14–15. Stacks are used in situations and algorithms in which the last element into a data structure needs to be the first element out of the data structure (LIFO).

Queues are often used in simulations, or in situations that require a fair, first-come, first-serve handling of data. Queues are used in situations and algorithms in which the first element into a data structure needs to be the first element out of the data structure (FIFO). Both stacks and queues are often used as a part of more complex algorithms.

The exercises at the end of this chapter are important to do. You will gain experience in writing your own linked-list functions, as well as gain experience in writing larger programs. If you get stuck while trying to implement the pull function in Exercises 16–17, you may need some more brainwashing, and you should go over Section 7.3 again.

EXERCISES

1. What is an abstract data type? Why is it important to be able to conceive of a data structure without thinking about code?
2. Why is a dynamic array implemented instead of a fixed-length array?
3. Using shift operators, write short programs to perform the following:

    a. Multiply the value of num by 8.
    b. Divide the value of num by 4.
    c. Multiply the value of num by 32 and save the result in num.

    Output the result of each of these programs.
4. Why are shift operators sometimes used instead of multiplication and division (when multiplying or dividing by a power of 2)?
5. Write a class template for a linked-list implementation of a stack. The stack class must have the same functions as the one used in Section 8.2, but with four additional functions: destructor, copy constructor, overloaded assignment operator, and deepCopy. The private section shall only have one data member: a pointer called top. Be sure to have the pointer of the last node (at the bottom of the stack) set to NULL at all times. (This condition wasn't necessary in the linked-list implementation of the queue, because the back pointer signified the last node—but it is generally necessary in linked lists). At the top of the class implementation file, include iostream (important because NULL is defined here) and use the std namespace.
6. Make a new Stack class template in which, on the basis of memory waste, the constructor determines whether an array implementation or a linked-list implementation of the stack should be used. Use the sizeof operator in the constructor to get the number of bytes in the DataType used. Also, use the sizeof operator on a pointer type to get the number of bytes

used in an address, in case the size of an address changes in the future. For example, use size-of(int *). On the basis of the number of bytes in DataType, the constructor will determine whether or not the array implementation or linked-list implementation should be used. (See Section 7.4.2.) The constructor will set a flag in the private section to indicate which implementation was selected. Every function in the Stack class will use either the array implementation or the linked-list implementation, on the basis of the flag that was set by the constructor. You will place two different top data members in the private section, with different names, so that either implementation can be used. (Remember that one top data member stores the index of an array and the other is a pointer.)

7. What does enqueue mean? What does dequeue mean? What is FIFO?

8. In the linked-list implementation of a queue, why is it important to maintain a pointer called back that points to the end of the queue?

9. Why is a destructor, a copy constructor, and an overloaded assignment operator provided in the linked-list queue implementation?

10. A programmer would like to write an isFull function for the Queue class, which returns true only if there is no more heap memory left to enqueue another element. The function tries to create a node; if it is successful, there is more heap memory, the node is freed, and the isFull function returns false. If the node can't be created because of a lack of heap memory, the is-Full function returns true. What is the difficulty with such an isFull function?

11. Why have both a destructor and a makeEmpty function in the linked-list implementation of a queue?

12. In the array implementation of a queue, what would be the problem with keeping the back index after the front index and then doubling the size of the array when the back index reaches the last index?

13. In an array implementation of a queue, how do you know when the array is full? How do you know when the array is empty?

14. Why do the elements in a queue sometimes need to be rearranged when the size of the array is doubled or cut in half?

15. Make a new Queue class template in which on the basis of memory waste, the constructor determines whether an array implementation or a linked-list implementation of the queue should be used. Use the sizeof operator in the constructor to get the number of bytes in the DataType used. Also, use the sizeof operator on a pointer type to get the number of bytes used in an address, in case the size of an address changes in the future. For example, use size-of(int *). On the basis of the number of bytes in DataType, the constructor will determine whether or not the array implementation or linked-list implementation should be used. (See Section 7.4.2.) The constructor will set a flag in the private section to indicate which implementation was selected. Every function in the Queue class will use either the array implementation or the linked-list implementation, on the basis of the flag that was set by the constructor. You will place two different front data members in the private section, with different names, so that either implementation can be used. (Remember that one front data member stores the index of an array and the other is a pointer.) You can also do the same with the back data member.

16. Make a data structure similar to a queue, except that it is possible to pull an element from the middle if it meets some special condition. Note that we cannot call this a queue anymore because of this allowance, so we will call it a pull-queue. Use a linked-list implementation of the pull-queue.

   The PullQueue class will be like the Queue class, except that you will be required to make one more member function. This function, called pull, pulls (deletes) an element anywhere in the PullQueue that meets some special condition. The pull function passes in a variable **item** of type DataType and a variable **pulled** of type DataType, both passed by reference, that will return the info deleted (like dequeue). We will use **item** for comparison purposes, to see if there is any node in the PullQueue that meets the special condition. Overload the equality operator to find the first node in the PullQueue that meets the condition. For example, you might use the code

```
template <class DataType>
bool PullQueue<DataType>::pull( const DataType & item, DataType & pulled )
{
        Node<DataType> *ptr;
        // other possible code
        while ( ptr->next != NULL ) {  // search for an element that meets the condition
            if ( ptr->next->info == item ) { // check info for special condition,
                                // using overloaded operator ==
                        // Delete the node here and return the info in pulled

            }
        }
        ...
}
```

The overloaded equality operator will be defined in the struct used for DataType. The struct and special condition are chosen by the main programmer, so when you test PullQueue, you can make your own struct and special condition. The special condition should apply to some member of the struct you choose. When you pass in item, the usual practice would be to pass in a struct which meets that special condition and then compare item with the info section, using your overloaded operator == (as shown in the example). With this technique, the main programmer can have more than one special condition; the one to use at any particular time is passed in as item. The return type for your binary operator must be a bool, since it is used as a condition (which must always evaluate to true or false). The pull function also has a bool return type. It returns true if there was some node that met the special condition, and it returns false if there was no node in the PullQueue that met the special condition.

The pull function pulls only the first node that meets the condition. (The rest of the PullQueue is ignored.) Make sure that the pull function works (1) when the PullQueue is empty, (2) when the first element is pulled, (3) when the last element is pulled, (4) when an element in the middle is pulled, (5) when the pulled item is the only element in the PullQueue, and (6) when there is no special item in the PullQueue to pull (in this case, pull will return false, as stated earlier). Be careful that the pointers of the private section are set correctly in each case. Whenever you write a class function, you should always consider the state of the data members.

The main programmer now has a choice as to whether to remove an item from the PullQueue. An item can be removed normally by dequeue, or a special item (if one exists) can be removed by pull.

Write a printPullQueue, which will print each member of the PullQueue for debugging purposes. Once you are sure that the pull function is working, delete the printPullQueue function.

Test PullQueue by enqueuing nodes, trying the pull function on the six conditions discussed and then printing the PullQueue after each pull.

*17. Do exercise 16, except have the PullQueue class inherit from the Queue class.

18. This exercise will be about creating a simulation, which is a technique that is used to make a model behave as a real object. Queues are often useful in simulations. A queuing system is made up of both servers and elements on the queue to be served. Everyday life is filled with

all kinds of queuing systems. For example, when you stand in line to check out at a supermarket or wait in line at a car wash, you are inside a queuing system.

Nobody wants to stand in line. If there were one checkout counter for every customer in a supermarket, the customers would be deliriously happy. The supermarket, however, would be feeling a financial pinch. So the supermarket and the customers need to find some middle ground: The store doesn't hire any more cashiers than it can handle, and the average customer may have to wait a little while.

The supermarket would like to determine what the average wait time of a customer will be. If the customers like the average wait time, the number of customers will increase, boosting profits. If the customers don't like the average wait time, the supermarket can lose customers and lose profits. If a supermarket can determine the average wait time, on the basis of how often customers arrive and how many cashiers the supermarket has, then the supermarket can adjust the number of cashiers as appropriate to keep a good average wait time and keep those profits rolling in.

But how *does* a supermarket manager determine the average wait time of the customers? One way is by trial and error: The supermarket tries out different numbers of cashiers. Collecting data with such an approach, however, can take a long time. Also, the average arrival time of the customers can change as a function of how happy they are with the average wait time, throwing another monkey wrench into the picture. When the average arrival time of the customers changes, you can expect that the average wait time will change. Another, perhaps better, way of dealing with this problem is to use a computer simulation that has a queuing system; queuing systems run through the same types of scenarios much faster, enabling data to be obtained much faster. Every time the environment changes in a new way, a new type of simulation might be devised to deal with it.

Our simulation program can be used for a variety of queuing systems. It will ask the user to enter the following data:

1. The length of the simulation (an integer). We can think of this as being in seconds. However, a second in a simulation is much faster than a real second.
2. The number of general-purpose servers.
3. Whether or not there is a special-purpose server (a "yes" or "no" answer) that can pull a customer off the queue if the customer meets a special condition.
4. The number of different types of transactions. As an example, a bank line might have two different types of transactions: making a deposit and making a withdrawal.
5. The average transaction time for each type of transaction (an integer array). That is, how long does it take, on average, to serve a customer seeking to make a particular transaction. The times might be different for each type of transaction.
6. The average time between customer arrivals (an integer). For example, a new customer might come into a bank line once every 600 seconds, on average.

The program will output the average amount of time it took for a customer to be served. This time can be computed by

Average wait time = (total wait time for all customers served) / (number of customers served)

Note from the formula that the wait time for customers that have not been serviced (but are waiting in line when the simulation ends) should not be used in computing the average wait time.

When asking for "average transaction times", the program should just ask the user to enter the average time for transaction 0, the average time for transaction 1, and so on. For the average transaction times, use a dynamic array whose length depends on the number of different types of transactions the user enters.

This program will use the ServerGroup class completed in Chapter 5, Exercise 10, and the PullQueue class in Exercise 16 or 17 here. The declaration for the ServerGroup will need to be made after the user enters the data described, because the constructor you made for that task has the number of general-purpose servers as a parameter.

The main program will contain a simulation loop, each iteration of which will do three things: (1) update a "clock" and the servers (the word "server" alone will always be used to refer to both general-purpose servers and the special-purpose server if any), (2) possibly receive a new customer, and (3) possibly serve one or two waiting customers.

The clock is just an integer that starts off at zero and is incremented by 1 each time through the loop. (Each iteration of the loop signifies the passing of a second.) A server is available if it stores 0. Otherwise, it stores an integer that indicates how long it will take to serve the customer it is working on. Therefore, to update the servers in the simulation loop, you decrease the time by 1 second for each server, except for the servers that are free. (You wrote some functions for completing this task.)

After updating the clock and servers, the PullQueue might receive a new customer. How do we know whether or not a new customer has arrived at any particular second? The answer depends on two things: the average time between customer arrivals (that the user had entered) and chance. First, we need to know the probability that a customer will arrive in any given clock unit. Probabilities range from 0.0 (no chance of arrival) to 1.0 (a customer will definitely arrive). If, on average, a customer arrives every 5 seconds, then the chance of a customer arriving in a given second is 0.2 (1 chance in 5). Therefore, the probability of a new customer arriving in a particular second of the simulation loop is

ArrivalProb = 1.0 / (average time between customer arrivals)

For the chance factor, we will make use of a random-number generator. To start the generator, the first line of code in your main program should be

srand(unsigned(time(NULL)));

Make sure to use

#include <time.h>

at the top of the main program. (The .h extension is necessary.) Once the srand function has been used to start the random-number generator, it should never be used again throughout the rest of the program.

First, we will generate a random number between 0.0 and 1.0, using the fragment of code

float(rand( )) / RAND_MAX

(The random number output by this function must be assigned to a variable.) The rand( ) function returns a random integer from 0 to RAND_MAX (a maximum random number defined in cstdlib; be sure to #include <cstdlib>) . Therefore, this code will give us a value from 0.0 (if rand( ) returns 0) to 1.0 (if rand( ) returns RAND_MAX). This fragment of code can be used again and again (in the simulation loop).

Now we can apply the following rules:

1. If the random number is between 0.0 and ArrivalProb (calculated earlier), a customer has arrived and we put the customer on the PullQueue.
2. If the random number is greater than ArrivalProb, then no customer arrived during this clock unit.

What exactly should be placed on the PullQueue? It will be the object of a struct defined in the main program (encapsulated in a Node by PullQueue, of course). For our purposes, the struct should have at least two members: a time stamp, which is the time of the clock when the customer first entered the PullQueue, and the transaction type (an integer).

The overloaded operator == would usually be used to check the transaction type for a particular transaction that should be "pulled" off the PullQueue. In fact, a special condition can always be defined as being some particular type of transaction. In the main program, use transaction 0 as the transaction type representing the special condition. (Typically, in real-life situations this would be a transaction type having one of the shortest average transaction times: Customers fume when they have a transaction that takes only a few seconds, but they have to wait in line a long time.)

For simplicity, we will assume that all transactions have an equal chance of occurring. Then the transaction type for a customer, before it is enqueued, can be randomly determined with the code

```
transactionType = rand( ) % numTransTypes;
```

where numTransTypes is the number of different transaction types entered by the user. Since the modulus operator (%) gives a remainder, the result of this calculation is guaranteed to be a random number between 0 and (numTransTypes −1).

One more part of the simulation loop remains: possibly serving one or two waiting customers. In order for this to occur, a server must be free. If a transaction time stored by a server is nonzero, then the server is not free. If no servers are free, then a customer at the front of the PullQueue has to wait a number of loop iterations until a server's transaction time is decremented all the way to zero. (As described earlier, it is decremented by 1 in the first part of the simulation loop.) After that, the server is free to serve a waiting customer. The second condition that must exist is that there is actually a customer waiting to be served in the PullQueue. (The PullQueue might be empty at this time, particularly if the transaction times are quick and the customer arrivals are slow.) If these two conditions are met, the customer can be dequeued. The struct returned during the dequeue has some important information: (1) the transaction type, which will be used to determine the average transaction time passed to the free server. (You wrote some functions in ServerGroup to do this; recall that the average transaction times for each transaction type was entered by the user); and (2) the time stamp, which is used to determine how long the customer had been waiting. (Subtract it from the present clock value.) Remember, you will output the average waiting time for all the customers at the end of the simulation.

If the user has chosen to use a special-purpose server, this is the server that should be checked first to see if it is free. If it is, then an attempt is made to "pull" an item from the Pull-Queue. Remember to use the pulled customer in the average waiting-time calculation also. If the PullQueue is empty or no customer meets the special condition, then the special-purpose server remains free. Afterwards, the general-purpose servers should be checked and used if the PullQueue is not empty. For simplicity, we will only use up to one free general-purpose server per clock second (depending on whether the PullQueue is empty).

The simulation stops when the clock is incremented to the simulation length, which was entered by the user.

When you get results, how do you know whether the program is working correctly? Since random numbers are used, results will be different every time. You can count your blessings, because I have also created this program, running it and obtaining some results that you can use as a guideline. However, keep in mind that your results may be slightly different, due to randomness. Here are my results:

Results of Test Runs on Simulation Project

All test runs used a simulation length of 10,000 and three transactions, such that the average transaction times were as follows:

type 0   15 sec.

type 1   200 sec.

type 2   300 sec.

Six test runs were made on each set of conditions, giving a range of average wait times for a given set of conditions (this doesn't mean that a correct program will always land in the range):

GP = general-purpose server

SP = special-purpose server

Test Run 1

2 GP

no SP

average arrival time: 30 sec.

range of average wait times: 2725–3682 sec.

Test Run 2

2 GP

no SP

average arrival time: 170 sec.

range of average wait times: 21.00–62.11 sec.

Test Run 3

2 GP

SP enabled

average arrival time: 30 sec.

range of average wait times: 1237–1509 sec.

Test Run 4

3 GP

no SP

average arrival time: 30 sec.

range of average wait times: 1859–2592 sec.

Test Run 5

3 GP

SP enabled

average arrival time: 200 sec.

range of average wait times: 0.03–11.54 sec.

Test Run 6

5 GP

SP enabled

average arrival time: 30 sec.

range of average wait times: 184–653 sec.

CHAPTER 9

Introduction to Time Complexities

Sometimes, a particular data structure is a part of a well-known algorithm, just as the stack was in the expression evaluation algorithm. In this case, we may choose between the array implementation and the linked-list implementation, but we pretty much know that we are going to have to use a stack. At other times, we are developing an algorithm and we have a choice among two or more different data structures to use for the algorithm—and it is not always the case that one data structure is better than another. Someone who has a lot of experience with data structures eventually realizes that one data structure is better than another in some situations, but not in others. Each data structure seems to have its own situation in which it is more advantageous among the others. Data structures are like the tools in a toolbox: When you need a hammer, you might have a choice between a rubber mallet and a sledgehammer. Both might work for a given task, but one would probably work better; each has a situation in which one works better than the other.

One critical factor in the decision about which data structure to use lies in the speed of the operations (or functions) of each data structure. Other factors can be important, but speed is almost always important. Therefore, to aid in making an informed decision about which data structure to use, we need to have an intelligent way to compare the speeds of the functions involved.

There is more to this comparison than meets the eye, so let's understand what we are dealing with. Consider an array of elements and an algorithm (within the function of a data structure) that does something with the array. The amount of time the function takes to execute may vary with the number of elements in the array. We might expect that when we have more elements in the array, the algorithm will take longer to execute; there are more elements to process, and processing each element takes some

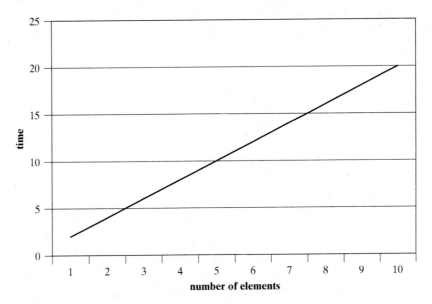

FIGURE 9.1

A line graph of number of elements vs. time.

amount of time (if we are indeed processing each element). Our expectation about the number of elements in the array and the time required for execution might look something like the graph in Figure 9.1.

In the figure, each point on the line gives the number of elements (on the *x*-axis) and the amount of time the algorithm takes to execute (on the *y*-axis). Thus, if we take a point higher on the line, the number of elements is greater, and so is the time for execution. Conversely, a point lower on the line gives us a lesser number of elements, but a smaller amount of time for execution.

An algorithm, however, does not always produce the nice, straight line that we see in Figure 9.1: Sometimes the graph is more like that in Figure 9.2 or Figure 9.3. In both of these figures, as the number of elements increases, the time the function takes to execute also increases. However, the *behavior* is different: In Figure 9.2, the time increases dramatically as the number of elements increases; in Figure 9.3, the time increases as the number of elements increases, but it seems about to level off, although it never quite does. If we had to choose which figure has the better behavior, it would be Figure 9.3. In that figure, if we increase the number of elements in the array, we are not going to pay a heavy price in the amount of time the algorithm takes to execute. The *time complexity* of an algorithm describes its behavior in such a manner. The different behaviors that we see in Figures 9.1, 9.2, and 9.3 are really different time complexities.

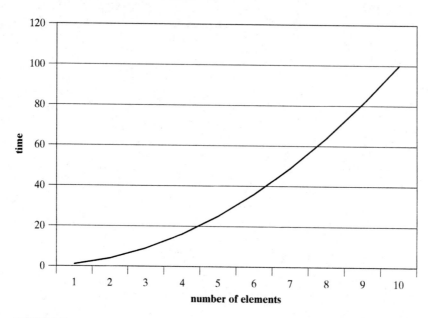

FIGURE 9.2

Another plot of number of elements vs. time. The time scale is higher and increases substantially as the number of elements increases.

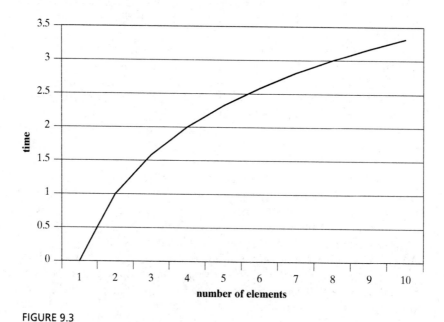

FIGURE 9.3

Another way of plotting number of elements vs. time. The time scale is very small, and an increase in the number of elements results only in a slight increase in time.

9.1 TIME COMPLEXITY BASICS

Suppose we have two different data structures to choose from, one with function A and one with function B. Both functions accomplish the same thing with an array, but they take very different approaches. (There may be only one mountaintop, but there are many ways up the mountain.) Let's suppose that Alan needs to make a decision about which data structure to use. (We need *some* scapegoat.) Now, Alan doesn't know much about computer science, but after carefully weighing all the factors, he realizes that the data structure with the faster function, A or B, should be chosen for the program. He can't really tell which is faster by looking at them, because their approaches to solving a particular problem are radically different. So Alan decides to time them. He uses an array size of 100 and runs each one a million times (automated in a program test, of course). Let's say that function B turned out to be faster. Then its data structure is chosen.

Little does Alan know that if we were to examine the behaviors of functions A and B, they would compare as shown in Figure 9.4. At 100 elements (the array size that Alan used for the test), function B is clearly faster than function A, as shown by the dots. So Alan was right. However, when the program is finally given to the customer, the customer always uses it with a lot of data, filling the array to 500 elements or more; notice that function A would be much faster in this situation, so the customer was shortchanged. The example shows that time complexities would help us to make a more informed decision about which data structure to use.

Whenever we compare two algorithms that have different time complexities, their graphs often intersect as shown in Figure 9.4. The point of intersection is called

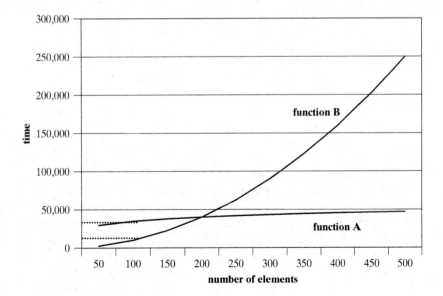

FIGURE 9.4

A comparison of the behaviors of functions A and B for number of elements vs. time.

the **cross-over** point, the number of elements at which both algorithms take the same amount of time to execute. In this case, to the left of the cross-over point function B is faster than function A, but to the right of the cross-over point the situation is reversed and function A is faster. So how do we determine which function is better? Computer scientists often ignore what happens to the left of the cross-over point. The reason is that the number of elements is relatively low here, and *any* algorithm that executes with a low number of elements is probably going to be fairly fast. In other words, the user of the algorithm won't really notice the difference in speed. It is when the number of elements is high that computer programs start to take a longer time to execute. Here, the user really *can* notice the difference between the speeds of the algorithms. Therefore, we often base decisions about data structures on what happens to the right of the cross-over point, where the number of elements can be high.

Often, we are not really sure about the number of elements at which a cross-over point occurs between two algorithms with different time complexities. The cross-over point rarely occurs at a high number of elements, but when it does, we should pay attention to the left of the cross-over point, because all practical uses of the program might occur there. In the vast majority of cases, the cross-over point occurs at a relatively small number of elements. Although we frequently are not sure about the precise location of the cross-over point, we know which time complexity is going to eventually be better with an increasing number of elements. As the number of elements increases, the number is really "approaching infinity", so we use this kind of language very often. Sometimes people think of "approaching infinity" as being extremely high, but you can increase the number of elements from 5 to 6 and be approaching infinity. However, "approaching infinity" is eventually going to pass to the right of the cross-over point. We say that we are considering the **asymptotic running times** of algorithms when we think about their running times as the number of elements approaches infinity (which is just a fancy way of saying that we are considering numbers to the right of any possible cross-over point).

The main purpose of a time complexity is to compare the amount of time algorithms take to execute when that amount of time can vary. If we never had to make a decision about which algorithm to use or which data structure to use, then time complexities would probably not be discussed in any textbook.

At this point, we would like to examine how we can determine the time complexity of an algorithm. But there is quite a bit to this undertaking, so we will have to lead up to it. First of all, in discussing time complexities, we often use the variable n to represent the number of elements. It is just easier to say n than to keep saying "the number of elements." The variable n can represent the number of elements in an array, but it might also represent the number of elements in something else, such as a linked list. In reality, n is used for anything that has a pronounced effect on the execution time of an algorithm as that thing is varied; it just turns out that, in the vast majority of cases, this happens to be the number of elements that we are working with. We often refer to n as being the *problem size* for the algorithm.

In determining time complexities, the time that an algorithm takes to execute is represented by the number of instructions that are executed in the algorithm. The rationale for adopting this method of representing time is that the more instructions algorithms have, the longer they take to execute. It is not a perfect method, because, in reality, each instruction can take a different amount of time to execute. Therefore, we cannot really think of the execution time of one instruction as being one time unit (although it is often perceived that way during analysis). This method, however, works surprisingly well in determining time complexities.

Let's look at an example and count the number of instructions executed:

```
1   sum = 0;
2   i = 0;
3   while ( i < 3 ) {
4       sum += A[ i ];
5       i++;
6   }
```

Lines 1–2 constitute 2 instructions. We'll consider the checking of the condition in the while loop as another instruction, giving us 3 instructions up to this point. Then, we have an iteration of instructions. We repeat line 4, line 5, and the condition check on each iteration, so 3 instructions are involved on each iteration. The loop repeats three times, giving us 9 instructions for all iterations. Adding this on to the other 3 instructions at the beginning gives us a total of 12 instructions. (We are assuming that there are no overloaded operators; otherwise there would be more instructions to count.)

The interesting thing about the number of instructions is that it can often be represented as a function of n. That is, for a value of n put into the function, the function produces a certain number of instructions. To see an example of this, let's take the same code as before, but use a variable numElements instead of 3:

```
sum = 0;
i = 0;
while ( i < numElements ) {
        sum += A[ i ];
        i++;
}
```

We still have the first 3 instructions, counting the initial condition check in the while loop. But this time, the number of iterations will be numElements instead of 3. So the code is adding all the elements in the array A. Realizing that numElements is really n, we know that the number of instructions in all the iterations is $3n$. Therefore, the function for this algorithm would be

$$f(n) = 3n + 3$$

The function $f(n)$ gives us the number of instructions executed in the algorithm. For example, if n is 5, the total number of instructions executed is $f(n) = 3 \times 5 + 3 = 18$. If n is 2, the total number of instructions executed is $f(n) = 3 \times 2 + 3 = 11$. Hence, this is a nice parallel to the number of elements and execution time that we discussed earlier. But the fact that we can represent the number of instructions executed as a function of n is significant, as we will see later. By the way, the function for the first example of this chapter would be

$$f(n) = 12$$

assuming that the algorithm is correctly written (i.e., that the array will always have at least three elements).

Let's take a look at a slightly more complex algorithm:

```
1    sum = 0;
2    i = 0;
3    while ( i < n ) {
4        j = 0;
5        while ( j < n ) {
6              sum += i * j;
7              j++;
8              }
9        i++;
10    }
```

Let's examine lines 4–9 first. We start off with 2 instructions on lines 4–5. Then we iterate n times with 3 instructions in each iteration, giving us $3n + 2$ instructions so far. When line 9 is executed, we have a total of $3n + 3$ instructions for lines 4–9. But all of these instructions are repeated n times in the while loop of line 3, giving us a total of $n(3n + 3)$ instructions. The while loop condition on line 3 is also involved on each iteration, so we have $n(3n + 3) + n$ instructions. Finally, the first 3 instructions, counting the initial condition check, are added in, giving us $n(3n + 3) + n + 3$, which reduces to $3n^2 + 4n + 3$, so our function for this algorithm is

$$f(n) = 3n^2 + 4n + 3$$

As you can probably imagine, for more complex algorithms we could have a lot of fun finding a function for the number of instructions executed. You will see shortly that we don't really have to go through all of this tedious work to determine a time complexity, but it was necessary to show it to you so that you get a feel for what is going on.

If we graph these functions out, we can see their behavior. As you probably know from algebra, the function $f(n) = 3n + 3$ will have the shape of a straight line, as in Figure 9-1. (The figure shows the *shape*, not what the actual line would look like.) The function $f(n) = 3n^2 + 4n + 3$ gives us half of a parabola, like the shape in Figure 9.2. (It won't be a full parabola, because n, the number of elements, can't be negative.) But these functions aren't really time complexities. A time complexity is actually a *set* of functions. So these functions are really *elements* of time complexities.

Now, in order to understand how a time complexity is actually derived, you need to recall from algebra the meanings of the words **term** and **coefficient**. The terms of a function are the parts of it that are added together, as shown in Figure 9.5a. The coefficients of a function are the leading constants of each term, shown in blue in Figure 9.5b.

If the function has at least one term with an n, then, in order to derive the time complexity, we remove the least significant terms from the function, leaving only the most significant term—the term that would be the largest number if n were a very high

(a)

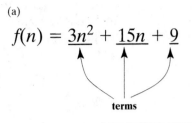

terms

(b)

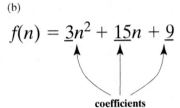

coefficients

FIGURE 9.5

(a) The terms of a function. (b) The coefficients of a function.

value. Then we remove the coefficient from the most significant term. For the function $f(n) = 3n + 3$, the most significant term is $3n$, and removing its leading coefficient would give us a time complexity of n. For the function $f(n) = 3n^2 + 4n + 3$, the most significant term is $3n^2$, and removing its most significant term would give us a time complexity of n^2. There is a special notation that we use for time complexities. A time complexity of n is written as $\Theta(n)$, and a time complexity of n^2 is really written as $\Theta(n^2)$, pronounced theta-n and theta-n squared, respectively. This is called **theta notation**. It is used so that when we see n or n^2, we know that we are talking about, not the number of instructions in an algorithm, but rather, the time complexity.

A time complexity should be thought of as a set. An infinite number of functions would belong to the set $\Theta(n)$. For example, $3n + 4$, $10n + 1$, $5n$, $2n + 100$, n, $\frac{1}{2}n + 25$, and $n - 2$ are all examples of functions that belong to the $\Theta(n)$ time complexity. The last two examples might surprise you a little. However, the coefficients can be less than 1, as in $\frac{1}{2}n + 25$. In this case, we might go only halfway through an array before stopping a loop. It is also possible to have negative signs in the function, as in $n - 2$. A negative sign in a function would occur, for example, in this algorithm:

```
sum = 0;
i = 0;
while ( i < size – 2 ) {
        sum += sum + A[ i ];
        i++;
}
```

Here, we stop the loop after size -2 iterations. Since size is presumably n, the loop stops after $n - 2$ iterations. There are three instructions on each iteration, so the function for this algorithm would be $3(n - 2) + 3$, which works out to

$$f(n) = 3n - 3$$

If you have a negative sign in the most significant term of a function, however, it is an indication that something went awry. If n is high enough, it would give you a negative number for the number of instructions, which is nonsensical.

When one gains experience in determining time complexities, one realizes that it is not really necessary to count every single instruction in an algorithm. All that is necessary is that you have an understanding of how the time complexity is derived, so you know what you can ignore and what you can't ignore. Let's take a look at the second algorithm again:

```
sum = 0;
i = 0;
while ( i < numElements ) {
        sum += A[ i ];
        i++;
}
```

Once we notice that the while loop executes n times, we have the time complexity. We don't really need to count the number of instructions in the while loop if it is a constant number, because it will just end up being the coefficient of n that we throw out. The first three instructions will be an insignificant term that we throw out.

In the example

```
sum = 0;
i = 0;
while ( i < n ) {
        j = 0;
        while ( j < n ) {
                sum += i * j;
                j++;
                }
        i++;
        }
```

the nested loops, with each loop iterating n times, tells us that the time complexity will be $\Theta(n^2)$. If a loop iterates n times, and all those iterations are repeated n times, it's going to give us an n^2 term. There is nothing here to give us an n^3 term or higher. Once we realize that the n^2 term will be the most significant term, we have the time complexity.

Sometimes, we'll have one loop followed by another loop in an algorithm. (The second loop starts after the first finishes executing.) In sequential cases like this, we would *add* the time complexities of the individual components that are in sequence. For example, suppose that the first loop, by itself, has a time complexity of $\Theta(n)$. Once the first loop finishes executing, the second loop starts, and it has a time complexity of, say, $\Theta(n^2)$ (possibly, it contains a nested loop). Adding the time complexities of these components together gives us $\Theta(n) + \Theta(n^2)$. Remember that we can add these time complexities because one finishes executing before the other one starts. If one looks at this sum, one realizes that, in the instruction function, the highest term would be the n^2 term. Therefore, the overall time complexity would be $\Theta(n^2)$. We often use this technique to come up with an overall time complexity—the highest time complexity of those components which are in a sequence.

We rarely have a need to count up the exact number of instructions, as a function of n, in an algorithm. On occasion, however, we are interested in where the cross-over point occurs between two algorithms. The cross-over point between two algorithms can often be approximated by the functions that represent the number of instructions. For example, let's consider the functions of two different algorithms:

$$f(n) = n^2 + n + 2$$

$$g(n) = 4n + 2$$

The cross-over point would occur where the number of elements and the number of instructions are exactly the same for both functions. Since the number of instructions would be the same, and each function gives us the number of instructions, we can equate the two functions:

$$n^2 + n + 2 = 4n + 2$$

When we solve for an n that makes this equation true, we have the point at which the number of elements and the number of instructions is exactly the same. Subtracting the right side from both sides of the equation yields

$$n^2 - 3n = 0$$

which factors to

$$n(n - 3) = 0$$

There are two solutions: $n = 0$ and $n = 3$. But $n = 0$ is a nonsensical answer, since the number of elements is 0. Thus, at $n = 3$, we have a cross-over point between the two algorithms that we are interested in. We can check that the number of instructions is the same by using $n = 3$ in both functions. This yields 14 instructions for each function. (Such a calculation should be considered only a ballpark approximation of a cross-over point.) At $n = 2$, we would presume that $f(n)$ is faster than $g(n)$, since $f(n) = 8$ instructions while $g(n) = 10$ instructions. But at $n = 4$, we would presume that $g(n)$ is faster, since $g(n) = 18$ instructions while $f(n) = 22$ instructions. We can see that, for larger values of $n, g(n)$ will continue to be faster.

However, $g(n)$ will do more than continue to be faster. Since $g(n)$ and $f(n)$ belong to different time complexities, the larger n gets, the faster $g(n)$ will get over $f(n)$. This situation, which always occurs when two algorithms have different time complexities, is illustrated in Table 9.1. At $n = 10$, $g(n)$ is 2.7 times faster than $f(n)$. At $n = 100$, $g(n)$ is 25.1 times faster, and at $n = 1000$, $g(n)$ is 250.1 times faster. The greater the number of elements, the more benefit that we get out of an algorithm that has a better time complexity. However, don't read more into this than you see. If one algorithm has more speedup over another as n increases, it does not mean that the algorithms belong to different

TABLE 9.1 Amount of speedup of $g(n)$ over $f(n)$ as n increases.

n	$f(n) = n^2 + n + 2$ (number of instructions)	$g(n) = 4n + 2$ (number of instructions)	How many times faster $g(n)$ is over $f(n) : [f(n)/g(n)]$
10	112	42	2.7
100	10102	402	25.1
1000	1001002	4002	250.1

time complexities (consider $3n^2 + 5n$ and $3n^2$). But if two algorithms have different time complexities, then one will have more speedup over another as n increases.

Let's consider two functions: $f(n) = 3n$ and $g(n) = 9n$. These functions belong to the same time complexity, $\Theta(n)$. As Table 9.2 shows, $f(n)$ is always three times faster than $g(n)$ as n increases. But we don't need a table for that; we can see that it's true just by looking at the functions, right? When the speedup of one function over another remains the same as n increases, the two functions belong to the same time complexity. Again, however, don't read more into this than you see: If the speedup of one function over another increases as n increases, it doesn't mean that the algorithms *don't* belong to the same time complexity. (Consider, once more, $3n^2 + 5n$ and $3n^2$.) However, if two algorithms belong to the same time complexity, then any speedup of one over another as n increases won't be significant.

These principles apply to any two time complexities. In theory, there are an infinite number of time complexities—for example, $\Theta(n)$, $\Theta(n^2)$, $\Theta(n^3)$, $\Theta(n^4)$, etc. However, the only time complexities that we will need to deal with in this textbook are listed in Table 9.3, which also gives the names that are sometimes used for these time complexities. It may be surprise you that the time complexities in Table 9.3 are really quite common. We will be discussing these other time complexities a little later.

For now, we are still building on the notion of what a time complexity is. Let's consider why the function $f(n) = 4n^2 + 6n$ belongs to the $\Theta(n^2)$ time complexity and not some other time complexity. In the light of the discussion we just had, it might seem that it should belong to another time complexity. However, let's consider the function $g(n) = 4n^2$. We can see clearly that $g(n)$ is faster than $f(n)$ for all $n > 0$. That is,

$$4n^2 < 4n^2 + 6n$$

Let us also consider the function $h(n) = 12n^2$. The relationship

$$4n^2 + 6n \leq 4n^2 + 6n^2 = 10n^2 < 12n^2$$

TABLE 9.2 The amount of speedup of $f(n)$ over $g(n)$ stays the same as n increases. (This can also be seen just by looking at the functions: $g(n) = 3f(n)$, so $g(n)$ always has three times as many instructions as $f(n)$.)

n	$f(n) = 3n$ (number of instructions)	$g(n) = 9n$ (number of instructions)	How many times faster $f(n)$ is over $g(n) : [g(n)/f(n)]$
10	30	90	3
100	300	900	3
1000	3000	9000	3

TABLE 9.3 Time complexities used in this book and their common names.

Time complexity	Common name
$\Theta(1)$	constant
$\Theta(\lg n)$	logarithmic
$\Theta(n)$	linear
$\Theta(n \lg n)$	n-log-n
$\Theta(n^2)$	quadratic

makes it clear that $f(n)$ is faster than $h(n)$ for all $n > 0$. Thus, $4n^2 + 6n < 12n^2$ for all $n > 0$. So now we have a situation in which $g(n) = 4n^2$ is always faster than $f(n) = 4n^2 + 6n$, but $f(n)$ is always faster then $h(n) = 12n^2$. That is, $f(n)$ is always sandwiched in between the two as n approaches infinity. But if you look closely at the "bread slices," $g(n)$ and $h(n)$, you will see that they definitely belong to the same time complexity and, further, that $g(n)$ will always be three times faster than $h(n)$. We can see that in the function $f(n) = 4n^2 + 6n$, the $6n$ term is really not significant at all; we say that it is **absorbed** into the time complexity of the most significant term.

It can further be shown that *any* term which is not the most significant term of a function can be absorbed into the time complexity of the most significant term, although some of the proofs are quite involved. But that is the reason we always remove the terms of lesser significance from the function in deriving the time complexity. It can also be shown that a function which belongs to one time complexity cannot be sandwiched in between the functions of another time complexity. You will see such proofs at the beginning of a course or textbook on algorithm analysis.

Once we have removed all terms of lesser significance, the coefficient of the remaining most significant term is also not a part of the time complexity. Recall that the speedup between this term and a term of equal significance will be the same, regardless of the coefficient, as was illustrated in Table 9.2. When the amount of speedup does not change as n increases, the functions belong to the same time complexity. So the coefficient is not a part of the time complexity either.

If we are comparing two algorithms and we find that they have two different time complexities, we can tell quickly which will be faster to the right of the cross-over point (if there is one). It is obvious, for example, that $\Theta(n)$ is a better time complexity than $\Theta(n^2)$. After all, when we look at n, it is really giving us an indication about the number of instructions that need to be executed. The shapes of the graphs of these two time complexities also tell you which will be better. In the $\Theta(n^2)$ algorithm, we pay a heavy price in execution time as the number of elements is increased, as shown in Figure 9.2.

Sometimes a time complexity of an algorithm is called the running time of the algorithm, but this is really a misnomer. We can tell nothing about how long the algorithm will actually take to run simply by looking at its time complexity. If an algorithm has a $\Theta(n)$ time complexity, we often say that the algorithm runs in $\Theta(n)$ time, language that seems to be a bit more palatable.

There is a long, formal definition of time complexity that relates closely to what we have been talking about, but there is no need to examine it. As long as you have a basic idea of what a time complexity is, and you are familiar with the time complexities that we need to use, that is all that is required for this textbook. So, let's summarize the notion of a time complexity:

1. Time complexities describe the pattern of how an algorithm's execution time changes as some other factor or factors, usually the number of elements, change.
2. Time complexities are useful in comparing algorithms, because the execution time of an algorithm will sometimes differ depending upon some other factor or factors; thus, time complexities are used as an aid in making an informed decision about which algorithm or data structure to use.
3. When two algorithms have different time complexities, one will have an increasingly significant speedup over another as n increases. If two algorithms have the same time complexity, there will be no significant difference in the speedup of one over another as n increases.

In determining which algorithm will be better as far as speed goes, we always look at their time complexities first. If their time complexities are the same, then we sometimes time them to see which one is better.

9.2   THE CONSTANT TIME COMPLEXITY

A $\Theta(1)$ (pronounced theta-1) time complexity is the best possible time complexity. In this time complexity, an increase in n does not affect how long the algorithm will take to execute. An example of a $\Theta(1)$ time complexity is the time complexity of the algorithm that dequeues an element from a queue implemented with a linked list. It does not matter if the queue has a hundred elements, a thousand elements, or even a billion elements: The dequeue operation works just with the front of the linked list and takes the same amount of time.

Sometimes a $\Theta(1)$ time complexity is called *constant time*. This, however, is a misnomer. Time is hardly ever constant for such algorithms, and many factors including the architecture of the computer, can affect the time one way or another.

The only thing that is true about a $\Theta(1)$ time complexity is that it has an upper limit to the number of instructions, regardless of how high n is increased. Take, for example, the following code:

```
if ( a > b ) {
        x = A[ 0 ] + 2;
        z = x * 3;
        }
x++;
y = x + 1;
```

This is code that has a $\Theta(1)$ time complexity. It does not matter how many elements are in array A, because we access only the first element. However, the number of instructions can be different, depending on whether a > b. If a > b, then five instructions are executed, counting the condition. If a <= b, then only three instructions are executed.

However, the number of instructions in this code can be no more than five. Therefore, five is an upper limit on the number of instructions. When code has a constant upper limit on the number of instructions, the code has a $\Theta(1)$ time complexity. You will sometimes hear the expression that an algorithm is **bounded** by a constant. This means the same thing as having a constant upper limit in instructions.

It is considered improper to use notations such as $\Theta(5)$ for a constant time complexity. No matter how high the constant is that bounds the algorithm, the correct notation is always $\Theta(1)$.

9.3   BIG-OH NOTATION

Sometimes, not only the number of elements used in an algorithm, but even the time complexity itself, can vary with the situation. For example, let's look at the templated code presented next, which searches for an element in a **sorted** array. Recall that a sorted array is an array in which the elements are placed in order. If the elements are objects, then they are ordered according to some data member within the objects.

```
1   i = 0;
2   found = false;
3   while ( ( i < size ) && itemToFind > A[ i ] )
4       i++;
5
6   if ( itemToFind == A[ i ] )
7       found = true;
```

We are assuming templated code here, so that itemToFind and the elements within A[i] can be of any DataType. The operators $>$ and $==$ are overloaded if DataType is an object.

We know that the array A is in sorted order, so as long as itemToFind is greater than A[i], we should keep searching. If itemToFind is no longer greater than A[i], then one of two things has occurred: (1) We have found the item in A, and they are equal, which causes us to exit the while loop, or (2) the item is not in A; then, since A is in order, itemToFind will be less than the rest of the elements in A, and we should stop searching. The last two lines of the code test for the situation that has occurred and set found to true if appropriate. It is also possible that we will search through the whole array and never find itemToFind, because itemToFind is greater than every element in A. In this case, i will eventually reach the last element. When i becomes equal to size, we also exit the while loop. Short-circuiting is used here: If the condition i < size is false, the condition itemToFind < A[i] won't be checked; if short-circuiting were not used, we could get a runtime error.

In the best case, the algorithm finds itemToFind right away, in the first element of the array. So the best case is bounded by a constant number of instructions, six in this case (counting the two conditions in the while loop heading as two instructions). Therefore, the best case runs in $\Theta(1)$ time.

In the worst case, we would go through all of the elements of the array without finding itemToFind. Since we would have *n* iterations, the worst case runs in $\Theta(n)$ time. So, in this example, the time complexity can vary with the situation.

A type of time complexity notation that we can use for this situation is $O(n)$, which is pronounced big-oh-of-n. When we use big-oh notation, we are saying that the time complexity might not be exactly what we have written, but it will be no worse. So $O(n)$ means that the time complexity won't be any worse than $\Theta(n)$. The $O(n)$ set of algorithms would include all of those algorithms whose time complexity is either $\Theta(n)$ or better than $\Theta(n)$. Thus, if we have a $\Theta(1)$ algorithm that executes only, say, six instructions, regardless of the size of *n*, then this function belongs to $O(n)$ as well as to $\Theta(1)$. Such an algorithm would also belong to $O(n^2)$.

The $O(n)$ time complexity applies to the previous search algorithm, since its time complexity, depending on the situation, might not be $\Theta(n)$, but can be no worse than $\Theta(n)$. We would also be correct in using the $O(n^2)$ notation for this search algorithm, but it would be misleading. When using big-oh notation, we should always use the best time complexity that applies correctly to the situation. We should always use theta notation when the time complexity cannot vary and we know exactly what it is. Sometimes it is considered to be an abuse of big-oh notation when we use it while knowing the best-case, average-case, and worst-case time complexities for an algorithm, all in theta notation. The reason is that if the best- and average-case time complexities are much better than the worst-case time complexity, big-oh notation can be misleading.

There are three other time complexity notations, but there is no need to cover them here. You will see them in a course or textbook on algorithm analysis.

9.4 THE LOGARITHMIC TIME COMPLEXITY

The last time complexity we will discuss is the logarithmic time complexity, $\Theta(\lg n)$.

Logarithms are really quite simple if you look at them in the right way. A logarithmic equation is just another way of rewriting an equation that has an exponent. Figure 9.6 shows two equivalent equations and how they translate. The equations mean exactly the same thing; what you see are just two different ways of writing it. And it is really not too hard to remember how these equations translate. You just have to remember two things:

1. The base of the logarithm in one equation is also the base for the exponent in the other equation. In Figure 9.6, the base is 3 in both equations.
2. The result of applying a logarithm is an exponent.

$$\log_3 9 = 2$$
$$3^2 = 9$$

FIGURE 9.6

Conversion from a logarithmic equation to an exponential equation and vice versa. The two equations have exactly the same meaning, but are written in different forms.

These are the only two things you have to remember. If you are translating from an equation with an exponent to an equation with a logarithm, or vice versa, once you know where the base and the exponent go, there is only one other place for the third number to go.

In computer science, the abbreviation lg is often used for a logarithm of base 2. So let's look at an example. What is the result of lg 16? First, think about the equation with the exponent. If you diligently memorized the two points just presented, you know that the result (let's call it x) is an exponent. The base is 2, so we have

$$2^x$$

There is a 16 left and there is only one place for it to go:

$$2^x = 16$$

We know that when x is 4, this equation is true. So 4 is the result of lg 16. Try your hand at translating $\log_3 9$. Once you get the hang of this, you can do it in your head by visualizing the equation.

The logarithmic time complexity $\Theta(\lg n)$ is a highly desirable time complexity. Although it is not as good as $\Theta(1)$, it is the next best thing among the most common time complexities. It is much better than $\Theta(n)$. Its shape is shown in the graph of Figure 9.3.

The nice thing about the logarithmic time complexity is that n can be very large, but the number of instructions executed, represented by $\lg n$, is still rather small. Let's suppose we have an algorithm whose function for the number of instructions is exactly $\lg n$; that is $f(n) = \lg n$. We know that

$$2^{10} = 1024$$

so we may write it as the equivalent logarithm

$$\lg 1024 = 10.$$

Since our function is $f(n) = \lg n$, if 1024 elements were used by this algorithm, only 10 instructions would be executed. It gets better: If n is 1,048,576, then $\lg n$ is only 20 instructions. What if n is the number of atoms in the known universe?

The number of atoms in the known universe is estimated to be 10^{80}. Since 10 is approximately $2^{3.32}$, $10^{80} \approx (2^{3.32})^{80}$. Multiplying the exponents together gives us approximately 2^{266} for the number of atoms in the known universe. So what is the result of $\lg 2^{266}$? Well, if we set it equal to x, we have

$$\lg 2^{266} = x$$

Remembering that lg is another way to write $\log_2$, we know that the base is 2 and x is an exponent, giving us

$$2^x$$

There is only one place for the large number 2^{266} to go:

$$2^x = 2^{266}$$

This means that $x = 266$. (Actually, we should have known that. Why?) But since our function is $f(n) = \lg n$, if n (the number of elements used by our algorithm) is equal to the number of atoms in the known universe, 2^{266}, then the number of instructions executed in the algorithm is only 266. (You've now got to have some respect for the $\Theta(\lg n)$ time complexity!)

Now that we've talked about how tantalizing the $\Theta(\lg n)$ time complexity is, let's discuss how an algorithm can achieve such a time complexity in its worst case. Basically, the idea is to somehow set up a loop that reduces the size of the problem by half on each iteration. That is, on the first iteration of the loop, the size of the problem is n; on the second iteration, the size is $\frac{1}{2}n$; on the third iteration, the size is $\frac{1}{4}n$, and so on, until the size of the problem becomes 1 element. Let's take a look at how many iterations would be required in such a loop. Suppose we have t iterations and we want to solve for t. Since each iteration reduces the size of the problem by half until we reach 1 element, we need to figure out how many times we need to multiply $\frac{1}{2}$ by n in order to reach 1 element. On the first iteration, we have n elements. On the second iteration, we have

$$\tfrac{1}{2}n$$

elements. On the third iteration, we have

$$\tfrac{1}{2} \times \tfrac{1}{2}n$$

elements. We keep multiplying by $\frac{1}{2}$ until the size of the problem is equal to 1:

$$\tfrac{1}{2} \times \tfrac{1}{2} \times \tfrac{1}{2} \times \ldots \times \tfrac{1}{2}n = 1$$

Since each iteration reduces the size of the problem by half, and we have t iterations, we obtain

$$(\tfrac{1}{2})^t n = 1$$

which is the same as

$$\left(\frac{1^t}{2^t} \right) n = 1$$

This equation reduces to

$$\left(\frac{1}{2^t} \right) n = 1$$

Multiplying both sides by 2^t yields

$$n = 2^t$$

When we convert this formula into its equivalent logarithm form, we get

$$\lg n = t$$

Since t is the number of iterations of the loop, we have $\lg n$ iterations of the loop, thereby achieving the $\Theta(\lg n)$ time complexity (assuming that the number of instructions inside the loop is bounded by a constant).

Sometimes, multiplying by $\frac{1}{2}$ continuously does not give us exactly 1. But if we need to multiply by $\frac{1}{2}$ an extra time to get less than 1 element, it does not affect the time complexity. That is, if we have $(\lg n) + 1$ iterations, we would end up throwing out the least significant term to get the time complexity. So, in the end, the time complexity is still $\Theta(\lg n)$.

9.5 THE BINARY SEARCH ALGORITHM

Let's take a look at an algorithm called the *binary search algorithm*, which runs in $O(\lg n)$ time (i.e., its time complexity can vary, but is no worse than $\Theta(\lg n)$). Let's call the previous search algorithm we examined the linear search algorithm. The linear search algorithm is often slower, running in $O(n)$ time. In both algorithms, we work with a sorted array. (In fact, the binary search algorithm will not work if the array is *not* sorted.)

The operation of the binary search algorithm is shown in Figure 9.7, which illustrates searching for a value of 33 in an array of integers. We first get the middle index of the array by adding the first and last indexes and dividing their sum by 2. If the result

FIGURE 9.7

(a) A sorted array that we want to search for the key value 33, using the binary search algorithm; we start by looking at the middle location. (b) After comparing 33 with the value at the middle location, we need not consider the keys 23 and lower anymore. (Locations are darkened.) We look at the middle location of the remaining section. (c)–(d) The search narrows until the key value 33 is found.

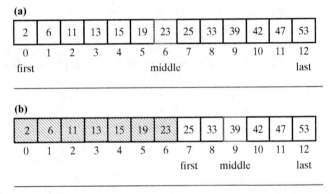

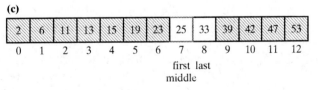

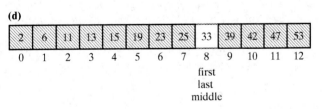

does not work out to an integer, the next lower integer is used for the middle index. We compare the value at that middle index, A [middle], with 33. Since the array is sorted, if A[middle] <33, then we must search in the right half of the array, and if A[middle] >33, then we must search in the left half of the array. This feature is significant, because we are eliminating about half the array from the search. When we restrict ourselves to one-half of the array for the search, the size of the problem essentially reduces to that half. We then take the middle index of that half and compare it with 33. We can then reduce the size of *this* problem by half, using the same technique. Each time we eliminate half of what remains, we are going through an iteration of the binary search algorithm. Eventually, we will get down to 1 element. If it isn't the number 33, then 33 is not in the array.

The templated binary search algorithm is as follows:

```
1    int first = 0;
2    int last = size – 1;
3    int middle;
4    bool found = false;
5
6    while ( first <= last && !found ) {
7        middle = ( first + last ) >> 1;
8        if ( itemToFind == A[ middle ] )
9                found = true;
10       else if ( itemToFind < A[ middle ] )
11               last = middle – 1;
12       else // itemToFind must be greater than A[ middle ]
13               first = middle + 1;
14   }
```

The itemToFind and the elements of array A might be objects. If so, the == and < operators will be overloaded. The first two lines show the index variables used as place markers for the first and last elements of any array section we might be dealing with. Initially, first is set to the first index of the entire array and last is set to the last index of the entire array. We also declare an index for the middle of the array on line 3. We use a found variable, which is set to true if the value is found. When found is set to true, the while loop condition will be false on line 6 and the program will exit the loop.

Line 7 calculates the middle index with the use of the current first and last indexes by taking their average. The average, in this case, gives the midpoint, so the current first and last indexes are added together and divided by 2. (See the discussion of the shift operator in Section 8.2.) The division is integer division, so if the division is not even, an integer result is still given (by truncating the right of the decimal point).

Then, if itemToFind is equal to A[middle] on line 8, we have found the value, so found is set to true on line 9. On line 10, if itemToFind is less than A[middle], we know that we need to search the left half of this array section. The current first index is still the first index in the left half; we just need to reset the last index. The new last index will be the next position to the left of the middle. (We don't need to include the current middle again, since we know it is not the value we seek.) The new last index is set on line 11.

If we execute line 13, we must have had the case that itemToFind was greater than A[middle]. So we know that we need to search the right half of this array section. In this case, the current last index will still be the last index in the right half; we just need to reset the first index. The new first index will be the next position to the right of the middle. The new first index is set on line 13.

If itemToFind still has not been found, then, when we continue into the next iteration of the loop, we will do so with the first and last indexes set appropriately to the section of the array that we need to search. The middle index of that section is then recalculated on line 7, and we compare itemToFind with the value at this index on line 8. Hence, the process repeats itself, narrowing the search down by resetting the first and last indexes as appropriate.

The first and last indexes will be approaching the same value as they get closer and closer together. If itemToFind is not found, eventually the first index will be higher than the last index, causing the condition on line 6 to be false, and the while loop is exited. For example, if the first and last indexes become equal, the middle index will be calculated at that same index. Then, if itemToFind is not equal to A[middle], it is not in the array. Notice, however, that if itemToFind is less than A[middle], the last index is set to middle -1 on line 11, which would make it less than the first index. By contrast, if itemToFind is greater than A[middle], the first index is set to middle $+1$, which would make it greater than the last index. Either situation will cause an exit from the while loop, since we have the condition "first $<=$ last" in the while loop heading on line 6.

We may not have to go through all lg n iterations of the binary search algorithm to find the element we are looking for. If we are lucky, we will find it on the first attempt, at the first A[middle]. So its best-case time complexity is $\Theta(1)$. This is the reason we say that the binary search algorithm runs in $O(\lg n)$ time.

You can probably win a $10 bet with one of your friends. Tell them to think of a number between 1 and 1 billion, and tell them that you can get it within 30 attempts, as long as they tell you whether each guess you make is higher or lower than the actual number. Then, just use the binary search algorithm. Since 2^{30} is greater than a billion, you'll be able to find it within the 30 attempts. (On the first attempt, you eliminate 500 million numbers right off the bat!) Just don't make a mistake! Figure 9.8 shows that starting with a billion elements and eliminating half the elements on each step will get you down to 1 element after 29 attempts. Note that when the number of elements remaining is odd, the binary search algorithm eliminates half the elements +0.5, an integer, if the element is not found at the middle index. When the number of remaining elements is even, the binary search will eliminate either half the elements or half the elements +1 (the worst case is assumed in Figure 9.8). The binary search algorithm is something to keep in mind when you're short on cash. Your friends will learn not to mess with a computer scientist!

Attempt Number	Elements Remaining
1	500,000,000
2	250,000,000
3	125,000,000
4	62,500,000
5	31,250,000
6	15,625,000
7	7,812,500
8	3,906,250
9	1,953,125
10	976,562
11	488,281
12	244,140
13	122,070
14	61,035
15	30,517
16	15,258
17	7,629
18	3,814
19	1,907
20	953
21	476
22	238
23	119
24	59
25	29
26	14
27	7
28	3
29	1
30	Give me my $10.

FIGURE 9.8

A number between 1 and 1 billion can be guessed within 30 attempts with the use of the binary search algorithm.

9.6 COMPUTER SPEED: WHERE DOES IT REALLY COME FROM?

The contents of the while loop of the binary search algorithm are bounded by a constant. We may have to check up to two conditions inside the loop, and the while loop heading has two conditions to check. Add these to the instructions on line 9 and line 11 (or line 13), and we have a bound of six instructions on each iteration of the binary search. In the linear search algorithm, we had a bound of three instructions in the loop. Thus, each iteration of the linear search can be about twice as fast as each iteration of the binary search algorithm. But the most important thing is the number of iterations.

Here is a problem to think about: If we have a million elements in an array, then which algorithm would be faster, a binary search on a 500-MHz computer or a linear search on a faster 5-GHz computer? Assume that each instruction on the 5-GHz computer is 10 times faster than each instruction on the 500-MHz computer and that each iteration of a linear search will be twice as fast as each iteration of a binary search, as we learned in the previous paragraph.

Well, first of all, let's think about the number of iterations we might have. A binary search of 1 million elements is only 20 iterations at the most. (Let's assume this worst case.) Using a linear search on a million elements, we might assume, on average, that we would go halfway through the array before we find the element. That would be 500,000 iterations. If each iteration took the same amount of time, the binary search would be 500,000/20 = 25,000 times faster than the linear search. However, as we've said, an iteration of a linear search is assumed to be about twice as fast as an iteration of a binary search *on the same computer*. So if we were on the same computer, the binary search would be 25,000/2 = 12,500 times faster.

The binary search is working on the slower, 500-MHz computer, while the linear search is working with the faster, 5-GHz computer. Therefore, each instruction of the binary search will be 10 times slower. On these different computers, the binary search will be 12,500/10 = 1,250 times faster. So, when we have a million elements, a binary search on a 500-MHz computer is 1,250 times faster than a linear search on a 5-GHz computer.

This example was brought up for an important reason: to show that algorithmic improvements can make a computer much faster than typical hardware improvements can. As computer scientists, we have a tremendous impact on computer speed whenever we develop algorithms. Through our own improvements in software, we have the capability of making computers run much faster even without any hardware improvements at all. So whenever you study time complexities, don't take them with a grain of salt.

Our ingenuity in improving computer speed doesn't apply just to algorithms like the binary search algorithm; it applies to the data structures that use the algorithms, too. Consider the linked-list implementation of the queue in Chapter 8. With most linked lists, the only thing we are concerned about is having a pointer to the front of the list. However, if we just had a pointer to the front of the linked list in a queue, as is traditional, then whenever we needed to enqueue, we would first have to travel through the entire linked list, node by node, until we found the last node with a pointer to NULL. Then we would enqueue the new element at the end of the linked list. The problem is that the procedure would require a loop to find the last node, and the time complexity would be $\Theta(n)$. Ingeniously, however, the standard implementation of a queue has a back pointer to the last node added into the data structure, so that we would not have to travel node by node through the linked list to find the last node. Thus, the enqueue operation is turned into a $\Theta(1)$ algorithm. This is nothing to scoff at: If a linked list has a thousand nodes, this little idea of having a back pointer might make a run through the algorithm about a thousand times faster.

9.7   TIME COMPLEXITIES OF DATA STRUCTURE FUNCTIONS

If we take a look at most of the stack and queue functions that we have talked about in Chapter 8, we see that most of them turn out to have $\Theta(1)$ algorithms. In the linked-list implementations, the exceptions turn out to be the copy constructors, overloaded assignment operators, destructors, and makeEmpty functions. The copy constructors and overloaded assignment operators must make deep copies of the linked lists; in so doing, they process the list node by node and are thus $\Theta(n)$ algorithms. The destructor and the makeEmpty function must free the entire linked list node by node; therefore, these also run in $\Theta(n)$ time.

In the array implementations, the copy constructors and overloaded assignment operators must copy an array element by element, too. There is no way to do it all at once if we are making a deep copy. This causes them to run in $\Theta(n)$ time. The makeEmpty functions and destructors in the array implementations, however, run in $\Theta(1)$ time, because the dynamic array does not have to be freed element by element.

In the array implementation of a stack, the push and pop algorithms run in $\Theta(1)$ time if the dynamic array does not need to be expanded or contracted. If the dynamic array needs to be expanded or contracted at the time of the push or pop, respectively, then these algorithms run in $\Theta(n)$ time, because when they make a new dynamic array, all of the elements of the old array must be copied over to it one at a time. Thus, the loop for copying runs in $\Theta(n)$ time. But this copying is not done often enough to significantly affect the time complexities of the push and pop operations, *on average*. Indeed, it can be proven that the time complexities of the push and pop algorithms are still $\Theta(1)$, on average. This proof is given in the next (optional) section for the mathematically inclined.

*9.8   AMORTIZED ANALYSIS OF ARRAY EXPANSION AND CONTRACTION

When a part of an algorithm is executed over and over again, and the time complexity of that part of the algorithm can vary with the conditions under which the algorithm executes, it is helpful sometimes to estimate the average time complexity of all the times the algorithm is executed. Such an estimation is called an **amortized analysis**. The pop and push functions in the array implementation of a stack are examples illustrating when this type of analysis comes in handy. They are $\Theta(1)$ algorithms, unless the size of the array needs to change; then they are $\Theta(n)$ algorithms.

The analysis in this section will apply generally to any algorithm that inserts or removes an element such that the size of the array might change on the basis of the technique described in Section 7.1: The size of an array is doubled whenever it is full and another element needs to be added, and it is cut in half whenever the number of elements in the array is 25% of its capacity. We will also assume that the capacity is always a power of 2. In this section, we will show that the number of elements that are copied per insertion or removal operation is no worse than a constant number, *on average*.

First, consider Figure 9.9, which illustrates adding and removing an element, alternating between the two operations continuously. During this alternation, no expansion or contraction of the array needs to take place. It is clear that we need to consider the worst case, using the most expansions or contractions that are possible, in this analysis.

To avoid the alternation in Figure 9.9, we will first examine what happens when we add elements continuously. Consider adding $n + 1$ elements, where n is a power of 2.

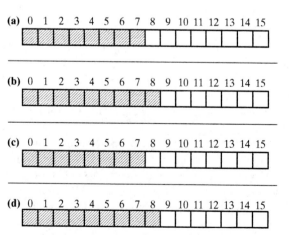

FIGURE 9.9

An alternation between adding and deleting an element from an array. The shaded section shows the used part of the array, while the white section is the unused part. The used section grows by one element in parts b and d, but shrinks by one element in parts a and c. No expansions or contractions of the array take place during this continuous alternation. The array never becomes full to cause an expansion, and the used section never shrinks to 25% of the array's capacity to cause a contraction.

This is the point at which we copy elements over from one array into the new array. Thus, the number of elements copied up to this point is the worst case for continuous additions; if n is not a power of 2, then we are at a point where no elements needed to be copied. To analyze how many copies we had with each addition of an element, we will first analyze the situation for n elements and then consider adding the next element.

For n elements that have been added to the array, where n is a power of 2, it is clear that the number of elements that have been copied thus far is

$$\frac{1}{2}n + \frac{1}{4}n + \frac{1}{8}n + \ldots + 1 =$$

$$\frac{1}{2}n + \frac{1}{4}n + \frac{1}{8}n + \ldots + \frac{1}{2^{\lg n}}n =$$

$$n\left(\frac{1}{2} + \frac{1}{4} + \frac{1}{8} + \ldots + \frac{1}{2^{\lg n}}\right) =$$

$$n\left(\frac{1}{1} + \frac{1}{2} + \frac{1}{4} + \frac{1}{8} + \ldots + \frac{1}{2^{\lg n}}\right) - n =$$

$$n\left(\left(\frac{1}{2}\right)^0 + \left(\frac{1}{2}\right)^1 + \left(\frac{1}{2}\right)^2 + \left(\frac{1}{2}\right)^3 + \ldots + \left(\frac{1}{2}\right)^{\lg n}\right) - n$$

To reduce this equation, we can use the geometric series summation formula

$$\sum_{k=0}^{m} x^k = \frac{x^{m+1} - 1}{x - 1}$$

with $x = \frac{1}{2}$ and $m = \lg n$. Thus, we have

$$n\left(\left(\frac{1}{2}\right)^0 + \left(\frac{1}{2}\right)^1 + \left(\frac{1}{2}\right)^2 + \left(\frac{1}{2}\right)^3 + \ldots + \left(\frac{1}{2}\right)^{\lg n}\right) - n =$$

$$\left(n\sum_{k=0}^{\lg n}\left(\frac{1}{2}\right)^k\right) - n =$$

$$n\left(\frac{\left(\frac{1}{2}\right)^{\lg n+1} - 1}{\frac{1}{2} - 1}\right) - n =$$

$$n\left(\frac{\frac{1}{2}\left(\frac{1}{2}\right)^{\lg n} - 1}{-\frac{1}{2}}\right) - n =$$

$$n\left(\frac{\dfrac{1}{2n}-1}{-\dfrac{1}{2}}\right) - n =$$

$$n\left(\frac{\dfrac{1-2n}{2n}}{-\dfrac{1}{2}}\right) - n =$$

$$n\left(\frac{2n-1}{n}\right) - n =$$

$$n - 1$$

To add n elements to the array, then, we copied exactly $n - 1$ elements. To add an additional element to the array, which is now full, will require copying n elements, giving us a total of $2n - 1$ copied elements per $n + 1$ insertions, where n is a power of 2. The number of copies per insertion (in this worst case for continuous insertions) is now

$$\frac{2n-1}{n+1} < \frac{2n-1}{n} < \frac{2n}{n} = 2$$

Thus, in the worst case for continuous insertions, we have fewer than 2 copied elements per insertion, on average. This is $\Theta(1)$ time, on average.

The worst case for continuous deletions is just the reverse analysis, and we also have fewer than 2 copied elements per deletion, on average.

When combining expansions and contractions, we must consider one more worst-case scenario: an alternation between expansion and contraction as quickly as possible, over and over again.

This scheme of expansion and contraction, where n is at least 2, does not allow alternating between an expansion and contraction on a pattern of one insertion followed by one removal. If it did, we would have a serious problem. But if an insertion causes an expansion, a following deletion cannot cause a contraction; we must wait until the number of elements falls to 25% of the capacity.

If we have n, where n is a power of 2 greater than 1, the next insertion causes an expansion during which n elements are copied; after n elements are copied, we add the new element, giving us $n + 1$ elements. Then, to cause the next contraction as fast as possible, we would need to have $\frac{1}{2}n + 1$ deletions. These would then be followed by a copying of n elements. (technically, only $\frac{1}{2}n$ elements need copied, but all n elements are copied to the new array in the Array implementation of changeSize.) Then, inserting $\frac{1}{2}n$ elements would get us back to where we were at the beginning. Thus, we will have completed one cycle. The next cycle would start by inserting an extra element, causing an expansion and a copying of n elements. Figure 9.10 shows a cycle.

In one cycle, therefore, we have $2n$ copied elements and $n + 2$ insertions or deletions. The number of copied elements, on average, per insertion or deletion would then be

$$\frac{2n}{n+2} < \frac{2n}{n} = 2$$

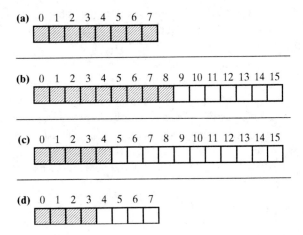

FIGURE 9.10

A cycle that alternates between expansion and contraction as quickly as possible for an arbitrary value of n. (a) All n elements of the array are used. (b) When another element needs to be added, the array is expanded to twice its capacity, n elements are copied from the old array to the new array, and then the new element is added in. (c) The result after deleting $\frac{1}{2}n$ elements. One more deletion will cause the array to contract. (d) One more element is deleted, and a new array is made that is one half of the capacity of the array in c. There are n elements copied from the old array to the new array (in the Array implementation of changeSize). At this point, inserting $\frac{1}{2}n$ elements will complete the cycle, giving (a) again.

Thus, on average, in the worst-case alternation between expansion and contraction, we also have fewer than 2 copied elements per insertion or deletion. This, too, is $\Theta(1)$ time, on average.

SUMMARY

A study of time complexities is essential in making an informed decision about which data structure should be used in a given situation. Each function of each data structure has its own time complexity. We will apply time complexity considerations to the data structures discussed in the chapters that follow.

We have introduced an important algorithm in this chapter called the binary search algorithm. Its time complexity is a very good $\Theta(\lg n)$. It is used in searching for elements in arrays, but it can be used only on sorted arrays.

We have noted that our ingenuity in improving algorithms can make computers perform faster, even if no hardware improvements have taken place. An improvement in time complexity can make computers perform thousands of times faster—or even more—for large numbers of elements.

When dynamic arrays are used in data structures and they are expanded and contracted, elements are copied from the old dynamic array to the new dynamic array, a process that takes $\Theta(n)$ time. However, when the technique discussed in Section 7.1 is used, this copying does not happen often enough to affect the time complexity of the average insertion or removal of a data element.

EXERCISES

1. What is the problem with timing two algorithms to see which one is faster?

2. What is the cross-over point? Why do computer scientists often ignore the left side of the cross-over point in determining which algorithm is better?

3. Determine a function of n for the number of instructions executed in the following code:

```
i = 0;
while ( i < n – 2 ) {
    cout << "Enter a number: ";
    cin >> num[ i ];
    sum += num[ i ];
    i++;
}
```

4. Given the following functions, which represent the number of instructions required for the execution an algorithm, determine the time complexities:

   a. $5n + n^2 - 2$
   b. 7
   c. $4n + 10 \lg n + 25$
   d. $3 + 4 \lg n$
   e. n^2

5. A program's main function consists of two function calls in sequence. The first function that is called has a time complexity of $\Theta(n \lg n)$, and the second function has a time complexity of $\Theta(n)$. What is the overall time complexity of the program?

6. Is this statement true or false? "An algorithm with a constant time complexity must execute the same number of instructions each time the algorithm executes." Explain why.

7. What is the difference between theta notation and big-oh notation (other than a symbolic difference)?

8. Given the following equations, find the equivalent equation that solves for n:

   a. $\log_5 n = 6$
   b. $\lg n = 25$
   c. $\log_{99} n = 2$

9. Given the following equations, find the equivalent logarithmic equation:

   a. $2^a = n$
   b. $a^{10} = n$
   c. $3^n = 81$

10. How can a logarithmic time complexity be achieved by an algorithm? Give an example of an algorithm that achieves a logarithmic time complexity.

11. Given the functions $f(n) = 12\lg n + 10$ and $g(n) = 3n + 10$, which produce the number of instructions of two different algorithms, approximate the cross-over point.

12. Which is faster and by how much, a sequential search of only 1000 elements on a 5-GHz computer or a binary search of 1 million elements on a 1-GHz computer. Assume that the execution of each instruction on the 5-GHz computer is five times faster than on the 1-GHz computer and that each iteration of the linear search algorithm is twice as fast as each iteration of the binary search algorithm.

13. Is this statement true or false? "An improvement in computer hardware is the only thing that can make a computer execute a program significantly faster." Explain.

CHAPTER 10

The Linked List as a Data Structure

It might at first seem contrary to intuition, but using a linked list as a data structure it-self is a lot more involved than using a linked list for a queue or a stack. The reason is that we want clients to have a lot of flexibility in the way that they wish to use the linked list. Clients need to be able to insert elements as they do in any data structure, but they also need to access, change, or remove any element of the linked list in any po-sition at any time.

Sometimes a client wants to use a linked list because he or she has large objects as elements. In this case, linked lists do a lot to conserve memory, as was discussed in Section 7.4. The linked-list data structure is also sometimes used as a part of other larger data structures, such as hash tables and graphs. These data structures will be discussed in Chapters 11 and 15, respectively. In addition, a general linked list can be used to im-plement other data structures that have a simple linked-list structure, similarly to the way the Array class is used in the array implementation of a stack. Exercises 14 and 15 at the end of the chapter have you explore this idea a little more.

10.1   THE LIST ADT

If we wanted to divorce the C++ linked-list implementation from the linked-list ADT completely, then we wouldn't be talking about a linked-list ADT per se; instead, we would be talking about a *list* ADT. This is because some programming languages might not have the capability to join nodes with pointers or by some other means, but they may have the capability of forming a list, perhaps by using an array or another method.

The list operations act upon the set of data in the list, but they also act upon a current, or active, position in the list. As an example, if we are reading through a grocery list of items that we want to get, then the position of any item our eyes focus on at any particular moment becomes the current position. The list operations are typically as follows:

- insert, to insert a new item into the list; there is no current position after an insertion.
- an iterator, for retrieving (by copying instead of removing) each item from the list, one at a time; at any particular moment an item is retrieved, that item becomes the current position in the list.
- find, to determine whether a certain item exists in a list; if the item exists, it becomes the current position.
- retrieve, to retrieve (by copying instead of removing) a certain item; that item becomes the current position.
- replace, to replace the item at the current position with another item; the current position remains unchanged.
- remove, to remove an item from a list; there is no current position after a removal.
- an operation to determine whether the list is empty; the current position is unchanged.
- an operation to empty out the list; the current position is lost.

The reason there is no current position after an insertion is because a current position is sometimes associated with the beginning or end of the list. The place of insertion is left to the implementation, so the association could be muddled. Likewise, there is no current position after a removal: The item being removed might be the one at the current position!

This is the first time an *iterator* has been introduced. Iterators are common in other data structures and are used to process each item in a data structure. In the preceding list, we use an iterator just to retrieve items from the list, one at a time.

10.2   USING KEY VALUES IN RECORDS OF INFORMATION

As the list ADT shows, we often need to search through a list for a particular item. The item might be something simple, such as an integer, or it might be a record of information. If it is a record of information, our search is often restricted to the value of a data member in the record. The values of the other data members are frequently ignored in the search. Furthermore, such a search is usually for a *key*, which has a unique value for each record. In a list of employees, for example, a good key would be a Social Security number, since it is different for each person. In a list of books, a good key would be the ISBN number, because, on occasion, different books have been given the same title. In a list of automobile parts, a good key might be the part number. For a type of value other than a key, more than one record in the list might have that value (but this property is sometimes useful).

In real life, if, for example, you are calling your insurance company because you have a discrepancy in the amount of coverage it provided for an operation, the insurance representative would probably ask you for a claim number, which would be the key. After you give the claim number and the representative types it into the computer, the computer program looks through the data structure(s) to find the object with that key. Then, once the object is found, the other data members of the object are revealed on the computer screen. The insurance representative can then see what you are talking about.

The retrieve operation of a list data structure works the same way. It (usually) looks through the list for a certain key value and then returns the object that has that value back to the client. The client can then display the other data members on the screen or do whatever else he or she may want to do with them.

10.3   LINKED-LIST IMPLEMENTATION

A retrieve operation would not make sense if all the items retrieved were simple, like integers, because we would already have the values we want to retrieve. Accordingly, when we implement a list, we want to make the list general enough so that it will be able to have these simple items (even though some functions might not be useful), but in order to be practical, we need to take a key-oriented approach to the implementation. Elements with keys, however, tend to be large, especially if strings are used for the keys or for other data members. As the discussion in Section 7.4 shows, the linked list conserves more memory than the array with large element sizes. In Section 7.4, it was also shown that a linked list is faster in situations where we need to remove an element from the middle of the list, yet keep the elements contiguous. Therefore, it is more likely that a linked list would be used to implement a list, whereas an array might be used for simple types, such as integers, that do not need to be removed from the middle. Of course, there may be exceptions to both of these uses of linked lists and arrays (there usually are), but given the likelihood of such uses, it is compelling just to focus on the linked-list implementation of a list (at least when using C++), yet make the list implementation general enough that it can handle simple types. Since "linked list" already has "list" in the name, we will refer to the "linked-list implementation of a list" simply as a "linked list", for short.

10.3.1   The Linked-List Specification File

The linked-list data structure class template is as follows:

```
1   // LinkedList.h - - class for a linked list as a data structure
2
3   template <class DataType>
4   struct Node {
```

```
5        DataType info;
6        Node<DataType> *next;
7    };
8
9    // LinkedList maintains a current position in list after each function call
10   // If an object of a struct is used for DataType, the == operator must be
11   // overloaded for it; the left and right operands are both DataType objects
12   // the == comparison is used for finding elements, usually by key value
13   // For find, retrieve and remove functions, if you are using an object as an element, a
14   // typical use would be to set the key of the desired object to find or remove, then pass
15   // the object into the function.
16   // The constructor, copy constructor, overloaded assignment operator, and insert function
17   // can throw an exception if out of heap memory.
18
19   template <class DataType>
20   class LinkedList
21   {
22   public:
23       LinkedList( );
24       LinkedList( const LinkedList<DataType> & aplist );
25       ~LinkedList( );
26       LinkedList<DataType> & operator =( const LinkedList<DataType> & rlist );
27       void insert( const DataType & element ); // no current position after use
28       bool first( DataType & listEl );         // returns first element of list in listEl
29                                                 // and current position is set to this element;
30                                                 // if list is empty, returns false and there is
31                                                 // no current position; otherwise, returns true
32       inline bool getNext( DataType & listEl );     // retrieves the next element of a linked list
33                                                 // beyond the last element that was retrieved
34                                                 // by first or getNext functions and returns
35                                                 // it in listEl;
36                                                 // current position is set to this element.
37                                                 // if no element exists at this position,
38                                                 // getNext returns false and there is no
39                                                 // current position; returns true otherwise
40       bool find ( const DataType & element ); // returns true if element is found
41                                                 // returns false if element is not found
42                                                 // if found, found element becomes current
43                                                 // position in list; if not found, there is
44                                                 // no current position
45       bool retrieve( DataType & element ); // like find, except returns found element
46       bool replace( const DataType & newElement ); // replaces element at current position
47                                                 // in list with newElement; returns false if
48                                                 // there is no current position (no list
49                                                 // modification occurs); returns true otherwise
```

```
50      bool remove( DataType & element );  // returns true if element is found
51                                          // returns false if element is not found
52                                          // if found, element is set to found element;
53                                          // no current position after use
54      bool isEmpty( ) const;              // returns true if linked list is empty
55                                          // returns false otherwise; current position
56                                          // unchanged
57      void makeEmpty( );                  // no current position
58  private:
59      Node<DataType> *start;
60      Node<DataType> *current;            // points to node at current position
61      inline void deepCopy( const LinkedList<DataType> & original );
62  };
63
64  #include "LinkedList.cpp"
```

In the private section, on lines 59–60, there are two data members. One is a pointer called start, which is the pointer to the beginning of the linked list. The second pointer, called current, points to the current node in the linked list and, in so doing, maintains a current position into the linked list. The client can then work with this current position as he or she sees fit.

In this implementation, we choose not to use a header node. A header node can simplify code—a property that is more evident in the remove function and the deep-Copy function. However, there is an advantage to not having a header node in the LinkedList class. Data structures are sometimes made with the use of arrays of linked lists, and quite a few linked lists in the array can be empty. If a linked list is empty and there is a header node, much space can be wasted, depending upon the size of the element. The data members in the header's info section are still there; they just haven't been set to anything. However, in this implementation, an empty linked list will just waste 8 bytes: 4 for the start pointer and 4 for the current pointer. (The functions don't waste any memory inside the element.) It would do us no good to make a dynamic header node within the constructor: When an array of LinkedList objects are made, the constructor for each LinkedList is called during the formation of the array.

When you are maintaining a current position in a linked list, you should clearly define how the current position is set in each class function, and you should convey that definition to the client through some form of commenting. In C++, we have all sorts of situations to think about for the current position (other than in the list ADT). In the constructor, the current position is obviously not set, since there are no positions in an empty linked list. If there is no current position, the current pointer should be set to NULL to indicate that. Likewise, there is no need for a current position after calling a destructor. In the copy constructor and overloaded assignment operator, the current position of the new linked list should be the same as the current position of the old one. Otherwise, the entire object with all its characteristics wasn't really copied.

The first and getNext functions, on lines 28 and 32, respectively, are usually used in conjunction to implement the iterator described in the list ADT. The first function returns the first element of the linked list, if there is one, in the parameter listEl provided. The current pointer is then set to the first node. Afterwards, the getNext function can be used to retrieve the next element past the current position, adjusting the current position (current pointer) to the next element. In the getNext function, the element found is returned in the reference parameter listEl provided. Thus, the two functions can be used together to process an entire linked list. The getNext function usually returns true, but will return false when it tries to retrieve an element beyond the end of the list. Therefore, the return value of the getNext function can be used as the stopping condition for a loop that processes all elements of the linked list. The getNext function also returns false if there is no current position, so before using getNext, one should call the first function to set the current position to the beginning of the linked list. The first function will return false if the linked list is empty and will return true otherwise.

If one looks at the retrieve function prototype on line 45, it is not so obvious how the key is supplied to this function, although one can see that the element to be retrieved is passed in by reference and is, therefore, retrieved that way. What actually happens is that the client declares an object from the struct that he or she designed. Then, only the key in that object is set by the client, leaving all other data members uninitialized. The client then passes this (otherwise empty) object containing the key into the retrieve function, which uses the key to look for the object in the list. When retrieve finds an info section that has that key, it uses a simple assignment to set the other data members of the reference parameter to what is in the info section. Thus, the client gets the other information about the record he or she wants to retrieve. There are a couple of advantages to this method. The first is that the client does not need to declare a separate key variable to pass into the retrieve function; the client needs to declare an object of the struct anyway (since it needs to hold the information returned), and there is a key data member already within the struct. The second advantage is that the client doesn't need to have a DataType2 parameter for the key, in addition to the one for the element. A DataType2 parameter would be a little awkward for the client if he or she is using elements that don't have keys (but it could be done). The same technique of providing a key in an empty object is also used in the find and remove functions.

In this kind of design, the current position and how it is affected needs to be considered within the design of each function. This statement is, however, generally true about any data member, and it is something you should keep in mind when designing a data structure. The start pointer, for example, will need to change its value if the first element is removed, and such a possibility must be considered when you write each function. In designing a class that has something abstract like a current position, however, it is best to make the design as intuitive as possible. That is, the client should be able to guess, in most cases, how the current position would be affected after a particular function is called. This design will prevent the client from having to memorize too much about the way the class works.

10.3.2 The Linked-List Implementation File

Let's take a look at the top of the class implementation file:

```
1    // LinkedList.cpp - - function definitions for the linked list data structure
2
3    #include <iostream>
```

```
4
5   using namespace std;
6
7   template <class DataType>
8   LinkedList<DataType>::LinkedList( )
9   {
10      start = current = NULL;
11  }
```

Line 3 is used to recognize NULL, since it is defined in iostream. As expected, the constructor sets both pointers in the private section to NULL, on line 10.

The copy constructor, destructor, and overloaded assignment operator look similar to the ones for the linked-list implementation of the queue:

```
12  template <class DataType>
13  LinkedList<DataType>::LinkedList( const LinkedList<DataType> & aplist )
14  {
15      deepCopy( aplist );
16  }
17
18  template <class DataType>
19  LinkedList<DataType>::~LinkedList( )
20  {
21      makeEmpty( );
22  }
23
24  template <class DataType>
25  LinkedList<DataType> & LinkedList<DataType>::operator =(
26                                      const LinkedList<DataType> & rlist )
27  {
28      if ( this == &rlist )
29              return *this;
30      makeEmpty( );
31      deepCopy( rlist );
32      return *this;
33  }
```

The insert function is as follows:

```
34  // inserts at the beginning of the linked list
35  // no current position after use
36  template <class DataType>
37  void LinkedList<DataType>::insert( const DataType & element )
38  {
39      current = NULL;
40      Node<DataType> *newNode = new Node<DataType>;
41      newNode->info = element;
```

```
42      newNode->next = start;
43      start = newNode;
44  }
```

The insert function does the fastest thing: Since order in this linked list is not important, it places the new element at the start of the linked list. Thus, it is a $\Theta(1)$ function. If it were to travel all the way through the linked list to place the new element at the end, it would be a $\Theta(n)$ function. When designing a function, we like its time complexity to be as low as possible.

Current is set to NULL on line 39 so that there is no current position after the insertion, as specified in the list ADT. Figure 10.1 shows how the new element is inserted at the beginning of the list.

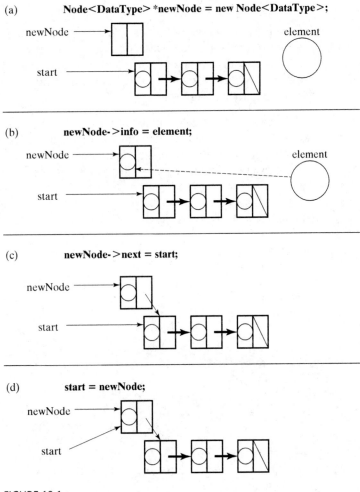

FIGURE 10.1

How a node is inserted into a linked list. The line of code involved is shown at the top of each part. Elements are shown abstractly as circles.

The first function is shown next:

```
45  // returns first element of list in listEl and current position is set to this element;
46  // if list is empty, returns false and there is no current position;
47  // otherwise, returns true
48  template <class DataType>
49  bool LinkedList<DataType>::first( DataType & listEl )
50  {
51      if ( start == NULL )
52              return false;
53
54      current = start;
55      listEl = start->info;
56      return true;
57  }
```

The case of an empty list is handled on lines 51–52. If the list is not empty, line 54 sets the current position to the first node. Then, on line 55, the listEl object (passed in by reference) is assigned the data members of the info object member of the first node. Finally, true is returned to indicate that the element was retrieved.

Following is the getNext function:

```
58  // retrieves the next element of a linked list beyond the last element that was
59  // retrieved by first or getNext functions and returns it in listEl;
60  // current position is set to this element.
61  // if no element exists at this position, getNext returns false and there is no
62  // current position; returns true otherwise
63  template <class DataType>
64  inline bool LinkedList<DataType>::getNext( DataType & listEl )
65  {
66      if ( current == NULL )
67              return false;
68      if ( current->next == NULL ) {
69              current = NULL;
70              return false;
71              }
72
73      current = current->next;
74      listEl = current->info;
75      return true;
76  }
```

The getNext function is inlined because its main use will probably be in loops. (See Chapter 5.) The getNext function is supposed to retrieve the next element beyond the current position. If there is no current position, then current == NULL on line 66 and false is returned on line 67.

If we try to retrieve an element beyond the end of the linked list, then current->next will be NULL. In this case, as the function comments indicate, there should be no current position. So current is set to NULL on line 69 and false is returned on line 70.

If there is an element beyond the current position, then we are in business. The current position is set to that element on line 73. The information from the element is then retrieved and assigned to listEl (passed in by reference) on line 74. Then, finally, true is returned on line 75, indicating success.

The find function is shown next:

```
77  // returns true if element is found; returns false if element is not found
78  // if found, found element becomes current position in list;
79  // if not found, there is no current position
80  template <class DataType>
81  bool LinkedList<DataType>::find( const DataType & element )
82  {
83      DataType item;
84      if ( !first( item ) )
85          return false;
86      do if ( item == element )
87          return true;
88      while ( getNext( item ) );
89
90      return false;
91  }
```

Here, we make use of the first and getNext combo. The first item in the list is retrieved on line 84. If the list is empty, false is returned on line 85. On line 86, in the do . . . while statement, we check to see if the first item is equal to the element passed in. If it is, then true is returned to indicate a successful find. If not, we check the while condition on line 88, which just calls getNext. The getNext function will return true if there is another item in the list. Then the item will again be checked against element on line 86. When the getNext function call on line 88 tries to get something beyond the end of the list, the loop will end, because its return value will be false. In this case, element was not found and false is returned on line 90. When the getNext function tries to go beyond the end of the list, it will set current to NULL. Thus, if the element is not found, there will be no current position, as was specified in the list ADT.

Note that when the comparison is made on line 86, the equality operator is an overloaded operator in the struct that the client is using. In a typical use, the overloaded operator == would be written by the client just to compare the keys in the objects for equality and return true if they are equal. If DataType were something unusual, such as an integer, the == operator would be used normally to compare two integers. But this might not be the recommended use of a linked list, because, like an integer, a pointer has 4 bytes; thus, 50% of the memory in the linked list would be wasted on pointers.

Note also that this is one of those rare cases where the do ... while loop seems to work better than a normal while loop. If we were to use a normal while loop in this function, the heading might be

```
while ( !getNext( item ) )
```

but this would mean that the if statement on lines 86–87 would need to be copied above the while loop. Otherwise, we would get the first item on line 84, and then, before we checked it for equality, we would get the next item in the while loop heading. The way the do ... while loop is written is also the way the client might typically use first and getNext, except with the object specifier added, as for example, in

```
list.first( item );
```

The retrieve function, shown next, makes use of the find function:

```
92   // returns true if element is found; returns false if element is not found
93   // if found, found element becomes current position in list;
94   // if not found, there is no current position
95   template <class DataType>
96   bool LinkedList<DataType>::retrieve( DataType & element )
97   {
98      if ( !find( element ) )
99            return false;
100     element = current->info;
101     return true;
102   }
```

If, on line 98, the element is not found, we simply return false on line 99. If the element was found, the current pointer will point to the node that contains the key of element. (The current pointer is set in the first and getNext functions.) Therefore, we assign element (passed in by reference) the info at the current position on line 100; this assignment copies the data members from info into element, other than the key. Then we return true on line 101.

In comparing the find and retrieve functions, notice that the find function could have been written differently. Only the key value of the object needs to be passed in, and no object needs to be retrieved. Sometimes it is less confusing for the client, however, if the usage of the two functions is consistent.

The replace function is as follows:

```
103  // replaces element at current position in list with newElement;
104  // returns false if there is no current position (no list modification occurs);
105  // returns true otherwise
106  template <class DataType>
107  bool LinkedList<DataType>::replace( const DataType & newElement )
```

```
108 {
109     if ( current == NULL )
110             return false;
111     current->info = newElement;
112     return true;
113 }
```

The replace function is supposed to replace the element at the current position with newElement that is passed in. If there is no current position, then current is equal to NULL and false is returned on line 110. Otherwise, the info member at the current position is set to the newElement object that is passed in, and true is returned on line 112.

The replace function is useful in a number of situations. If the client wanted to update an object with a certain key, the client can call the find function first and then call the replace function. If information from the object needs to be obtained before the object can be updated, the client can call the retrieve function, perform the necessary modification on the retrieved object, and then call the replace function. If the client would like to update every object in the linked list, the client can use the first–getNext combo and call the replace function within the do...while loop.

The remove function is shown next:

```
114 // returns true if element is found; returns false if element is not found
115 // if found, element is set to found element;
116 // no current position after use
117 template <class DataType>
118 bool LinkedList<DataType>::remove( DataType & element )
119 {
120     current = NULL;
121     if ( start == NULL )
122             return false;
123     Node<DataType> *ptr = start;
124     if ( ptr->info == element ) {
125             element = ptr->info;
126             start = start->next;
127             delete ptr;
128             return true;
129             }
130     while ( ptr->next != NULL ) {
131             if ( ptr->next->info == element ) {
132                     Node<DataType> *tempPtr = ptr->next;
133                     element = tempPtr->info;
134                     ptr->next = tempPtr->next;
135                     delete tempPtr;
136                     return true;
137                     }
138             ptr = ptr->next;
139             }
```

```
140
141        return false;
142  }
```

In the remove function, we cannot use the first and getNext combo, because the first and getNext functions return just elements. To remove a node, we must have the actual address of the node, once the node is found. As specified in the list ADT, there is no current position after a removal, so current is set to NULL right away on line 120, never to be set again in this function.

Lines 121–122 handle the case where the list is empty. After that, on line 123, a pointer ptr is declared and initialized to the address of the first node. This pointer will be used to move through the linked list and find the node to remove.

When we want to remove a node that we first need to find, we want to keep the pointer one node in front of the node we want to remove. Otherwise, we cannot link the nodes on each side of it, because we no longer have the address of the node in front of it. This strategy was discussed in Section 7.3.6. So first, we see if ptr is pointing to the node containing element already on line 124. If DataType is an object, the overloaded operator == is used. If the node we want to remove is the first node, it is a special case, because start will need to be reset. We assign the info member to element (passed in by reference) on line 125, in case the client would like this information. Then the start pointer is advanced on line 126, and the first node is freed on line 127. Finally, true is re-turned on line 128.

The condition in the while loop on line 130 keeps the pointer one node behind the node that needs to be removed. On line 131, we examine the info member of the next node (now that it is safe to do so). This line uses the overloaded operator == for objects. If ptr->next->info and element are equal, the node in question is removed. Figure 10.2 illustrates the removal operation of lines 132–135.

If you are having trouble understanding this section of code, don't forget that pointers store addresses and you need to think about those addresses. (Refer back to Section 7.3.) And by the way, if you can't write this section of code yourself, then you don't really understand it. Try to write the section yourself without memorizing it; use logic to figure out what the code should be.

If true has not been returned by line 136, then, on line 138, ptr is advanced to the next node. Then the next node beyond this is checked on line 130, and the process re-peats. If there is no node beyond the current one, the while loop exits. Here, the node that ptr is pointing to cannot contain element, because it would have been found on the previous iteration. If the remove function does not find the node it is looking for, then false is returned on line 141.

The isEmpty function is no big surprise:

```
143  template <class DataType>
144  bool LinkedList<DataType>::isEmpty( ) const
145  {
146    return start == NULL;
147  }
```

(a) **ptr->next->info ==element**

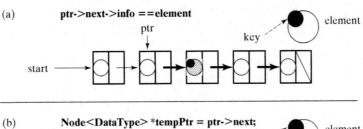

(b) **Node<DataType> *tempPtr = ptr->next;**

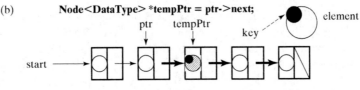

(c) **element = tempPtr->info;**

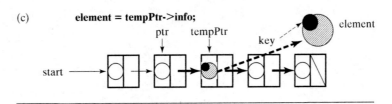

(d) **ptr->next = tempPtr->next;**

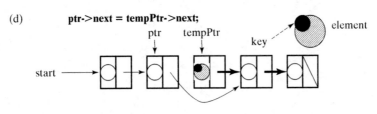

(e) **delete tempPtr;**

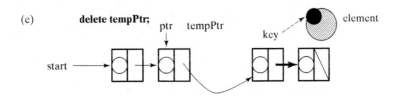

FIGURE 10.2

How the remove function works for the linked list.

The makeEmpty function looks a little different from the simple makeEmpty functions that you have seen before for linked lists:

```
148   template <class DataType>
149   void LinkedList<DataType>::makeEmpty( )
150   {
151     while ( start != NULL ) {
152         current = start;
```

```
153              start = start->next;
154              delete current;
155    }
156
157    current = NULL;
158 }
```

In the makeEmpty function, the nodes are freed one by one. If the list is empty, start is NULL and we don't even enter the while loop. If the list is not empty, we enter the while loop. Figure 10.3 shows the execution of lines 152–154. We continue the iterations of the loop until the advancement of the start pointer on line 153 sets it to NULL (i.e., we have reached the end of the linked list). Then the while loop is exited. When the start pointer is NULL, it indicates an empty list. The current pointer is set to NULL before returning, so the conditions for an empty list are complete.

(a)   **start != NULL**

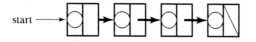

(b)   **current = start;**

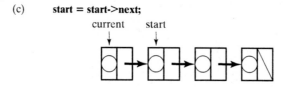

(c)   **start = start->next;**

(d)   **delete current;**

FIGURE 10.3

How the body of the loop in the makeEmpty function works.

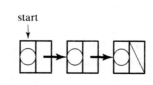

Finally, the last function, called the deepCopy function, is shown:

```
159 template <class DataType>
160 inline void LinkedList<DataType>::deepCopy( const LinkedList<DataType> & original )
161 {
162     start = current = NULL;
163     if ( original.start == NULL )
164             return;
165     Node<DataType> *copyptr = start = new Node<DataType>;
166     Node<DataType> *originalptr = original.start;
167     copyptr->info = originalptr->info;
168     if ( originalptr == original.current )
169             current = copyptr;
170     while ( originalptr->next != NULL ) {
171             originalptr = originalptr->next;
172             copyptr->next = new Node<DataType>;
173             copyptr = copyptr->next;
174             copyptr->info = originalptr->info;
175             if ( originalptr == original.current )
176                     current = copyptr;
177     }
178     copyptr->next = NULL;
179 }
```

Line 162 starts off by creating an empty list, as the constructor would do. If the original list is also empty, we are done, and we return on line 164. Otherwise, similar to the linked list implementation of the queue, a copyptr and an originalptr are set up on lines 165–166. On line 165, we also create a new node for the original list, since we know that it will not be empty at this point. The code isn't as simplified as it was in the linked-list implementation of the queue, because of the absence of a header node (but we'll be glad later that we didn't use such a node in the LinkedList class). The information in the first node is copied on line 167. Then, if the current pointer happens to be pointing to the first node in the original (line 168), the current pointer of the copy is set to its first node on line 169.

If the node beyond originalptr is not NULL (line 170), then the while loop is entered. Figure 10.4 shows the execution of lines 171–174. Then, on line 175, the same check is made for the current node, possibly to set the current pointer for the copy on line 176.

When there is no node beyond originalptr to copy, the while loop is exited and copyptr points to the last node in the copy. Finally, we need to do one more thing: set this node's pointer to NULL (indicating the end of the list), on line 178.

(a)   **originalptr->next != NULL**

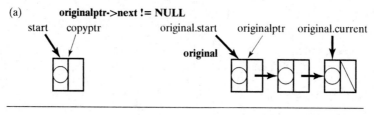

(b)   **originalptr = originalptr->next;**

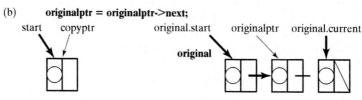

(c)   **copyptr->next = new Node<DataType>;**

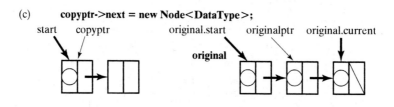

(d)   **copyptr = copyptr->next;**

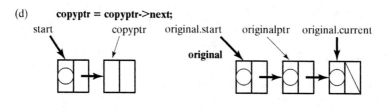

(e)   **copyptr->info = originalptr->info;**

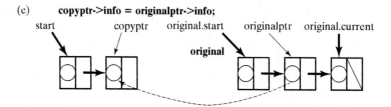

FIGURE 10.4

What transpires in the body of the while loop of the deepCopy function in the linked list.

10.4   OTHER IMPLEMENTATIONS

This section discusses some implementations of a linked list other than those we have examined up to now. Some implementations have a length function that returns the number of elements in a linked list. This information is useful mainly in the condition of a loop that processes all of the elements of the linked list. In such an implementation, a count of the number of elements is kept in the private section. The count is initially set to 0 in the constructor. Any time an element is added to the linked list, the count must be incremented, and any time an element is removed, the count is decremented. When the length function is called, the count is returned, and then it can be used in the condition of a loop. In the implementation presented in this chapter, the getNext function returns false when there are no more elements to process in the list, so the getNext function call can be used in the condition of a loop. However, there may be other reasons for needing to know the number of elements in the list.

Some linked-list implementations have an isFull function, which can be used by the client before inserting a new node. The function would typically try to create a new node in the heap. If an exception is thrown as a result of the *new* operation, the exception is caught in the isFull function, which does nothing except return true. If the new node can be created, it is immediately freed, and then the isFull function returns false. Such a function, however, can be misleading to the client: The heap memory might be close to being exhausted, but enough heap memory might be left so that the isFull function returns false. After this, the client might inadvertently use more heap memory by doing something else, before trying to insert a new node. Then, when a new node is inserted, a runtime error results. The problem here is that there is no guarantee that a client will insert a node immediately after checking to see whether the linked list is full.

Some people might not view a linked list as being full just because there is no heap memory left. It is a little like blowing up a balloon inside a jar, and then, when you can't get any more air into it, saying that the balloon is full of air. Some people would say yes, and some would say no.

Sometimes, a linked-list implementation lacks a replace function. Such a function, however, is a handy one that is simple to write, and it allows the client to update a linked list as it is being processed. Let's say, for example, that we have a linked list of Employee objects and the Employee struct has data members for performance and salary. Then if the client would like to give all employees with excellent performance a 10% raise, he or she might write code like this:

```
Employee emp;
list.first( emp );
do if ( emp.performance == "excellent" ) {
            emp.salary *= 1.1;
            list.replace( emp );
            }
while ( getNext( emp ) );
```

Sometimes, implementations of linked lists will be circular. In a *circular linked list*, the last node in the list points to the first node of the list instead of pointing to NULL. Circular linked lists have been used in editors and are sometimes used in advanced data structures such as Fibonacci heaps. A circular linked list is shown in Figure 10.5.

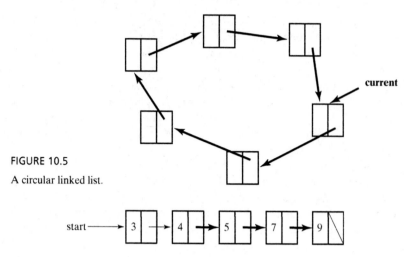

current

FIGURE 10.5

A circular linked list.

start ——→ 3 | → 4 | → 5 | → 7 | → 9 |

FIGURE 10.6

A sorted linked list. Only the key values are shown in the elements. The key values are in order from the beginning of the list to the end.

An implementation of a linked list can also be **sorted**. In a sorted linked list, the elements of the list are put in order, usually by key value. A sorted linked list is shown in Figure 10.6. Such an implementation affects the way that the insert, find, and remove functions work. More work needs to be done in the insert function, because any time an element is inserted, we must search for the correct position in the list into which to insert it. Therefore, the worst-case time complexity of the insert function is no longer $\Theta(1)$, but $\Theta(n)$. On average, we would expect to go halfway through the list before inserting, sometimes more and sometimes less. But if we went halfway through the list, that would give us $\frac{1}{2}n$ iterations, and we throw out the coefficient when determining a time complexity. So, on average, the insert function would run in $\Theta(n)$ time in a sorted linked list.

The find and remove functions search for an element in the linked list. In a sorted linked list, once the value sought is less than the element of the current node, there is no point in searching further, and the search can be stopped, saving time. However, if we assume that this occurs halfway through the list, on average, it also still gives us a $\Theta(n)$ time complexity. Thus, time is saved in the find and remove functions (and consequently in the retrieve function), but the amount of time saved is not significant.

It would be nice if we could do a binary search on a sorted linked list, just as we use a binary search on a sorted array. But if you look at the binary search algorithm in Section 9.5, you will see that it uses array indexes to access elements. If we want to access the middle element of a linked list, for example, we have to get the address of the node first; and unless we had some external pointer pointing to it already, we have to travel halfway through the list to get it. This requires a loop with $\frac{1}{2}n$ iterations. So just getting to the middle node would use $\Theta(n)$ time. Once we're done with this binary search, the $\Theta(\lg n)$ complexity would be absorbed into the larger $\Theta(n)$ complexity. We could have an array of pointers with a pointer to each node in the linked list, in order. We could even form an array of pointers easily, by traversing through the linked list and assigning the address of every node to the next element in the array. And we could do a binary search on the array of pointers, accessing the info of each node pointed to. This procedure would involve a $\Theta(\lg n)$ algorithm. However, a problem arises when we want to insert new nodes and remove nodes from the linked list: The array would be too expensive (in time) to maintain. But what if we had an unchanging number of elements in the linked list? Well, then we should use a dynamic array to store the elements. If we have an unchanging number of elements, a dynamic array set to that size will waste no memory whatsoever internal to the array!

Don't feel depressed about not being able to do a binary search on a linked list. Chapter 11 will demonstrate that a much faster $\Theta(1)$ algorithm can be used to search a linked list for an element.

Also, in a sorted linked list, it can be proven that it takes $\Theta(n^2)$ time to insert n elements, even though n starts off small and increases by 1 on each insertion. In an unsorted linked list, it provably takes only $\Theta(n)$ time to insert n elements.

The main advantage of a sorted linked list is that it can provide the elements in order. In an unsorted linked list, to provide the elements in order, you would have to use one of the many sorting algorithms (to be discussed in Chapter 14). In addition, in an unsorted linked list, the elements are generally inserted at the front of the list for speed. However, no check is made in the insert function to see if an element of the same key is already in the list. In the sorted linked list, where elements must be inserted in order, it can be easily checked whether or not there is an element of the same key before the insertion.

The insert function of an unsorted list is used when the client is sure that there is no other key with the same value in the linked list. For example, the client might be reading a list of parts from a file, each element with a different key (perhaps a part number), and inserting them into a linked list. Sometimes, upon an insertion, the client might not be sure that there is no other key in the linked list with the same value. In this case, the client should call the find function before performing the insertion. If the find function returns false, the item can be inserted. If the find function returns true, the client may want to either use the replace function (for an update, perhaps) or leave the linked list unchanged.

Other implementations of linked lists will be **_doubly linked_**. In such linked lists, there are two pointers in each node: a *next* pointer and a *back* pointer. Each node points to the node after it, but also points to the node before it, with the back pointer. Thus, the node struct looks something like this:

```
template <class DataType>
struct DLNode {
        DataType info;
        DLNode<DataType> *next;
        DLNode<DataType> *back;
};
```

FIGURE 10.7

A doubly linked list. Each node is divided intro three sections. The left section is a back pointer, and the right section is the *next* pointer. The middle section is the info section.

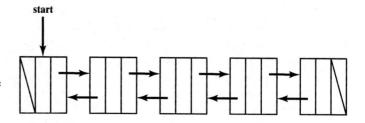

Figure 10.7 shows a figure of a doubly linked list.

In some implementations of a doubly linked list, the *next* pointer of the last node is set to NULL as in an ordinary linked list; the back pointer of the first node is also set to NULL. A disadvantage of the doubly linked list is that there are 8 bytes of wasted memory per node instead of 4 bytes per node. However, 8 bytes is not a whole lot of wasted memory if the object used for an element is fairly large.

Doubly linked lists allow retrievals, insertions, and removals to be done in $\Theta(1)$ time, as we shall see in the next chapter. For now, let's suppose that we pass the address of a node as a parameter into a class function and that the function is supposed to remove that node. The parameter must be a pointer, of course, so that an address can be passed into it. As shown in Figure 10.8, if the list is singly linked, we don't have access to the node in front of it (the dashed node); but we need such access in order to set its pointer *next* to the node that follows it (the dotted node). In other words, we would have to travel through the linked list, from the beginning, comparing the address of each node with the address that is passed in, so that we could get the right node to remove. If we assume that, on average, we would travel halfway through the list, this would be a $\Theta(n)$ function.

However, if we have the same situation with a doubly linked list, it would be a $\Theta(1)$ function. To see this, consider Figure 10.9. The code to handle the removal would be as follows:

```
ptr->back->next = ptr->next;
ptr->next->back = ptr->back;
delete ptr;
```

The first line of code sets the pointer *next* of the dashed node to the address of the dotted node. The second line of code sets the back pointer of the dotted node to the address of the dashed node. This action links together the two nodes on both sides of

FIGURE 10.8

The ptr node's address, which is to be deleted, is passed in as a parameter of a function and stored in ptr. It can't be safely deleted in $\Theta(1)$ time, because the dashed node can't be linked with the dotted node.

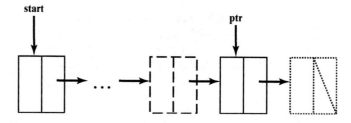

start

ptr

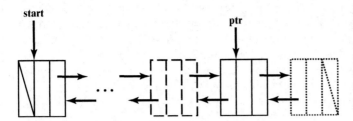

FIGURE 10.9

The ptr node's address, which is to be deleted, is passed in as a parameter of a function and stored in ptr. It *can* be safely deleted in $\Theta(1)$ time, because the dashed node can be accessed with the back pointer of the ptr node.

the ptr node. Then we can free the ptr node with the third line. Notice, however, that this code would not work if the ptr node were the first node or the last node of the list. These special situations can be handled by (1) testing for these special conditions and writing code for them or (2) using empty nodes at the beginning and end of the doubly linked list—called header and trailer nodes, respectively. If header and trailer nodes are used, an empty doubly linked list will contain these two empty nodes linked together.

A node of a doubly linked list wastes a little more memory than a node of a singly linked list, since there are two pointers instead of one. Currently, it usually takes about 4 bytes to store an address, so a doubly linked list would waste 8 bytes per node instead of 4 bytes per node. There is also more work to be done in writing each function, since we must maintain a back pointer and a *next* pointer of each node. However, doubly linked lists are important for achieving $\Theta(1)$ time complexities on all their list operations (except makeEmpty, destructor, overloaded assignment operator, and copy constructor, of course), as we shall see in the next chapter.

SUMMARY

This chapter has presented a general linked list used as a data structure. Data structures in previous chapters had only specialized uses of a linked list—uses that inserted and removed elements only from certain locations—such as the stack and the queue. In the generalized linked list, one needs to be able to access any node, a feature that makes it a little more difficult to write the linked list class. Accordingly, the general linked list introduced the idea of a key, because, in a general linked list, elements often need to be found; when elements are objects, there is some data member that we are most interested in when we do the search. Often, we are interested only in one particular element in the data structure, so the data member we are searching for needs to be unique—hence the importance of the key.

A general linked list is important for a number of reasons. For one, it can be used instead of an array for conserving memory when large elements are used, as discussed in Section 7.4. It is also faster if elements need to be removed from the middle of the list, while keeping the elements contiguous. Arrays of linked lists will be used in the hash table data structure of Chapter 11 and in the graph data structure of Chapter 15. Both of these data structures become considerably easier to write when we can use the LinkedList class in them. A general linked list can also be used for simple linked-list implementations of data structures, similarly to the way the Array class was used in the array implementation of the stack. Using such a general linked list might save time in writing destructors, copy constructors, and overloaded assignment operators, similarly to the way they did not need to be written in the array implementation of the stack and queue when an Array object was used. Exercises 14 and 15 will explore this idea a little more.

The generalized linked list introduced the concept of an iterator, implemented by the first and getNext functions. When the getNext function is used by the client, it always retrieves the element in the next position of the list, beyond the one that was retrieved last.

In writing a function for a data structure, it is always important to consider what the state of each data member in the class should be after the function is finished executing. While we have done this in the past—for example, in maintaining a back pointer in a queue—the importance of doing it became more prominent in considering how to maintain the current pointer in the LinkedList class.

EXERCISES

1. What is a key? Explain how a client uses a key to retrieve information from a data structure.
2. When you write a function for a class, do you need to consider what the state of each data member should be in the object when the function stops executing? Why or why not?
3. Why does inserting an element at the beginning of a linked list have a faster time complexity than inserting it at the end of a linked list? (Assume that no pointer to the last node of the linked list is maintained in the private section.)
4. Why couldn't the first and getNext functions be used to implement the remove function?
5. Why couldn't the first and getNext functions be used to implement the deepCopy function?
6. Why is there no current position after the insert function is called? Why is there no current position after the remove function is called?
7. Why was inlining used on the getNext function?
8. Why does the do … while construct work better with the first/getNext duo than a regular while loop does?
9. Why doesn't the retrieve function pass in the key of an object instead of the object itself?
10. Implement a sorted linked list. Use the same functions as were used in the LinkedList class. The insert function needs to insert a new element in its proper position, an action that will require one of the overloaded relational operators, such as $>$, $<$, $>=$, or $<=$. Also, check to make sure that the key isn't already in the sorted linked list before inserting. The find function can and should stop sooner if the element is not in the linked list (as soon as a greater element is found). Use the same function prototypes as in the LinkedList class.
*11. Do exercise 10, but have the sorted linked list inherit from the LinkedList class template.
12. Implement a circular linked list. Maintain a current pointer and a marker pointer (we don't want to call it start anymore!) in the private section. Use the same function prototypes as in the LinkedList class. When there is only one node, the node points to itself.

   One issue that you will need to deal with is the use of the first and getNext functions. The client cannot use them the same way as in the LinkedList class; otherwise there will be an infinite loop! A way of handling this problem is to start out at the marker pointer node and have the getNext function return false when you get back to it.
*13. Do Exercise 12, but have the circular linked list inherit from the LinkedList class template.
14. The LinkedList class can be used for the linked-list implementation of a stack (Chapter 8, Exercise 5), similarly to the way the Array class was used for the array implementation

(Section 8.2). This is because, when we insert an item at the top of a stack's linked list, we really insert it at the beginning of the list, similarly to the LinkedList insertion. Write the linked-list implementation of a stack with a single data member in the private section: a LinkedList object. Don't forget to remove the destructor, the copy constructor, the overloaded assignment operator, and the deepCopy function from the stack class. (You won't need them anymore.) How much shorter are your stack class files?

15. Think about how you would need to make the LinkedList class of Exercise 14 more general, so that it can be used efficiently in the linked-list implementation of a queue (Section 8.5). Some data structures, such as hash tables and graphs, need to have an array of linked lists. What would be the disadvantage of the modified LinkedList class compared with the old one?

CHAPTER 11

Hash Tables

The binary search algorithm discussed in Section 9.5 is a very fast way of searching for data—achieving a $O(\lg n)$ time complexity in the search—but it is not as fast as we can get. **Hash tables** are about the fastest data structure that we have available for searching, often achieving a $\Theta(1)$ time complexity, on average, in a search for data. Get ready for some high-powered stuff!

11.1   THE HASH TABLE ADT

The hash table is a table of keyed elements—that is, elements that have keys. The hash table uses a function, called a **hash function**, for locating a position in the table. This table of elements is the set of data acted upon by the following operations (some of which make use of the hash function):

- insert, to insert an element into a table
- retrieve, to retrieve an element from the table
- remove, to remove an element from the table
- update, to update an element in the table
- an operation to empty out the hash table

11.2   HASH FUNCTIONS AND HASH TABLE DESIGN

Elements are stored in the positions of the hash table. In this discussion, we will assume that an array is used for the hash table, so the elements would be stored at the indexes of the array. The hash table uses a hash function to retrieve an element quickly. There are two important things you have to remember about a hash function when retrieving an element: (1) The input (or parameter) to a hash function is a key of the element we wish to find, and (2) the output of a hash function is the index of the hash table array in which the element is found. An example of a hash function might be

$h(k) = k \% 100$

In algebra, this function would more than likely be written as $f(x) = x \% 100$. In talking about hash functions, h is often used instead of f, because h is short for "hash function"; and k is often used instead of x, because k represents the key. Remember that k is a key and $h(k)$, the result, is an index into the hash table array. So if k were, for example, 214, the remainder when 214 is divided by 100 is 14, so the result of the hash function would be 14, which stands for index 14 of a hash table array. This means that if we have a key value of 214, the object which has that key is located at index 14 of the hash table array. Thus, by using the hash function, we can achieve a $\Theta(1)$ time complexity to find an element with a certain key.

Hash functions are used not only to retrieve elements, but also to insert an element into a hash table to begin with. Suppose, for example, that we have a hash table of Employee objects, for employees that work in a corporation, and the key we are using is a four-digit Employee id. Let's illustrate how the preceding hash function h would be used. The hash function h assumes that our hash table array has 100 elements. If we wanted to insert an Employee object with an employee id of 2134 into the table, we would use the hash function and get an index of 34. Then the employee would be stored at this index in the array. If we ever want to retrieve the stored information for the employee with id 2134, we use the hash function, obtain an index of 34, look in the array at that index, and find the employee information. Thus, information on employees can be placed into the hash table quickly and retrieved quickly. In the ideal hash table array of Employee objects, the employee id is placed into the array with two simple operations, namely,

```
location = employee.id % 100;
table[ location ] = employee;
```

and is retrieved from the array with two simple operations, namely,

```
location = employee.id % 100;
retrievedEmployee = table[ location ];
```

thus achieving a $\Theta(1)$ time complexity for both the insertion and the search. The hash function, as written, is guaranteed to provide an index between 0 and 99, inclusive, so that we will always have a valid index into an array of 100 elements.

A problem arises, however, when we want to delete an element. We don't just wipe an element out of an array the way we wipe out a node. Some implementations use an extra member of a record of information, called *deleted*. The *deleted* member indicates whether or not the element in that array is present. We would set *deleted* to one value if the element is present, and if we wanted to remove the element, we would set *deleted* to a different value to indicate that the element is no longer present. Then, if we are searching for the element in the hash table, we (1) find its position with the hash function and (2) check the *deleted* member to see whether or not it still exists. With this implementation, all of the array elements would initially have their *deleted* members set to the not-present value before any elements are inserted.

There is, however, a fly in the ointment of this magnificent scheme. Suppose we would like to insert the employee id's 2169 and 3369 into a hash table. We use the hash function on these id's to see where in the table they should be inserted, and the hash function gives us index 69 for both of them. This is called a ***collision***.

Various schemes and implementations have been used to resolve collisions. Some implementations use probing techniques. One such technique would use the hash function, as usual. But if an element is already present at the position in question (and note that the presence of the element can be observed through the use of the *deleted* member), then the hash table array is examined sequentially from that position until an unoccupied position is found. The element is then placed in that unoccupied position. In searching for an element, if the element is not located at the index that the hash function provides, a search is made sequentially through the array until the element is found; but when the element is found, we must check the *deleted* member, of course, to see whether or not the element exists. In such a scheme, if the end of the array is encountered during a search for an unoccupied position or an element, the search resumes at the beginning of the array. The problem here is that when you search sequentially through an array, your algorithm is starting to behave like a $O(n)$ algorithm instead of a $\Theta(1)$ algorithm. Other implementations use double hashing. When one hash function results in a collision, a second hash function is used for that element. If the use of the second hash function still results in a collision, a sequential search is initiated.

Another scheme for resolving collisions uses ***chaining***, a method in which every element of the hash table array is a linked list. When an element needs to be inserted, the hash function produces an index and the element is then inserted at the beginning of the linked list at that index. Thus, a linked list at an index is a list of all the elements that have "hashed" at that index. If there is more than one node in the linked list, it is a list of all elements that have collided at the position in question. We will call such a list a ***collision list***. Figure 11.1 shows how chaining is used to insert a group of elements into a hash table.

When an element must be found, the hash function produces the index identifying where it can be found, and then the linked list at that index is searched for the element. With this technique, a *deleted* member of a struct is not needed. When an element needs to be removed, its node is simply removed from the linked list. There is also no danger of the hash table becoming full in the chaining scheme. By contrast, in the probing schemes, a hash table can become full.

The chaining method works reasonably well if the elements are evenly spread among the array positions, a situation called ***uniform hashing***. For example, if we have 300 employees and an array size of 100, and if there are about 3 employees per position, give or take an employee, then we still have a search function that operates in $\Theta(1)$ time, since no more than 3 or 4 comparisons will be needed to find the right employee. When chaining is used, the insert function is guaranteed to run in $\Theta(1)$ time, since new elements are placed at the beginning of the linked list.

We can see that the time complexity of hashing really depends on the length of the collision list. The longer the collision list, the more time it will take. In this discussion, we assume that uniform hashing is employed and that the design and use of the hash table will keep the length of the collision list bounded by some

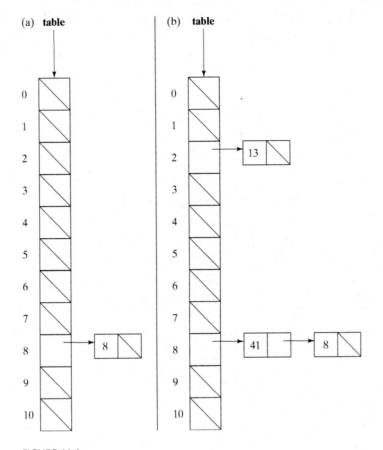

FIGURE 11.1

The key values 8, 13, 41, 14, 45, 47, 4, 49, and 30 are to be inserted into a hash table by means of chaining with the hash function $h(k) = k \% 11$. Every element in the array is a linked list. (Only the start pointer is used in the drawing.) (a) 8 % 11 is 8, so key 8 is inserted at index 8. (b) 13 is inserted (13 % 11 is 2) and then 41 is inserted; 41 % 11 is 8, causing a collision. 41 is inserted at the beginning of the linked list, since this is the fastest way to insert nodes into a list.

small constant. Thus, without getting into too much detail, we can regard the time complexity as being $\Theta(1)$ under these assumptions. Such a situation is entirely theoretical, of course, and may not pan out in practice. Yet, the science of hashing should advance so that we can reach this theoretical goal. Even at the present time, hashing is very fast.

It is the quality of the hash function that will largely determine whether the elements are evenly spread. A poor hash function may cause all of the elements to be placed at the same position, creating a long linked list. An obvious example of a poor hash function is

$$h(k) = 5$$

which places all of the elements at index 5. The insert function still operates in $\Theta(1)$ time, but we are back to a $\Theta(n)$ time complexity for the search. This hash function is obviously bad, though, and no one in his or her right mind would use it.

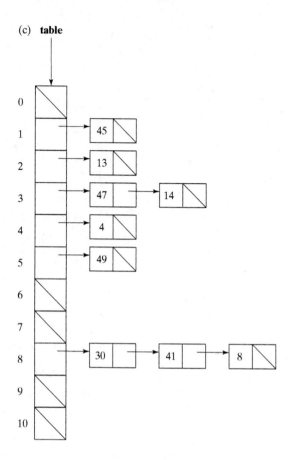

FIGURE 11.1 (*continued*)

(c) The completed hash table.

There are hash functions, however, that are bad, but not obviously so. For example, the function

$$h(k) = k \% 100$$

may, in fact, be horrible if meaning is attached to the parts of a key. For instance, in the four-digit employee id, let's suppose that the last two digits represent the state where the employee was born. For Pennsylvania, the two-digit code might be 12 in the last two digits of the id. Now, if we have a corporation in Pennsylvania, and 95% of our employees were born in Pennsylvania, the preceding hash function is almost always going to produce 12 for an index. The problem with keys is that very often there is some kind of meaning attached to parts of them.

For reasons that are beyond the scope of this text, a table size that is a prime number not too close to a power of 2 works reasonably well when the division method (i.e., the modulus operator, as before) is used for the hash function. Recall that a prime number is evenly divisible only by itself and 1, such that the result is not a negative number. The number 31, for example, is a prime number. But it would not make a good hash table size because it is close to 32, which is a power of 2. (It is 2^5.) If we chose a number such as 97, instead of 100, for our table size, then our hash function (using the division method) would be

$$h(k) = k \% 97$$

This function would usually give a decent method of spreading elements evenly in a hash table, even if meaning is attached to the parts of keys.

The division method is rather slow, however, because division is a slow operation for the hardware of a computer to perform. There are faster hash functions that are geared more to the machine's architecture, but this topic is best covered in a course or textbook on algorithm analysis. Sometimes the division method can't easily be used because the keys are types that are not numbers. Many types of keys are strings that include letters as well as numbers, or letters only.

When a key is a string, we can still design a hash function for it but a little more work is involved. For example, we can add together the ASCII values of all the characters of a string and then use the division method:

```
1       int sum = 0;
2       for ( int i = 0; i < int( str.length( ) ); i++ )
3               sum += str[ i ];
4       hash_index = sum % 97;
```

Since sum is of type int, the ASCII value of the character in str[i] will be added to sum on line 3. There is a loop involved here, but the operation should not be construed as taking any more time than a binary search algorithm would take. When the binary search algorithm compares two strings, it compares them character by character also. It's just that the algorithm for comparing strings is written in the string class of the library.

Designing a good hash function is an art as well as a science. It depends on many factors, including (but not limited to) the architecture of the computer, the types of keys that are being used, the meanings attached to parts of keys, and the number of keys expected as well. A good hash function will create uniform hashing, so that the elements are spread evenly throughout the hash table.

In using a hash table, there is often a trade-off between speed and memory conservation. More speed comes about by reducing the number of collisions. If there are no collisions, you can't ask for much more as far as speed is concerned. Memory is wasted if array positions are empty. If we assume that the chaining method is used, then each empty linked list still has two pointers in its private section: a start pointer and a current pointer. Thus, assuming that a pointer occupies 4 bytes, 8 bytes of wasted memory is used for an empty linked list. (No memory would be used for functions within the objects of the array elements.)

When there are, for example, 300 employees, an array size of 601 would certainly cut down on the number of collisions (although we would still probably have some). However, there will be at least 301 empty linked lists, wasting at least 2408 bytes of memory. By contrast, an array size of 149 would have far less empty linked lists, but there certainly would be collisions—at least two per array position, on average. So, for the array size, one must ask how important memory conservation is and how important speed is for the application being written. If you are looking for rules of thumb here, there really aren't any (the joys of art, once again).

If speed is of utmost importance, and we have keys that are nonnegative integers, then we can design a hash table that has absolutely no collisions. The hash function we use is

$$h(k) = k$$

No collisions are possible, because each key is unique; therefore, each index produced will be unique. Here, the size of the hash table must be set to (1 + largest key possible). Sometimes, we are in a lucky situation and we can use such a technique. For example, suppose we have 300 employees, and they each have an id from 0 to 299. Then the index of the array corresponds exactly to the employee id, and there is no wasted memory either. We set the array size of the hash table to 300 and use the preceding hash function, whereupon we have a very fast technique. We don't even need to use linked lists.

Sometimes we can use such a hash function, but doing so is not so great. For example, suppose that our employee objects use Social Security numbers as keys (without dashes, of course). We would need to create an array with a billion elements to use this hash function. And if there were only 300 employees, there certainly would be a lot of wasted memory. However, if speed is of utmost importance, and we have unlimited supplies of memory, we can certainly use that hash function.

In an ideal world, we would always have keys that are nonnegative integers and there would never be gaps in between the key numbers. Then hash table design would be simple and very fast, and no memory would be wasted. However, until we can get to this ideal world, much computer science literature will be devoted to the art and science of making hash tables and hash functions.

11.3 IMPLEMENTATION ISSUES FOR A HASH TABLE

If we use the hash function $h(k) = k$, and there are empty positions, sometimes it will still benefit us to use a linked list at every position, even though chaining is not necessary. Whether we should do so depends upon the element size. If, for example, the element size is 100 bytes, then, without using linked lists, an empty position of the array would waste 100 bytes—the data members of the element just haven't been set. If we use an empty linked list at that position instead, then the start and current pointers would waste just 8 bytes. Therefore, it is probably in the best interests of our client if we use the chaining scheme, even if the hash function $h(k) = k$ is applicable. (A situation like this is the reason for not using a header node in the LinkedList class of Chapter 10.)

The linked list will waste space, however, if we use the hash function $h(k) = k$ and there are no empty positions. This was the ideal situation discussed in the last section. But frankly, in this situation, the client would do well to use just the Array class for speed and forget about using a HashTable class. If you think about it, you will see that it would be very easy to do this.

The chaining technique has an additional advantage over probing in that the hash table cannot get filled up. For all of these reasons, the hash tables in this chapter will focus on using the chaining technique. (That is not to say that the probing techniques do not have their uses.) In the private section, we use the Array class, discussed in Chapter 5, for the hash table. The size of the array will be passed into the constructor from the client. The array will, of course, be an array of linked lists. We will use the LinkedList class, discussed in Chapter 10, for the elements of the array. Thus, an Array of LinkedList data structures will be a part of the HashTable data structure. This approach illustrates something that a beginning programmer eventually learns: When you design a class, your clientele is not just restricted to the people who write the main programs, but also includes programmers who make other classes.

But we have a little added twist that we have to consider as well: What about the hash function for the HashTable data structure? Should we simply make one that we think is a good, all-purpose hash function? If the client doesn't think so, will he or she just have to live with it? We will probably not have a popular HashTable data structure if we just make a hash function that the client has to use. After all, the keys can take a variety of forms: We've seen that they can be strings and numbers, but we're not going to pretend to be omniscient about this. A key can be anything a client wants it to be; it might even be an object of a struct.

We have to face it: The only person who should write the hash function should be the client. The client knows what the application that will use the hash table is all about. The client knows what the keys will be like and may even know what the architecture of the computer using the program will be like. The client might have some very good ideas about what hash function will work best.

But if we accept all this knowledge on the part of the client, then we have an interesting situation: If the client writes a hash function, he or she shouldn't write it in the HashTable class. Rather, the client should just write it wherever he or she is writing the code that uses the hash table. It is poor class design when the client has to go into the class, which may be in the library, to change code so that the program will work.

As long as we use a class template for a HashTable data structure, the client can write a hash function in his or her main program that the compiler will recognize when it makes a class out of the class template. The reason for this is that the compiler doesn't make the class out of the template until it encounters the declaration of the object. But when it does encounter the declaration of the object, it has already seen the hash function prototype and knows that it exists. Of course, we would have to specify in the comments of the class definition what the hash function should be called, so that we can call it in the class functions. We know that it has to return an integer, but what about the parameter passed in? We can tell the client that the parameter must be whatever type the client uses for DataType. Then the parameter will either contain the key or be the key itself, so there is no problem. When the client calls the insert function, for example, the client will pass in an object which contains the key that the hash function needs. Then we will pass the object into the hash function that the client made, which will be recognized by the compiler. The hash function will return an index that we will use in the hash table.

These ideas make a pretty good picture of how we will use the hash function. There is a little problem with this approach, however: What if the client wants to make more than one hash table and wants a different hash function for each hash table, but wants to use the same struct or type for DataType in all of the hash tables? We've already specified what the hash function must be called so that we can call it. It must return an integer and pass in a parameter of the type that the client is using for DataType. But these characteristics limit the client to just one hash function. The client must be able to name the different hash functions with whatever name he or she wishes to use if the parameter passed into all of them is of the same type.

If the client uses different names for the hash functions, however, we will not know how to call the functions within our class functions. But there is a solution to this dilemma: a *pointer to a function*. Pointers typically hold the addresses of variable locations, but they can hold the addresses of functions, too. The client can write a hash function, calling it any name he or she wishes, and then the client will pass the name of the function into the constructor. Our pointer will be set to point to the function that gets passed in. Now, if the client makes another HashTable object and uses the same type for DataType, then the client can write a hash function with a different name for use with this HashTable object. The function still returns an integer and still passes in a parameter of the type used for DataType, but has a different name. This name is passed into the constructor of the second HashTable object, and a pointer in that object is set to point to the second hash table function.

Read the previous paragraph as many times as needed to get a clear picture of what is going on. As soon as you're sure you understand it, let's look at how pointers to functions are declared and used.

11.4 POINTERS TO FUNCTIONS

A pointer to a function has a declaration that is rather different looking from other declarations. As an example, the following declaration is for a pointer which points to a function that returns a float type and takes a string parameter:

```
float (*funcptr) (string);
```

The pointer's name is funcptr. The parentheses around *funcptr are necessary. The return type of a function that funcptr can point to appears to the left of the pointer's name, and the type(s) for the parameter list of such a function appear to the right. With this in mind, try to write the declaration of a pointer called fptr that can point to a function with a return type of void and that passes in two parameters, both of type int. Have you written it? Take a look at this code, and see if you got it:

```
void (*fptr) (int, int);
```

Now, suppose we have written a function foo:

```
void foo( int a, int b )
{
        cout << "a is: " << a << endl;
        cout << "b is: " << b << endl;
}
```

This function luckily has the same return type and parameter types as our pointer fptr, so we can assign the address of foo to fptr:

fptr = foo;

To execute the function by using the pointer, we do not dereference fptr:

fptr(10, 25);

This function passes 10 into a and 25 into b. Thus, the result of executing the preceding line of code is

a is 10
b is 25

Thus, the use of pointers to functions is different, but simple.

11.5   A HASH TABLE IMPLEMENTATION

Let's take a look at the class template for HashTable:

```
1   // HashTable.h - - class template for a hash table using chaining
2
3   #include "LinkedList.h"
4   #include "Array.h"
5
6   // client must provide a hash function with the following characteristics:
7   //            1 input parameter of DataType (see below), passed by const reference
8   //            returns an integer between 0 and size - 1, inclusive, where size is the
9   //            number of elements in the hash table
10  //            the name of the function is passed as the first parameter to the HashTable
11  //            constructor
12  //            client may make as many hash functions for as many HashTables as desired
13  // if a struct is used for DataType, a typical use of retrieve, remove, and update would
14  // be to set the key of an object and then pass the object into the function
15  // retrieve, remove, and update will return false if:
16  //            (1) the hash function supplied above does not return a valid index
17  //            (2) the supplied key or element cannot be found in the hash table
18  // otherwise, these functions will return true if successful
19  // For retrieve, remove and update functions, if you are using an object as an element, a
20  // typical use would be to set the key of the desired object to retrieve, remove, or
21  // update; then pass the object into the function.
22  // If an object of a struct is used for DataType, the == operator must be
23  // overloaded for it; the left and right operands are both DataType objects
24  // the == comparison is used for finding elements, usually by key value
25  //            Exceptions can be thrown in the constructor, the (default) copy constructor,
```

```
26  // the (default) assignment operator, or the insert function if out of heap memory.
27
28  template <class DataType>
29  class HashTable
30  {
31  public:
32      HashTable( int (*hf)(const DataType &), int s );
33      bool insert( const DataType & newObject );    // returns true if successful; returns
34                                                    // false if invalid index was returned
35                                                    // from hash function
36      bool retrieve( DataType & retrieved );        // see description above class template
37      bool remove( DataType & removed );            // see description above class template
38      bool update( DataType & updateObject );       // see description above class template
39      void makeEmpty( );
40  private:
41      Array< LinkedList<DataType> > table;
42      int (*hashfunc)(const DataType &);            // pointer to hash function supplied by client
43  };
44
45  #include "HashTable.cpp"
```

Notice on lines 3–4 that the LinkedList.h and Array.h files are included. The LinkedList.h, LinkedList.cpp, Array.h, and Array.cpp files must be in the same directory as the HashTable.h and HashTable.cpp files. The header files are included at the top of this file so that the use of LinkedList and Array on line 41 will be recognized by the compiler.

Notice also that, before the class template, some comments are provided on how to make the hash function and on the general usage of some of the hash table functions. In the private section, we have an Array called table on line 41. This will be our hash table. Each linked list in the hash table is made from the LinkedList<DataType> class, where DataType is the type of element stored in the linked list. The client chooses the type of element. The declaration on line 41 states that each element of our Array object will be a LinkedList<DataType> object. When using this type of template notation, you must be very careful to include the space shown in Figure 11.2. If you do not put the space in, the symbols " >> " will be interpreted as the >> operator (often used with cin), and you will get a compiler error that will make absolutely no sense to you.

The pointer to the hash function is declared on line 42. It will point to a hash function that returns an integer, of course. Notice how the parameter of the function is set: We simply put DataType in the parameter list. Then, when the compiler makes a

FIGURE 11.2

A space needs to be inserted here when you are
using nested angle brackets in a declaration.

class out of the template, the compiler will replace all occurrences of DataType with the type used by the client in the declaration of the object (in angle brackets). At that time, the pointer declaration will be complete. The client knows (by the comments) that the hash function must accept a parameter of the type that he or she uses for DataType, so the pointer will work. Note that we don't need a size variable in the private section for the hash table size, because this information is saved in the Array class.

In the constructor declaration on line 32, the first parameter is a pointer to a function. This pointer was declared in the same manner that the pointer in the private section was declared, so that DataType would be replaced by the type chosen by the client when the compiler makes a class out of the template. The client will pass the name of the hash function that he or she wrote into this parameter. The second parameter of the constructor is the size of the hash table, also chosen by the client. There is no default constructor (a constructor that has no parameters). When the client declares a HashTable object, the client must pass in these two parameters.

We have a pointer in the private section, so we start to think about writing a copy constructor, a destructor, and an overloaded assignment operator. We soon realize, however, that we do not need a destructor, because the pointer doesn't point to dynamic memory (allocated with the *new* operator). Instead, it points to a function. We also realize that a copy constructor isn't needed, since, in this case, we *want* the address of the function pointer in the actual parameter to be copied to the function pointer in the formal parameter. We want to use the same hash function after passing a HashTable object by value. This is one of those rare instances where we want a shallow copy instead of a deep copy. The same thing is true about the assignment operator. Therefore, in this special case, we do not need a copy constructor, a destructor, or an overloaded assignment operator.

Next, we have insert, retrieve, remove, and update functions on lines 33–38. These functions were described in the hash table ADT and will return true if successful; the comments above the class template explain when the retrieve, remove, and update functions will return false. The client should thoroughly test the hash function to make sure that it returns a valid index; but if it doesn't, we don't want our class functions to crash the program, so we will check for a valid index in those functions.

Let's take a look at the implementation file, starting with the constructor:

```
1    // HashTable.cpp - - function definitions for a hash table using chaining
2
3    template <class DataType>
4    HashTable<DataType>::HashTable( int (*hf)(const DataType &), int s )
5         : table( s )
6    {
7         hashfunc = hf;
8    }
```

Line 5 shows an initializer list. Recall from Section 6.1 that an initializer list is necessary when there is no default constructor for an object in the private section. The Array object's constructor must have a size passed into it, so this takes place in the initializer list. On line 4, the variable s is passed in as the second parameter of the

HashTable constructor. It is used to set the capacity of the Array object when its constructor is called on line 5.

The address of the hash function that the client has written is saved on line 7; here, the function pointer declared in the private section, called hashfunc, is assigned the address passed into the function pointer parameter called hf. When the client uses the HashTable constructor, the client passes in the name of the hash function that he or she wrote. The name is passed in without parentheses or parameters, as in the code

HashTable<MyStruct> ht1(hash1, 97);

where hash1 is the name of the hash function.

One other thing should be pointed out about what happens in this constructor: A dynamic array of LinkedList objects (of length s) is formed on line 5 when the Array constructor is called. It is important to realize that, at the time that this dynamic array is formed in heap memory (in the function body of the Array constructor), the constructor for each LinkedList object will be called for each element of the array.

Next, the insert function is shown:

```
9    template <class DataType>
10   bool HashTable<DataType>::insert ( const DataType & newObject )
11   {
12       int location = hashfunc( newObject );
13       if ( location < 0 || location >= table.length( ) )
14             return false;
15       table[ location ].insert( newObject );
16       return true;
17   }
```

The integer *location* on line 12 will be used as the index into the hash table. The hash function that the client has written is called on line 12, using the function pointer that was declared in the private section and passing in newObject (which was passed into the insert function). On line 13, if the hash function returns an invalid index, false is returned on line 14. If *location* is valid, we use it in the table on line 15, giving us a LinkedList object at that location. The insert function in the LinkedList class is called, using the dot operator and passing in newObject. Then true is returned on line 16, indicating a successful insertion.

The retrieve and remove functions are written similarly to the insert function:

```
18   template <class DataType>
19   bool HashTable<DataType>::retrieve( DataType & retrieved )
20   {
21       int location = hashfunc( retrieved );
22       if ( location < 0 || location >= table.length( ) )
23             return false;
24       if ( !table[ location ].retrieve( retrieved ) )
25             return false;
```

```
26        return true;
27 }
28
29  template <class DataType>
30  bool HashTable<DataType>::remove( DataType & removed )
31  {
32      int location = hashfunc( removed );
33      if ( location < 0 || location >= table.length( ) )
34            return false;
35      if ( !table[ location ].remove( removed ) )
36            return false;
37      return true;
38  }
```

The only difference is that if the retrieve and remove functions in the LinkedList class (called on lines 24 and 35, respectively) return false, it is because the object was not found.

The update function is shown next:

```
39  template <class DataType>
40  bool HashTable<DataType>::update ( DataType & updateObject )
41  {
42      int location = hashfunc( updateObject );
43      if ( location < 0 || location >= table.length( ) )
44            return false;
45      if ( !table[location].find( updateObject ) )
46            return false;
47      table[location].replace( updateObject );
48      return true;
49  }
```

This function is also written somewhat similarly, except two functions in the LinkedList class are called instead of one. The first function is the find function, on line 45. If it returns false, the object could not be found; this would cause the condition on line 45 to be true, so false is returned from the update function on line 46. If the object was found, the current position in the LinkedList object has been set to it. (Remember the current pointer in the LinkedList class.) Therefore, we can simply call the replace function of the LinkedList class on line 47. Finally, true is returned on line 48.

The makeEmpty function is as follows:

```
50  template <class DataType>
51  void HashTable<DataType>::makeEmpty( )
52  {
53      for ( int i = 0; i < table.length( ); i++ )
54            table[ i ].makeEmpty( );
55  }
```

An empty hash table would still have the array, but each array position must have an empty linked list. Therefore, a loop is set up to call the makeEmpty function in the LinkedList class for every LinkedList object in the array.

11.6   USING THE HASH TABLE IMPLEMENTATION

Because the HashTable class template is a little different from other class templates (it has function pointers), we should probably take a look at a main program that illustrates the use of hash tables:

```
1    // useHashTables.cpp - - code that demonstrates the use of the hash tables
2
3    #include <iostream>
4    #include <string>
5    #include "HashTable.h"
6
7    using namespace std;
8
9    struct MyStruct {
10       string str;
11       int num;
12       bool operator ==( const MyStruct & r ) { return str == r.str; }
13   };
14
15   const int SIZE1 = 97, SIZE2 = 199;
16
17   int hash1( const MyStruct & obj );
18   int hash2( const MyStruct  & obj );
19
20   int main( )
21   {
22       HashTable<MyStruct> ht1( hash1, SIZE1 ), ht2( hash2, SIZE2);
23
24       MyStruct myobj;
25
26       myobj.str = "elephant";
27       myobj.num = 25;
28       ht1.insert( myobj );
29
30       myobj.str = "giraffe";
31       myobj.num = 50;
32       ht2.insert( myobj );
33
34       MyStruct myobj2;
35
```

```
36        myobj2.str = "elephant";
37        ht1.retrieve( myobj2 );
38        cout << "retrieved from ht1: " << myobj2.num << " for num." << endl;
39
40        myobj2.str = "giraffe";
41        ht2.retrieve( myobj2 );
42        cout << "retrieved from ht2: " << myobj2.num << " for num." << endl;
43
44        return 0;
45   }
46
47   int hash1( const MyStruct & obj )
48   {
49        int sum = 0;
50        for ( int i = 0; i < 3 && i < int( obj.str.length( ) ); i++ )
51               sum += obj.str[ i ];
52        return sum % SIZE1;
53   }
54
55   int hash2( const MyStruct & obj )
56   {
57        int sum = 0;
58        for ( int i = int( obj.str.length( ) ) - 1;
59                       i > -1 && i > int( obj.str.length( ) ) - 7; i- - )
60               sum += obj.str[ i ];
61        return sum % SIZE2;
62   }
```

This program doesn't really accomplish anything, and its hash functions are not particularly well written, but its main purpose is to illustrate the mechanics of how hash tables are used.

A struct called MyStruct is defined on lines 9–13. Objects of this struct will become elements in the hash tables. The equality operator is overloaded on line 12. Recall that the equality operator must be overloaded for the use of the LinkedList class template. This requirement is listed above the LinkedList class template in a comment. The equality operator is not used to compare objects in the HashTable implementation file, but it is still important to include a comment above the HashTable class template stating that the equality operator must be overloaded (which was done). Whenever you use another class in designing a class, comments on the overloaded operators should be added to the new class from the old one (if DataType ends up being used in the old class).

Two hash functions were created on lines 47–62. Both of these pass in an object of MyStruct. We are going to have two hash tables of MyStruct objects, but we are going to use a different hash function for each hash table, as discussed earlier. In both hash tables, the string called str is going to be the key. In the hash1 function, it adds together the ASCII values of the first three characters of the string and then uses the division method with SIZE1, which was set to 97 on line 15. In the hash2 function, str adds together the ASCII values of the last six characters of the string and then uses the division method with SIZE2, which was set to 199 on line 15.

The addresses of these functions will be passed into the hash table data structures. Notice that the functions are defined normally, and there is nothing unusual about them. Their prototypes, on lines 17–18, are also normal.

Line 22 declares two HashTable objects. A class using MyStruct for DataType is made from the HashTable class template. The objects are named ht1 and ht2. The constructor for ht1 passes in the name of the hash1 function as the first parameter and SIZE1 as the second parameter. The constructor for ht2 passes in the name of the hash2 function as the first parameter and SIZE2 as the second parameter. Notice that any change to SIZE1 or SIZE2 on line 15 will update both the parameter that is passed into the constructor and the corresponding hash function (lines 52 and 61).

An object of MyStruct is declared on line 24, for use with the hash tables. After setting the data members in it on lines 26–27, it is inserted into ht1 on line 28. Its data members are changed on lines 30–31, and it is then inserted into ht2 on line 32. Another object of MyStruct called myobj2 was declared on line 34 (although this was not necessary). We set the key of myobj2 on line 36, to retrieve the entire object from ht1 on line 37. Afterwards, the value of the num data member is printed out on line 38. The process is repeated for ht2.

11.7   A HASH TABLE IMPLEMENTATION OF A DOUBLY LINKED LIST

If you look closely at the description of the hash table ADT in Section 11.1, you will see that it is very close to the description of the list ADT given in Section 10.1. In fact, we wouldn't have far to go in order to call a hash table a kind of list; I believe it was Shakespeare who said "A rose by any other name smells just as sweet". We would just need a few more operations:

- find, to determine whether an element is in the "list"
- an operation to determine whether the "list" is empty
- an iterator, to retrieve each item from the "list", one at a time

We would also need a current position. These are all it would take, and it would be a fast list, indeed.

All of these features can all be easily implemented, but the iterator is not guaranteed to be $\Theta(1)$ for one retrieval of an element. We could process a collision list easily enough, but as shown in Figure 11.3, there might be large gaps of empty collision lists between the one we are on and the next one we have to find. Certainly, if we are thinking about making a very fast list, we would need to speed up this iteration process.

One solution would be to run an "iterator" list through all of the collision lists. Sure, each collision list node already has a pointer to the next node, but we're not limited to just one pointer to a node: We can use a pointer for a node of the iterator list, so that each node has more than one pointer. If we wanted to remove a collision list node now, however, it would help to make the iterator list a doubly linked list. As we saw in

table

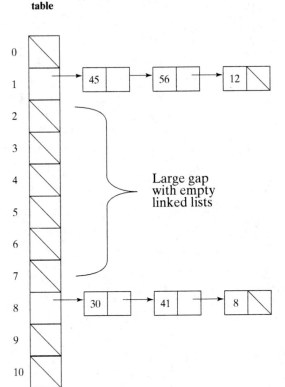

FIGURE 11.3

How large gaps might exist between collision lists, so that an iterator is not guaranteed to be $\Theta(1)$ upon each retrieval of an element.

Section 10.4, if we have the address of a node of a doubly linked list, we can remove it from the list in $\Theta(1)$ time. Figure 11.4 illustrates this idea.

The ADT description of the doubly linked list is the same as that of the list ADT described in Section 10.1. However, because of the double links, many of the list operations, such as retrieve and remove, are sped up significantly. Now we have a fast iterator, too—and the operation to determine whether the data structure is empty would be fast: It is empty if the header node points to the trailer node. We can maintain a current position within the doubly linked list. So, with this idea, everything seems to fall into place.

It is important to realize that the way the pointers in the doubly linked list are arranged is independent of the way the collision list pointers are arranged. We can maintain the doubly linked list as an unsorted list, a sorted list, or a circular list if we want. All of these ways of maintaining the doubly linked list may have important uses. Figure 11.5 shows the same collision lists as Figure 11.4, but the doubly linked list is maintained as a sorted list.

The new, improved speed of the list operations does come at the expense of some memory usage, however. In each collision node, we now have three pointers instead of one: We have a next pointer to the next node in the collision list, a dlnext pointer to the next node in the doubly linked list, and a dlback pointer, wasting 12 bytes of memory. The node, therefore, will look like this:

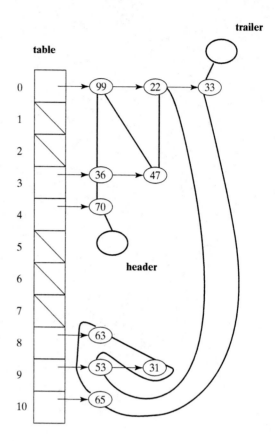

FIGURE 11.4

How the following key values would be inserted into the hash table with an $h(k) = k \% 11$ hash function: 33, 65, 63, 31, 53, 22, 47, 99, 36, 70. The nodes are represented by ovals, and each has three pointers. The bold lines show the doubly linked list. Each bold line indicates that both nodes point to each other (i.e., they are doubly linked). The header node marks the beginning of the doubly linked list, and the trailer node marks the end. Nodes are inserted at the beginning of the list, so the last node inserted will be closest to the header. If you follow the doubly linked list from trailer to header, you will see the nodes as they were inserted.

```
template <class DataType>
struct Node {
        DataType info;
        Node<DataType> *next;
        Node<DataType> *dlnext;
        Node<DataType> *dlback;
};
```

Now we can't really regard the hash table array as being negligible housekeeping information, the way we regard a start pointer. We must count it as being part of the housekeeping information per node, described in Section 7.4.2. This is because collision lists are expected to be short, perhaps even one element long. In the implementation discussed here, each table element takes 8 bytes for a LinkedList object, using a start pointer and a current pointer. We can ignore the overhead in an Array object, since it is trivial when divided up among large numbers of elements. The header and trailer nodes use space for one element, even though the data members of that element aren't set to anything. (Those nodes are empty.) But we

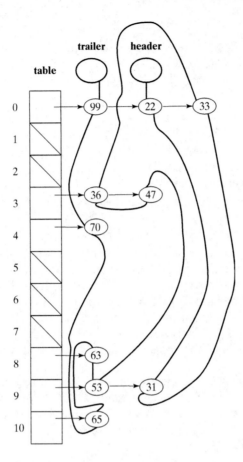

FIGURE 11.5

The same collision lists that would be formed as in Figure 11.4, by the insertion of the same keys in the same order with the same hash function. However, here the pointers of the doubly linked list have changed to reflect a sorted order of the keys, from the header node to the trailer node.

can ignore this, too; if we have about 10,000 nodes, it pales in comparison. But if we assume that the size of the hash table is less than the number of elements, we can see that we are using between 12 and 20 bytes worth of pointers (wasted memory) per element.

Assuming the worst case of 20 bytes for memory waste, if an element is about 20 bytes in size, roughly 50% of the memory in the data structure is wasted on overhead. When an element is 60 bytes in size, only 25% of the memory is wasted, a percentage that compares more favorably with an array, which wastes 25–50% of memory, on average. (See Section 7.4.) Of course, for very large elements, our doubly linked list is still highly advantageous: An element 1980 bytes in size in this data structure would cause only 1% of memory waste in overhead. So, depending on element size, the speed gained from such an implementation of a doubly linked list may be well worth it.

The question is what to call this data structure. It is not really a triply linked list; it is still a doubly linked list running through the collision lists of a hash table. It seems reasonable that we call this data structure either a doubly linked list or an enhanced hash table. As you can see by the title of the section, I'm choosing to call it a doubly linked list.

11.7.1 Implementation Issues

In order to make the implementation easy, we're going to make some slight modifications to the LinkedList class (used for the collision lists), and it won't really be for clients anymore. Rather, it will just be a specialized "helper" class for the doubly linked list class. Following are the changes we are going to make:

- We are going to change the name of the class from LinkedList to CollisionList.
- We are going to modify the Node struct so that it looks like the Node struct shown a few paragraphs ago.
- We are going to make a function called getcurrent to retrieve the current pointer.
- Instead of eliminating the current position when we insert a node, we will set the current position to the node we inserted.

When we insert or remove a node, we need to get the address of the node of interest from the CollisionList object. That is the purpose of the getcurrent function. We cannot eliminate the current position now when we insert a node into a collision list (but a collision list isn't like a normal list anyway). The current position needs to be set to the inserted node, so we can get the address of that node with getcurrent and work with it directly in the insert function of the doubly linked list, in order to set up the dlnext and dlback pointers. (We'll be inserting the node at the head of the doubly linked list, for speed.)

But we want to use a HashTable as a data member in the doubly linked list for convenience. And it is the HashTable object that will be working with the CollisionList objects. Therefore, we'll need to make some changes to the HashTable class, which will now be a helper class, having features that are not generally useful for normal clients. The changes we will make are as follows:

- Rename the HashTable class to DLHashTable, short for "Doubly Linked Hash Table."
- Keep the location, used throughout the class, as a private data member
- Have a function getcurrent, which retrieves the current pointer of the CollisionList that was used in the last use of location; that is, return table[location].getcurrent( ).
- Include a function called gethashfunc, which will return the hash function pointer.
- Include a function called sethashfunc, which will set a hash function pointer.
- Include a function called getsize, which will get the Array size of the hash table.
- Include a function called changeSize, which will change the Array size of the hash table.

The last four bulleted items will be useful in the copy constructor and deepCopy functions of the doubly linked list class. These are all straightforward implementations that you should have no problem with, except for the gethashfunc function. When a function pointer is used as a return type of a function, as in the gethashfunc function, the proto-type for it looks like this:

int (***gethashfunc( ) const**)(const DataType &);

The part shown in bold is what we would normally think of as the function heading, apart from the return type. (We are not modifying a data member of the hash table, so const is used at the end of the function heading.) The part not shown in bold is, collec-tively, the return type of the function pointer (specifically, the pointer to a hash func-tion). Correspondingly, the function definition in the implementation file looks like this:

```
template <class DataType>
int (*DLHashTable<DataType>::gethashfunc( ) const)(const DataType &)
{
        return hashfunc;
}
```

11.7.2   The Specification File for the DoublyLinkedList Class

The following is the class template for the DoublyLinkedList class:

```
1    // DoublyLinkedList.h - -  class for a doublylinked list
2
3    #include "DLHashTable.h"
4
5    // DoublyLinkedList maintains a current position in list after each function call
6    // If an object of a struct is used for DataType, the == operator must be
7    // overloaded for it; the left and right operands are both DataType objects
8    // the == comparison is used for finding elements, usually by key value
9    // For find, retrieve and remove functions, if you are using an object as an element, a
10   // typical use would be to set the key of the desired object to find or remove, then pass
11   // the object into the function.
12
13   // client must provide a hash function with the following characteristics:
14   //       1 input parameter of DataType (see below), passed by const reference
15   //       returns an integer between 0 and size - 1, inclusive, where size is the
16   //       number of elements in the hash table
17   //       the name of the function is passed as the first parameter to the DoublyLinkedList
18   //       constructor, the size of the hash table is passed as the second parameter
19   //       client may make as many hash functions for as many DoublyLinkedLists as desired
20   // The insert, find, retrieve, and remove functions will return false if an invalid index
21   // is obtained from the hash function.  The copy constructor and overloaded
22   // assignment operator will produce an empty list if an invalid index is obtained
23   // from the hash function
24   // The constructor, copy constructor, overloaded assignment operator, and insert
```

```
25   // functions will throw an exception if out of heap memory.
26
27
28   template <class DataType>
29   class DoublyLinkedList
30   {
31   public:
32       DoublyLinkedList( int (*hf)(const DataType &), int s );
33       DoublyLinkedList( const DoublyLinkedList<DataType> & aplist );
34       ~DoublyLinkedList( );
35       DoublyLinkedList<DataType> &
36               operator =( const DoublyLinkedList<DataType> & rlist );
37       bool insert( const DataType & element ); // no current position after use
38       bool first( DataType & listEl );          // returns first element of list in listEl
39                                                  // and current position is set to this element;
40                                                  // if list is empty, returns false and there is
41                                                  // no current position; otherwise, returns true
42       inline bool getNext( DataType & listEl ); // retrieves the next element of a linked list
43                                                  // beyond the last element that was retrieved
44                                                  // by first, getNext or getPrevious functions
45                                                  // and returns it in listEl;
46                                                  // current position is set to this element.
47                                                  // if no element exists at this position,
48                                                  // getNext returns false and there is no
49                                                  // current position; returns true otherwise
50       bool last( DataType & listEl );           // returns last element of list in listEl
51                                                  // and current position is set to this element;
52                                                  // if list is empty, returns false and there is
53                                                  // no current position; otherwise, returns true
54       inline bool getPrevious( DataType & listEl );  // retrieves the previous element of a list
55                                                  // before the last element that was retrieved
56                                                  // by last, getNext or getPrevious functions
57                                                  // and returns it in listEl;
58                                                  // current position is set to this element.
59                                                  // if no element exists at this position,
60                                                  // getPrevious returns false and there is no
61                                                  // current position; returns true otherwise
62       bool find ( const DataType & element );   // returns true if element is found
63                                                  // returns false if element is not found
64                                                  // if found, found element becomes current
65                                                  // position in list; if not found, there is
66                                                  // no current position
67       bool retrieve( DataType & element );      // like find, except returns found element
68       bool remove( DataType & element );        // returns true if element is found
69                                                  // returns false if element is not found
```

```
70                                              // if found, element is set to found element;
71                                              // no current position after use
72        bool replace( const DataType & newElement ); // replaces element at current position
73                                              // in list with newElement; returns false if
74                                              // there is no current position (no list
75                                              // modification occurs); returns true otherwise
76        bool isEmpty( ) const;                // returns true if linked list is empty
77                                              // returns false otherwise; current position
78                                              // unchanged
79        void makeEmpty( );                    // no current position
80   private:
81        DLHashTable<DataType> table;
82        Node<DataType> *current;              // points to node at current position
83        Node<DataType> headerNode;
84        Node<DataType> trailerNode;
85        Node<DataType> *header;               // points to headerNode
86        Node<DataType> *trailer;              // points to trailerNode
87        inline void deepCopy( const DoublyLinkedList<DataType> & original );
88   };
89
90   #include "DoublyLinkedList.cpp"
```

In the private section, we have a DLHashTable on line 81. There is also a current pointer defined on line 82, similar to the current pointer of the LinkedList class. The Node type shown on line 82 is declared in the CollisionList class and comes along for the ride, by the inclusion of "DLHashTable.h" on line 3. The empty header and trailer nodes are declared on lines 83–84. These nodes will come in handy in the implementation, because we won't need to consider removing the first or last nodes from the doubly linked list as special cases. The header pointer on line 85 will point to the headerNode, while the trailer pointer on line 86 will point to the trailerNode. The header and trailer pointers do not need to be in the implementation, but without them, to access the first node in the doubly linked list, we would have to use the notation "headerNode.next", instead of "headerNode->next", which might be confusing to some. In this implementation, we will be using "header->next". When there is no current position, the current pointer will be set to the address of the trailerNode, which will make the implementation slightly easier. (For one thing, we won't have to worry about accessing a NULL current pointer.)

The functions of the DoublyLinkedList class are almost the same as those of the LinkedList class, but there are some exceptions. We have the addition of the last and getPrevious functions, which are the counterparts of the first and getNext functions. The DoublyLinkedList constructor must pass in both the address of a hash function and the size to be used for the hash table, and it is possible that the client's hash function is not designed correctly and will return an invalid index. The consequences of using the DoublyLinkedList class functions in that situation are described in the comments on lines 20–23.

11.7.3 The Implementation File for the DoublyLinkedList Class

The constructor of the DoublyLinkedList class template is shown first:

```
1   // DoublyLinkedList.cpp - - function definitions for the linked list data structure
2
3   template <class DataType>
4   DoublyLinkedList<DataType>::DoublyLinkedList(int (*hf)(const DataType &), int s )
5   : table( hf, s ), header( &headerNode ), trailer( &trailerNode )
6   {
7       current = header->dlnext = trailer;
8       trailer->dlback = header;
9   }
```

The parameters of the constructor on line 4 are passed directly into the DLHashTable constructor in the initializer list on line 5. The intializer list also sets the header to point to the headerNode and the trailer to point to the trailerNode. The header and trailer nodes are linked together on lines 7 and 8. The current pointer is set to trailer on line 7 to indicate that there is no current position.

The copy constructor is shown next:

```
10   template <class DataType>
11   DoublyLinkedList<DataType>::
12       DoublyLinkedList( const DoublyLinkedList<DataType> & aplist )
13   : table( aplist.table.gethashfunc( ), aplist.table.getsize( ) )
14   {
15       deepCopy( aplist );
16   }
```

The copy constructor is really just a special constructor. We therefore need an initializer list on line 13 to initialize the DLHashTable. We use our new functions gethashfunc and getsize, from aplist.table, to pass in the hash function and the size of the table.

The destructor and overloaded assignment operator functions look the same as in other data structures:

```
17   template <class DataType>
18   DoublyLinkedList<DataType>::~DoublyLinkedList( )
19   {
20       makeEmpty( );
21   }
22
23   template <class DataType>
24   DoublyLinkedList<DataType> & DoublyLinkedList<DataType>::
25       operator =( const DoublyLinkedList<DataType> & rlist )
26   {
27       if ( this == &rlist )
```

```
28            return *this;
29        makeEmpty( );
30        deepCopy( rlist );
31        return *this;
32  }
```

The insert function is shown next:

```
33  // inserts at the beginning of the linked list
34  // no current position after use
35  template <class DataType>
36  bool DoublyLinkedList<DataType>::insert( const DataType & element )
37  {
38      if ( !table.insert( element ) )
39              return false;
40
41      current = table.getcurrent( );
42      current->dlnext = header->dlnext;
43      current->dlback = header;
44      header->dlnext = header->dlnext->dlback = current;
45      current = trailer;
46
47      return true;
48  }
```

We first insert the element into the hash table on line 38. If the insert function returns false because of a faulty hash function from the client, we don't want to do anything else but return false on line 39.

We will insert the new node at the head of the doubly linked list, which really means that we insert it after the headerNode at the beginning. The insert function of the CollisionList now causes the current position of the collision list to be saved as the inserted node, so we make use of that property and get the address of the inserted node, assigning it to current on line 41. Using the node layout in Figure 11.6, we show the operation of lines 42–44 in Figure 11.7. There is no current position after this insertion (from the client's perspective), so current is set to trailer on line 45.

The first function is as follows:

```
49  // returns first element of list in listEl and current position is set to this element;
50  // if list is empty, returns false and there is no current position;
51  // otherwise, returns true
52  template <class DataType>
53  bool DoublyLinkedList<DataType>::first( DataType & listEl )
54  {
55      if ( header->dlnext == trailer )
56              return false;
57
```

FIGURE 11.6

The convention we will use for the components of the Node struct in the DoublyLinkedList.

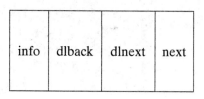

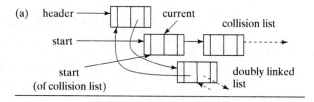

(a)

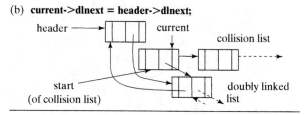

(b) **current->dlnext = header->dlnext;**

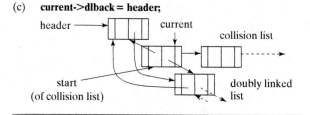

(c) **current->dlback = header;**

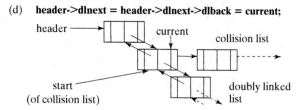

FIGURE 11.7

How a node is inserted. In part (a), the node has been inserted at the head of the collision list, but has not yet been inserted in the doubly linked list. In part (d), the second assignment is done before the first one.

(d) **header->dlnext = header->dlnext->dlback = current;**

```
58      current = header->dlnext;
59      listEl = current->info;
60      return true;
61  }
```

If the doubly linked list is empty (line 55), then we return false. Otherwise, we start with the first node after the header, on line 58. The parameter listEl (passed by reference) gets the info at this position on line 59, and then true is returned on line 60.

The getNext function is now shown:

```
62   // retrieves the next element of a linked list beyond the last element that was retrieved
63   // by first, getNext, or getPrevious functions and returns it in listEl;
64   // current position is set to this element.
65   // if no element exists at this position, getNext returns false and there is no
66   // current position; returns true otherwise
67   template <class DataType>
68   inline bool DoublyLinkedList<DataType>::getNext( DataType & listEl )
69   {
70       if ( current->dlnext == trailer )
71               current = trailer;
72       if ( current == trailer )
73               return false;
74
75       current = current->dlnext;
76       listEl = current->info;
77       return true;
78   }
```

We stop advancing current when current->dlnext is trailer, checked on line 70. In this case, there is no current position anymore, so current is set to trailer on line 71. There are two reasons the condition on line 72 can be true: (1) It was set that way on line 71, or (2) the client misused the getNext function (before calling the first function or some other function that sets a current position), and there is no current position. In either case, we want to return false on line 73.

The current position is advanced on line 75. We know that there is an element there: otherwise, we would have returned from the getNext function. The parameter listEl is assigned the element there on line 76, and then true is returned on line 77.

The last and getPrevious functions are opposite in nature to the first and getNext functions, but are written similarly:

```
79   // returns last element of list in listEl and current position is set to this element;
80   // if list is empty, returns false and there is no current position;
81   // otherwise, returns true
82   template <class DataType>
83   bool DoublyLinkedList<DataType>::last( DataType & listEl )
84   {
85       if ( header->dlnext == trailer )
86               return false;
87
88       current = trailer->dlback;
89       listEl = current->info;
90       return true;
91   }
```

```
92
93
94    // retrieves the previous element of a linked list before the last element that was
95    // retrieved by last, getNext or getPrevious functions and returns it in listEl;
96    // current position is set to this element.
97    // if no element exists at this position, getPrevious returns false and there is no
98    // current position; returns true otherwise
99    template <class DataType>
100   inline bool DoublyLinkedList<DataType>::getPrevious( DataType & listEl )
101   {
102       if ( current->dlback == header )
103             current = trailer;
104       if ( current == trailer )
105             return false;
106
107       current = current->dlback;
108       listEl = current->info;
109       return true;
110   }
```

Next, we'll examine the find function:

```
111   // returns true if element is found; returns false if element is not found
112   // if found, found element becomes current position in list;
113   // if not found, there is no current position
114   template <class DataType>
115   bool DoublyLinkedList<DataType>::find( const DataType & element )
116   {
117       DataType el = element;
118       if ( table.retrieve( el ) ) {
119             current = table.getcurrent( );
120             return true;
121       }
122
123       current = trailer;
124       return false;
125   }
```

We need to call the retrieve function of the hash table on line 118, but we can't change element on line 115, because find is not supposed to retrieve. Therefore, we create a DataType el to retrieve on line 117. (An exercise will ask you to write a find function for DLHashTable, eliminating element copying.) If the retrieval is successful, the current location is set to the node on line 119 and true is returned. Otherwise, the current location is set to trailer on line 123, because there is no current position if the element is not found. In this case, false is returned on line 124.

The retrieve function is as follows:

```
126  // returns true if element is found; returns false if element is not found
127  // if found, found element becomes current position in list;
128  // if not found, there is no current position
129  template <class DataType>
130  bool DoublyLinkedList<DataType>::retrieve( DataType & element )
131  {
132     if ( !find( element ) )
133            return false;
134
135     element = current->info;
136     return true;
137  }
```

We make use of the find function on line 132. If the element is not found, false is returned on line 133. Otherwise, the current pointer points to it, and we set element (passed in by reference) to the info at the current pointer in line 135. This is successful, so true is returned on line 136.

Next, the remove function is shown:

```
138  // returns true if element is found; returns false if element is not found
139  // if found, element is set to found element;
140  // no current position after use
141  template <class DataType>
142  bool DoublyLinkedList<DataType>::remove( DataType & element )
143  {
144     if ( !retrieve( element ) )
145            return false;
146     current->dlback->dlnext = current->dlnext;
147     current->dlnext->dlback = current->dlback;
148     current = trailer;
149     table.remove( element );
150
151     return true;
152  }
```

The element that is to be removed will be returned to the client. So we might as well use the element parameter (passed in on line 142) in the retrieve function on line 144, so the parameter will be set correctly. The retrieve function will also perform another function, however: It will use the find function to find the element to remove and will set the current position to that element (unless it could not be found, in which case false is returned on line 145). Figure 11.8 shows how current is used to splice the node out of the doubly linked list on lines 146–147. The current pointer is set to trailer on line 148, indicating there will be no current position after the

(a)

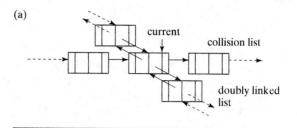

(b)   **current->dlback->dlnext = current->dlnext;**

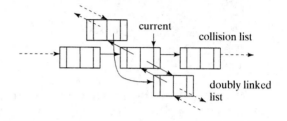

FIGURE 11.8

How the current node is spliced out of the doubly linked list. In part (c), the current node still points to nodes in the doubly linked list in both directions. However, these are only addresses stored in the current node. Once the current node is removed from the collision list, the removal will be complete.

(c)   **current->dlnext->dlback = current->dlback;**

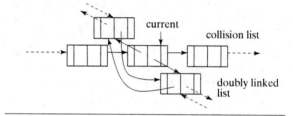

removal. Then the hash table remove function is used on line 149 to remove the element from the collision list.

Note that the insert, find, retrieve, and remove functions operate by using hash table functions in $\Theta(1)$ time. We must keep in mind, however, that this time complexity holds only under the theoretical assumption that we have uniform hashing and that the design and use of the hash table will keep the length of the collision list bounded by some small constant. Regardless of how this situation is realized in practice, we can expect that the DoublyLinkedList operations will be much faster than the LinkedList operations.

The replace function and the isEmpty function are simple and need no explanation:

```
153  // replaces element at current position in list with newElement;
154  // returns false if there is no current position (no list modification occurs);
155  // returns true otherwise
156  template <class DataType>
157  bool DoublyLinkedList<DataType>::replace( const DataType & newElement )
```

```
158 {
159    if ( current == trailer )
160            return false;
161    current->info = newElement;
162    return true;
163 }
164
165
166 template <class DataType>
167 bool DoublyLinkedList<DataType>::isEmpty( ) const
168 {
169    return header->dlnext == trailer;
170 }
```

The makeEmpty function is shown next:

```
171 template <class DataType>
172 void DoublyLinkedList<DataType>::makeEmpty( )
173 {
174    table.makeEmpty( );
175    current = header->dlnext = trailer;
176    trailer->dlback = header;
177 }
```

We just call the makeEmpty function for the hash table on line 174, freeing all the collision list nodes, but also freeing all the doubly linked list nodes (since each doubly linked node is a collision node). Lines 175–176 mimic the constructor for creating an empty list.

Finally, the deepCopy function is shown:

```
178 template <class DataType>
179 inline void DoublyLinkedList<DataType>::
180    deepCopy( const DoublyLinkedList<DataType> & original )
181 {
182    if ( original.table.getsize( ) != table.getsize( ) )
183            table.changeSize( original.table.getsize( ) );
184    table.sethashfunc( original.table.gethashfunc( ) );
185    header = &headerNode;
186    trailer = &trailerNode;
187    Node<DataType> *save = header->dlnext = trailer;
188    trailer->dlback = header;
189    Node<DataType> *originalptr = original.trailer->dlback;
190    if ( (originalptr == original.header) || !insert( originalptr->info ) )
191            return;
192    while ( originalptr->dlback != original.header ) {
```

```
193            originalptr = originalptr->dlback;
194            if ( !insert( originalptr->info ) ) {
195                    makeEmpty( );
196                    return;
197            }
198            if ( original.current == originalptr )
199                    save = header->dlnext;
200    }
201
202    current = save;
203 }
```

Lines 182–183 are used to make sure that the table Array has the same length in the copy that it has in the original. In the copy constructor, we don't need to worry about this length because of the initializer list, but it is important to include this line for the overloaded assignment operator. Line 184 ensures that we are using the same hash function as in the original. Lines 185–188 essentially start the copy as an empty doubly linked list, mimicking the constructor, except for the save pointer, which will be described shortly. Line 189 sets originalptr to point to the last node in the doubly linked list (assuming that the list is not empty). On line 190, the first condition checks to see if the original is an empty list, and if it is, we return.

The reason we want originalptr to start at the last node in the doubly linked list (not the trailer) is that we can then access the element there and use the insert function to insert it at the head of the list in the copy. The same element transfer will take place when we move the originalptr in the back direction through the doubly linked list. In this manner, we'll make an exact copy of the list, and the insert function will create a hash table similar to the hash table of the original. The first insertion takes place on line 190 and will cause a return if it fails because of a faulty hash function. The rest of the insertions take place in the while loop on line 192. If at any point we cannot insert because of a faulty hash function, the makeEmpty function is called on line 195 to free all the dynamic memory in the copy, and then we return.

There is a little issue concerning the current pointer of the original that we need to deal with. When we find the position in the list that the original current pointer has been set to (line 198), we save the corresponding position of the copy in the save pointer. Since we use the insert function, we cannot set the current position in the copy right away, because it will be lost after the next insertion. Once we are done making the deep copy, we set current to the address stored in save on line 202. If there wasn't any current position in the original, the save pointer is set to trailer on line 187, and current is set to trailer (via save) on line 202.

Although the hash table will be similar to the original hash table in functionality, will it be similar physically? Fortunately for us, every time we insert a node at the head of the doubly linked list, we do the fast thing and insert it at the head of the collision list in the hash table. This correspondence ensures that the hash table will be duplicated physically. If it weren't similar physically (just similar in functionality), it might not be a big deal except in cases of timing.

SUMMARY

This chapter has introduced hash tables, one of the fastest data structures available for searching. Hash tables can search for an element in $\Theta(1)$ time, a better time complexity than the $O(\lg n)$ time of the binary search.

In the implementation of the hash table, some important issues came up. One was that the client should make his or her own hash function. Using function pointers, the functions of the hash table can call the hash function that the client writes. Another issue was that an Array object in which each element is a LinkedList object was used. This issue demonstrates that when you write a class, your clientele extends beyond the main program, to people who write other classes.

Whenever you write a class that will have a contained object as a data member, you should look at the comments in the class for the contained object. If a client needs to know about any of these comments, the relevant ones should be copied at the top of your new class. You should always look, for example, for the use of overloaded operators in the contained class and supply comments at the top of your class, so that the client knows that he or she needs to overload these operators (if DataType is used in the contained object). This suggestion is easy to overlook, because you may not be using these operators within the functions of the container object.

A hash table implementation of a doubly linked list was also provided in this chapter. This is an important implementation, since, if we have uniform hashing, 11 of the functions called by the client in the DoublyLinkedList class execute in $\Theta(1)$ time. The only ones that execute in $\Theta(n)$ time are obvious: the copy constructor, the overloaded assignment operator, the destructor, and the makeEmpty functions (assuming that the number of table positions is less than or equal to the number of elements). Nothing can be done to get these functions to execute at a faster time complexity, unless you are a renegade and you accept memory leak and make shallow copies.

EXERCISES

1. What are hash tables used for? Why are they fast?
2. What is the input for a hash function? What is the output?
3. What is a collision? How are collisions resolved?
4. Using the hash function $h(k) = k\% 13$, show how the following keys would be inserted into the hash table with the chaining method: 24, 43, 28, 37, 4, 20, 14, 2, 15, 13. Assume that the table has 13 positions.
5. How is it possible to have a hash table that doesn't have collisions and doesn't waste memory?
6. In the HashTable implementation, how and when are the constructors for the LinkedList objects called?
7. Suppose you have about 800 key values and you would like to have an average of about 3 elements in a chain of the hash table. More importantly, however, you would like to have uniform hashing. Select a hash function using the division method, based on the guidelines in this text. What is the hash table size?

8. Suppose you are designing your own data structure and you realize that the behavior of one of the class functions should differ with the application the client is using the data structure for. Suppose that the best possible behavior of the function might differ in a multitude of ways, depending on the application. Furthermore, suppose the function doesn't access any data members in the private section. What method would you consider in writing this function?

9. Suppose that you have the same situation as in Exercise 8, but the function needs to access private data members. What method would you consider in writing this function? (*Hint*: Don't forget that the functions of a class can be used to access and change data members; consider passing the keyword *this* as a parameter, and don't forget that you can provide the client with instructions on writing the necessary parts of the function.)

10. Declare pointers to functions that meet the following descriptions:

   a. A function that returns a float and that has an int for a first parameter, a float for a second parameter, and a string for a third parameter.
   b. A function that has a void return type and no parameters.
   c. A function that returns a Car struct and has only one parameter, which is another Car struct.

11. Suppose you have a pointer called fncptr which points to a function that has one int parameter and a void return type. Suppose you also have two functions, called foo1 and foo2, both of which have void return types and one int parameter. Write a section of code that will use fncptr to call both of these functions, passing 5 into foo1 and 10 into foo2.

12. Let's consider calling the data structure in Section 11.7 a hash table. Write a class for a doubly linked list, and then use an object from your list as a data member of the HashTable class to implement this data structure. How does your implementation compare with the implementation in Section 11.7?

13. Implement a circular, doubly linked list with a hash table implementation. Don't use header and trailer nodes in the list, as those nodes were supplied only for easy removal of the first and last nodes from a *noncircular* list; the first and last nodes didn't need to be considered as special cases. In a circular list, there aren't any first and last nodes, so this is not a problem. Be careful about the way you insert nodes, so that an exact physical copy of the hash table is made in the copy constructor and overloaded assignment operator.

*14. Do Exercise 13, but have the circular, doubly linked list class inherit from the DoublyLinkedList class.

15. Implement a sorted, doubly linked list with a hash table implementation. Your insert function can be $\Theta(n)$, on average. Don't worry about duplicating the hash table exactly in the deepCopy function, as long as it is similar in functionality to the original. (The collision list should have the same elements, but the order in the collision list is not important.)

*16. Do Exercise 15, but have the sorted, doubly linked list class inherit from the DoublyLinkedList class.

17. Write a find function for DLHashTable, passing in the element (of DataType) by const reference. Then, take advantage of this find function by using it in the find function of the Doubly Linked List class. (This will eliminate the need for the el variable, and no element copying should take place.)

CHAPTER 12

Priority Queues, Trees, and Heaps

Sometimes, we would like to retrieve the maximum element or the minimum element of a data structure. If the element is an object, there might be some particular data member of the object for which we are interested in the maximum or minimum value, and we would like to retrieve the object which has that value.

A *priority queue* is a data structure that allows such a retrieval. However, a priority queue does not unconditionally allow the maximum or minimum value to be retrieved; usually, it allows only the current maximum value to be retrieved on every retrieval or only the current minimum value to be retrieved on every retrieval. Different priority queues are generally used for the maximum values and the minimum values. In this chapter, we will refer to priority queues that give only maximum values. The ones that give minimum values are similar, with slight modifications.

12.1 PRIORITY QUEUE ADT

Although the name *priority queue* implies that this structure takes the form of a queue, the queue structure is often only conceptual. That is, we can think of a priority queue as being a queue of elements, with the following typical operations on the queue:

- enqueue, an operation to add an element to the queue
- dequeue, an operation to take the largest element from the queue
- an operation to determine whether or not the queue is empty
- an operation to empty out the queue

Abstractly, we can think of the largest element as being first in line, the second-largest element next in line, and so forth. Whenever we insert a new element, it takes its proper place in the line and we say the element is enqueued. When we remove an element, we remove it from the front of the line and we say the element is dequeued. But this is just how we might view these operations abstractly; the actual implementation of a priority queue is often nothing like that.

12.2 PRIORITY QUEUE DESIGN

There are many different ways to design a priority queue. One thing that comes to mind is an array, sorted in descending order. When we try to decide which way we should design a priority queue, our decision is often governed by the speed of the operations (or functions) involved in the priority queue. We try to get that implementation which would make the functions of the priority queue the fastest. If our decision is based on the speed of the functions involved, something called a **heap** is often considered for the design. We won't be able to get a handle on what a heap is right away, but we can talk about why it is used in the design of a priority queue.

An array sorted in reverse order is great for dequeuing elements in a priority queue. We simply dequeue the element at the front of the array and set the front index to the next position of the array for the next dequeue. This is a $\Theta(1)$ operation. In a heap, each dequeue has a slightly worse time complexity of $O(\lg n)$. This makes the heap look bad, but it is more advantageous for inserting elements.

There are two ways of inserting an initial group of elements into a priority queue: (1) They can be provided all at once; then the client can enqueue additional elements one at a time, using an enqueue operation. (2) The initial group can be provided one at a time; in this case, an enqueue operation is used to enqueue them one at a time. However, the time complexities can be different for both of these methods; in other words, the time complexity of providing n elements at once for insertion into a priority queue can be different from the time complexity of enqueuing n elements one at a time. The heap, for example, can insert n elements in $\Theta(n)$ time if the elements are provided all at once. But if elements are enqueued, $O(\lg n)$ time is required for each enqueue into a heap. Therefore, enqueuing n elements would require $n \times O(\lg n)$ time, which is $O(n \lg n)$ time. This can be a worse time complexity than the $\Theta(n)$ time required to insert a group of n elements all at once.

In the implementation of a priority queue that uses a sorted array, if n elements are provided all at once, then the array has to be sorted. Sorting the array can take $\Theta(n)$ time if the conditions are right, but sometimes takes as long as $\Theta(n \lg n)$ time. It can be proven, however, that if the elements are enqueued one at a time into a sorted array, then the time complexity of enqueuing the n elements is $O(n^2)$, even though n starts off small and changes with each enqueue. This can be a worse time complexity than the $O(n \lg n)$ time required by the heap.

After the initial insertion of elements, whether as a group or one at a time, each additional enqueue into an array takes $\Theta(n)$ time, on average. This is because the element must be inserted into its proper place in an array. If we assume, on average, that this place is the middle of the array, then $\frac{1}{2}n$ elements will need to be moved to insert the element, as Figure 12.1 shows. Thus, we will need a loop with $\frac{1}{2}n$ iterations to move

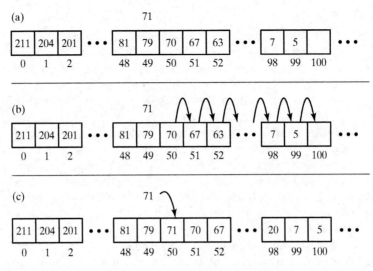

FIGURE 12.1

(a) Element 71 needs to be inserted into the middle of a sorted array with 100 elements. (b) Each element from the insertion point onward needs to be copied one position to the right, starting with the element at index 99. A loop must be used to copy the elements one at a time. Since $\frac{1}{2}n$ elements need to be copied, where $n = 100$, the loop will iterate $\frac{1}{2}n$ times, which is a $\Theta(n)$ time complexity. (c) The elements at the insertion point onward have been copied over one position to the right, and element 71 is inserted at index 50.

the elements, giving us the $\Theta(n)$ time complexity. Each enqueue into a heap, however, is guaranteed to be in $O(\lg n)$ time.

Often, when making a decision based on time complexities, we avoid a data structure with a high time complexity in a commonly used function, even if other commonly used functions have very low time complexities. This is because the lower time complexities are often absorbed into the higher one. For example, if we consider each enqueue and dequeue as a pair, then the sorted array takes $\Theta(n) + \Theta(1)$ time, on average, and the $\Theta(1)$ time complexity is absorbed into the $\Theta(n)$ time complexity, giving a $\Theta(n)$ time complexity for each enqueue–dequeue pair of operations, on average. In a heap, an enqueue–dequeue pair of operations takes $O(\lg n) + O(\lg n)$, which is a $O(\lg n)$ time complexity overall for an enqueue–dequeue pair. Thus, the heap has a better time complexity per pair of operations.

We can see, however, that an array is excellent for a priority queue when (1) the elements can be provided all at once, (2) the elements can be sorted in $\Theta(n)$ time, and (3) the only operation that needs to be done afterwards is removal (no more insertions). If we do not have these conditions, then a heap is considered.

Although a heap has an extremely fast $O(\lg n)$ operation time for both the enqueue and dequeue operations, we have to do a little work to understand what it is all about. Since a heap is a member of a class of data structures called *trees*, let's talk about trees first.

12.3 TREES

In defining exactly what a tree is, we use the word *edge* and the word *path*. An edge is a direct link between two nodes. An edge between two nodes indicates that we can *travel* from one node to get to the next node. Sometimes, this traversal can be done only in one direction and is indicated by an arrow in figures, pointing in the direction that can be traveled. We call such an edge a *directed edge*. A *path* exists between two nodes A and B if it is possible to follow edges to get from node A to node B. Figure 12.2, which is *not* a tree, shows that there is a path from node A to node B using directed edges, but no path from node C to node B. Note that there is more than one path from node D to node B.

A tree has a special node called the *root node*. There is one and only one path from the root node to any other node in the tree. Figure 12.3 shows a tree with root node A. As you can see, there is a path from node A to every other node in the tree. However, to get to another node from the root node, only one path can be followed. Another characteristic of trees is that they can have no *cycles* of three or more nodes. A cycle is a path that starts at one node, traverse edges without passing through the same node twice, and comes back to the original node. A cycle of four nodes is shown in Figure 12.4, which is not a tree.

In a tree, two nodes that are linked together have a parent–child relationship. The *parent* is the node that is closer to the root, while the *child* is further from the root. In Figure 12.3, for example, A is a parent of B, while E and F are children of D. There are many parent–child relationships in a tree, one for every link. Cycles involving only two nodes are allowed in a tree; some designs have a directed edge from the parent to the child and another directed edge from the child to the parent. Nodes that do not have any children are called *leaf* nodes, or *leaves*, for short. The root node is the only node

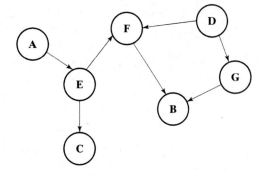

FIGURE 12.2

Different paths between nodes. Not shown are the info section and the pointer section of each node. There is one path from A to B. There is no path from C to B. There are two paths from D to B: [D, F, B] and [D, G, B].

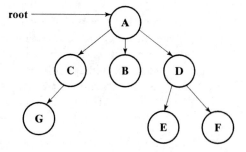

FIGURE 12.3

A tree with root node A.

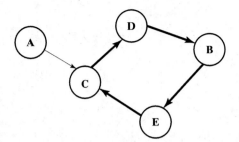

FIGURE 12.4

A cycle (links shown in bold). Node A is not part of the cycle.

that has no parent. A tree is normally drawn upside down from a biological tree, with the root at the top and the leaves at the bottom, a little oddity that prevents us from thinking of it as similar to a biological tree.

A *subtree* is a part of a tree that is, in itself, a tree. Figure 12.5 shows a subtree. We often think of a subtree as including every node that is reachable from the root of that subtree. Thus, in Figure 12.5, we wouldn't normally think of a subtree as just being nodes C, D, and E, but all of the nodes reachable from C (so that the subtree comprises nodes C, D, E, F, G, and H).

A *binary tree* is a tree in which each node can have up to two children, but no more. Figure 12.5 is not a binary tree, because node C has three children. However, Figure 12.6 is a binary tree. Each node has either two children, one child, or no child.

The *level* of a node is the number of edges in the path from the root node to that node. The root node is at level 0, while the children of the root node are at level 1, etc. Figure 12.7 shows the levels of a tree. In a *full binary tree*, every node has exactly two children, except for the last level, in which each node is a leaf. Figure 12.8 shows a full binary tree.

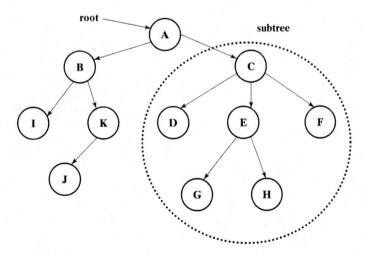

FIGURE 12.5

A tree with root node A. One of its subtrees is shown, in a dotted circle. This subtree is rooted at C.

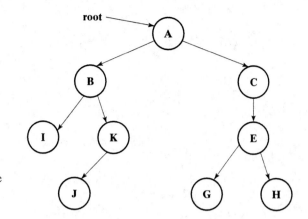

FIGURE 12.6

A binary tree with root node A. Each node has either two children, one child, or no child.

A *complete binary tree* is a binary tree that is either a full binary tree or a tree that would be a full binary tree except for the fact that it is missing the rightmost nodes of the last level. Figure 12.9 shows three examples of complete binary trees.

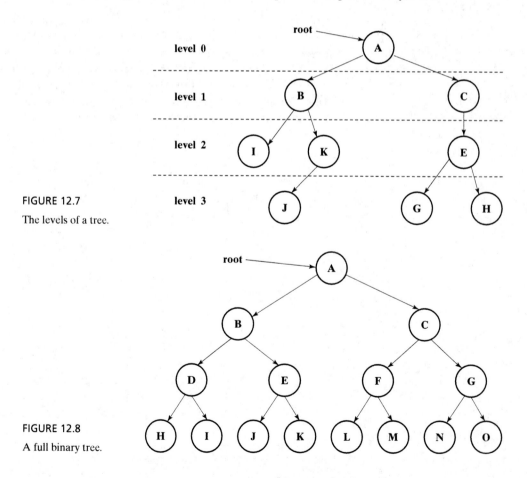

FIGURE 12.7

The levels of a tree.

FIGURE 12.8

A full binary tree.

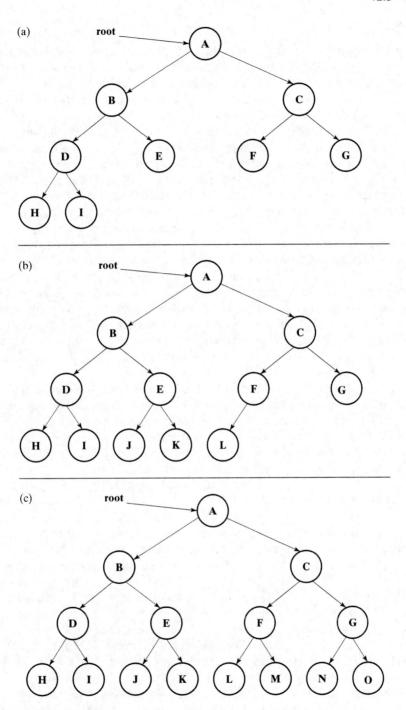

FIGURE 12.9

Three examples of complete binary trees. The last example is also a full binary tree.

12.4   HEAPS

A *heap* is a complete binary tree in which each parent has a value that is greater than or equal to each of the values of its children. Technically, this is called a *maxheap*, used for dequeuing the maximum value. In a *minheap*, each parent has a value that is less than or equal to each of the values of its children. A minheap is used for dequeuing the minimum value. When we talk about values, we may be talking about objects that contain a data member whose value we want to prioritize. For example, we may be interested in the maximum or minimum value of a key. We will limit our discussion to maxheaps in this chapter, since minheaps are easily designed once you know the design of a maxheap. Therefore, when we use the word *heap*, it will refer to a complete binary tree in which each parent has a value that is greater than or equal to each of the values of its children. A heap is shown in Figure 12.10a. (Ignore the dotted line.)

Because a heap has this ordering property in which the value of a parent is always greater than or equal to the value of its children, the greatest value in the heap is always found in the root node. Thus, the dequeue operation of a heap would appear to be a $\Theta(1)$ operation. If all we did was return this value, though, then the next time we wanted to dequeue, it would be a more expensive operation. In fact, every time we dequeued, it would be more and more expensive, until we essentially would have a $\Theta(n)$ operation. Therefore, on each dequeue, we have to remove the node that was dequeued and then spend some time turning what remains back into a heap again. Fortunately, it only takes $O(\lg n)$ time to form a new heap. Thus, a dequeue in a heap is considered to take $O(\lg n)$ time.

The formation of a new heap during the dequeue operation is done in kind of a surprising way: We take the element in the last node of the heap—that is, the rightmost node in the bottom level. We replace the root element with this element (after saving the root element, of course). Then we remove the last node of the heap. This sequence of operations is shown in Figure 12.10 for a heap of integers. The result, of course, will probably not be a heap, as it is not in Figure 12.10c. Figure 12.11 illustrates the process of forming a new heap in $O(\lg n)$ time with the result from Figure 12.10c. If the root is less than the value of one of its children, we swap the element of the root with the element of the child with the largest value. At that point, the root will be greater than or equal to each of the values of its children. The value that is now in the root was larger than the value it was swapped with, and it was the largest child, so it is larger than the other child.

At this point, however, the new value that was put in the largest child might not be greater than both of the children below *it*. So we work with this node, repeating the process. That is, we look at the greatest value of its children. If the greatest value is greater than its own value, then we swap its value with that of the largest child again. Now its value is guaranteed to be greater than or equal to each of the values of its children, for the same reasons as before. However, the new value that was put into the largest child might not be greater than the children below *it*. So now we work with this node. We stop swapping when, on the last swap, the child that was swapped with has a value that is greater than or equal to each of the values of its children. At that point, we have a new heap. Sometimes, we have to swap all the way down through the heap until we swap with a leaf. Then, at that point, we can stop and we have a heap.

This process is called *heapifying*. When we heapify, it is important that the rest of the tree be a heap, except for the root node that we are starting off with. Otherwise,

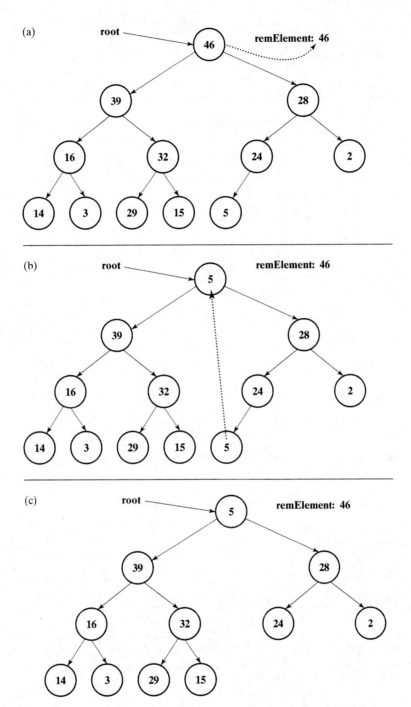

FIGURE 12.10

How an element is dequeued from a heap. (a) The element in the root node (which has the maximum value) is copied to remElement (of type DataType for templates). (b) The element of the last node of the heap is copied into the root node. (c) The last node of the heap is removed. The result is not a heap, but can be made into one in $O(\lg n)$ time.

(a)

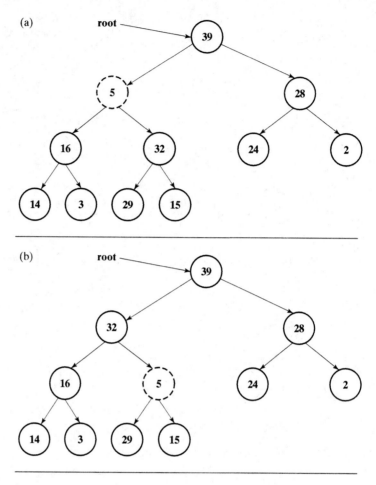

(b)

FIGURE 12.11

How a heap is formed from the diagram in Figure 12.10c. (a) In Figure 12.10c, the largest child of the root node has the value 39, which is greater than 5; therefore, the values of 39 and 5 are swapped, as shown. (b) In part (a), the largest child of the node containing 5 is now 32, which is greater than 5, so the values of 32 and 5 are swapped. (c) In part (b), the largest child of the node containing 5 is now 29, which is greater than 5, so the values of 29 and 5 are swapped. The result is a heap.

(c)

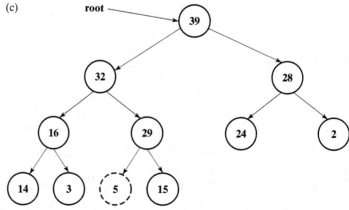

heapifying won't form a new heap. However, when we dequeue, we are starting off with a heap. When we replace the element at the root node with the element of the last node, it is probably not a heap anymore, but it will be heap *except* for the root node. It is only under this condition that heapifying is successful.

A loop is used for heapifying; we swap elements each time through the loop. The number of times the loop executes, though, is always lg n or less—hence the $O(\lg n)$ time complexity.

Recall from Section 9.4 that a loop which reduces half the problem size on each iteration executes in $\Theta(\lg n)$ time. To understand why the number of times the loop executes is lg n or less, think about starting at the root node and about how many nodes can be traveled to from the root node. We have a path to all n nodes (if we include the root). Now, suppose that we pick one of the two nodes below the root node and travel to that one. We can no longer travel to about half the nodes in the heap. Thus, the problem size has been reduced by about half. When we travel to the next node, we throw out about half the problem size that is left. Eventually, when we reach a leaf node, we can travel to only one node (the node we are on). When we swap nodes down through the heap, as we do in heapifying, we are traveling, in a sense, from the root node to a leaf node. Thus, the loop for heapifying is a $O(\lg n)$ loop (not necessarily $\Theta(\lg n)$, because we may stop before we get to a leaf).

Notice that, in a heap, the number of nodes on a level (if the level is filled with nodes) is 2^{level}. We start off with 2^0, which gives us 1 for the root node. But, for each full level, we double the number on the previous full level above it, since each node in that level above has 2 children. Thus, the number of nodes on a full level is the next power of 2 from the level above it. If the last level in the heap is level 30 and it is a full level, then that means we have $2^{30} > 1$ billion nodes on that level. Thus, the value of n, in the heap, would be far more than a billion, yet it would take us only 30 swaps to get to the last level from the root node when heapifying. But I've already talked about the wonders of the $\Theta(\lg n)$ time complexity in Section 9.4. It is the reason, however, that heaps are noted for their speed. (Actually, not just heaps, but binary trees in general, are noted for their speed.)

We've talked about the dequeue operation on a heap, but we haven't yet discussed the enqueue operation, which also takes $O(\lg n)$ time. This process is shown in Figure 12.12. When we insert a new node into a heap, what we come up with must be a heap, and fortunately, it takes only $O(\lg n)$ time to make one with the new node. We first place the new node in the last position of the heap, which probably won't make a heap unless we are very lucky. We compare the element in the last node with the element of its parent. If its parent has a smaller value, then we swap elements. Now the parent has a larger value, but it still might not work for *its* parent. (After all, the value we inserted might be the largest value in the heap.) So if *its* parent has a smaller value, we swap upwards again. We keep repeating this process until we find a parent with a value greater than or equal to that of the element we just swapped with. If we never find such a parent, we will stop when we finally swap at the root node.

Every time we swap, we guarantee that the parent will have the largest value after the swap. The reason is that it was a heap before, so the parent's element before the swap is greater than or equal to the other child's element. Since the child we are on has an even greater value than that of the parent, it will have a greater value than the

(a)

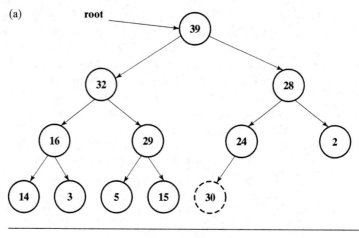

(b)

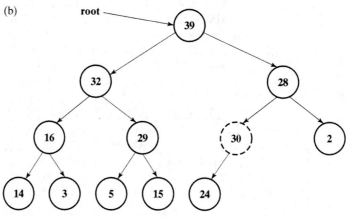

FIGURE 12.12

How a new element is enqueued into a heap, starting with the diagram in Figure 12.11c. (a) The new element is inserted into a new node placed at the last position of the heap. (b) In part (a), the new element, 30, is greater than the parent element, 24, so 30 is swapped with 24, as shown. (c) In part (b), 30 is greater than 28, so 30 and 28 have been swapped. At this point, 30 is less than the root parent element, 39, so no other swap is necessary. The result is a heap.

(c)

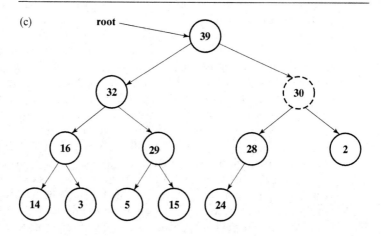

value of other child after the swap. And of course, the parent's new element will be greater than the element of the child it swapped with; otherwise we wouldn't do the swap in the first place.

We also need a loop for the enqueue operation, with a swap taking place on each iteration. The maximum number of swaps is no more than that in the heapify operation; it is just swapping in reverse. So this is also a $O(\lg n)$ loop.

In order to understand how the heap is actually implemented, we need to talk about a remarkable property of heaps. If we number the nodes of a heap, starting with 0, from top to bottom and left to right, as in Figure 12.13, the numbers in the parent–child relationships exhibit a pattern. The number of the left child of a node is always

(number of left child) = 2(number of parent) + 1

For example, in Figure 12.13, look at the node numbered 4. Using the preceding formula, we can predict that the number of its left child (if there is one) will be $(2) \times (4) + 1 = 9$, and looking at Figure 12.13, we can verify that this is true. Furthermore, the number of the right child of a node is always

(number of right child) = 2(number of parent) + 2

Also, if we have a child, we can get the number of the parent with another formula:

$$\text{(number of parent)} = \frac{\text{(number of child} - 1)}{2}$$

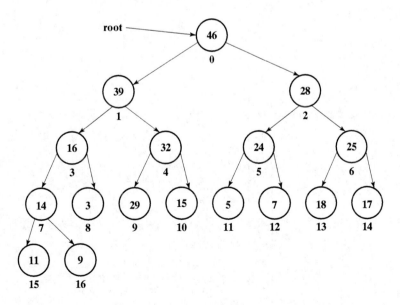

FIGURE 12.13

Numbering the nodes of a heap (numbers shown below each node).

This division is intended to give an integer result, however, so if the number of a child is 6, the number of the parent is $(6 - 1)/2 = 5/2$, which gives an integer result of 2. (The decimal portion is truncated.) When the number of a child is 5, it also gives an integer result of 2 for the number of the parent. You can verify this property by looking at Figure 12.13 again.

This wonderful property has an important ramification: It means that the *heap can be placed into an array*, with each index of the array corresponding to the number of a node. Thus, the elements in the heap of Figure 12.13 are simply placed into the array of Figure 12.14.

Now, wait a minute: If we have the heap in an array, how are we supposed to heapify? Aren't we supposed to be able to get the left child and the right child of a node, so that we can see if we need to do a swap? How are we supposed to do that with just an array? I know you can answer this question. Look at those wonderful formulas again. If I am at the node in index 6 of the array, I can get the left child of that node by the formula $(2)(6) + 1 = 13$. That is, 13 is the index of the left child. Similarly, the right child of the node at index 6 can be found at index $2 \times 6 + 2 = 14$. And the parent of the node at index 6 can be found at index $(6 - 1)/2 = 2$ (integer division). So, for any node in the array, as long as we have the index of that node, we can find its left child, its right child, and its parent.

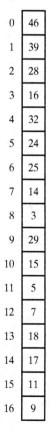

FIGURE 12.14

The heap elements in Figure 12.13 are placed into this array. The numbers shown below each node in Figure 12.13 are used as the indexes of the array. This is the array representation of the heap.

But what happens if we are heapifying and we reach a leaf node? We have the index of that leaf node, and we try to get the left child of it by using the formula, but we get a runtime error, because that place in the array for the left child doesn't exist. Well, we have to keep track of the number of nodes in the heap, storing this number in a variable called heapsize. When we enqueue, we have to increase heapsize by 1, and when we dequeue, we have to decrease heapsize by 1. If we ever find that the index of a left child is greater than the heapsize, we don't bother accessing that array position. At that point, we know we are at a leaf node and we stop. But what if the index of the left child that we come up with is equal to heapsize? Well, we're still outside of the heap, because the last index that is being used in the array is heapsize -1 (that old array trick from easier programming times).

It is worth noting that in some programming languages the array index may start at 1 instead of 0. This does not mean that heaps cannot be placed into the array with those languages. The formulas are just different and, in fact, are simpler: We just multiply the node number by 2 to get the left child and multiply by 2 and add 1 to get the right child. To get the parent, we perform integer division by 2. These simpler formulas motivate some people to just start the heap at index 1 in C++ and leave index 0 blank!

By now, you can see that if we enqueue n elements one at a time, it will take us an overall time complexity of $n \times O(\lg n) = O(n \lg n)$ to do all the enqueuing. This time complexity is provable, even considering that n starts off small. But there is a way to place the elements in the heap in $\Theta(n)$ time if the n elements are provided all at once. If the client is able to supply all n elements at once, it is wise to do so, because it will probably save time.

To explain the process of building a heap from an initial array, we just think of the array as starting off as a complete binary tree. It is not a heap initially, of course, because in each parent–child relationship, the value of the parent's element might not be greater than or equal to the value of the child's element. The heapify function is used, but it is used in a different way than we saw before. Back then, we were using it starting with the root node, but it can be used starting at *any* node. Recall that we stated that, in order for the heapify function to be successful, the tree it is working on must be a heap, *except* for possibly the root node. We can be more general now and say that, in order for the heapify function to be successful, the subtree it is working on must be a heap, except for possibly the root of that subtree. We cannot use the heapify function, therefore, if we don't have this type of subtree.

We can use the heapify function if we use it on the last parent in the tree. This node will then have one or two nodes underneath it, but the subtree won't consist of any more than three nodes. And the subtree is a heap, except for the root node of that subtree. That is, if the root node of this subtree had a high enough value, it would be a heap. Therefore, we use the heapify function on the last parent and make a small heap. We decrement the index of the parent to get the next-to-the-last parent and then use heapify on that, creating another small heap. We continue decrementing the index and calling heapify on the new index, making new heaps. When we get to an index that is a last grandparent, its children will be roots of heaps that have more than one element. That is, the subtree rooted at the last grandparent will be a heap, except for possibly the grandparent node. Thus, heapify can be called on the subtree. So, we just keep decrementing the index and calling heapify, combining the smaller heaps that were made previously. Eventually, when we get to the root node and call heapify, the whole tree will be a heap. Although this looks like a time-consuming process, most of the heaps are made at the bottom of the tree and don't take long to make. It can be proven that this whole process takes $\Theta(n)$ time, but the proof belongs in a course or textbook on algorithms. (It is beyond the scope of this text.)

We are ready to look at an implementation of a priority queue that uses a heap. Before we do, however, let's talk about some implementation issues that can make heap algorithms a little faster.

12.5   USING A ONE-ASSIGNMENT SWAP

When we use the heapify function in Section 12.4, or when we swap upwards, as we do in the enqueue function of Section 12.4, a little work is involved. For example, if we want to swap elements[i] with elements[j], the following code won't work:

```
elements[ i ] = elements[ j ];
elements[ j ] = elements[ i ];
```

In this code, the value of elements[j] is assigned to elements[i]. Thus, the value of elements[i] has been lost, and that value won't be assigned to elements[j] on the second line. Both elements[i] and elements[j] end up with the value in elements[j]. In order to do the swap, three assignments can be used, with elements[i] saved first in temp:

```
temp = elements[ i ];
elements[ i ] = elements[ j ];
elements[ j ] = temp;
```

The heapify operation and the algorithm to swap upwards can be written to execute faster if we realize that we don't need to do a complete swap. Figure 12.15 shows an example for the enqueue operation, using integers as elements. The value to enqueue is saved in a variable that we will call newElement. The next node in the heap can be created, but it doesn't have to be assigned newElement. We keep comparing newElement with the parent, and if the parent is smaller, we simply overwrite the element in the child with the element of the parent, without doing any three-assignment swap. (We make just one assignment). We then compare newElement with the next parent, and if the next parent is smaller, we overwrites *its* child. Conceptually, we are doing a swap, but we don't have to write the value of newElement anywhere, because the value is saved in newElement. When we finally find the place in which newElement is to be put, it is written in, as in Figure 12.15d. The same thing can be done when we use the heapify operation.

12.6   A HEAP IMPLEMENTATION OF A PRIORITY QUEUE (ARRAY-BASED)

In the C++ heap implementation of a priority queue, we can take advantage of the shift operators and the Array class. In calculating the formulas, we are lucky, because there is a lot of multiplying and dividing by 2. Thus, we can use the shift operators for greater speed, as discussed in Section 8.2. We have

(number of left child) = 2(number of parent) + 1

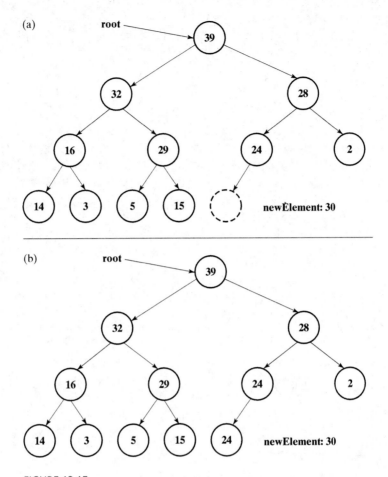

FIGURE 12.15

Enqueuing into a heap with one-assignment swaps. (a) A new node is placed into the last position of the heap, with no value written into it. The new element is saved in newElement, shown in red. (b) newElement is compared with the parent element of the new node; newElement is greater, so the parent element is assigned to the new node.

which can be written as

(number of left child) = ((number of parent) << 1) + 1

where we shift by 1 to the left in order to multiply by 2. Also, the formula for calculating the number of the right child can be simplified to

(number of right child) = (number of left child + 1)

because, in finding the greatest child, we can always calculate the number of the left child first. Finally,

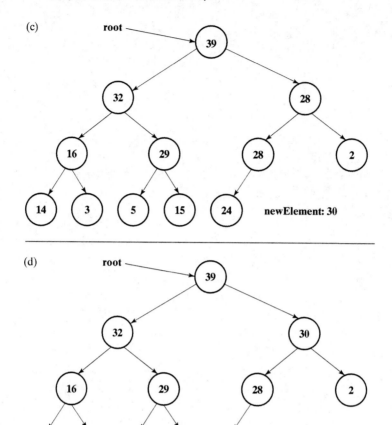

FIGURE 12.15 (*continued*)

(c) newElement is compared with 28; newElement is greater, so 28 is assigned to its left-child node. (d) newElement is compared with 39; newElement is less, so newElement's value is written into the root node's right child.

$$\frac{\text{(number of parent)} = \text{(number of child} - 1)}{2}$$

can be written as

(number of parent) = (number of child – 1) >> 1

If (number of child − 1) is an even number, the last digit in the register is 0, so shifting to the right by 1 divides the result evenly by 2. If (number of child − 1) is an odd number, however, there is a 1 in the last digit of the register, and that 1 becomes shifted out. This is essentially the same thing as truncating the .5 in integer division. The reason is that the 2^0 position (the last position in the register) would become 0.5 (which is 2^{-1}) when it is shifted to the right if it wern't lost. Therefore, the expression (number of child − 1) >> 1 has the same effect as the integer division that we need in the formula.

The Array class contains capabilities for expanding and contracting the array, as needed for memory conservation. We may need to double the size of the array if it becomes full after a number of elements are enqueued. We should cut the size of the array in half if only 25% of the array is being utilized. Doubling the size of the array will take place in the enqueue function, if necessary, while cutting the size of the array in half might take place after dequeuing. Every time we expand or contract the array, it takes $\Theta(n)$ time, since n elements are copied from the old dynamic array to the new one. However, as was proven in Section 9.8, this doesn't happen often enough to affect the time complexity of the enqueue and dequeue operations, *on average*. Using this strategy of expansion and contraction of the array contributes only $\Theta(1)$ time, on average, to the enqueue and dequeue functions.

The class template for the priority queue using the heap implementation is as follows:

```
1   // PriorityQueue.h - -  a heap (array) implementation of a priority queue
2
3   #include "Array.h"
4
5   // if a struct is used as DataType
6   //            operator > must be overloaded for comparing two elements of DataType
7   // if a PriorityQueue is constructed passing in an Array object, the length function of the
8   //            Array object must return exactly the number of elements to be put in the heap
9   //            (use the changeSize function if necessary)
10  // The constructors, the enqueue function, the (default) copy constructor, and
11  // the (default) assignment can cause an exception to be thrown if out of heap memory
12
13  template <class DataType>
14  class PriorityQueue
15  {
16  public:
17      PriorityQueue( );
18      PriorityQueue( const Array<DataType> & arr );
19      void enqueue( const DataType & newElement );
20      bool dequeue( DataType & remElement );    // returns false if heap is empty
21                                                // otherwise returns true; use isEmpty before
22                                                // use if necessary
23      bool isEmpty( ) const;
24      void makeEmpty( );
25  private:
26      Array<DataType> elements;
27      int heapsize;
28      inline void heapify( int i );    // assumes the subtree rooted at i is a heap, except for
29                                       // node i; turns this subtree into a heap
30  };
31
32  #include "PriorityQueue.cpp"
```

The use of the Array in the PriorityQueue class is similar to the way it was used in the array implementation of the Stack. We have a dynamic array in the Array class, but we have no pointer to dynamic memory as a data member in the PriorityQueue class. Therefore, on passing a PriorityQueue object by value, or on assignment of PriorityQueue objects, the copy constructor and the overloaded assignment operator of the Array class are called, respectively, as they were with the Stack class. Also, upon the destruction of the PriorityQueue object, there is no destructor written for it, but the destructor of the Array object will be called automatically.

The Array is declared on line 26. The compiler makes an Array class out of the Array template, after it starts making a PriorityQueue class out of the PriorityQueue template. This is the time when DataType changes to the type chosen by the client in the declaration of the PriorityQueue object. A heapsize variable is provided on line 27 for keeping count of the number of elements in the heap. Thus, in heapifying, if the index of the left child is greater than or equal to heapsize, we have a leaf node.

Two constructors are provided on lines 17–18. The one that gets called depends on the declaration. If a PriorityQueue object is declared without passing parameters, the constructor on line 17 is used. In this case, all elements will have to be enqueued one at a time. The second constructor is used if an Array object is passed as a parameter. The client is forced to pass an Array object instead of a regular array to help prevent run-time errors during the execution of the constructor. The Array object gives the capacity of the array by calling the length function. If a smaller, wrong capacity were to be passed in as a second parameter, the constructor will try to access elements beyond the end of the array, causing a program crash. As the comment above the class template states, the length function of the array must give the exact number of values to be inserted into the heap. If it doesn't, some values will be missing in the heap, or there will be some funny values in the heap, but neither will cause a program crash within the class functions.

There is a heapify function in the private section, which means that it can't be called by the client. Such functions are called *auxiliary functions* or *helper functions*. They are used by other class functions, but the client has no business using them. The heapify function is called a number of times by the second constructor, which constructs a heap with the use of an initial array, as we just discussed. (This is why it was inlined.) The heapify function is also called by the dequeue function. Rather than writing the same heapify code in the constructor and the dequeue function, it is best to make a separate inline function in the private section that can't be called by the client.

Next, we'll examine the class implementation file, starting with the first constructor:

```
1   // PriorityQueue.cpp - - function definitions for the heap (array) implementation of
2   // a priority queue
3
4   template <class DataType>
5   PriorityQueue<DataType>::PriorityQueue( )
6        : elements( 2 ), heapsize( 0 )
7   {
8   }
```

In this constructor, we use the initializer list on line 6 to initialize the elements data member to an Array object with two elements. Of course, the array will be doubled when it is filled, so the small size is not important. The initializer list is also used to set the heapsize to 0.

In the second constructor, we pass in an Array object:

```
9    template <class DataType>
10   PriorityQueue<DataType>::PriorityQueue( const Array<DataType> & arr )
11       : elements( arr ), heapsize( arr.length( ) )
12   {
13       for ( int i = ( heapsize - 2 ) >> 1; i >= 0; i- - )
14               heapify( i );
15
16       // change elements capacity to the next power of 2, for use in dequeue function
17       int tryPower = 2;
18       for ( ; tryPower < elements.length( ); tryPower <<= 1 );
19
20       if ( tryPower != elements.length( ) )
21               elements.changeSize( tryPower );
22   }
```

In the initializer list on line 11, the elements data member is initialized to the Array object passed in as parameter arr. (This would be done with the copy constructor of the Array class, not the constructor.) The heapsize is set to the length of the arr object in the initializer list.

Lines 13–14 convert the array into a heap. In this for loop, we start off by setting index i to the index of the last parent in the array. Since heapsize gives the number of elements in the array, heapsize − 1 will be the index of the last node in the array. We then use the formula for finding the parent, namely,

((heapsize – 1) – 1) / 2

to find the index of the last parent. (After all, the last parent will be the parent of the last node.) The preceding formula is simplified to

(heapsize – 2) >> 1

This formula produces the same thing as integer division by 2, as discussed earlier. So i starts at this value, and heapify is called on line 14. The index i is decremented on line 13, calling heapify each time. When i becomes 0, it is the root node. Therefore, the for loop terminates at i = −1.

Lines 16–21 change the size of the array to the smallest power of 2 that is greater than or equal to the current size. The for loop heading is followed by a semicolon, so it doesn't have a body. Each time through the loop, tryPower is multiplied by 2 and the result in tryPower is saved with the use of operator ≪=. Therefore, each time through the loop, tryPower becomes the next power of 2. Eventually, tryPower will become greater than or equal to the length of the elements array. Then the for loop stops, and the capacity of this array is changed on line 21 if tryPower is not equal to the current capacity.

The capacity of the array was changed to keep it at a power of 2. This may not have been necessary, but whenever maintenance becomes necessary, it helps to know that there are rules which are consistently followed, such as that the capacity is always a power of 2. Consistency greatly aids in maintenance. Inconsistency can cause confusion and hinder maintenance.

The enqueue function is shown next:

```
23  template <class DataType>
24  void PriorityQueue<DataType>::enqueue( const DataType & newElement )
25  {
26      if ( heapsize == elements.length( ) )
27              elements.changeSize( elements.length( ) << 1 );
28
29      // reheap upwards from the bottom
30      int i = heapsize;
31      for ( ; (i != 0) && newElement > elements[ (i - 1) >> 1 ]; i = ( i - 1 ) >> 1 )
32              elements[ i ] = elements[ ( i - 1 ) >> 1 ];
33
34      elements[ i ] = newElement;
35      heapsize++;
36  }
```

The enqueue function passes in newElement, to be enqueued. On line 26, if the number of elements in the heap is equal to the capacity of the array, then the array is full and we need to double the capacity. The expression elements.length( ) $\ll$ 1 multiplies the current capacity by 2 and passes the result into the changeSize function.

We then conceptually place newElement in the next position of the array, although we don't actually do it in the code. Lines 30–32 swap upwards, but use only one assignment per swap, as was discussed earlier. Index i conceptually holds the value of newElement, so it is initialized to heapsize (before heapsize is incremented). The for loop condition checks that i is not 0 (if it is already, it is the first element enqueued). Since the expression $(i - 1) \gg 1$ gives the index of the parent, we are comparing newElement with the value stored in the parent. If newElement is greater, we need to swap upwards. On line 32, the value of the parent of index i overwrites the value at index i, using only one assignment. Then, in the last section of the for loop, index i becomes the index of its parent. The condition of the for loop is checked again and the process repeats. We stop when either i becomes the index of the root (i == 0) or the parent is the greater of the two values being compared. In either case, we have found the place in the array to insert newElement. The insertion is performed on line 34, and heapsize is finally incremented on line 35.

If DataType is an object of a struct (and not just an integer, as we often imagine), then the operator > will need to be overloaded within the struct so that line 31 will not give an error in the condition. The client is free to pick out which data member should be compared. For example, if an Employee struct is used for DataType, the client might want to dequeue the object with the largest salary and then write the overloaded operator > for the salary. If the client wants to dequeue the employee with the greatest age, the client can write the overloaded operator > for the age. The fact that the operator > will need to be written for a struct was pointed out in the comments above the class template.

The dequeue function is shown next:

```
37  // returns false if trying to dequeue from an empty heap; otherwise returns true
38  template <class DataType>
39  bool PriorityQueue<DataType>::dequeue( DataType & remElement )
40  {
41      if ( !heapsize )
42          return false;
43      remElement = elements[ 0 ];
44      heapsize- - ;
45      elements[ 0 ] = elements[ heapsize ];
46      heapify( 0 );
47
48      // try to get the lowest power of 2 which is at least 2 and at least twice the
49      // size of the used portion of the array; use this for the new capacity to conserve
50      // memory
51      int trysize = elements.length( );
52      while ( ( heapsize <= trysize >> 2 ) && trysize > 2 )
53              trysize >>= 1;
54
55      if ( trysize < elements.length( ) ) {
56              try {
57                      elements.changeSize( trysize );
58              }
59              catch ( ... ) { }
60      }
61
62      return true;
63  }
```

If heapsize is 0, !heapsize will be false on line 41, because the client is trying to dequeue from an empty queue. Therefore, false is returned on line 42.

The parameter remElement, passed in by reference, is assigned the largest element in the heap (which is the root node, elements[0]) on line 43. Then, heapsize is decremented on line 44. It needs to be decremented because an element is being dequeued, but it is decremented here so that the last node in the heap can be accessed with heapsize on line 45. The root node is assigned this element on line 45, and then heapify is called, starting with the root node 0, on line 46.

Lines 48–60 try to reduce the capacity of the array if the number of elements in the heap has fallen to 25% or less than capacity. Recall that, in the array implementation of the Stack class, these same lines appeared in the pop function. In fact, I had actually copied them from the Stack class and then changed the expression top + 1 (which gave the number of elements in the stack) to heapsize (which gives the number of elements in the heap). The same code works as it did in the Stack class (see Section 8.2 for a refresher on how the code works in the pop function) and can work in any class that uses the same strategy of array expansion and contraction. Experienced programmers are always looking for code that they can copy and paste, knowing that it will save time. Finally, true is returned on line 62, indicating a successful dequeue.

The isEmpty function is not a great source of bewilderment:

```
64   template <class DataType>
65   bool PriorityQueue<DataType>::isEmpty( ) const
66   {
67       return !heapsize;
68   }
```

The makeEmpty function is as follows:

```
69   template <class DataType>
70   void PriorityQueue<DataType>::makeEmpty( )
71   {
72       heapsize = 0;
73       try {
74               elements.changeSize( 2 );
75       }
76       catch( ... ) { }
77   }
```

In this function, heapsize is set to 0 on line 72, and this is really enough to make an empty heap. The array positions will be overwritten during enqueuing. However, we also desire to conserve memory, so we try to change the array capacity to 2 on line 74. If we are unsuccessful because of a lack of heap memory in forming the new, smaller array, we still desire to continue unscathed; therefore, we catch the exception that would be thrown on line 76 and do nothing with it.

The heapify function, called from the second constructor and the dequeue function, is shown next:

```
78   // assumes that the subtree rooted at i is a heap except for node i;
79   // turns this subtree into a heap
80   template <class DataType>
81   inline void PriorityQueue<DataType>::heapify( int i )
82   {
83       int leftChild, rightChild, largest;
84       bool stop = false;
85
86       DataType temp = elements[ i ];
87
88       leftChild = (i << 1) + 1;
89       while ( leftChild < heapsize && !stop ) {
90           rightChild = leftChild + 1;
91           largest = ( rightChild == heapsize )? leftChild :
92                   (( elements[ leftChild ] > elements[ rightChild ] )? leftChild : rightChild );
```

```
93              if ( elements[ largest ] > temp ) {
94                      elements[ i ] = elements[ largest ];
95                      i = largest;
96                      leftChild = (i << 1) + 1;
97                      }
98              else
99                      stop = true;
100             }
101
102   elements[ i ] = temp;
103 }
```

Recall that heapify is an auxiliary function in the private section and hence can't be called by the client. We declare a leftChild index, a rightChild index, and a largest index on line 83. The largest index is to be set to the larger of the leftChild and rightChild indexes of a node. We also have a stop variable, set to false, that will be used to help stop the while loop at the right time.

The value of node i is not saved to any variable, like the value of newElement in the enqueue function. Therefore, it can be overwritten when we perform our one-assignment swap, and it must be saved. Line 86 saves elements[i] to temp, so that one-assignment swaps can be performed.

We get the index of the left child of i by using the expression on line 88. In the while loop, we check to make sure that the index of the left child is less than heapsize. (If it isn't, we are already at a leaf node.) The index of the right child can be found just by adding 1 to the left child, saving computation time, as on line 90.

Lines 91–92 are really just one statement that finds the larger element at the left-Child and rightChild indexes and assigns the index of the larger element to largest. This statement uses a ternary operator nested within another ternary operator. The outer ternary operator is the one with the first condition, rightChild == heapsize. If this condition is true, it represents an unusual case. The left child is the last node in the heap. When 1 was added to it on line 90 to get the right child, we are outside of the heap. If the condition expressed in the outer ternary operator is true, then the left child is the largest, as shown in the second section of this ternary operator. If the right child is within the heap, we use another ternary operator in the false section of the first one to determine which of the children is greater. The value at the left-child index is compared with the value at the right-child index. If the value of leftChild is greater, it is returned as the result of the nested ternary operator and is assigned to largest. Otherwise, rightChild is assigned to largest. The operator > on line 92 is an overloaded operator if a struct is used for DataType. We are careful to use the overloaded operator > again, as we did in the enqueue function. If we reversed the condition on this line to read elements[rightChild] < elements[leftChild], the client would have to overload two operators instead of one in order to use a struct for DataType.

On line 93, we compare the value of the largest child with temp, the value that we eventually must insert into the heap in the proper position (just as newElement was eventually inserted in the enqueue function). We are careful to use the overloaded operator > again.

If the value at the largest child is greater than temp (the parent, conceptually), then the value of the parent is overwritten with the value of the child on line 94. The variable i needs to be changed to the child that was the largest, for the next time when this might happen, so i is set to largest on line 95. Then, on line 96, the index of the left child of the new i is found, after which use repeat the process.

There are two ways that this loop can stop. If the largest child is not larger than temp (the parent, conceptually), then we should stop. In this case, the condition on line 93 will be false, and stop is set to true on line 99. The while loop condition is thereby rendered false, and the while loop is exited. The other way we should stop is when the index of the left child is found and it is greater than the last index of the heap. If that is the case, we have reached a leaf node and should stop. In either case, we have found the right position of the heap to place the value stored in temp. On line 102, we overwrite the value at elements[i] with temp, and we are done heapifying.

A linked version of a priority queue is discussed in the next two (optional) sections for those who would like to drink deeply from the pointer waters.

*12.7 THE DESIGN OF A LINKED (EMBEDDED) HEAP

Let's consider designing a linked heap. We want it to have the same time complexities for all operations as did the array-based heap in the previous section. Moreover, there should not be any significant difference in speed between the two. Essentially, we want the linked heap to mimic the array-based heap.

In order to perform a dequeue in the linked heap, we need

- left and right pointers in a node, so that we can get the children for swapping
- a pointer to the last node in the heap, which needs to be maintained (updated) in $\Theta(1)$ time

In order to perform an enqueue that mimics the array-based heap, we can use

- a parent pointer in a node, for swapping upwards if necessary
- a $\Theta(1)$ method of finding the place to put the initial node

The dequeue and enqueue $\Theta(1)$ requirements can be met by realizing that, in the array-based heap, we are really working only with the end of the array. Therefore, we can use a linked list instead of an array and just work with the end of the linked list. We can use a "next" pointer in each node, to point to the next node in the linked list.

Figure 12.16 illustrates the idea. Figure 12.16a shows the edges that are used in the parent–child relationships. They are not directed edges, because there is a pointer from child to parent and a pointer from parent to child. Figure 12.16b shows the edges that are used in the linked-list relationships. As we will see shortly, the list is doubly linked, so its edges are not directed either. Now, keep in mind that each node has all of the pointers (used for the edges) shown in Figures 12.16a and 12.16b. Figure 12.17 combines Figures 12.16a and 12.16b. Technically, we can't call the structure shown a heap anymore, because it isn't even a tree; it is loaded chock full of cycles. But we can think of a heap as being embedded in this data structure, so we'll refer to it as an "embedded heap."

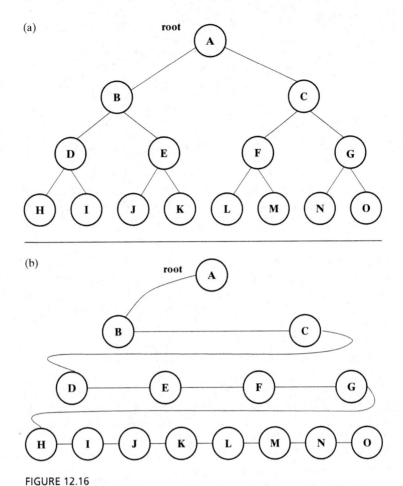

FIGURE 12.16

(a) The parent–child relationships in the linked heap. (b) The linked list that runs through the linked heap.

We'll maintain a last pointer as a private data member. Every time we enqueue, we are going to have to start with a new node as the next node in the linked list of Figure 12.16b. We then need a way to hook this node to its parent, again in $\Theta(1)$ time. The problem can be solved by maintaining another node pointer as a data member which points to the parent that the enqueued node would be attached to. By using this node pointer, we can attach two successively enqueued nodes to it, one for its left child and one for its right child. Thus, the pointer can be regarded as a "last parent" pointer — a pointer to the last parent (or parent-to-be) in the heap. For the next enqueued node, we'll just move this "last parent" pointer to the next node in the linked list. Figure 12.18 shows that it will then become the parent of the next enqueued node.

When we dequeue, we still need to maintain the last pointer in the heap in $\Theta(1)$ time. If we had a singly linked list running through the embedded heap, we might be able to find it by going through its parent, as in Figure 12.19. But what if we had the situation shown in

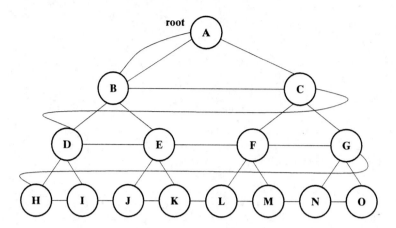

FIGURE 12.17

Figures 12.16a and 12.16b combined.

Figure 12.20? Using a doubly linked list would allow us just to use the back pointer of the last node to update the "last" pointer in a dequeue. When we dequeue a node, we'll have to make sure to move the "last parent" pointer back a node when appropriate, too.

Thus, the cost of having an embedded, linked heap that mimics the array-based version is having five node pointers in a priority queue node: left, right, parent, next, and back. However, if the element size is large enough, this strategy may well be worth it. (See Section 7.4.) An element size of 60 bytes would cause about 25% of the memory space to be wasted, comparing favorably with the array, which wastes 25–50% of its memory space, on average. An element size of 180 bytes would mean that only 10% of the memory space is wasted in the linked priority queue.

One would think that setting all these node pointers would make the performance of the linked priority queue significantly worse, even though the time complexities are the same. Surprisingly, this does not seem to be the case. Part of the reason is due to the array management code that does not need to be done in the linked priority queue. In the array-based heap, when we change the size of an array, an array with the new size is created, and then the elements from the old array are copied over into the new array. Section 9.8 illustrates that, on average, we just copy a couple of elements (due to array resizing) for a single enqueue or dequeue function when the whole collection of enqueue and dequeue function calls is considered. But if the element size is large, even copying a couple of elements can be far worse than just updating five addresses for a new node (or a dequeued node). Once again, large element sizes appear to benefit from linked implementations.

To make the implementation run as fast as possible, we would like to have a rapid way of determining when the "last parent" pointer should be moved to the next node in the linked list. We can achieve this aim by maintaining a data member called "left", set to one value if the next enqueued node should be the left child and a different value if it should be the right child. After each enqueue and dequeue, we need to toggle "left" between its two values. Then we can easily tell (by observing left) whether we need to move the "last parent" pointer when enqueuing or dequeuing.

To build a heap from an array in $\Theta(n)$ time, such as the second constructor of the array implementation, we can process the array as we did before, but this time, for every

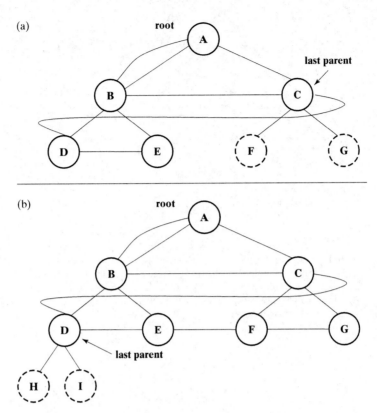

FIGURE 12.18

(a) The "last parent" pointer points to node C. Nodes F and G are dashed and show where the next two nodes will be enqueued (before swapping upwards). b) After nodes F and G have been enqueued, the "last parent" pointer moves from node C to node D, the next node in the linked list. You can see that nodes H and I will be the next to be enqueued, whereupon they will both be children of the "last parent" node. Once nodes H and I have been enqueued, the "last parent" pointer will move from node D to node E, the next node in the linked list. This node will, of course, be the parent of the next two nodes that are enqueued.

element, we'll just lay a node into the tree without swapping upwards. We can lay all of the nodes into the tree in $\Theta(n)$ time. Then, starting a current pointer off with the parent of the last node, we can call the heapify function, passing in the current pointer instead of an index. Each time through the loop, we move current back a node in the doubly linked list.

A final consideration is that, to improve performance, we would like to avoid testing for special cases. The special cases involve the root node, such as when the heap is initially empty. So we'll use an empty root node—something like a header node in a linked list; in fact, we might as well call it a "root header." We'll have the actual root come off as a child of this node, and it will be the only child of the root header node. When I started doing this, I was thinking of having the actual root start off at the left child of the root header. But it turns out that it is better to start the actual root as the

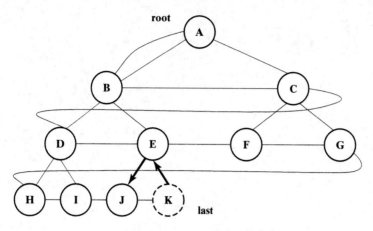

FIGURE 12.19

Node K (dashed) will take part in a dequeue operation. This node needs to be removed (after its element is copied to the root node), and the "last" pointer needs to be updated to node J. In this case, node J can be easily accessed by following the bold arrow pointers, so that the address of node J can be assigned to the "last" pointer.

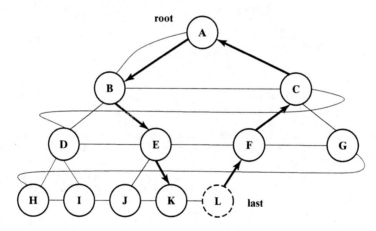

FIGURE 12.20

Node L (dashed) will take part in a dequeue operation. This node needs to be removed (after its element is copied to the root node), and the "last" pointer needs to be updated to node K In this case, node K cannot be easily accessed. One possible path for accessing it is shown by following the bold arrow pointers. However, there is now no path from node L to node K that will give a $\Theta(1)$-time access. The solution would be to turn the linked list that runs through the heap into a doubly linked list. Then node L will contain a "back" reference to node K, and node K will easily be able to be accessed in $\Theta(1)$ time.

right child of the root header. If we used the actual root as the left child, then the next enqueue would naturally take place as the right child of the root header, something we don't want. We can use special-case code to handle this, but such code is avoided by having the actual root come off as the right child of the root header.

*12.8   A LINKED (EMBEDDED) HEAP IMPLEMENTATION OF A PRIORITY QUEUE

In light of the discussion of the last section, the PQNode (Priority Queue Node) struct and the PriorityQueue class using a linked, embedded heap shouldn't contain any surprises:

```
1    // PriorityQueue.h — implementation of a priority queue with a linked (embedded) heap
2
3    #include "Array.h"
4
5    template <class DataType>
6    struct PQNode {
7        DataType info;
8        PQNode<DataType> *left;
9        PQNode<DataType> *right;
10       PQNode<DataType> *parent;
11       PQNode<DataType> *back;
12       PQNode<DataType> *next;
13   };
14
15   // if a struct is used as DataType
16   //   operator > must be overloaded for comparing two elements of DataType
17   // if a PriorityQueue is constructed passing in an Array object, the length function of the
18   //   Array object must return exactly the number of elements to be put in the heap
19   //   (use the changeSize function if necessary)
20   // The constructors, the enqueue function, the copy constructor, and the overloaded
21   // the assignment operator can cause an exception to be thrown if out of heap memory
22
23
24   template <class DataType>
25   class PriorityQueue
26   {
27   public:
28       PriorityQueue( );
29       PriorityQueue( Array<DataType> & arr );
30       PriorityQueue( const PriorityQueue<DataType> & appq );
31       ~PriorityQueue( );
32       PriorityQueue<DataType> & operator =( const PriorityQueue<DataType> & rpq );
33       void enqueue( DataType & newElement );
```

```
34     bool dequeue( DataType & deqElement );
35     bool isEmpty();
36     void makeEmpty();
37  private:
38     PQNode<DataType> rootNode;
39     PQNode<DataType> *root;
40     PQNode<DataType> *last;
41     PQNode<DataType> *lastParent;
42     bool left;
43     inline void insertNode( const DataType & inf );
44     inline void heapify( PQNode<DataType> *current );
45     inline void deepCopy( const PriorityQueue<DataType> & original );
46  };
47
48  #include "PriorityQueue.cpp"
```

There is a private insertNode function on line 43, for putting a node with inf (the parameter) into the end of the heap. This function is called from three places: the second constructor (which passes in the array), the enqueue function, and the deepCopy function.

The two constructors are shown next:

```
1   // PriorityQueue.cpp - -  function definitions for a Priority Queue implemented
2   // with a linked (embedded) heap
3
4   #include <iostream>
5
6   using namespace std;
7
8   template <class DataType>
9   PriorityQueue<DataType>::PriorityQueue( )
10  {
11      last = lastParent = root = &rootHeader;
12      root->next = NULL;
13      left = false;
14  }
15
16  template <class DataType>
17  PriorityQueue<DataType>::PriorityQueue( Array<DataType> & arr )
18  {
19    last = lastParent = root = &rootHeader;
20    left = false;
21
22    for ( int i = 0; i < arr.length( ); i++ )
23              insertNode( arr[ i ] );
24
```

```
25   for ( PQNode<DataType> *current = last->parent; current != root; current = current->back )
26      heapify( current );
27 }
```

On line 11, in the first constructor, all three node pointer data members (last, lastParent, and root) are set to point to the root header node. Thus, the heap will be empty when root is equal to last. Surprisingly, the only pointer member of rootHeader that we have to set is the root->next pointer, set to NULL on line 12. The left data member starts off at false, so we want to enqueue the first node (the actual root) to the right of lastParent (which will be the right of the root header).

The second constructor starts off the same on lines 19–20, except that we don't even need to set root->next to NULL. Lines 22–23 contain a loop that will add a node to the end of an embedded complete binary tree, on each iteration, keeping the tree complete, until all the array elements are exhausted. We don't worry about whether or not we have an embedded heap at this point; we just keep the embedded binary tree complete. This loop takes $\Theta(n)$ time.

When the for loop stops (on lines 22–23), the "last" data member will point to the last node in the embedded complete binary tree; then lines 25–26 turn the embedded complete binary tree into an embedded heap in $\Theta(n)$ time, using the same technique as in the array-based implementation. Notice that the for loop heading starts with the parent of the last node, the for loop stops when current is the header root node, and the trailer on the for loop heading moves current back one spot in the doubly linked list. The heapify function is called on line 26, passing in a node pointer instead of an index. (Recall that an index was passed in in the array-based heap.) If the heapify function could be called by the client, this would have changed the class interface—but it can't be, since it is a private function.

The copy constructor, destructor, and overloaded assignment operator shouldn't contain any surprises:

```
28 template <class DataType>
29 PriorityQueue<DataType>::PriorityQueue( const PriorityQueue<DataType> & appq )
30 {
31      deepCopy( appq );
32 }
33
34 template <class DataType>
35 PriorityQueue<DataType>::~PriorityQueue( )
36 {
37      makeEmpty( );
38 }
39
40 template <class DataType>
41 PriorityQueue<DataType> & PriorityQueue<DataType>::
42      operator =( const PriorityQueue<DataType> & rpq )
43 {
44      if ( this == &rpq )
```

```
45            return *this;
46      makeEmpty( );
47      deepCopy( rpq );
48      return *this;
49  }
```

The enqueue function is shown next:

```
50  template <class DataType>
51  void PriorityQueue<DataType>::enqueue( DataType & newElement)
52  {
53       insertNode( newElement );
54
55       // reheap upwards from the bottom
56       PQNode<DataType> *current = last, *parent = current->parent;
57       while  ( parent != root && newElement > parent->info ) {
58               current->info = parent->info;
59               current = parent;
60               parent = current->parent;
61       }
62
63       current->info = newElement;
64  }
```

Line 53 inserts the node at the end of the heap, and lines 56–63 perform the "swap-up-ward" part of the operation, in a manner similar to the way it works in the array-based implementation, except that we do not need to calculate the parent index. The one-assignment swaps are still used. The code is the same, except that where we used indexes on the elements array, we instead access the info member of the appropriate node pointer. Also, instead of setting indexes to new values, we now set node pointers to point to other nodes. The use of the overloaded operator $>$ on line 57 is the same here and in the following functions as it is in the array-based implementation.

The dequeue function is also similar in operation to the way it works in the array-based implementation:

```
65  template <class DataType>
66  bool PriorityQueue<DataType>::dequeue( DataType & deqElement )
67  {
68      if ( root == last )
69              return false;
70
71      PQNode<DataType> *current = root->right;
72      deqElement = current->info;
73      current->info = last->info;
74      if (left) {
```

```
75              lastParent = lastParent->back;
76              lastParent->right = NULL;
77      }
78      else
79              lastParent->left = NULL;
80      last = last->back;
81      delete last->next;
82      last->next = NULL;
83      left = !left;
84
85      if ( root != last )
86              heapify( current );
87
88      return true;
89 }
```

Lines 68–69 handle the empty priority queue condition. On line 71, we assign current the actual root node. This doesn't actually need to be done, but cuts down on the number of member accesses. (Otherwise root->right would have to be used instead of current on lines 72, 73, and 86). On line 72, we assign the info in the actual root to deqElement (passed in by reference). Line 73 copies the info in the last node to the actual root node.

Now we are ready to remove the last node, a procedure handled by lines 74–82. In order to eliminate the node without having dangling pointers, the child pointer to it has to be set to NULL first. On the one hand, if left is true on line 74, lastParent has no children, but was ready to assign the next enqueued node to its left child. Therefore, we have to move lastParent back one node on line 75, so that its right pointer points to the last node. On line 76, the pointer to the last node is broken. On the other hand, if left is false, lastParent has a left child, but no right child, so the left pointer is broken on line 79. To free the node, on line 80 we move "last" back one node (where it will need to be anyway) and then finally free the node on line 81. Line 82 sets last->next to NULL, signifying the new end of the list.

Finally, we need to toggle the truth value of the bool "left" data member on line 83. (In the enqueue function, this is handled by the insertNode function call.) If the priority queue is not empty at this point (line 85), we heapify at the actual root (line 86).

The isEmpty function is, again, refreshingly simple:

```
90  template <class DataType>
91  bool PriorityQueue<DataType>::isEmpty()
92  {
93      return root == last;
94  }
```

The makeEmpty function is quite short as well:

```
95  template <class DataType>
96  void PriorityQueue<DataType>::makeEmpty()
```

```
97   {
98       while ( root != last ) {
99                lastParent = last->back;
100               delete last;
101               last = lastParent;
102      }
103
104      root->next = NULL;
105      left = false;
106  }
```

We execute a loop that starts at the end of the doubly linked list; the loop uses last-Parent to mark the node before the last node on line 99, frees the node on line 100, and then sets "last" to the new last node on line 101. At the end of the loop, root, last, and lastParent will all point to the root header. The "last" pointer does, or the loop wouldn't have ended, and since the "last" pointer does, the lastParent pointer does by virtue of line 101. Lines 104–105 mimic the constructor for creating an empty priority queue.

The final three functions are all private functions, beginning with insertNode:

```
107  template <class DataType>
108  inline void PriorityQueue<DataType>::insertNode( const DataType & inf )
109  {
110      last->next = new PQNode<DataType>();
111      last->next->back = last;
112      last = last->next;
113      last->left = last->right = last->next = NULL;
114      last->parent = lastParent;
115      if (left)
116              lastParent->left = last;
117      else {
118              lastParent->right = last;
119              lastParent = lastParent->next;
120      }
121      last->info = inf;
122      left = !left;
123  }
```

On line 110, the node is created and pointed to by the "next" member of the "last" node. Then we need to move "last" to the new last node, as on line 112, but before we do, on line 111 we set the "back" pointer member of the new last node to point to the node that "last" is currently on. (Once we move "last", we won't have a pointer to the node to set the "back" pointer of the new last node.) On line 113, we set the appropriate pointers to NULL in the last node. Then the only pointers left to set are the parent–child relationships between last and lastParent. The parent relationship is set on line 114. The child relationship depends on whether the new last node is the left child or right child, as we discussed earlier. The "left" bool data member is tested on line 115 to see if we should set the left or right child relationship of lastParent. If left is true, we set the left relationship on line 116. If left is false, we set the right relationship on line 118 and then move lastParent to the next node in the linked list on line 119. On line 121, inf (passed in by reference) is assigned as the element of the last node. Finally, line 122 toggles "left" to its opposite truth value for the next operation.

The next function is the heapify function:

```
124  // assumes that the subtree rooted at current is a heap except for current;
125  // turns this subtree into a heap
126  template <class DataType>
127  inline void PriorityQueue<DataType>::heapify( PQNode<DataType> *current )
128  {
129      DataType temp = current->info;
130
131      PQNode<DataType> *leftc = current->left, *rightc = current->right, *largest;
132      largest = (rightc == NULL)? leftc : ((leftc->info > rightc->info)? leftc : rightc );
133      while ( (leftc != NULL) && largest->info > temp ) {
134              current->info = largest->info;
135              current = largest;
136              leftc = current->left;
137              rightc = current->right;
138              largest = (rightc == NULL)? leftc : ((leftc->info > rightc->info)? leftc : rightc );
139      }
140
141      current->info = temp;
142  }
```

This heapify function is similar in structure to the heapify function in the array-based implementation. The differences between the two stem from the fact that node pointers are used instead of indexes. For example, a node pointer is passed into the heapify function (here), instead of passing an index into it (there). Also, instead of using an index on the elements array, we access the info section of the appropriate node, as on line 132.

In the array-based heapify function, we checked to see if we were at a leaf node by examining the left index and finding out whether it was greater than or equal to heapsize. In the heapify function set forth here, we are at a leaf node when the left child pointer (leftc) is NULL, which is somewhat more obvious. Other than these considerations, the two heapify functions are basically the same.

Finally, we have the deepCopy function:

```
143  template <class DataType>
144  inline void PriorityQueue<DataType>::
145      deepCopy( const PriorityQueue<DataType> & original )
146  {
```

```
147      last = lastParent = root = &rootHeader;
148      root->next = NULL;
149      left = false;
150
151      PQNode<DataType> *originalptr = original.root->next;
152      for ( ; originalptr != NULL; originalptr = originalptr->next )
153           insertNode( originalptr->info );
154 }
```

Lines 147–149 mimic the first constructor for creating an empty priority queue. Line 148 is necessary because the original might be an empty priority queue as well. We use originalptr on line 151 to march through the doubly linked list of the original, starting with the actual root node. Then the for loop on lines 152-153 place the info in each node of the original into the copy. The pointer originalptr moves through the doubly linked list (the trailer in the for loop heading) until it becomes NULL.

SUMMARY

This chapter introduced priority queues, trees, and heaps. Heaps are often considered for the implementation of priority queues when speed is an issue. Heaps have very fast enqueuing and dequeuing operations, each taking $O(\lg n)$ time.

Since heaps are considered to be a form of a tree, much tree terminology was introduced. The tree terminology is important, since quite a few data structures are trees (many of them rather advanced).

Remarkable formulas were introduced in this chapter that enable us to place a heap into an array. The formulas can be used to find any child or parent of an element, as long as we know the index of that element.

The chapter presented a heap implementation of a priority queue, which placed the heap into an array. We noted that, in the heap array, extra speed can be gained by using shift operators in swapping upward or downward. We've also noted that, in swapping upward or downward, it is not necessary to use three assignments on each swap. A technique was presented that uses only one assignment per conceptual swap.

We also saw a linked, embedded heap implementation of a priority queue that may be worth using for large elements. Each operation of the linked priority queue (except for the destructor and makeEmpty) had a time complexity similar to that of each operation in the array-based heap.

EXERCISES

1. When it comes to implementing priority queues, how does an array (sorted in descending order) compare with a heap?
2. When a heap is first made, why is it advantageous to provide a group of initial elements all at one time instead of enqueuing these elements one at a time?
3. Why is an enqueue–dequeue pair better for a heap than for an array sorted in descending order?
4. In a tree, is it possible for a node to have more than one parent? Why or why not?

5. Suppose we have a binary tree in which the value of each parent is greater than or equal to the value of its children. Explain why this tree might not be a heap.

6. Determine whether or not the arrays that follow are heaps. If not, explain why.

    a. [50, 29, 47, 16, 19, 46, 39, 5, 7]
    b. [46, 37, 45, 27, 5, 43, 39, 29, 6]

7. How many heaps can be made from the elements 5, 7, 9, 11, and 15?

8. Suppose an array stores a heap that has 100 elements. Find the following:

    a. the left child of index 24
    b. the right child of index 45
    c. the parent of index 37

9. Suppose a heap has 727 elements. How many levels does it have?

10. Suppose a heap has 9 levels (level 0 through level 8). How many nodes are on level 7?

11. Draw the heap that results from dequeuing three nodes from the heap in Figure 12.13.

12. Show the result of inserting the following elements, in the order shown, if the elements are enqueued one by one:

$$3, 28, 47, 23, 17, 21, 36, 25, 16, 49$$

13. Show the result of forming a heap from an array of elements in $\Theta(n)$ time when the elements have the values in Exercise 12 in the order shown.

14. Show how an element with key 43 would be enqueued into the heap of Figure 12.13, by showing how the heap looks after each "one-assignment swap."

15. Rewrite the PriorityQueue class template for the array-based heap so that it will remove the minimum element on each dequeue instead of the maximum element on each dequeue.

16. Rewrite the PriorityQueue class template for the linked (embedded) heap so that it will remove the minimum element on each dequeue instead of the maximum element on each dequeue.

17. Make a new PriorityQueue class template in which the constructor determines, on the basis of memory waste, whether an array implementation or a linked, embedded implementation of a heap should be used. Have the sizeof operator in the constructor get the number of bytes in the DataType used. Also, use the sizeof operator on a pointer type to get the number of bytes used in an address in case the size of an address changes in the future. For example, use sizeof (int*). On the basis of the number of bytes in DataType, the constructor will determine whether or not the array implementation or linked-list implementation should be used. (See Section 7.4.2.) The constructor will set a flag in the private section to indicate which implementation was selected. Every function in the PriorityQueue class will use either the array implementation or the linked-list implementation, determined by the flag that was set by the constructor. It is all right to have two heapify functions in the private section, both with the same name (as long as the parameter is different).

CHAPTER 13

Recursion

Binary search trees, a data structure discussed in Chapter 15, are often written with *recursive functions*. A recursive function is a function that calls itself. Because you will undoubtedly encounter recursion in data structures, it is important to talk about what recursion is and how it works.

13.1 A RECURSIVE FACTORIAL FUNCTION

It seems like the most popular function to begin a discussion of recursion with is the factorial function. A factorial of a positive integer is computed by multiplying all positive integers together that are less than or equal to the given positive integer. To express a factorial mathematically, we write the integer, followed by an exclamation mark. For example, 5! is 5 factorial, and the result of 5 factorial is $5 \times 4 \times 3 \times 2 \times 1 = 120$. The result of 3! is $3 \times 2 \times 1 = 6$. The factorial of 0, 0!, is defined to be 1. The factorial of a negative number is undefined.

We can write a recursive function to compute a factorial:

```
1   int factorial( int num )
2   {
3       if ( num == 0 || num == 1)
4               return 1;
5       return num * factorial( num – 1 );
6   }
```

The factorial function can also be written with a loop, of course, but its use with recursion enables one to become familiar with how recursion works.

The recursive function call is on line 5: The factorial function calls itself. As written, the factorial function produces the correct result when the parameter passed in gives a valid (defined) result. For example, for the section of code

```
int x = factorial( 4 );
cout << x << endl;
```

the value 24 which is 4!, will be printed out.

A lot of people get confused with how recursive functions work, but if you look at them the right way, they are not confusing at all. The important thing to keep in mind is that when a recursive function calls itself, what essentially happens is that another function is made, exactly like the recursive function, and that is the one called.

Let's take, for example, the function call factorial(4) in the preceding code. When this function call is made, num becomes 4 in the factorial function, as shown in Figure 13.1. The condition of the if statement is obviously false, so line 5 is executed. The function call factorial (num − 1) is then made, passing 3 into the factorial function, but at this point, *another factorial function is made*, as shown in Figure 13.2. The variable num is replaced with 3 in *this* factorial function, which is made during runtime.

The if statement is false, so the function call factorial (num − 1) is made again. At this point, *another* factorial function is made, as shown in Figure 13.3. This time, 2 is passed into the function, so num is replaced with 2. The if statement is still false, so the function call factorial (num − 1) is made again. Yet another factorial function is made, as shown in Figure 13.4. Now a 1 is passed into the factorial function, replacing num.

The if statement is *true* in *this* function, causing a 1 to be returned. The 1 replaces the function call that called *this* function, as shown in Figure 13.5. When the function call is replaced, the expression

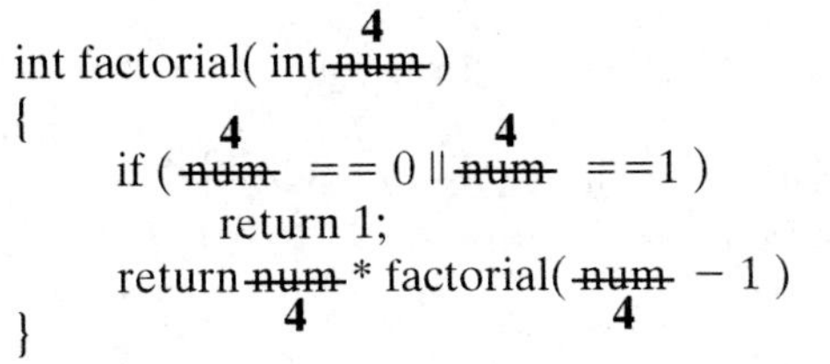

```
int factorial( int num[4] )
{
        if ( num[4] == 0 || num[4] ==1 )
            return 1;
        return num[4] * factorial( num[4] − 1 )
}
```

FIGURE 13.1

The factorial function is called by factorial(4). The variable num has been replaced by 4 throughout the function.

```
int factorial( int num[4] )
{
        if ( num[4] == 0 || num[4] == 1 )
            return 1;
        return num[4] * factorial( num[4] − 1 )
}
```

```
int factorial( int num[3] )
{
        if ( num[3] ==0 || num[3] == 1 )
            return 1;
        return num[3] * factorial( num[3] − 1 )
}
```

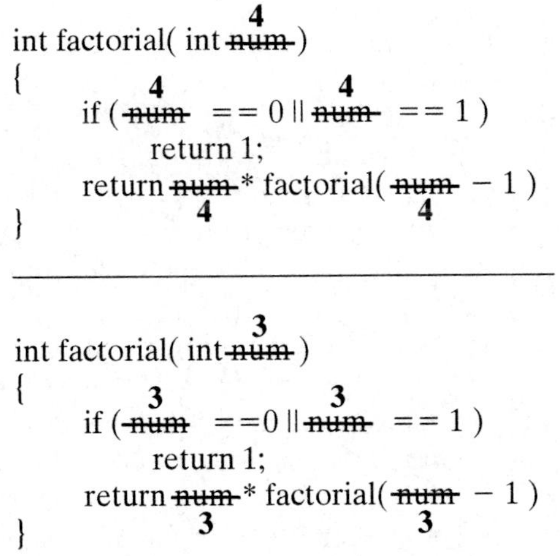

FIGURE 13.2

The factorial function is called recursively from Figure 13.1, passing 4 − 1 = 3 into num. A copy of the factorial function is made, replacing num with 3 throughout the function.

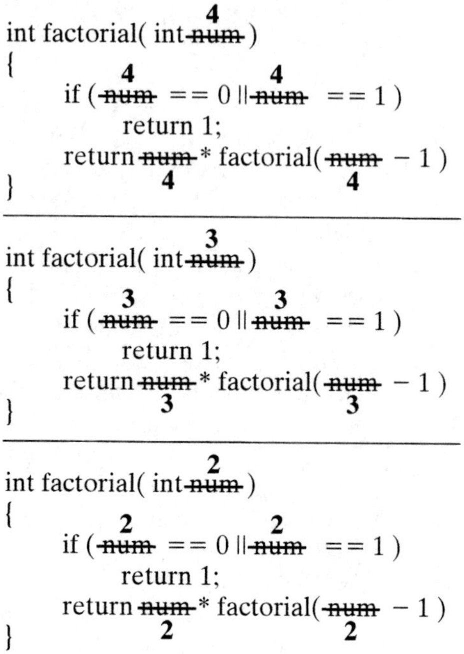

```
             4
int factorial( int num )
{
        4             4
    if ( num == 0 || num == 1 )
        return 1;
    return num * factorial( num − 1 )
        4               4
}
```

```
             3
int factorial( int num )
{
        3             3
    if ( num == 0 || num == 1 )
        return 1;
    return num * factorial( num − 1 )
        3               3
}
```

FIGURE 13.3

The factorial function is called recursively from the last statement in Figure 13.2, passing 3 − 1 = 2 into num. The variable num has been replaced with 2 throughout the function.

```
             2
int factorial( int num )
{
        2             2
    if ( num == 0 || num == 1 )
        return 1;
    return num * factorial( num − 1 )
        2               2
}
```

```
return num * factorial( num − 1 );
```

can now be computed and returned. The result is 2, of course. The return at the front of the expression causes it to replace the function call that called *this* function, as shown in Figure 13.6. Then, this function returns the value 6, replacing the function call that called *this* function, as shown in Figure 13.7. Finally, this function returns 24 to the function call,

```
int x = factorial( 4 );
```

and assigns 24 to x. So, you see, recursion is completely logical and works just as any other functions work.

Notice that lines 3–4 of the factorial function are really what stops all this recursion from happening. If we had written the recursive function without these lines, the function would call itself on and on in a process called *infinite recursion*. Actually, the computer runs out of memory when these functions are created over and over again, and when it does, the program aborts. So infinite recursion isn't really the same thing as an infinite loop.

In a correctly written recursive function, there is always some condition that, when true, causes the recursive function calls to come to an end; after that, there is usually a series of returns, as in our example. The condition that causes the recursive calls to come to an end is called the ***base case***. The condition that causes a recursive function call to be made is called the ***recursive case***.

If one makes a mistake and inputs −1 into the recursive factorial function, what will happen? The next function call will input one number less, which is −2. Then, the

```
int factorial( int num⁴ )
{
      if ( num⁴ == 0 || num⁴ == 1 )
          return 1;
      return num⁴ * factorial( num⁴ − 1 )
}
```

```
int factorial( int num³ )
{
      if ( num³ == 0 || num³ == 1 )
          return 1;
      return num³ * factorial( num³ − 1 )
}
```

```
int factorial( int num² )
{
      if ( num² == 0 || num² == 1 )
          return 1;
      return num² * factorial( num² − 1 )
}
```

```
int factorial( int num¹ )
{
      if ( num¹ == 0 || num¹ == 1 )
          return 1;
      return num¹ * factorial( num¹ − 1 )
}
```

FIGURE 13.4

The factorial function is called recursively from the last statement in Figure 13.3. The call passes $2 - 1 = 1$ into num. The variable num has been replaced with 1 throughout the function. The if condition is true now, so 1 is returned.

next will input −3, then −4, then −5, etc. But, you can see that we have a problem here, too. Sometimes, in order to safeguard this situation, a ***driver*** function is made:

```
int factorial( int num )
{
      if ( num < 0 ) {
          cout << "The factorial of a negative number is undefined" << endl;
          return 0;
          }
      return factorial2( num );
}
```

```
int factorial2( int num )
{
      if ( num == 0 || num == 1 )
          return 1;
      return num * factorial2( num − 1 );
}
```

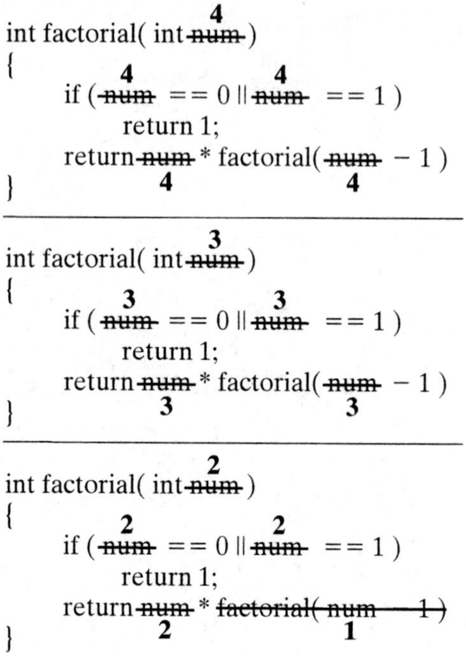

```
int factorial( int num )    // 4
{
    if ( num == 0 || num == 1 )    // 4    4
        return 1;
    return num * factorial( num - 1 )    // 4    4
}
```

```
int factorial( int num )    // 3
{
    if ( num == 0 || num == 1 )    // 3    3
        return 1;
    return num * factorial( num - 1 )    // 3    3
}
```

FIGURE 13.5

The 1 that is returned from Figure 13.4 replaces the function call, similarly to the way return values always replace function calls. The function call is replaced with the return value 1. The last line now returns 2 * 1 = 2.

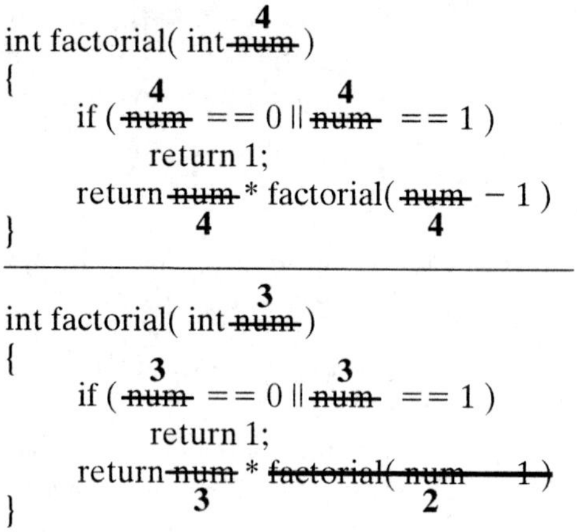

```
int factorial( int num )    // 2
{
    if ( num == 0 || num == 1 )    // 2    2
        return 1;
    return num * factorial( num - 1 )    // 2    1
}
```

```
int factorial( int num )    // 4
{
    if ( num == 0 || num == 1 )    // 4    4
        return 1;
    return num * factorial( num - 1 )    // 4    4
}
```

FIGURE 13.6

The 2 that is returned from Figure 13.5 replaces the function call which called the function that the 2 returned from. The last line of this function now returns 3 * 2 = 6.

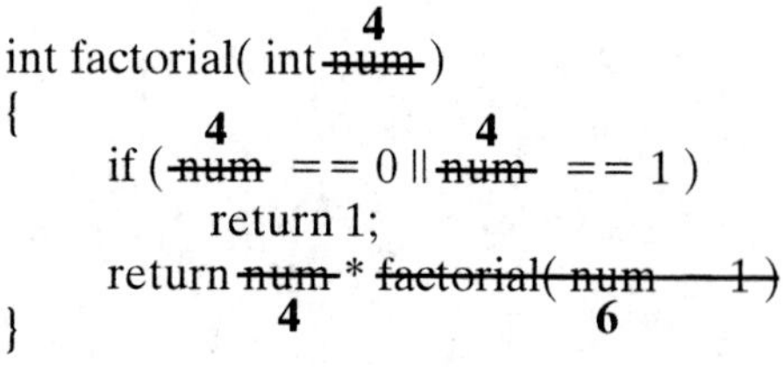

```
int factorial( int num )    // 3
{
    if ( num == 0 || num == 1 )    // 3    3
        return 1;
    return num * factorial( num - 1 )    // 3    2
}
```

FIGURE 13.7

The 6 that is returned from Figure 13.6 replaces the function call from the previous function. This factorial function now returns 4 * 6 = 24. The value 24 replaces the original function call, which was factorial(4). Thus, the correct value of 4 factorial, 24, replaces the function call.

```
int factorial( int num )    // 4
{
    if ( num == 0 || num == 1 )    // 4    4
        return 1;
    return num * factorial( num - 1 )    // 4    6
}
```

The function factorial is the driver function, while factorial2 is the recursive function. The driver function makes sure that the input is correct and, if so, calls the recursive function, returning the result to the original function call. The driver and recursive functions can be combined into one recursive function, but it would slow down program execution. The check for a negative number would be made over and over again, on each recursive function call. When the driver is separate, a check for a negative number is made only once. Recursive functions should be as small and as simple as possible, avoiding local variable declarations if at all possible, in order to conserve memory. (Don't forget that a new function is created in memory on each recursive call.)

Recursive functions can sometimes be written tersely by using the ternary operator:

```
int factorial( int num )
{
        return ( num == 0  || num == 1)? 1 : num * factorial( num – 1 );
}
```

The problem that some people have with understanding recursion is that they try to think of only one function in use during the whole recursive process. As you can imagine, this can be quite confusing. The function copying that we described here is actually achieved by making an activation record for each function, not by copying the function in machine language. But what happens physically in the computer matches the recursive process that we just described.

13.2   GUIDELINES FOR WRITING RECURSIVE FUNCTIONS

When you write a recursive function, it can be a little challenging to try to evaluate whether it will work. Here are some guidelines:

1. There must be some base case that stops the recursive function calls from taking place (obviously).
2. Each recursive function call should approach the base case. When we call factorial(4), for example, the next recursive call uses factorial(3), substituting 3 for num. The base case occurs when num == 1, so 3 is closer to the base case than 4 is; that is, the recursive function call *approaches* the base case. If you don't approach the base case, you're in trouble. For example, if the next recursive function call uses factorial(5), we are getting further from the base case and there is something wrong with the way our function is written.
3. The recursive function should work for the base case. That is, if our original function call is factorial(0) or factorial(1), it should produce the right result. And it does in this case: Such calls will produce a result of 1.
4. The last recursive function call before reaching the base case should produce the right result. In our example, we would need to verify that factorial(2) produces the right result. You have to walk through the code a little to verify this, but it is not too inconvenient, and it is worth it for peace of mind.

5. If we assume that a recursive function call will do everything that it should do after it finishes executing, the logic of the function should make sense. To understand this fifth guideline, let's take another look at the factorial function and imagine that num could be any nonnegative integer:

```
1   int factorial( int num )
2   {
3   if ( num == 0 || num == 1)
4           return 1;
5   return num * factorial( num – 1 );
6   }
```

Lines 3–4 make logical sense. If we have 0! or 1!, the result is 1. If num is not 0 or 1, however, does line 5 make logical sense? The guideline is telling us that we have to assume that factorial (num − 1) does everything it is supposed to do. If num is 10, for example, we assume that factorial (num − 1) will definitely return 9!. If num is 10, then we want the result of 10! Line 5 says that we will return the result of $10 \times 9!$. This makes logical sense only if $10 \times 9!$ is 10!. After a little reflection, we see that that is true. For any $n > 1$, in fact, $n! = n(n − 1)!$. So the factorial function makes logical sense, *assuming that the recursive function call does everything it is supposed to do.*

It might seem that if the fifth guideline is followed, you are just taking it "on faith" that the recursive function will work for all nonnegative integers. If you've followed guideline (5), you've essentially got the rule that says if factorial(a) produces the correct result, then factorial (a + 1) produces the correct result. After all, (a + 1)* factorial(a) is the same as factorial (a + 1). If you've followed guideline (4), you've got the fact that factorial(2) works. If factorial(2) works, then guideline (5) tells you that factorial(3) will work. Because factorial(3) works, guideline (5) tells you that factorial(4) will work, etc., etc.

13.3   USING RECURSION ON LINKED STRUCTURES

Sometimes recursive functions are used for linked structures, such as binary search trees. Let's suppose we wanted to search for a Mercedes in a linked list, using a recursive function. The linked list is made out of Node<Car> objects, where the info section in each node is an object of a Car struct. Suppose we know that a Mercedes is definitely in the list. Then our recursive function might look like this:

```
1   Car search( Node<Car> *ptr, Car mercedes  )
2   {
3       if ( ptr->info == mercedes )
4               return ptr->info;
5       return search( ptr->next, mercedes );
6   }
```

Here, the operator == is overloaded. We might make the initial function call with a line like

Car auto = search(start, mercedes);

where start is a pointer to the beginning node in the linked list. The pointer ptr is going to move down through the list. Since we know that Mercedes is definitely in the list, we don't have to worry about ptr getting set to NULL at the end of the list. So ptr in the search function is set to point to the beginning of the linked list. If Mercedes is in the first node, then the if statement will be true right away and we return the Car object in that node on line 4. If Mercedes isn't in the first node, then line 5, which makes a recursive function call, is executed. The pointer ptr->next is passed into ptr, so ptr points to the next node. To understand why, think of the function call

foo(3);

where the function heading is

void foo(int a)

The result of passing 3 into a is essentially the same as the assignment a = 3. Likewise, if we pass ptr->next into ptr of another function, the result is essentially the same as the assignment ptr = ptr->next. Thus, when a copy of the search function is made, we essentially look at the next node for Mercedes. Note, however, that both ptr's are not the same pointer, because ptr is not passed by reference into the search function copy. You know from experience, for example, that if you pass a variable a into the function foo, both a's have the same name, but they are not the same variable.

Let's consider the guidelines. First, what is the base case? When Mercedes is found, it stops the recursion. So the base case occurs when ptr->info == mercedes. Does a recursive function call approach the base case? Yes, when we look at the next node, we are one node closer to the node that contains Mercedes. Does the base case work? Yes, the Car object that contains Mercedes at that node is returned. Those are the three easy questions to answer.

Now, does the last recursive call, before reaching the base case, work? We begin at the node right before the node with Mercedes. The if statement is false, so we pass ptr->next to ptr, and now ptr has the address of the node with Mercedes. The if statement in the second search function is true, so ptr->info is returned. It replaces the function call in the first search function, and then info is returned again. So, yes, the last recursive call before reaching the base case works.

Finally, assuming that the recursive call does what it is supposed to do, does the function make logical sense? The base case certainly makes logical sense, as we have verified. For the recursive case, sometimes it helps to imagine that we are about a thousand nodes away from the Mercedes node, so you wouldn't possibly want to walk through the code. We assume that search (ptr->next, mercedes) does what it is supposed to do—that is, start at the node pointed to by ptr->next and find and return the Car object with Mercedes. This makes sense, because, since Mercedes wasn't in the current node, the only place you can find it is in the rest of the list. To search through the rest of the list thoroughly, you would have to start at the first node of the rest of the list (assuming that the list is not doubly linked).

Now, what if we want to search for a Mercedes in a linked list, but we are not sure whether there is one in there? We could have our function return false if it isn't in the list and return true if it is, but that only takes care of the return type. What about returning the Car object? We could have a Car object passed by reference into the recursive function, which then might look like this:

```
bool search( Node<Car> *ptr, Car & auto, Car mercedes )
{
        if ( ptr == NULL )
                return false;
        if ( ptr->info == mercedes ) {
                auto = ptr->info;
                return true;
                }
        return search( ptr->next, auto, mercedes );
}
```

This function is a little more complicated. There are two base cases, each of which stops the recursive calls from taking place. In one base case, ptr is NULL; in another, ptr->info == mercedes. Each recursive call approaches one base case or the other; if Mercedes is in the linked list, we move a node closer to it. If Mercedes is not in the list, we move a node closer to the end of the list.

If the second base case is true, since auto was passed by reference into each recursive function call, the changes to auto will be reflected all the way back through the function calls.

Notice how important it is to place the keyword "return" in front of the recursive function call (in the last line of the function). A common mistake is to leave it out. But once we start a chain of returns, as in our factorial example, if "return" is left out, the chain is broken. True or false might be returned from the last function in the chain, but it wouldn't be returned by the next-to-last function in the chain. The compiler should catch this error, but would probably give a warning that not all paths in the function return a bool type. It is a common mistake to leave "return" out.

As one final example, let's take a look at a recursive function that discounts the prices of all of the cars in the linked list by 10%. We don't want to return anything from the function, so it has a void return type:

```
1   void discount( Node<Car> *ptr )
2   {
3   if ( ptr != NULL ) {
4       ptr->info.price -= 0.1 * ( ptr->info.price );
5       discount( ptr->next );
6       }
7   }
```

What is the base case in this function? It is unusual, but the base case still exists; it just doesn't need to be written. The base case occurs when ptr == NULL. In that case, control returns from the function. This causes a series of returns through all of the recursive function calls that were made; after returning to another discount function, the line after line 5 would be executed, but there is nothing left to do, so it returns again ... and again ... and again.

13.4   TIME COMPLEXITIES OF RECURSIVE FUNCTIONS

When analyzing the time complexities of recursive functions, we determine how many times a recursive function is called in the recursive process. The example in the last part of Section 13.3 would execute in $\Theta(n)$ time, because the discount function is called $n + 1$ times, one time for each node and one additional time when ptr is set to NULL. Of course, looping inside a recursive function can increase the time complexity further.

The factorial function demonstrates that the number of elements isn't the only factor that can make programs take longer to execute. In the factorial function, the magnitude of num, not the number of elements, would be used for n. The factorial function executes in $\Theta(n)$ time, where n is the magnitude of num.

Finally, note that recursion is never necessary in order to write a program. In other words, whatever you can do with recursion you can also do with a loop. Recursion is not common in data structures, but is encountered occasionally, as some programmers prefer to use it. Binary search trees, discussed in Chapter 15, are often implemented with recursion, which allows the functions of a binary search tree to be written rather elegantly. Sometimes people convert recursive functions to loops for the sake of speed (There is some time used in making function calls.)

In data structures, recursion is often applied to linked structures. Some examples of this application were given in this chapter.

SUMMARY

Recursion is sometimes used in data structures. Even though you may never intend to write recursive functions yourself, some programmers prefer to write them. Therefore, you need to know about recursion, because you will almost certainly encounter it and need to deal with it.

People get confused about recursive functions when they try to think of only one function being used throughout the whole recursive process. You should never think of recursion that way, because it is not even what happens physically. The best way to think about recursion is to think about *copies* of recursive functions that execute independently. Making such copies matches what happens physically.

Some guidelines for writing recursive functions have been presented in this chapter. Occasionally, there are going to be exceptions to these guidelines (which is why they are called guidelines, and not rules). However, when you become an expert in recursion, you will realize what you need to do to handle any exceptions.

When analyzing the time complexity of a recursive function, we have to remember that it is really an alternative to writing a loop. Each recursive function call corresponds to an iteration of the loop, so, to come up with a time complexity, we analyze how many times the recursive function is called. In data structures, this number can often be described in terms of n, the number of elements.

EXERCISES

1. Describe what a base case is and what a recursive case is.
2. Explain what happens if there is no base case in a recursive function.
3. What is a driver for a recursive function?
4. What are the guidelines for writing a recursive function?
5. Describe how pointers are advanced through a linked data structure in recursive function calls.
6. How are time complexities of recursive functions evaluated?
7. Write a recursive function to calculate x^a, where $a \geq 0$ and a is an integer.
8. For the recursive function of Exercise 7, write a driver that checks the parameter a to see if it is nonnegative or negative. The driver should use the same recursive function in either case and then return the correct result.
9. Suppose we have a linked list of integers, and a pointer called start points to the first node. Write a recursive function that adds all the integers in the linked list.
10. Write a recursive version of the binary search algorithm in Section 9.5. (*Hint*: There will be two recursive function calls in the function.)
11. Sometimes it is obvious how we can reduce a fraction (4/8 = 1/2), and sometimes it isn't (2491/3127 = ?). The *Euclidean algorithm* will find the greatest common divisor (gcd) of two numbers, so that we can divide both numerator and denominator by the gcd and reduce the fraction. The Euclidean algorithm for two nonnegative integers a and b, where $a > b$, is as follows:

```
r = a % b
while r is not 0
        a = b
        b = r
        r = a % b
b is the gcd
```

In the fraction 2491/3127, the Euclidean algorithm reveals that the gcd is 53, so dividing both the numerator and denominator by 53 yields 47/59. Write a recursive function for the Euclidean algorithm.

12. Write a driver for the recursive Euclidean function in Exercise 11. The driver should test a and b to see whether or not they are nonnegative and should call the recursive function so that the greatest of the two numbers is in the correct parameter position.

CHAPTER 14

Introduction to Sorting Algorithms

On occasion, we need to *sort* elements—that is, put them in order. If the elements are objects of structs, then a certain data member is chosen for the sort. For example, an array of Employee objects might be sorted by the employees' last names: the objects are placed in order in the array according to the data member used for the last name. By contrast, we may want to sort the Employee objects by salary, with highest salary first and lowest salary last. There are numerous sorting algorithms available, and choosing the right one (that will be the most efficient or effective for the data being sorted) requires careful consideration. Hundreds of pages can and should be written about this, and this topic is covered extensively in textbooks on the analysis of algorithms. In this chapter, we'll take a look at some of the most important sorting algorithms, to help get you ready for a course in algorithm analysis.

14.1   HEAPSORT

When the heap is used in the priority queue, we can use a simple algorithm to sort an array. This algorithm, which has a very good time complexity as far as sorting algorithms go, is known as the *heapsort algorithm*. The section of code for the heapsort algorithm is as follows:

```
PriorityQueue< float > pq( arr );
for ( i = arr.length( ) – 1; i >= 0; i-- )
        pq.dequeue( arr[ i ] );
```

The first line assumes that we are using an Array<float> object called arr which has been assigned floating-point numbers. The object arr is passed into the second constructor of the priority queue, which makes a heap out of the array. We then set up a for loop, starting with the last position i of the array. (When we dequeue the largest value, we want to place it in that position.) The index i is decremented in the last section of the loop. Each time through the loop, the largest remaining value is dequeued from the priority queue and is assigned to the appropriate array element. The condition in the for loop is i $>=0$, since we want to stop when i becomes -1. Thus, at the end, arr will have its elements in sorted order, from smallest to largest.

Heapsort gets its speed from the fact that an array can be turned into a heap in $\Theta(n)$ time, as is done in the second constructor, although the proof of this proposition is beyond the scope of the text. Then, heapsort makes use of the incredibly fast [$O(\lg n)$ time] dequeue function, to dequeue all of the elements back into the array. Heapsort provably runs in $O(n \lg n)$ time, the gold standard for a general-purpose sorting algorithm. It can run as fast as $\Theta(n)$ time in the unusual case where all of the elements have the same value. Although such a case rarely occurs, heapsort should be considered if you suspect that the array has a number of values that are the same, even if it has multiple occurrences of two or more values. For example, in an array in which 25% of the elements have one value and another 20% have another value, heapsort should be considered. Some work will be eliminated from the sorting because a swap does not need to take place when values are equal.

Sorting algorithms can be implemented in client programs with the use of function templates. These templates work like class templates, except that a compiler makes a function out of a function template, when the function is used. The following main program shows the heapsort algorithm converted into a function template:

```
1    #include <iostream>
2    #include "PriorityQueue.h"
3
4    using namespace std;
5
6    struct MyStruct {
7        int id;
8        float amount;
9        bool operator >(const MyStruct & right ) { return amount > right.amount; }
10   };
11
12   template <class DataType>
13   void heapsort( Array<DataType> & arr );
14
15   int main( )
16   {
17       int num;
18
19       cout << "How many records do you want to enter? ";
20       cin >> num;
21       Array<MyStruct> objs( num );
22       for ( int i = 0; i < objs.length( ); i++ ) {
```

```
23                    cout << "Enter id for record " << i + 1 << ": ";
24                    cin >> objs[ i ].id;
25                    cout << "Enter amount for record " << i + 1 << ": ";
26                    cin >> objs[ i ].amount;
27                    }
28      heapsort( objs );
29      cout << "Records in sorted order:" << endl;
30      for ( int i = 0; i < objs.length( ); i++ ) {
31                    cout << "record " << i << ":" << endl;
32                    cout << "id:      " << objs[ i ].id << endl;
33                    cout << "amount: " << objs[ i ].amount << endl;
34      }
35
36      return 0;
37  }
38
39  template <class DataType>
40  void heapsort( Array<DataType> & arr )
41  {
42      PriorityQueue<DataType> pq( arr );
43      for ( int i = arr.length( ) - 1; i >= 0; i-- )
44                    pq.dequeue( arr[ i ] );
45  }
```

A struct is defined on lines 6–10. We will have an Array of objects made from these structs and use a function template for heapsort to sort the array of objects. The way the operator > function was written in the struct by the client on line 9, it is apparent that the client would like to sort the objects by amount and not by the id key.

The function template for heapsort is shown on lines 39–45. Unlike the situation for a class, the compiler will determine what type DataType should be by the type of parameter that is passed in. All occurrences of DataType in the function template are replaced by the type the compiler determines that the actual parameter has. This is the way the compiler makes a function out of a function template. The compiler can, however, make more than one heapsort function out of this function template. For example, if we also had an Array of floats that we wanted to sort in the same program, then when we call heapsort, passing in the Array of floats, the compiler would make another function for the program, replacing all occurrences of DataType with float.

The prototype for the heapsort function template is shown on lines 12–13. It must be templated, too. Interestingly, the function call on line 28 does not look like a template is being used, but the compiler uses this line to determine what function to make out of the template.

Lines 19–27 of the main function just get some records from the user and store them into the Array of MyStruct objects, declared on line 21. The heapsort function is then called on line 28. Finally, the records, in order by amount, are output on lines 29–34.

Sorting algorithms are good algorithms to put in function templates, because we can use them for any type of element without having to rewrite them. They are fully transplantable into another program by copy and paste. But we must make sure they are working before we do a lot of copying and pasting. Otherwise, any mistakes we make will be duplicated!

14.2   INSERTION SORT

Insertion sort is another important sorting algorithm to have in your toolbox. When insertion sort is used on an array, the array is conceptually divided into two sections, as shown in Figure 14.1a: a sorted section on the left and an unsorted section on the right. With each iteration of the algorithm, an element from the unsorted section is inserted into its proper place in the sorted section, as shown in Figure 14.1b. This is what gives rise to the name "insertion sort". Thus, on each iteration of the algorithm, the sorted section grows by one element and the unsorted section shrinks by one element, until the elements are sorted. So how do we get that sorted section on the left to begin with? Insertion sort starts off with the leftmost element being the only element in the sorted section. (A section with only one element is a sorted section.)

The algorithm for insertion sort is as follows:

```
1       for each j, from 1 to the length of A – 1
2           i = j – 1
3           while i is greater than -1 and A[ i ] is greater than A[ i + 1 ]
4               swap( A[ i ], A[ i + 1 ] )
5               i--
```

On line 1, j marks the beginning of the unsorted section, so it increases by 1 every time a new iteration starts, reflecting the fact that the sorted section is increasing by

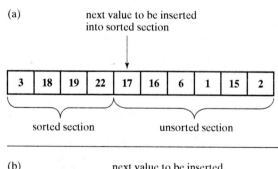

FIGURE 14.1

(a) The sorted and unsorted sections in an array when insertion sort is in progress. The next value to be inserted in the sorted section is 17. (b) The value 17 was inserted into the sorted section. The sorted section grows by one element, and the unsorted section shrinks by one element. The next value to be inserted into the sorted section is 16.

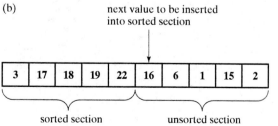

one element on each iteration. Then, on line 2, a separate index i is used to find where A[j] should be inserted. Notice now that A[j] is really A[i + 1]. So A[i] is compared with A[i + 1], and if A[i] is greater, a swap takes place on line 4. This is how the value that was in A[j] will eventually find its right position—by being swapped backwards through the array on each iteration of the while loop until it is greater than or equal to the element before it. This backwards swapping is illustrated in Figure 14.2, which shows how Figure 14.1b was achieved.

We can analyze the time complexity of insertion sort by thinking about **inversions**. An inversion occurs between two elements when they are out of order. Figure 14.3 shows an example, listing the inversions that occur in a particular array. Notice that every time a swap occurs on line 4 of the preceding code, exactly one inversion is removed from the array—the inversion that occurred between the two elements that were swapped. No other inversions can be removed or created by this swap. So, if we think about the number of times that line 4 is executed, we readily see that it has to be equal to the number of inversions that existed in the original array. This reasoning is significant, because line 4, being in the innermost loop, would tell us what the time complexity is if we knew how many times it would be executed (as a function of n). Note, however, that the time complexity is at least $\Theta(n)$, because of the outer loop. (The inner loop may never be executed.) But the only way the time complexity can be more than $\Theta(n)$ is if the function of the number of times line 4 is executed has a term greater than n.

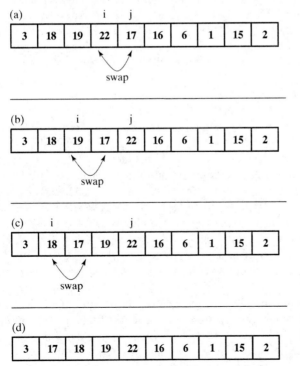

FIGURE 14.2

(a) The array from Figure 14.1a. A swap needs to take place between A[i] and A[i + 1]. (b) The swap took place, the index i is decremented, and now another swap needs to take place between A[i] and A[i + 1]. (c) The process repeats. (d) The final swap takes place, producing the sorted section shown in Figure 14.1b.

FIGURE 14.3

An inversion occurs between any two elements that are out of order. In this example, there are three inversions. The first is between element 0 and element 1. The second is between element 2 and element 3. The last is between element 2 and element 4.

So, realizing that the number of times line 4 is executed is equal to the number of inversions, we can ask, How do we get the number of inversions in an array as a function of n? There are a couple of ways to think about this. First of all, let's think about the worst thing that can happen: The array is in reverse order, sorted from largest to smallest. The number of inversions can't be any higher; every single element is inverted with every other element. So how many inversions do we have? Well, there are n elements, and every element is inverted with the other remaining $n - 1$ elements, so this would give us $n(n - 1)$ inversions. But it is only part of the picture: We are counting each inversion twice. For two elements a and b, we are supposing that element a is inverted with element b and also counting element b inverted with element a, but these are the same inversion. Therefore, the correct number of inversions is $n(n - 1)/2$. Hence, the number of times line 4 will execute in this absolute worst case is $n(n - 1)/2 = \frac{1}{2}n^2 - \frac{1}{2}n$ which is a $\Theta(n^2)$ time complexity for insertion sort—not so hot when you compare it with heapsort. But again, this is an absolute worst case.

What about the number of inversions in the average case? How would we even get an average case? For every two elements, we might suppose that they have a 50% chance of being inverted, on average. We already know that the number of possible inversions is $n(n - 1)/2$. If 50% (or half) of these inversions occur in the average case, it will give us $\frac{1}{2}n(n - 1)/2 = n(n - 1)/4$ But this is still a $\Theta(n^2)$ time complexity for insertion sort in the average case.

So what's so great about insertion sort? After all, heapsort is $\Theta(n \lg n)$ in its *worst* case. Well, insertion sort's claim to fame is that it is fast if the elements are already sorted (or nearly sorted). Surprisingly, some sorting algorithms perform poorly when the elements are close to being sorted. Heapsort, for example, still goes through all of the steps of the algorithm, making a heap out of the sorted elements first and then re-sorting them. Why is insertion sort fast when the elements are already sorted? Well, note that there are no inversions in a sorted array, so line 4 of the algorithm is never executed. The condition in the while loop on line 3 is never true, so the inner loop is not executed. If we just have the outer loop, then the algorithm has of $\Theta(n)$ time complexity. But it can also be a $\Theta(n)$ algorithm if it is *not* completely sorted to begin with. For example, if we just have n inversions, then line 4 in the innermost loop is executed only n times, so we still have a $\Theta(n)$ algorithm. So insertion sort should be considered if you suspect the elements of a list are close to being sorted.

One thing that sometimes confuses students is how the statements in an inner loop can be executed only n times throughout the whole algorithm when an outer loop is also executed n times. The confusion is cleared up when one realizes that, for each iteration of the outer loop, the inner loop has an average of one iteration.

In addition to using insertion sort for nearly sorted arrays, we often use insertion sort if there are a small number of elements in the array. Considering that, in the average case, there are $n(n - 1)/4$ inversions, we can solve

$$n = \frac{n(n - 1)}{4}$$

The solution of this equation is, in fact, $n = 5.3$ Thus, at around five elements, in the average case, we would expect insertion sort to behave more like a $\Theta(n)$ algorithm than a $\Theta(n^2)$ algorithm.

We can speed up insertion sort (without changing its time complexity) by realizing that there are three assignments in each swap and that we can use the same kind of "one-assignment" swaps as we did in the heap. Following is the algorithm for the improved insertion sort:

```
1        for each j, from 1 to the length of A − 1
2              temp = A[ j ]
3              i = j − 1
4              while i is greater than -1 and A[ i ] is greater than temp
5                      A[ i + 1 ] = A[ i ]
6                      i—
7              A[ i + 1] = temp
```

The trick is to save A[j] first in temp on line 2. (The one-assignment swap is shown on line 5, where the value in A[j] can be overwritten.) Once the correct position is found, the while loop terminates, and then temp is saved into the correct position. An example of such an insertion is shown in Figure 14.4.

14.3   QUICKSORT

Quicksort is a popular recursive sorting algorithm that has both a best-case and an average-case time complexity of $\Theta(n \lg n)$. Its worst-case time complexity is $\Theta(n^2)$. At first blush, it might seem that heapsort should be more popular, judging by the corresponding time complexities. But recall that when we determine time complexities, we take an instruction function, remove least significant terms, and then throw out the coefficient of the most significant term. For quicksort, this coefficient is rather small compared with those of other sorting algorithms. And since the average time complexity predominates, that accounts for the popularity. An analysis of how these time complexities are derived for quicksort is beyond the scope of this text, but we can at least discuss how quicksort works.

Quicksort is made up of a nonrecursive function and a recursive function. The nonrecursive function is usually called *partition*, and we'll discuss this function first. The partition function chooses something called a **pivot** from an array arr. A pivot is an element used for comparison purposes. When partition is finished executing, all elements less than or equal to the pivot will be on the left of the pivot and all elements

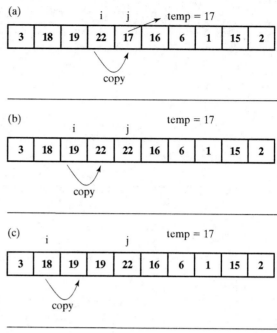

FIGURE 14.4

How swapping can take place in insertion sort with "one-assignment swaps." (a) The initial array from Figure 14.1(a). (b–c) One-assignment swaps taking place. (d) Index i is decremented, but A[i] is less than temp, so the loop stops. The value of temp is to be placed into A[i + 1]. (e) The value of temp is written in, producing the result of Figure 14.1b.

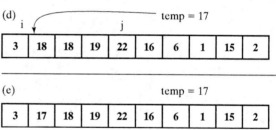

greater than the pivot will be on the right of it. These sections on the left and right of the pivot are not sorted in any way other than what was described. Note, however, that when partition is finished, the pivot will be in its proper position in the array when the array is finally sorted. The only thing that will remain is to sort the left section and the right section separately.

In the partition function we will be looking at, the last element is chosen as the pivot. Ignoring the last element of the array, we can conceptually divide the array into two sections during the operation of the partition function. There is a partitioned section on the left and an unpartitioned section on the right. Figure 14.5 shows an example of these sections, with the partition function in progress. Note that the index i is used to mark the end of the small-value section, while j is used to mark the beginning of the unpartitioned section. On each iteration of the for loop in the partition function, the element at j is placed on the proper side of the partition; thus, the partitioned section grows by 1, and the unpartitioned section decreases by 1, on each iteration. When there is no more unpartitioned section, the element at *r* will be placed between the sides of the partition.

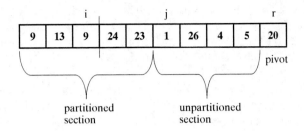

FIGURE 14.5

An array with the partition function in progress. The left section is a partitioned section, with the line acting as the divider. All of the elements to the left of the line in the partitioned section are less or equal to the pivot (on the right), while all of the elements to the right of the line in the partitioned section are greater than the pivot. The unpartitioned section is on the right. (The pivot is not included.) The index i marks the end of the small-value section of the partition, while the index j marks the beginning of the unpartitioned section. On each iteration of the partition function, the element at j is inserted into the partition. Thus, the partitioned section grows by 1, and the unpartitioned section shrinks by 1. If the element at j is less than or equal to the pivot, i is incremented and the element at i is swapped with the element at j. (The dividing line moves one element to the right.) If the element at j is greater than the pivot, the partitioned section includes the element at j in its large-value section. (j is just incremented.)

Next, we'll discuss how the partitioned section grows by 1, while the unpartitioned section shrinks by 1, on an iteration. The element at j is compared with the pivot. If it is less than or equal to the pivot, it should be placed on the left side of the partition. This is achieved by incrementing i and then swapping the element at j with the element at i. Thus, the element at j is placed into the left side of the partition, and i still marks the end of the small-value side of the partition. If the element at j is greater than the pivot, no swap is necessary; the element at j is already in the large-value side of the partition. When the unpartitioned section is gone, i is incremented and the pivot is swapped with the element at i—since the pivot was swapped with the first element in the large-value side, the pivot is where it belongs. It will be greater than or equal to everything to the left of it and less than everything to the right of it.

The algorithm for partition is as follows:

```
1       partition( arr, p, r )
2       i = p − 1
3       for all j from p to r − 1
4               if arr[ j ] <= arr[ r ]
5                       i++
6                       swap( arr[ i ], arr[ j ] )
7       swap ( arr[ i + 1 ] and arr[ r ] )
8       return i + 1
```

The parameters passed in are (1) arr, the name of the array; (2) p, the index of the first element; and (3) r, the index of the last element. Thus, arr[r] will be the pivot. At the beginning, there is no partitioned section. Since i marks the end of the small-value section, we don't want to start by setting i to 0; that would mean that the small-value section ends at element 0. So i is set to p − 1 on line 2. When we increment i and do the swap, the first small value will be at element 0, where it should be. But it might be that all elements are larger than the pivot; in that case, there is no small-value section and i will remain where it is.

The entire array (except for the pivot) starts off as being one large unpartitioned section, so j starts off at p on line 3. The comparison is made on line 4, and if the element at j is less than or equal to the pivot, i is incremented on line 5. Then the swap is made on line 6, as described earlier. (This could be just a swap of the element with itself the first time.) Notice that if the element at j is larger than the pivot, nothing is done—the element at j will already be on the large-value side of the partition.

Line 7 places the pivot in its proper position of the array. Then line 8 returns the index of that position.

One thing that can happen is that all elements might be less than or equal to the pivot. If this is the case, then index i keeps incrementing and the swap on line 6 swaps the element at i with itself. When we reach line 7, the pivot is swapped with itself. Although this would be bad luck, partition still makes progress in sorting the array, because the pivot will be in its proper position in the array when finally sorted.

Likewise, all elements might be larger than the pivot. If this is the case, the condition on line 4 is never true and i stays at p − 1. When the for loop terminates, the pivot is swapped with the first element on line 7.

The partition function is called many times during the execution of the quicksort algorithm. Throughout this discussion, I gave you the impression that partition is working with the entire array. This is so when the partition function executes for the first time. However, the next time partition is called, it will work only with the section on the left side of the pivot. The last element on that side will be chosen as the pivot for this section. Then the partition function will do the same thing with this section that it did with the entire array. Eventually, partition will be called to work with the right section and will partition it also. That is why p and r are passed as parameters into the partition function. Their index values will change, depending on which section of the array the partition function is working with. The partition function continues to be used with smaller and smaller sections of the array until the entire array is sorted. (Recall that the partition function will place whatever pivot it is working with into the correct position of the array when finally sorted.)

Let's take a look at the recursive quicksort algorithm, which will call the partition algorithm from within:

```
1       quicksort( arr, p, r )
2       if p < r
3               q = partition( arr, p, r )
4               quicksort( arr, p, q − 1 )
5               quicksort( arr, q + 1, r )
```

When quicksort is first called, p is the beginning index of the array arr and r is the ending index. The first call to partition on line 3 breaks the array into two pieces (with a piece possibly being empty), separated by the pivot at index i + 1, which is returned at the end of the partition algorithm. The index q is set to this index on line 3. All elements to the left of index q (if any) will be less than or equal to arr[q], while all elements to the right of index q (if any) will be greater than arr[q]. Thus, after this first call to partition, the element at arr[q] occupies its correct location in the final sorted array. The same process is then used on the left and right sides by a recursive call to quicksort on lines 4 and 5. Note that a section of an array that quicksort works with has no pivot in it from a previous use of partition.

The sections of the array that quicksort works with will get smaller and smaller until the array section is just one element long. When that happens, the partition function doesn't need to be called for it. That element *is* the pivot, and it is already in its correct position of the partition for this one element. (Both sides of the partition are empty.) Thus, this state of affairs serves as the base case to stop the recursion. Note that p is equal to r if the array section is just one element long. Hence, the condition on line 2 will not be true, and the base case has been reached. The quicksort function does nothing except return for the base case.

14.4   COUNTING SORT

Counting sort is a faster sorting algorithm than quicksort when the range of values is less than the number of elements in the array. The smaller the range, the more duplicate values the array has. Under this condition, counting sort is a $\Theta(n)$ algorithm, so it is a good tool to have in your toolbox. The following counting sort algorithm assumes that we want to sort an array A of integer values ranging from 0 to k:

```
1       COUNTING-SORT( A )
2       make an Array C of length k + 1
3       for each i, from 0 to k
4            C[ i ] = 0
5       for each j, from 0 to the length of A - 1
6            C[ A[ j ] ]++
7       j = 0
8       for each i from 0 to k
9            for each m from 1 to C[ i ]
10                A[ j ] = i
11                j++
```

Each index in the dynamic integer array C created on line 2 will keep a count of how many values which equal that index are stored in array A, the array to be sorted. For example, if C[5] is set to 3, then three elements in array A have the value 5. The elements in array C are initially set to 0 on lines 3–4. Then we march through the array A on line 5, incrementing the element of C whose index has the value of A[j] on line 6. Figure 14.6 shows an example of the C array after lines 5–6 execute.

Notice that after lines 5–6 execute, the C array contains all the information in array A. The element at each index has a count of the number of values which equal that index. Therefore, we can now write over array A, using the information in array C. This is what takes place on lines 7–11. The index j on line 7 is used for array A. The index i on line 8 is used for C. But note that even though i is an index, i is the value to store in array A. The number of i's to store in array A is given by C[i]. Therefore, the

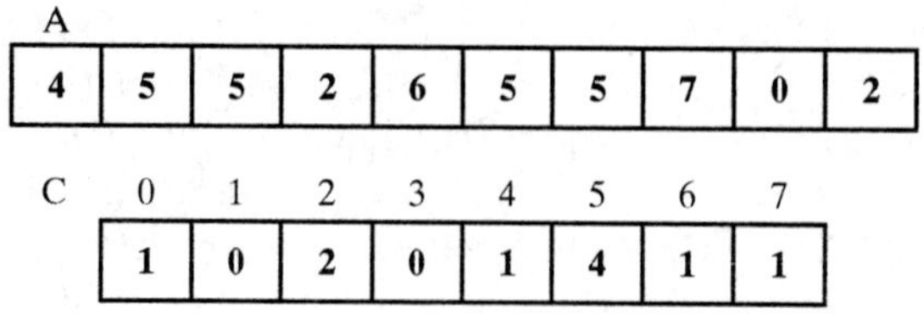

A

4	5	5	2	6	5	5	7	0	2

C   0   1   2   3   4   5   6   7

1	0	2	0	1	4	1	1

FIGURE 14.6

What the counting array C looks like after all the elements in A have been counted. The element at an index of C shows how many elements are in A which are equal to that index. For example, the element at index 5 of C is 4, because there are four 5's in the A array. There is only one 6 in the A array, so the element at index 6 in C is set to 1.

nested loop on line 9 will iterate C[i] times, each time writing i into the next element of A. Once i reaches the value of k in the outer loop, and this index is processed, A will contain the elements in sorted order.

Counting sort is an unusual algorithm because its time complexity depends not only on the number of elements in A, but also on the range of values in A. Other than this unusual characteristic, however, the time complexity of counting sort is easy to analyze. Lines 3–4 run in $\Theta(k)$ time. Lines 5–6 run in $\Theta(n)$ time.

Lines 8–11 are nested loops, but notice that j will not be incremented beyond the last element in A. This is because the total of all the values in array C is n, the grand total of all counts. Therefore, lines 10–11 execute exactly n times. This would appear to make lines 8–11 $\Theta(n)$, but notice that line 8 executes k times. If $k < n$, lines 8–11 would be $\Theta(n)$. But if k is much greater than n, then there are a number of elements of C that have a 0 count. For these elements, the inner loop won't be executed, but the algorithm still has to spend time considering them. How many times is line 9 executed? It is executed at least k times, because its implicit condition must be checked to see if the inner loop should be executed. It is also executed another n times for each iteration of lines 10–11. So line 9 is executed $k + n$ times. Putting it all together for lines 8–11, we see that they run in $\Theta(k) + \Theta(n)$ time.

This, in fact, is the time complexity for counting sort, but that time complexity makes it difficult to compare counting sort with other sorting algorithms. If k is less than or equal to n, however, we can think of counting sort as a $\Theta(n)$ algorithm in its best, average, and worst cases. Therefore, $k < n$ is often the condition when one would want to consider using counting sort.

It may seem as if counting sort can be used only on integer arrays whose values range from 0 to k. However, that is not really the case. If one knows the minimum and maximum values in the array, the values in array A can be adjusted so that they range from 0 to k, where k is maximum − minimum (the range between the minimum and maximum values). In this case, counting sort can be preceded by the following lines, where min is the minimum value in A and max is the maximum value in A:

```
for each j, from 0 to the length of A – 1
        A[ j ] = A[ j ] – min
    k = max - min
```

This code will adjust the values in array A to range from 0 to k even if min is negative. After counting sort executes, the following lines can adjust the values of A back to where they were:

```
for each j, from 0 to the length of A – 1
    A[ j ] = A[ j ] + min
```

These sets of lines don't add to the time complexity, because they are both $\Theta(n)$.

It may also be the case that one does not know the minimum and maximum values in array A, but can find them in $\Theta(n)$ time as well, using the following lines:

```
min = A[0]
max = A[0]
for each j, from 1 to the length of A - 1
        if A[ j ] > max
                then max = A[ j ]
        else if A[ j ] < min
                then min = A[ j ]
```

Putting it all together, our counting sort algorithm might look like this:

```
COUNTING-SORT( A )
min = A[0]
max = A[0]
for each j, from 1 to the length of A - 1
        if A[ j ] > max
                then max = A[ j ]
        else if A[ j ] < min
                then min = A[ j ]
for each j, from 0 to the length of A – 1
        A[ j ] = A[ j ] - min
k = max – min
make an Array C of length k + 1
for each i, from 0 to k
        do C[ i ] ;    0
for each j, from 0 to the length of A - 1
        do C[ A[ j ] ] ;    C[ A[ j ] ] + 1
j = 0
for each i from 0 to k
        do for each m, from 1 to C[ i ]
                do A[ j ] = i
                j = j + 1
for each j, from 0 to the length of A – 1
        A[ j ] = A[ j ] + min
```

The most common use of counting sort is just for integers, but with a little more modification of the algorithm, counting sort can be used in a variety of situations. For example, when sorting monetary amounts, the algorithm could be preceded by the lines

```
For each j, from 0 to the length of A − 1
    A[ j ] = A[ j ] * 100
```

and the following lines could come after the algorithm:

```
For each j, from 0 to the length of A − 1
    A[ j ] = A[ j ] * 0.01
```

These sets of lines don't add to the time complexity either. The main thing that can kill the practicality of counting sort is if the range k is much larger than n when converted to integers. If k is less than n, counting sort should definitely be considered for use.

14.5   SORTING A LINKED LIST

A linked list can be sorted by any sorting algorithm that can sort an array, without affecting the time complexity of the sorting algorithm. All you need to do is copy the linked list into an array, sort the array with the algorithm of your choice, and then copy the elements back into the linked list:

```
ptr = start
for all i from 0 to n − 1
    A[ i ] = ptr->info
    ptr = ptr->next
// sort array A with the sorting algorithm
ptr = start
for all i from 0 to n − 1
    ptr->info = A[ i ]
    ptr = ptr->next
```

Any sorting algorithm has to use at least $\Theta(n)$ time if nothing about the elements is known beforehand. This is basically because it takes $\Theta(n)$ time just to look at each element. Therefore, the sections of code above and below the sorting algorithm won't add to the time complexity of the sorting algorithm, since they are $\Theta(n)$ themselves.

Remember, however, that linked lists are often used to store large elements. There is an awful lot of element copying going on here, and there may be a lot in the sorting algorithm, too. When a large element, such as the object of a struct, is copied from one place to another, each member has to be copied over. Thus, even though the time complexity doesn't change, we may want to try to get better performance.

It is worth mentioning, then, that very often a linked list can be sorted with a sorting algorithm that can be used for an array, without affecting the time complexity and without copying any elements. The idea is to first set up an array of pointers to Nodes and then store the address of each successive node in the linked list in the next element in the array:

```
i = 0
ptr = start
while ptr is not equal to NULL
        A[ i ] = ptr
        ptr = ptr->next
        i++
```

Figure 14.7 shows what the array A of pointers will look like after this initial step is completed. The size of array A can be initialized to the number of elements in the linked list. If that number is not known, the Array class can be used and the size of the array can be extended if the array is filled. This loop would have a time complexity of $\Theta(n)$.

After that, a sorting algorithm of your choice can be used on the array, except that when an element is accessed, you would need to tack on -->info. For example, insertion sort is shown as follows for the array of pointers:

```
1       for each j, from 1 to the length of A – 1
2               tempPtr = A[ j ]
3               i = j – 1
4               while i is greater than -1 and A[ i ]->info is greater than tempPtr->info
5                       A[ i + 1 ] = A[ i ]
6                       i—
7               A[ i + 1] = tempPtr
```

Notice that no elements have been copied so far for the large elements in the linked list. On lines 2, 5, and 7, addresses are copied, which would take far less time. The ->info is tacked on, usually for comparison purposes, as shown on line 4. The "greater than" operator would need to be overloaded if these were objects of a struct. Figure 14.8 uses the initial array and linked list of Figure 14.7 to show what the array A looks like after the sorting algorithm has finished executing.

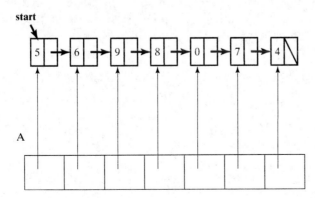

start

FIGURE 14.7

An array A of node pointers, where each element in A has been assigned the address of a corresponding node of a linked list.

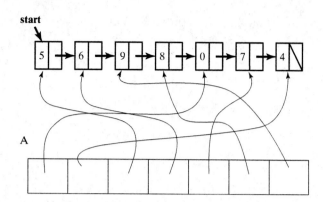

FIGURE 14.8

What the array A of node pointers
looks like after the sorting algorithm
is run on Figure 14.7.

At this point, notice that the linked list does not need to be linked together at all. The address of every node can be found in array A, so without the links between the nodes, there is no memory leak. All we really need to do now is relink the nodes in the linked list as indicated by the result in array A:

```
for all i from 0 to n – 2
        A[ i ]->next = A[ i + 1 ]
start = A[ 0 ]
A[ n – 1 ]->next = NULL
```

This relinking is also done in $\Theta(n)$ time without copying any elements. If the array A were declared locally in a function that does this, the array would be destroyed at the end of the function, and we would be left with the sorted linked list.

Putting it all together, we see that the resulting sorting algorithm for the linked list would look like this:

```
i = 0
ptr = start
while ptr is not equal to NULL
        A[ i++] = ptr
        ptr = ptr->next
// sort the array with a sorting algorithm (swap addresses instead of elements);
// use A[ i ]->info to look at an element
for all i from 0 to n – 2
        A[ i ]->next = A[ i + 1 ]
start = A[ 0 ]
A[ n – 1 ]->next = NULL
```

Thus, using such a technique would enhance the algorithm's performance with large elements.

As discussed in Chapter 10, it would take $\Theta(n^2)$ time, on average, to insert n elements into a sorted linked list. Therefore, one may want to consider whether it would be more efficient to insert elements into an unsorted linked list first (at the front of the list) in $\Theta(n)$ time and then use a sorting algorithm to sort the elements. The decision would, of course, depend entirely on the situation one is dealing with. If a function is added to an unsorted linked-list class for sorting purposes, it might be worth it to add a second function to insert an element in the proper position of the sorted linked list. Doing this would increase flexibility in the way one uses the (normally) unsorted linked list class.

SUMMARY

This chapter has presented some sorting algorithms to help you prepare for a course in the analysis of algorithms. Numerous sorting algorithms are available, and much has been written about them. Therefore, you should consider this chapter as only an introduction. As you can see, almost every sorting algorithm has some situation in which it will be more efficient than the others. You should carefully consider the right sorting algorithm for the situation you are dealing with.

The chapter also has introduced function templates, which are usually constructed by a client. A sorting algorithm in function template form can deal with any type of element without having to rewrite the sorting code. In sorting objects of structs (by one particular data member), it is often necessary to write overloaded comparison operators for the struct.

Sorting algorithms—both those presented here and others—can be used on linked lists as well as arrays. This versatility may or may not come in handy, but it is something to keep in mind.

EXERCISES

1. Why is a function template good to use for a sorting algorithm?
2. Recall from Chapter 9 that the binary search has a time complexity of $O(\lg n)$, while the sequential search has a time complexity of $O(n)$. However, in order to use the binary search on an array, the array must be sorted. Would you want to use a sorting algorithm on an array for the sake of doing a single binary search? Why or why not? If not, is there any situation where we would ever want to use a single binary search?
3. Given the following array, show what the array would look like after each iteration of the outer loop of insertion sort:
   [11, 5, 23, 10, 2, 3, 24, 5, 12, 13]
4. Show what the array of Exercise 3 would look like after using the partition function (from the quicksort algorithm) on it.
5. Show what array C (in the counting sort algorithm) would look like when the counting sort algorithm is applied to the following array:
   [4, 4, 1, 0, 4, 4, 1, 0, 1, 1]
6. Given the following linked list, show what the array of pointers into this list would look like after applying a sorting algorithm:
   10 -> 4 -> 25 -> 3 -> 9 -> 16 -> 8 -> 15 -> 2 -> 14
7. Write a function template for the insertion sort algorithm.
8. Recall that, during the progression of insertion sort, the first section of the array is the sorted section and the second section is the unsorted section. We take the element at index j and find the

place to insert it in the sorted section. Since this section is sorted, we could use the binary search on it to find the place where the element at j should be inserted. Would we have any gain in performance from using this technique? Why or why not?

9. Consider using an array of pointers into a linked list, but allow elements to be copied. Can we use the technique in Exercise 8 and insertion sort to sort the linked list and still get a gain in performance? (Think carefully!)

10. Recall that insertion sort behaves like a $\Theta(n)$ algorithm in the average case when the number of elements is around 5. Quicksort, by contrast, would still behave like a $\Theta(n \lg n)$ algorithm in the average case when the number of elements is around 5. Modify the quicksort algorithm so that when the array piece is five elements or less, quicksort is no longer called recursively on it. Instead, insertion sort is used to sort the array piece of five elements. (*Hint:* In the quicksort recursive function, instead of checking p $<$ r (a spread of at least two elements), you will be checking for a spread of at least six elements before calling quicksort recursively. The base case needs to use insertion sort.)

11. Devise an algorithm to use heapsort on a linked list without copying any elements. (*Hint:* Consider using an array of struct objects, where the struct contains a single data member: a pointer to a node of the linked list to be sorted. Then write the appropriate overloaded operator(s) for the struct.)

12. An array of 100 last names of people needs to be sorted. We notice that, for any letter of the alphabet, no more than 5 last names begin with that letter. Devise a $\Theta(n)$ algorithm to sort the array. (*Hint:* Consider using counting sort on only the first character of each last name. Then use insertion sort.)

13. Using quicksort, write a sort function for the DoublyLinkedList class (Section 11.7) that will sort the doubly linked list while keeping the collision lists intact.

14. Exercise 13 is interesting, but we should let the client write the sorting algorithm for the DoublyLinkedList class. After all, the client might have a good idea about which sorting algorithm to use for the application he or she is writing. Do Exercise 13, but use a function pointer as a parameter in the constructor, which will accept a sorting function written by the client. The sorting function should pass in an array of pointers to the doubly linked list. Be sure to test the function to make sure that the doubly linked list is sorted.

CHAPTER 15

Other Data Structures

In this chapter, we'll discuss some other data structures that are important tools to have in a data structures toolbox. One of these is the ***binary search tree***.

15.1 BINARY SEARCH TREES

A binary search tree is a binary tree, as you might guess from the name, but it differs somewhat from a heap. Unlike the way we use a heap, in a binary search tree we often search for values that can be anywhere in the tree. Therefore, when objects are used as elements, it frequently makes sense to search for the key value of an object. In the rest of this section, we will assume such an implementation, where each key is different for each object.

A binary search tree does not have to be a complete binary tree, and its ordering property is a little bit different from that of a heap. In a binary search tree, for each node, the value of the left child (if there is a left child) is less than the node's value, and the node's value is less than the value of the right child (if there is a right child). We don't consider nodes that have equal values, because we assume that keys are the values compared, and each key is different.

A binary search tree is usually implemented as a linked structure. Its node requires two pointers:

```
template <class DataType>
struct BSTNode {
        DataType info;
        BSTNode<DataType> *left;
        BSTNode<DataType> *right;
};
```

Here, "BST" is used as an abbreviation for "binary search tree". Often, the only data members needed in the private section of a binary search tree class are a pointer to the root (i.e., a pointer that can hold the address of a BSTNode<DataType> object) and, possibly, a variable for storing the number of elements in the tree.

There is a certain logic used when a new element is inserted into a binary search tree. If there is no root node, the new element's node becomes the root node, of course. But if there are one or more nodes in the tree, we start by comparing the new element with the element in the root. If it is less, then we examine the node to the left of the root (if there is such a node). If it is greater then we examine the node to the right of the root (if there is such a node). When objects are used as elements, it is necessary to overload one of the relational operators $<$ or $>$ for comparison purposes.

When we examine the left child or right child of the root, if the value of the new element is less, we look to the left node (if there is one) of *that* node. If the value of the new element is more, we look to the right node (if there is one) of *that* node. Every time we compare, we compare at the next level in the BST. We continue doing this same thing for each level, until we look to the left or the right of a node and there is no node there. (The left or right pointer is set to NULL.) This is the place where the new element is to be inserted (wrapped in a node, of course).

Figure 15.1 shows an example of inserting nodes that contain just integers. Placing the integers in a different order for insertion often (though not always) creates a different binary search tree. Figure 15.2 shows an example of a binary search tree that is produced when elements are inserted in order.

Recall from Section 12.4 that when we swap from the root of a heap all the way down to a leaf, the loop that does the swapping runs in $O(\lg n)$ time. Thus, if our binary search tree happens to take the shape of a complete binary tree, as a heap does, the insertion algorithm just described would run in $\Theta(\lg n)$ time. On each iteration of a loop (or on each recursive call if the algorithm is recursive), we would compare an element at the next level down. Thus, to reach the lowest level of a complete binary tree would require $\Theta(\lg n)$ iterations or recursive calls.

However, if we are unlucky and we get a binary search tree like that in Figure 15.2, and we tried to insert an element larger than any element in the tree, the insertion algorithm would run in $\Theta(n)$ time. A binary search tree for which an insertion can take as long as $\Theta(n)$ time can be formed by inserting elements in order or by inserting them in reverse order. Unfortunately, out of all the ways to place elements in different orders, the ways for in-order and in-reverse-order probably occur more frequently than any other type of ordering. However, the other types of ordering, *combined*, might be more frequent.

If the shape of a binary search tree provides a $\Theta(\lg n)$ time complexity for insertion, we say that the binary search tree is ***balanced***. A complete binary tree is the best of the balanced binary trees. If the shape of a binary search tree provides a $O(n)$ time complexity for insertion, where we are using the best time complexity that is applicable to the situation, we say that the binary search tree is ***unbalanced***. An unbalanced binary search tree does not have to be completely unbalanced, as in Figure 15.2; you might have a few nodes branching to the left. A binary search tree in a ∧ shape, as in Figure 15.3, would still be considered unbalanced. If you have to go

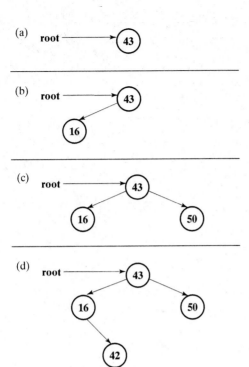

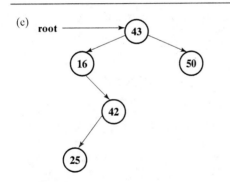

FIGURE 15.1

Elements with key values 43, 16, 50, 42, 25, 49, and 6 are inserted in that order into a binary search tree, starting with an empty tree. (a) When key 43 is inserted, it becomes the root node. (b) Key 16 is less than 43, so it is inserted to the left. (c) Key 50 is greater than 43, so it is inserted to the right. (d) Key 42 is less than 50; since we have an element on the left, we compare 42 with 16. Key 42 is greater than 16, so we insert it to the right of 16. (e) Key 25 is less than 50. (Go to the left.) Key 25 is greater than 16. (Go to the right.) Key 25 is less than 42. (Insert it on the left.)

through $\frac{1}{2}n$ elements to do an insertion, then $\frac{1}{2}n$ iterations is still a $\Theta(n)$ time complexity. Nor does a balanced tree have to be a complete binary tree: You can have a little slop and still have a balanced tree. As you might suspect, the line between the balanced tree and the unbalanced tree is more slender than the spider web.

To search for a node in a binary search tree, we use essentially the same process that we use when we insert the key that we are searching for. If we run into a NULL pointer during the search, the element wasn't in the tree. Otherwise, we will eventually run into the node that has the key. Figure 15.4 illustrates a search for a key. Thus, searching can take $O(\lg n)$ time in a balanced tree and $O(n)$ time in an unbalanced tree, again using the best time complexities, for big-oh notation, that apply to the balanced and unbalanced trees (which we will do throughout the section).

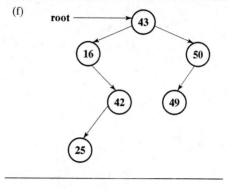

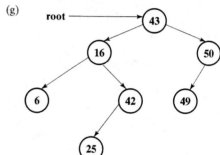

FIGURE 15.1 (*continued*)

(f) Key 49 is greater than 43 and less than 50. (Insert it to the left of 50.) (g) Key 6 is less than 43 and less than 16. (Insert it to the left of 16.) Note that we do an insertion at a pointer only when it is a NULL pointer. (If the pointer points to another node, we make another comparison.)

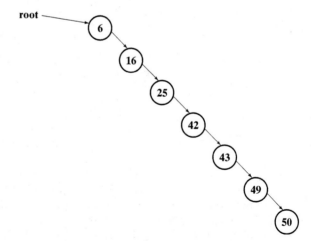

FIGURE 15.2

The key values used in Figure 15.1 are used to make this binary search tree. However, the values are inserted in a different order, namely, from lowest to highest: 6, 16, 25, 42, 43, 49, and 50.

One consequence of the scheme for inserting nodes is that all of the elements in the subtree on the left of a node will have values less than that of the node, and likewise, all of the elements in the subtree on the right of a node will have values greater than that of the node. This consequence helps us create a scheme for deleting nodes.

Deleting a node is a little tricky. There are three cases that we have to consider. In each case, we first have to find the node that we want to delete, using the searching

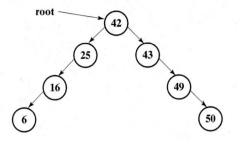

FIGURE 15.3

The same key values used in Figure 15.1 are used to make this binary search tree. They were inserted in the order 42, 25, 16, 6, 43, 49, and 50.

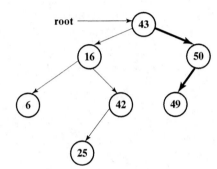

FIGURE 15.4

Searching for key 49 in the binary search tree formed in Figure 15.1. The search path is shown in bold, starting from the root node. We search by comparisons, similar to insertion. The key 49 is greater than 43, so we look to the right. The key 49 is less than 50, so we look to the left. If a NULL pointer is found at the place we look, then the key is not in the binary search tree.

algorithm described. After we find that node, what we do depends on how many children the node has. The first case, in which a node that we want to delete has no children, is the easiest. We just remove the node. To set its parent's child pointer to NULL, we may want to do a search staying one node above the node we want to delete; this method is similar to the one used for the LinkedList class of Chapter 10, where we stay one node in front of the node we want to delete.

The second case is where the node we want to delete has one child. In this case, we connect its parent to its child, thereby splicing the node out. Figure 15.5 shows an example in which the node we wish to delete is circled with a dotted line. Because of the consequence of the insertion scheme that we described earlier, we are guaranteed that when the address of the circled node's child is assigned to the right pointer of the circled node's parent, the child of the circled node will be greater than the parent of the circled node. The same is true if the circled node's child is the left child, as in Figure 15.6.

The third case is where the node we want to delete has two children. If so, then we can find either the greatest element in its left subtree or the least element in its right subtree. Let's assume the former. Then this element is found simply by going to the root node of the left subtree and then following the right pointers as far as we can go (until we find a NULL right pointer). Figure 15.7a shows an example in which the dashed node is the greatest node in the left subtree of the node we wish to delete. Once we find such a node, we just *replace* the element in the node we wish to delete (dotted in the figure) with the element in the dashed node. Then we remove the dashed node. The dashed node may have one left child, in which case we would remove it by splicing it out, described in the second case. The dashed node can't have a right child; otherwise the right child would have been the dashed node. If the dashed node has no children, we simply remove the node as described in the first case. The completed deletion is shown in Figure 15.7b.

(a)

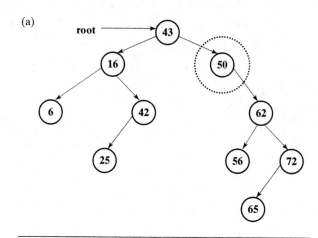

(b)

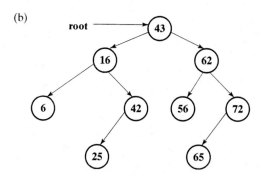

FIGURE 15.5

Deleting a node that has one child. (a) The node with 50, surrounded by a dotted circle, is the node we wish to delete. (b) It can just be spliced out as we reassign the right child pointer of the node with 43 to the address of the node with 62.

When we replace the node we wish to delete (the dotted node) with the element in the dashed node, we are guaranteed to have a binary search tree. The value in the dashed node was the greatest value in the left subtree, so it will be greater than all the values in the left subtree after it replaces the element in the dotted node. Because it was in the left subtree, it is less than all of the values in the right subtree of the dotted node, and it will continue to be so after it replaces the element in the dotted node.

In the first two cases of deleting a node, the time complexity is obviously $O(\lg n)$ for a balanced tree and $O(n)$ for an unbalanced tree. The only loop (or series of recursive calls) is involved in finding the node, as before. The actual deletion takes $\Theta(1)$ time, which is absorbed into the $O(\lg n)$ or $O(n)$ complexity.

In the third case, we search for the node we wish to delete and then search deeper for the greatest element in the left subtree. This is just a continuation of a path from the root node to the dashed node. Thus, the looping (or series of recursive calls) involved is $O(\lg n)$ for a balanced tree and $O(n)$ for an unbalanced tree. Replacing the element and deleting the dashed node are $\Theta(1)$ operations, which, again, are absorbed into the $O(\lg n)$ or $O(n)$ time complexities.

If we assume that (1) no deletions are done on a binary search tree and (2) all the possible orderings of the elements placed into the binary search tree are equally likely, then it can be proven that, *on average*, an insertion and a search in a binary search tree each take $O(\lg n)$ time. This property is important because it shows that, although the

(a)

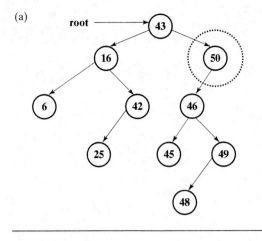

(b)

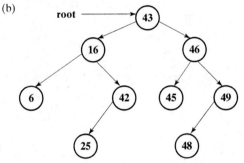

FIGURE 15.6

Another way of splicing out node 50, the node we want to delete.

$\Theta(n)$ time complexity is possible, in some situations it is not common. If deletions are allowed, the proof becomes incredibly difficult.

Even though all this looks pretty good, one may be wondering why on earth we would ever want to use a binary search tree for searching when we have hash tables that can often achieve searches in $\Theta(1)$ time. The reason is that binary search trees have another advantage: They can provide all the elements of the tree, in order, in only $\Theta(n)$ time, whether or not the tree is balanced.

Let's take a look at a recursive function to do just that:

```
1    template <class DataType>
2    void BinarySearchTree::InOrder2( BSTNode<DataType> *ptr ,
3                                                Array<DataType> & arr, int & i )
4    {
5        if ( ptr != NULL ) {
6                InOrder2( ptr->left, arr, i );
7                arr[ i ] = ptr->info;
8                i++;
9                InOrder2( ptr->right, arr, i );
10               }
11   }
```

(a)

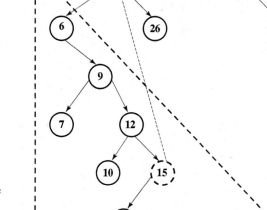

FIGURE 15.7

Deleting a node that has two children.
(a) The dotted node with 16 is the node we
wish to delete. To delete it, we find the
greatest value in its left subtree. The left
subtree of the node with 16 is shown with
a dashed border around it. The dashed
node has the greatest value in the left
subtree. It is found simply by following the
right-child pointers of the left subtree as
far as possible; when a right NULL
pointer is located, the node that we stop
on has the greatest value in the left
subtree. The value in the dashed node will
replace the value in the dotted node,
which we wish to delete. (Replacement is
indicated by the dotted arrow.) (b) The
value 15 has replaced the value 16. The
dashed node is now deleted. If the dashed
node has no children, it is simply removed.
If the dashed node has one left child, as it
does in this example, we simply splice the
dashed node out, using the method shown
in Figure 15.6. The dashed node cannot
have a right child: If it did, it would not be
the greatest value in the left subtree,
because we did not follow the chain of
right pointers as far as we could go.

(b)

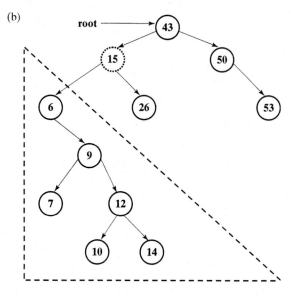

Since clients don't usually call functions by passing in pointers to nodes, this recursive
function would be in the private section. The driver for calling the function would be in
the public section:

```
12   template <class DataType>
13   bool BinarySearchTree::InOrder( Array<DataType> & arr )
14   {
15       if ( size == 0 )
```

```
16          return false;
17      arr.changeSize( size );
18      int i = 0;
19      InOrder2( root, arr, i );
20      return true;
21  }
```

We assume that size, on line 15, gives the current number of elements in the binary search tree. Thus, we set the size of the array so that it has the capacity to store all of the elements, in order. (The client may have done this, but we'll play it safe.) Then, i, used for the beginning index, is set to 0. The root of the tree is passed into the first call of the recursive function, along with the empty array and index i, both passed in by reference so that any changes to them will be reflected into each recursive function call. This approach is necessary because there are two recursive function calls, one on line 6 and one on line 9. The first call will get the changes to arr and i, thereby using them correctly on lines 7–8. Upon completion of all recursive calls, the Array object arr is returned to the client (passed in by reference), with the elements of the binary search tree, in order.

It may not be obvious how the recursive function works, so let's take a look at it, using our guidelines from Section 13.2. First of all, the base case occurs when ptr == NULL. Whether we make the recursive call on line 6 or the recursive call on line 9, we are moving down one level in the tree, thus getting closer to the base case for that call.

Does the recursive function work for the base case? Yes, if the driver will let it. The driver returns false if the binary search tree is empty. If, however, the driver called the InOrder2 function, no elements would be provided in order. InOrder2 would just return right away, because root would be set to NULL.

Does the function work for one recursive call? Well, we really have to make two recursive calls, since if the one is made on line 6, the other will certainly be made on line 9. But we can walk through the code if we assume that there is only one node in the binary search tree, at the root node, and see if the code works. The root, which is not NULL, is passed into the InOrder2 function. The if statement is true, so the recursive call on line 6 is made, passing in the pointer to the left child, which is NULL. When this InOrder2 function is made, it will return right away since ptr is NULL. Thus, we return back to the first InOrder2 function and continue. We store the info section at the root node into arr[0] on line 7 and then increment i to 1. Next, we make the recursive call on line 9, passing in the right pointer, which is again NULL. The next InOrder2 function that is made returns control right away back to the first InOrder2 function again. The InOrder2 function returns, and the InOrder function has the array with the info from the root node stored in arr[0]. So, yes, this function works for one recursive call.

Now, the next guideline is perhaps the most important for understanding how the recursive function works. We have to ask ourselves, whether or not the function makes logical sense with a large binary search tree, assuming that the function calls on lines 6 and 9 do everything they are supposed to do. Let's suppose that there are p nodes in the left subtree and r nodes in the right subtree. Then the first recursive call stores the p nodes in order in the first p positions of the array, and i is always incremented after storing an element, so i is set to the next position for storing an element. Line 7 stores the element in the node we are on. Well, we know that all the elements in the left subtree are less than the element of the node we are on; therefore, so far, all the elements are in order in the array. Then, the next recursive call, on line 9, stores the r nodes in the right subtree in the next r positions of the array, in order (Again, we assume that the call does what it is supposed to do.) Since all the elements in the right subtree are greater than the elements we have in the array so far, if they are placed in the next r positions of the array in order, then the whole array will be in order.

Since the two-call recursive case works, it follows that, for a binary search tree with three nodes, one on the left of the root and one on the right of the root, when we call the InOrder2 function from the root node, the one node on the left will be stored correctly. (This is just the two-call recursive case.) The same is true with regard to the right node. Now, if we have only two nodes in the binary search tree, we've established that the base case works, so this case will work, too. And if it works for two or three nodes, then it will work for a binary search tree with two or three nodes on the left side of the root node and with two or three nodes on the right side of the root node. We are assured of this because of the logical sense present in the previous paragraph and because we've already established that two or three nodes are stored in order correctly. You can see that when the function works with smaller binary trees, it works with larger ones, which are built by putting the smaller binary trees on each side of the root node.

But how do we know that the time complexity of all these recursive calls will be $\Theta(n)$? We need a way to count all of the recursive function calls that were made. Toward that end, we know, from the correctness of the algorithm, that an element will be stored in the array once and only once, in a unique array position. Therefore, the body of the if statement executes exactly n times. But what about all those recursive function calls that were made with ptr set to NULL? Well, we know that, in exactly n calls, the pointer ptr will *not* be set to NULL (since there are n elements). For each pointer that is not NULL, only two recursive function calls can be made, and these recursive calls may or may not be made with ptr set to NULL. So, once InOrder2 is called, only $2n$ function calls are possible: two recursive calls for each of the n nodes. When you combine these calls with the original call to InOrder2, you can easily see that InOrder2 will be called exactly $2n + 1$ times. This is, of course, $\Theta(n)$ time.

15.2   COMPARISON OF THE BST WITH OTHER DATA STRUCTURES

The binary search tree (BST) forms the basis of some more advanced data structures, including the red–black tree and the AVL tree. (The latter is named after its two originators, Georgy M. Adelson-Velsky and Yevgeniy M. Landis.) These data structures are more complicated than the BST, but they ensure that all insertions, deletions, and searches will be carried out in $O(\lg n)$ time. (There is no chance for $\Theta(n)$ time, as there is in the BST.) Although the workings of these more advanced data structures are beyond the scope of this textbook, you may see them in a more advanced text or course. Here, we can only give an overview of their comparison with a BST.

First of all, it may seem like the BST is inferior to the red–black tree and the AVL tree, but it is not. In fact, the BST usually has slightly better performance than either the red–black or the AVL tree. This is because the typical, run-of-the-mill BST is balanced well enough to be fairly fast. Slightly more balance is achieved by these more advanced trees, but the maintenance work that needs to be done to achieve that balance doesn't pan out. In other words, the maintenance costs more in time than the benefit of having a slightly more balanced tree than the typical BST. Also, these more advanced trees waste more memory than the BST, because more housekeeping information is required in each node.

The main reason the red–black tree and the AVL tree are useful is that the performance of the BST isn't consistent (even though its average performance is pretty darn good). Its performance depends on how balanced it is. In those less frequent cases in which a BST becomes unbalanced, the red–black or the AVL tree will outperform it. These more advanced trees have fairly consistent performance. With them, you don't get any surprises in performance lag, as you can with a BST. This is important in time-critical applications, in which each operation has to be done in a dependable amount of time.

We can also compare the BST with the DoublyLinkedList (DLL) data structure presented in Section 11.7. If we used the unsorted DLL, then, in order to provide the elements in order, we could use the iterator to read the elements into an array and then sort the array. We might be able to sort the array in $\Theta(n)$ time with counting sort (see Section 14.4) or another $\Theta(n)$ sorting algorithm that has not been discussed in this textbook. However, there will be a lot of element copying going on, which is not good with large element sizes. There are two reasonable alternatives to the unsorted DLL that would be better:

1. Maintain a sorted DLL (see Chapter 11, Exercises 15–16).
2. Use an unsorted DLL and sort the DLL itself with a sorting algorithm (see Section 14.5 and Chapter 14, Exercises 13–14) when the elements need to be provided in order.

We'll call these alternatives DLL(1) and DLL(2), respectively. When we compare DLL(1) and DLL(2) with the BST, we'll assume that the BST is fairly balanced (it usually is), and we'll assume that we have uniform hashing in the DLLs (the hashing is usually fairly close to uniform if the hash design is good). Under these assumptions, the average time complexities of the most commonly used operations are as shown in Table 15.1.

TABLE 15.1   Table showing how the time complexities of the important operations compare among the BST, DLL(1), and DLL(2). DLL(1) is a sorted DoublyLinkedList (Section 11.7), and DLL(2) is an unsorted DoublyLinkedList that is sorted only when the elements need to be provided in order; the sorting technique for DLL(2) is based on the algorithm presented in Section 14-5.

	BST	*DLL(1)*	*DLL(2)*
Insertion	$\Theta(\lg n)$	$\Theta(n)$	$\Theta(1)$
Deletion	$\Theta(\lg n)$	$\Theta(1)$	$\Theta(1)$
Search	$\Theta(\lg n)$	$\Theta(1)$	$\Theta(1)$
Providing elements in order	$\Theta(n)$	$\Theta(n)$	$\Theta(n)$-$\Theta(n \lg n)$

When we look at this table, it looks like DLL(1) would be a strong competitor with the BST. But the time complexities that you see in the table don't tell the whole story. For example, it would require $n * \Theta(\lg n) = \Theta(n \lg n)$ time to insert n elements into the BST, whereas it would provably require $\Theta(n^2)$ time, on average, to insert them into DLL(1). This difference is a strong factor to consider, because when a data structure will hold a lot of data, it requires quite a few insertions before the data structure becomes "established". DLL(2) would actually be more advantageous in this respect, as it would require only $\Theta(n)$ time for n insertions. In fact, as you can see from the table, DLL(2) should be strongly considered for use when the elements are such that they can be sorted in $\Theta(n)$ time with the sorting technique presented in Section 14.5.

Another factor to consider strongly is the search-intensive nature of the three data structures. Sure, it is nice to be able to insert and delete quickly, but when you come right down to it, these data structures are all about the fast search, and searching will be the most intensive operation of the three. Suppose we need to do n searches on a stabilized data structure (one having n elements and requiring no more deletions or insertions). Then we can expect the n searches to take $\Theta(n \lg n)$ time in the BST and $\Theta(n)$ time in DLL(1) and DLL(2).

Finally, providing the elements in order should be regarded as an important operation. The BST and DLL(1) can each provide the elements in order in $\Theta(n)$ time. The constant (in front of the n) will probably be lower in DLL(1) for execution of the machine language, since the getNext function of the iterator is inlined, but recursive functions (generally used for the BST) cannot be. In DLL(2), however, the situation looks grim: We might be able to sort in $\Theta(n)$ time, but it is more often the case that we cannot. We should expect DLL(2) to take $\Theta(n \lg n)$ time to provide the elements in order, but, as was pointed out earlier, DLL(2) should be strongly considered in those cases where it takes $\Theta(n)$ time to do the sort.

In conclusion, which data structure we should use depends entirely on the situation we are dealing with (as usual). If the elements are such that we can sort them in $\Theta(n)$ time, then DLL(2) deserves strong consideration. The following conditions would make it more advantageous to use the BST:

- The elements cannot generally be sorted in $\Theta(n)$ time.
- There will be a lot of elements.
- Providing the elements in order will be a highly intensive operation.
- There will be an occasional search, insertion, or deletion.

Under these conditions, the BST would be more advantageous than DLL(1) because DLL(1) performs poorly when a lot of elements need to be inserted, while it doesn't have much advantage in providing the elements in order (just a lower constant). We may want to consider DLL(1) if

- After the data structure has been "established" with a lot of elements, both providing the elements in order and searching will be intensive operations for a very long time.
- There will only be an occasional insertion.

Finally, we may want to consider DLL(2), even if it cannot generally sort the elements in $\Theta(n)$ time, if we have the following conditions:

- There will be a lot of elements.
- Searching will be, by far, the most intensive operation.
- We may occasionally provide the elements in order.

As a final word, if the time involved between the BST and the two DLL's appears to be a wash, we should strongly consider the BST, since it does not waste as much memory per node as the two DLL's.

15.3 GRAPHS

Entire textbooks are written about a data structure called a ***graph***. While in trees there are generally rules about which nodes other nodes can point to, there are no such rules in graphs. In a graph, a node is often called a ***vertex*** (plural: ***vertices***). Any vertex in a graph can point to any other vertex. It is possible that no vertices in a graph point to any other vertex; if so, then that graph has no connections between its vertices. It is also possible for each vertex to point to every other vertex in the graph, even if there are thousands of vertices or more; such graphs are called ***fully connected graphs***. Graphs are one of the most general data structures.

There are many graph algorithms that can, and should, be a part of a Graph data structure. Such algorithms, however, belong in a course or textbook on algorithms and are beyond the scope of this text. Therefore, you should consider this section to be only an introduction to graphs.

In graph terminology, when one vertex A points to another vertex B, we say that there is an ***edge*** from vertex A to vertex B. Such an edge is drawn as a pointer arrow, as is normally done in linked structures. Figure 15.8 shows a graph drawn with edges. Such a graph is called a ***directed graph***, or ***digraph*** for short.

Sometimes, every two vertices that are linked with an edge point to each other. That is, you can follow a pointer in vertex A to get from vertex A to vertex B and a pointer in vertex B to get from vertex B to vertex A. When this is true for every pair of vertices that have an edge between them, the graph is called an ***undirected graph***. To

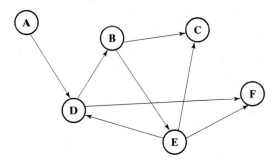

FIGURE 15.8

A directed graph (digraph).

show that there are pointers going in both directions between two connected vertices, we draw a line, rather than an arrow, between the vertices. An ***undirected graph*** is shown in Figure 15.9.

In a directed graph, some pairs of vertices can point to each other, while some pairs of vertices have a pointer only in one direction between them. If two vertices in a directed graph point to each other, two arrows are drawn between the vertices, with one arrow going in reverse; this notation is shown in Figure 15.10. It is considered improper to mix directed edges with undirected edges in the same graph.

Graphs can also be divided into ***cyclic*** and ***acyclic*** categories. A cyclic graph contains one or more cycles; a cycle is a group of three or more vertices such that we can start at one vertex, traverse edges through the other vertices in the cycle, and come back to the starting vertex without passing through any vertex twice. An acyclic graph is a graph that has no cycles. An acyclic, undirected graph that is not separated into two or more parts (by lack of edges) always qualifies as a tree, with any vertex as the root. An acyclic, directed graph may not always be a tree, because even if the graph is not separated into two or more parts, there may not be a way to get from any one vertex to all other vertices.

In a ***weighted graph***, each edge has some particular value, called a ***weight***, that is assigned to it. If the vertices represent, for example, cities, the weights might represent distances between the cities. Such an example is shown in Figure 15.11.

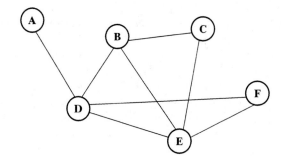

FIGURE 15.9

An undirected graph.

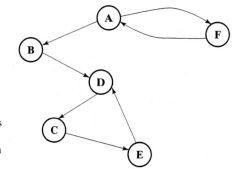

FIGURE 15.10

Another directed graph. In this example, vertex A points to vertex F and vertex F points to vertex A. It would be considered improper to draw just a straight line between vertices A and F in a digraph.

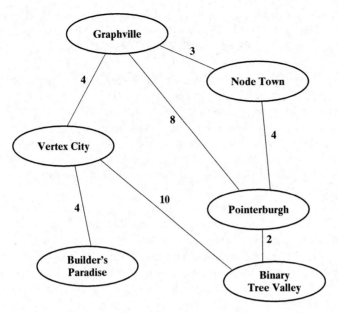

FIGURE 15.11

A weighted graph. Each edge has a value assigned to it. In this example, the vertices represent cities and the edges represent roads between the cities. Each weight is the distance in miles between two cities.

A graph that has few edges relative to the number of vertices is called a ***sparse graph***. A graph that has many edges relative to the number of vertices is called a ***dense graph***.

In discussing time complexities of graph algorithms, some textbooks do not use n for the number of elements. This is because there are two factors that can increase the execution time of a graph algorithm: the number of vertices and the number of edges. Since we can often vary one of these without varying the other, an individual factor can affect how long a graph algorithm takes to execute. V is often used to represent the set of vertices, so $|V|$ is the number of vertices. Similarly, E is used to represent the set of edges, so $|E|$ is the number of edges. Consequently, $|V|$ and $|E|$, rather than n, are used for the problem size in some textbooks. For example, the execution time of an algorithm that takes $\Theta(|V|)$ time to execute varies only with the number of vertices. Analogously, the execution time of an algorithm that takes $\Theta(|E|^2)$ time to execute (in this case, a rather bad time complexity) varies only with the number of edges.

There is a minor anomaly, however, that makes this use of $|E|$ and $|V|$ somewhat imprecise. A graph that has $|V|$ vertices can have, at most, $|V| - 1$ edges from a single vertex to other vertices. Since there are $|V|$ vertices, the total number $|E|$ of edges can be no more than $|V|(|V| - 1) = |V|^2 - |V|$. Therefore, $|E|$ cannot increase without bound independently of $|V|$, and time complexities that involve only $|E|$ are misleading (implying that there is no dependence on $|V|$). A time complexity such as $\Theta(|E|^2)$, for example, cannot make sense if $|V|$ is constant. This is because $|E|$ is bounded by $|V|^2 - |V|$, which would also be a constant. If $|E|$ is bounded by a constant, then $|E|^2$ is also bounded by a constant. (Recall that when the number of instructions is bounded by a constant, we have a constant time complexity.) Thus, such a time complexity is $\Theta(1)$ if $|V|$ is constant. The conclusion is that if $|E|$ and $|V|$

notation is used, time complexities for graph algorithms should either be in terms of $|V|$ or in terms of both $|E|$ and $|V|$, such as $\Theta(|V| + |E|)$.

By the same token, a time complexity such as $\Theta(|V|^3 + |E|)$ also does not make much sense. $|E|$ can be no higher than $|V|^2 - |V|$, so it is absorbed into the $|V|^3$ part of the time complexity. Thus, $\Theta(|V|^3 + |E|)$ is the same as $\Theta(|V|^3)$. A time complexity in terms of both $|V|$ and $|E|$, where the $|V|$ component is $|V|^2$ or higher, is the same as the time complexity with just the $|V|$ component.

If the $|V|$ component of such a time complexity is better than $|V|^2$, as in $\Theta(|V| + |E|)$, then the time complexity really depends on the type of graph we are dealing with. If it is a sparse graph, with $|E| < |V|$, then we have a best-case time complexity of $\Theta(|V|)$. If it is a graph with many edges, to the point of being fully connected, then we have a worst-case time complexity of $\Theta(|V|^2)$.

In light of this discussion, and because $|E|$ cannot really increase without bound independently of $|V|$, I am motivated to provide time complexities of graph algorithms in terms of n, where n is the number of vertices. Graph algorithms that run in a meaningful combination of $|V|$ and $|E|$ really have a best-case and worst-case time complexity in terms of n, depending on whether or we are dealing with a sparse or a dense graph.

One useful graph algorithm, called the *breadth-first search* algorithm, can find the path with the smallest number of edges between one chosen vertex, known as the source vertex, and any other vertex in the graph. One may be able to determine this number through an inspection of a simple graph, but if a graph has hundreds, or even thousands, of vertices, the path sought may not be so obvious. The breadth-first search algorithm is used on unweighted graphs, but forms the basis of more complex algorithms that work with weighted graphs. Such algorithms would find the shortest path, for example, to send a message on a network, in a graph in which each vertex represents a transfer point in the network (for example, a router) and each edge indicates a connection in the network. The breadth-first search algorithm runs in a best-case time of $\Theta(n)$ for sparse graphs and a worst-case time of $\Theta(n^2)$ for dense graphs.

Another graph algorithm, called the topological sort, can be used to order the vertices of a directed, acyclic graph, providing the order in a linked list. If two vertices A and B have a directed edge from A to B, then vertex A would come before vertex B in the ordering. The topological sort can be used to make sense out of an event graph, in which each vertex represents some event, or task, that must be taken care of. A directed edge from vertex A to vertex B means that the task represented by A must be taken care of before the task represented by vertex B can be performed. The topological sort would, therefore, provide the order in which the tasks can be performed in a complex event graph, where that order may not be so obvious. The topological sort runs in a best-case time of $\Theta(n)$ for sparse graphs and a worst-case time of $\Theta(n^2)$ for dense graphs.

Both the discussion of how graph algorithms work and their detailed analysis are beyond the scope of this textbook, but you can see how graphs and their algorithms can be useful in a number of situations. You will encounter more about graph algorithms in a course or textbook on algorithm analysis. In this chapter, we will just discuss how the graph data structure can be implemented.

Given that any vertex in a graph may or may not point to any other vertex, the implementation of a graph might seem rather difficult. But there are a couple of simple ways of making a data representation of a graph. In each representation, we focus on showing which pair of vertices has a connection.

When two vertices A and B have an edge between them, we say that vertex A is **adjacent** to vertex B. One way of representing a graph is to use something called an **adjacency matrix**. In explaining how the adjacency matrix works, we will first assume that the number of vertices in a graph will not change. The n vertices of a graph are numbered from 0 to $n - 1$, as shown in Figure 15.12. The adjacency matrix is a two-dimensional array, with each dimension being of size n. The indexes in each dimension correspond to the numbers of the vertices. The values of the two-dimensional array need to be only bool types, which use the least amount of memory space. An element of the two-dimensional array is set to true if there is an edge between the numbers of the vertices used in the indexes. For example, if there is an edge from vertex 5 to vertex 7, then, assuming that the name of the two-dimensional array is AdjMatrix, we would set the value at that corresponding position in the adjacency matrix to true:

AdjMatrix[5][7] = true;

If there is no edge from one particular vertex to another, then that corresponding position in the adjacency matrix would be set to false. Figure 15.13 shows the adjacency matrix for the graph shown in Figure 15.12.

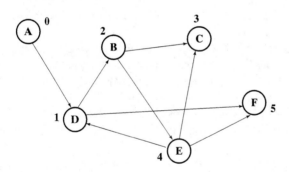

FIGURE 15.12

A graph with vertices numbered from 0 to $n - 1$. The numbering is arbitrary.

	0	1	2	3	4	5
0	T	T	F	F	F	F
1	F	T	T	F	F	T
2	F	F	T	T	T	F
3	F	F	F	T	F	F
4	F	T	F	T	T	T
5	F	F	F	F	F	T

FIGURE 15.13

Adjacency matrix for the graph of Figure 15.12. T is used to represent true, while F is used to represent false. The row numbers signify vertices that point to other vertices. For example, vertex 0 points to vertex 1, so 0 is used as the row while 1 is used as the column; at the place of intersection of the row and column, T is used to indicate a pointer from vertex 0 to vertex 1. In this example, it is assumed that a vertex is linked to itself. (In some situations, that assumption cannot be made.) For example, the intersection of row 0 and column 0 is marked as T.

One can determine how to draw the graph of Figure 15.12 just by looking at the adjacency matrix in Figure 15.13. The vertices might be drawn in different positions in constructing the graph, but the edges between the vertices will still be the same, and that is the important thing in order for two graphs to be equivalent.

If an adjacency matrix is used for a weighted graph, then the elements of the two-dimensional array can be numerical types, such as int or float. The weight on an edge between two vertices is then stored in the corresponding position of the two-dimensional array. If two vertices do not have an edge between them, the weight can be set to some value that can't be a correct weight. For example, if distances are used between vertices, the weight between two vertices that aren't connected might be set to −1, indicating that there is no pointer from the vertex with the first index to the vertex with the second index. Sometimes, all possible values of a data type may be used for a weight. In that case, each element can be a struct with a bool member and a number. The bool member is set to true if there is an edge and false otherwise; the number is set to the weight if the bool member is set to true. Of course, we want to form the representation that uses the least amount of memory.

Another way of representing a graph is to use something called an ***adjacency list***. We assume that vertices in a graph will not change, as before; thus, they are numbered from 0 to $n - 1$. Then we make a one-dimensional Array for the vertices, of size n, such that each index corresponds to a vertex number. Each element of the Array is a linked list, perhaps made with the LinkedList class of Chapter 10. The linked list is a list of vertices; the vertex represented by the index of the Array has an edge to every vertex in the linked list. Figure 15.14 shows an adjacency list representation of the graph illustrated in Figure 15.12. It is important to keep in mind that the vertices in a linked list are not necessarily connected to each other in the graph. Thinking that they are connected is a mistake that is easy to make because we normally think of elements in a linked list as being connected. But they simply represent the vertices that have an edge from the vertex represented by the index.

As with the adjacency matrix, we can construct a graph just by looking at its adjacency list. For weighted graphs, we would have a struct stored at each node in the

FIGURE 15.14

Adjacency list representation of the graph of Figure 15.12. The array is an array of linked lists. (We are looking only at the start pointer of each linked list.) Each index represents the numbered vertex of the diagram of Figure 15.12. A diagonal line, representing NULL, is drawn through cells 3 and 5, since their vertices do not point to any other vertices. A linked list at an index represents all the vertices that the vertex of that index points to. The nodes in the linked list do not need to be in any particular order.

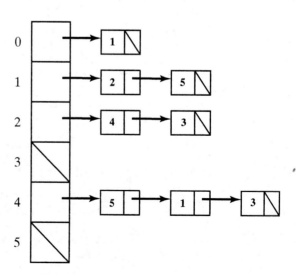

linked list, but the data members stored there should be minimal. All we need as data members are the number of the vertex and the weight of the connection. Figure 15.15 shows such an adjacency list for the weighted graph of Figure 15.11.

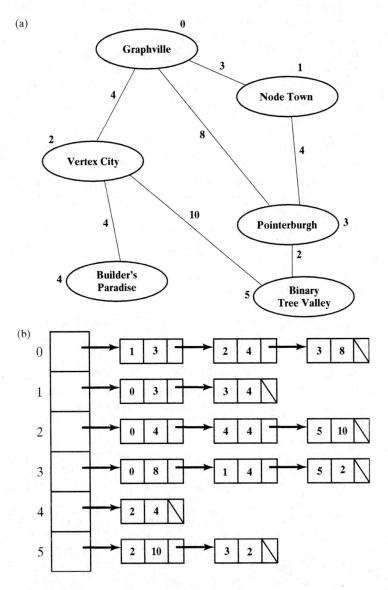

FIGURE 15.15

Adjacency list representation of the graph of Figure 15.11. (a) The graph of Figure 15.11, with vertices numbered from 0 to $n - 1$. (b) The adjacency list representation using the numbering provided in part (a) Each linked-list node is divided into three sections. The first section of a linked-list node in a linked list at an index is the number of a vertex that is pointed to by a vertex with the number of that index. The second section is the weight of the edge connecting the two vertices. These two sections would be put in a struct and used as the info data member of the Node struct. The third section represents the *next* pointer of the Node struct.

Both the adjacency matrix and the adjacency list specify the connections between vertices and the weights of the connections, if any. But neither of them addresses the info section that may be stored in a vertex. Graphs are a unique kind of data structure, because sometimes they don't even have an info section; we may be interested, for example, just in finding shortest paths between vertices. However, if an info section does exist, then, in the linked list, we could place the info section into the linked-list node that represents a particular vertex, but this would use a lot of unnecessary memory space. Such a vertex may appear in many of the linked lists, and the info section within it may be huge. It is best to use a separate array for storing the info sections of the vertices. The array would be of size n, where each index corresponds to the number of a vertex. The elements would be of type DataType, in a template. Thus, we can look up the info for a particular vertex number in $\Theta(1)$ time.

If the vertices can change in a graph, it puts a wrinkle on everything. The numbering scheme that we use for vertices falls apart. We may delete large numbers of vertices, creating gaps in the numbering sequence and wasting space in the array. We can use techniques to compact the array elements, but such techniques take linear time. When the number of vertices can change, we revert to methods that allow efficient processing while conserving memory. We use keys for the info within a vertex, where the key can be anything. Instead of having a simple array of n elements, we utilize a hash table with the chaining method, and we hash the key into an index of the array. Then we follow the linked list at that index to find the key of the vertex whose info we wish to extract. Thus, we can still extract the info for a vertex in $\Theta(1)$ time, while conserving memory. We will call this kind of hash table a ***vertex hash table.***

Let's discuss a possible implementation of the adjacency list representation when the vertices and edges can change. We can use a hash table for the adjacency list, and we hash the key of a vertex into an index. The linked list at that index is then searched for the key. This linked list is not a linked list of adjacent vertices, but rather, a linked list of all vertex keys that collided at the index. Once the key is found in a node of the linked list, that node contains another linked list; *this* is the linked list that contains the vertices that are adjacent to the vertex with the key. Under the assumption of uniform hashing, the adjacency list for a key is found in $\Theta(1)$ time. We will call this hash table an ***adjacency list hash table***.

The Graph data structure may contain functions for inserting vertices, deleting vertices, inserting an edge, and deleting an edge. Inserting a vertex is probably the simplest function if we assume that no edges are inserted with it at the time. All we do is add the vertex into the vertex hash table. If the graph application cannot assure us that this is a not a duplicate vertex, and we do not want duplicate vertices, we can search the linked list for the key, instead of inserting the info at the front of the linked list. If we have uniform hashing, this will still be a $\Theta(1)$ operation, but will be more time consuming.

Deleting a vertex is a little more complicated. We should delete the vertex from the vertex hash table, but we should also delete all the edges to the vertex and all the edges from the vertex in the adjacency-list hash table. Deleting all the edges *from* the vertex is not time consuming: We merely find the adjacency list for the vertex and call the makeEmpty function for that linked list. Deleting the edges *to* the vertex can be time consuming. We can call the delete function for each adjacency list in the hash table, but that would be quite time consuming. A faster, but more complicated, way is to keep a linked list of all keys of vertices that point to the vertex; we can maintain such a linked list in the pointed-to vertex node of the vertex hash table. Let's call this list the *fan-in list*, since it is a list of vertex ids that point inward to the vertex. If we use the DoublyLinkedList for the adjacency lists, deleting them will be quick if we use the implementation described in Section 11.7. It will also help to have a DoublyLinkedList for the fan-in list, because we will occasionally need to remove nodes from it. Once all of the relevant adjacency-list nodes have been deleted, the fan-in list for that vertex can be freed. Then the vertex node in the vertex hash table can be removed. This scheme, although faster, obviously uses more memory. The operation for deleting a vertex would take $\Theta(m)$ time, where m is the number of edges attached to the vertex.

To insert an edge into an adjacency list hash table, we need to know the key of the vertex that the edge points from and the key of the vertex that it points to. We use the key of the vertex that the edge points from in the adjacency-list hash table to get an index. Then we search the linked list for that key. Once it is found, we insert the edge at the front of the linked list found there. If we have a fan-in list, we insert the key of the new adjacency-list node to the front of the fan-in list for the vertex with the second key. If the graph application cannot assure us that this is not a duplicate edge, and we do not want duplicate edges, we can search the fan-in list first of the second key (of the vertex that the edge points to). If we have uniform hashing (when we use the DoublyLinkedList), this will still be a $\Theta(1)$ operation, but will be more time consuming.

Deleting an edge can be done with the use of the same representation of the edge. Once the (doubly linked) adjacency list for the first vertex is found, we simply call the delete function for the DoublyLinkedList to delete the edge. When that is done, we need to search the fan-in list of the second vertex for the key of the first vertex and remove that node as well. If we are using a DoublyLinkedList for the fan-in list, then deleting the edge would take $\Theta(1)$ time.

Implementing an efficient dynamic adjacency matrix representation is more challenging. We can use a dynamic two-dimensional array, as discussed in Section 7.1. But when a vertex is inserted, we must make $2n$ relationships, for possible edges to and from the n vertices that already exist, and set the bool members for each of these relationships (to false initially, assuming that no edges are provided with the new vertex). Thus, we would have at least a time-consuming $\Theta(n)$ method. We would also like to hash into the dimensions of the two-dimensional array, using a hash function that converts the key of a vertex to an index. Each element of the adjacency matrix could easily be a linked list (for collisions at that location), but forming the $2n$ relationships required for the insertion of a vertex would be more difficult and less efficient.

15.4 COMPARING ADJACENCY MATRICES WITH ADJACENCY LISTS

Since we have two ways of representing a graph—an adjacency matrix and an adjacency list—we often need to consider which representation is better for the situation we are dealing with. Our decision frequently (but not always) revolves around two factors:

speed (usually the foremost factor) and memory conservation. Let's consider issues of speed first.

First of all, if vertices as well as edges are to be added to and deleted from the graph, there isn't any doubt that the adjacency-list representation using hash tables would be the faster of the two methods. If the number of vertices is to remain the same, however, then they can be numbered from 0 to $n - 1$, with these values used as keys, and the simpler array schemes without hash tables can be employed. For these types of static graphs, we need to consider which would be the faster method.

The main reason for using an adjacency matrix would be that if we want to know whether or not there is an edge from one vertex to another, we can find out very quickly, in $\Theta(1)$ time. With an adjacency list, we would have to look through the linked list for a particular vertex to find out. However, if we used the DoublyLinkedList implementation of the adjacency list, we can achieve a $\Theta(1)$ time complexity if we have uniform hashing. But even though both implementations can take $\Theta(1)$ time, the adjacency matrix will be faster: With the adjacency list, we would have to search through the collision list of the hash table to get a pointer to the node in the DoublyLinkedList. We could keep the collision list as small as possible by using a large hash table, but then we still would need to execute the hash function.

Adjacency lists also have an advantage, however. In many graph algorithms, particularly searching algorithms (which are beyond the scope of this text), it is quite common for a line of the algorithm to read

for every vertex in the adjacency list of vertex B
      do such and such

where the variable B can denote any vertex. In this case, we can just process the linked list, node by node, so the time complexity of such a loop would be $\Theta(m)$, where m is the number of edges from vertex B. With an adjacency matrix, we don't have an adjacency list, of course, but we can use one row of the matrix to do the processing for this loop. For example, if vertex B is numbered 1, then we can look at all the elements in row 1. This will be more than the number of elements in an adjacency list, because it includes elements that are set to false. In fact, we would have to look at n elements, giving us $\Theta(n)$ time to implement this loop. So, in this case, the adjacency list is faster.

In short, our choice of method depends upon the algorithms used in the application for which we want to use a Graph data structure. Some algorithms never want to know if a connection exists between two particular vertices; some do. Some algorithms never process all the elements in an adjacency list; some do. But these are the main issues, as far as speed is concerned. If the application under consideration looks like a wash with regard to speed, then we may want to lean heavily on issues of memory conservation. For that, we get into issues of space complexity, which uses the same notation as that used for time complexity. In space complexity, one or more factors affect the amount of memory space used.

With the adjacency matrix, since each dimension is n, the space complexity is $\Theta(n^2)$, even though each element may just be a bool type. With the adjacency list, we have n linked lists, some of which may be empty. In the implementation of the LinkedList class in Chapter 10, there are only two pointers in the private section: a start pointer and a current pointer. Thus, a linked-list object uses 8 bytes all by itself, whether or not it is empty. But how many nodes do we have in all the linked lists? The nodes pointed to by these pointers take up even more space. If you think about it a little bit, you will realize that we put in exactly one node per directed edge. (In an undirected graph, we take each edge to be *two* directed edges.) Thus, the number of directed edges corresponds exactly to the number of nodes in all the linked lists. Consequently, the space complexity depends on whether we are dealing with a sparse graph (in which the number of edges is less than n) or a dense graph. If it is a sparse graph, the n linked lists dominate, and the space complexity is $\Theta(n)$. If it is a dense graph, the number of edges dominate, and the space complexity is $\Theta(n^2)$.

In both representations, we might also have an array of n elements used for vertex info, but this $\Theta(n)$ complexity is absorbed into the space complexities for both implementations. So we just need to consider the adjacency matrix vs. the adjacency list.

In conclusion, then, for sparse graphs, the space complexity of the adjacency list is better, while for dense graphs, the space complexity is the same for both the adjacency matrix and the adjacency list. When space complexities are the same, we can look at the number of bytes used per element. The adjacency matrix uses the bool type for its elements and hence 1 byte per element, while the linked-list node (dominant if the graph is dense) uses 8 bytes per node, assuming 4 bytes for the vertex number and 4 bytes for the pointer. Thus, the adjacency matrix uses less memory space in dense graphs, although the space complexities of the two methods are about the same.

Just as in comparing time complexities for algorithms, space complexities have a cross-over point. Therefore, even if a sparse graph is used, if the number of vertices is small, the adjacency matrix may be better. Let's suppose, for example, that we have a sparse graph in which the number of edges is equal to the number of vertices. Suppose further that each LinkedList object uses 8 bytes and each linked-list node uses 8 bytes. Therefore, we have $8n + 8n = 16n$ bytes of space being used (16 bytes per vertex). A bool type just uses 1 byte, so the adjacency matrix uses n^2 bytes. To find the cross-over point, we solve

$$16n = n^2$$

to get the number of vertices, where each side of the equation uses the same amount of memory. Subtracting $16n$ from each side gives

$$0 = n^2 - 16n$$

which factors to

$$n(n - 16) = 0$$

This equation has two solutions: $n = 0$, which is nonsensical, and $n = 16$. Thus, if the number of edges is equal to the number of vertices, then when the number of vertices is less than 16, the adjacency matrix is better; when the number of vertices is greater than 16, the adjacency list is better. Graphs in the real world often have a lot more than 16 vertices, so we wouldn't make use of the cross-over point very often.

Putting it all together, as far as memory conservation is concerned, we have to take a look at the number of bytes used in the linked-list object. If we are using the LinkedList class, the number of bytes is 8. Then, for sparse graphs with a small number of vertices or for dense graphs, the adjacency matrix would have a tendency to use less memory, while for sparse graphs with a large number of vertices, the adjacency list would have a tendency to use less memory.

Thus, deciding whether to use an adjacency matrix or an adjacency list for a graph depends on (1) whether the number of vertices and/or edges will need to change, (2) whether the graph application frequently processes adjacency lists or whether it frequently needs to know whether there is an edge between two vertices, (3) the number of expected vertices in a typical graph for the application, and (4) whether a typical graph in the application will be sparse or dense. There may, of course, be any of a multitude of other factors involved in the decision, but such factors will present themselves in the application or in the environment that the application is running in.

SUMMARY

This chapter has introduced two data structures: the binary search tree and the graph. Much of what is involved in the implementation of the graph data structure involves the study of the algorithms that are used for it; these algorithms, however, are beyond the scope of this text. You will encounter them in a course or textbook on algorithms. The basic concepts of graphs are presented here, and these concepts will help you understand the algorithms later. In the exercises that follow, you will explore making an implementation for a binary search tree and an incomplete, but challenging, implementation for a graph.

Two common implementations of graphs include adjacency matrices and adjacency lists. Depending on the algorithm used in the application of the graph, one technique may be faster than the other. We've also examined memory issues surrounding both of these implementations, to help you make an informed decision.

EXERCISES

1. Show the binary search tree that would be formed by inserting the following keys in the order shown:

29, 17, 8, 48, 26, 19, 1, 34, 40, 38

2. Show the result of removing the nodes with keys 10, 50, and 43 from the binary search tree in Figure 15.7b. Use the original binary search tree for each removal.

3. Why would one use a binary search tree for a search when a DoublyLinkedList can do so in $\Theta(1)$ time?

4. What is the difference between a balanced and an unbalanced binary search tree?

5. Suppose we wish to add a certain amount to the value of some data member (not the key) in each element of a binary search tree. Suppose that the client had overloaded the operator + to achieve this result. Write a recursive function that will accept an object of type DataType from the client and will add the object to each element in the binary search tree once and only once (*Hint*: Take a look at the InOrder and InOrder2 functions.)

6. Implement a binary search tree. Use a root pointer in the private section. Make sure that you have functions for insertion, removal, and retrieval. Also, put in the InOrder and In-Order2 functions described in Section 15.1. In addition, put in any functions that are needed when there is a pointer in the private section.

7. Add first and getNext functions to the binary search tree in Exercise 6. (These functions go through the binary search tree element by element, similarly to the way the LinkedList class does in Chapter 10.) To achieve this aim, place a Queue object, which stores pointers to binary search tree nodes, in the private section. The first function just returns the element at the root node (if any), and places the pointers to the children (if there are any) of the root node on the queue. Each time the getNext function is executed, a pointer is dequeued, the element at that pointer is returned, and pointers to the children (if there are any) of that node are placed on the queue. The getNext function should return false when the queue is empty, because there are no more elements on the binary search tree. In addition, write a re-place function so that the current element can be updated. (You might want to save its pointer in the private section.)

8. What is the difference between a directed graph and an undirected graph? When two vertices point to each other, how is this shown in a directed graph?

9. What is a weighted graph?

10. How does one decide whether to use an adjacency-matrix implementation or an adjacency-list implementation of a graph data structure?

11. Draw the adjacency-matrix representation of the graph in Figure 15.10.

12. Draw the adjacency-list representation of the graph in Figure 15.10.

13. Implement a graph by means of an adjacency-list representation. Using a vertex hash table and an adjacency-list hash table, put in functions that can add a vertex and add an edge. Use the HashTable class (Section 11.5) for the vertex hash table. In this table, each element of the LinkedList object will be of type DataType, where the client will make a struct containing information about a vertex and use this struct for Datatype. In a comment, instruct the client that the struct must contain an integer data member called id for storing the id of a vertex; id must be unique for each vertex in the graph. Ideally, the client would assign the next sequential id to any new vertex that is made. In the adjacency-list hash table, use the HashTable class, where each element of the LinkedList object will be a struct containing two data members: the id of a vertex and a DoublyLinkedList (Section 11.7) for storing the names of other vertices that this vertex points to. (In the declaration of this hash table in the private section of the graph, you will not need to use DataType or any other type from the client.) Put in first and getNext functions: The first function should pass in a vertex and retrieve the first vertex (if there is any) in the adjacency list that the passed-in vertex points to; the getNext function should retrieve the next value in that same doubly linked list.

14. To the graph in Exercise 13, add functions that can remove a vertex and remove an edge, using the scheme discussed in the text.

In each node of the vertex hash table, there will now be three data members: an info member of type DataType, a DoublyLinkedList of integers for the fan-in list, and a next pointer.

For small graphs with, say, fewer than a hundred vertices, this data structure has a lot of overkill. Even so, it is not really complete. There are quite a few functions that can and should be added to a Graph data structure, but the algorithms for such functions are beyond the scope of this text.

How to Compile and Work with Multiple-File Programs

MICROSOFT VISUAL STUDIO 2005 C++ COMPILER

The first thing you need to do is decide where you want to place your program files. By default, all program files that you create will be placed into a project folder inside the Visual Studio 2005 folder (which is inside the My Documents folder). In the Visual Studio 2005 folder, along with your .h and .cpp files, there will be other files created during project formation and compilation, which are not necessary in order to compile your .h and .cpp files. If you are going to submit homework, a cleaner place to put your .h and .cpp files is in a folder on your desktop. The other files created during project formation and compilation will still be placed in the project folder under the Visual Studio 2005 folder (by default), so that you will only have .h and .cpp files in your Desktop folder, allowing you to easily submit them when completed. (Often, your instructor will only ask for the .h and .cpp files; the other files can take up an incredible amount of disk space.) In this appendix, we'll assume that you want to use a folder on your Desktop; once you know how to do that, it is an easy matter to use the project folder.

COMPILING AND RUNNING CODE USING CLASSES (NOT CLASS TEMPLATES)

If you are new to the Microsoft Visual Studio 2005 C++ compiler, you will probably want to start off by compiling files that already make up a complete program, and then run the program. We'll assume that you've downloaded the files from chapter 1, example 2 (ch1ex2 folder) at http://www.prenhall.com/childs, and that you've placed them on the Desktop in a folder called ch1ex2.

To compile the program, you need to make a project for it first. Start up Microsoft Visual Studio 2005 by clicking on the Desktop icon for it (if it is not on the Desktop, it may be found in All Programs, using the Start menu). Using the File menu, select the New option, then select the Project option. This will give you a window, where you will select Visual C++ under Project Types on the left (you may need to expand the topics to see it). On the right, under Templates, select Win32 Console Application. Enter a name for the project, ch1ex2 for example, and then click on the "OK" button. You will get another window. Select "Application Settings" on the left side of the window. Check the Empty project box, then click the "Finish" button. You have now made a project for the source code files in the ch1ex2 folder on the Desktop. However, you must add these source code files to the project before you can compile it.

Using the Project menu, select "Add Existing Item . . . ". Then, in the window that opens, browse to the Desktop, and open the ch1ex2 folder *on the Desktop*. Make sure you get this right, because there will be a ch1ex2 project folder created under the Visual Studio 2005 folder, and this is the folder you will first see by default. The project folder is given the same name that you select for the project. Once you open the ch1ex2 folder on your Desktop, you should see the 3 source code files checkbook.h, checkbook.cpp, and useCheckbook.cpp. Select all three source code files by pressing the Shift key, and while holding the Shift key down, press the down arrow key. Then click on the "Add" button. If you have the Solution Explorer pane open on the right, you should see these files appear there. If you don't have the Solution Explorer pane open, you can select it from the View menu to open it.

You have now added all the source code files to your project and you are ready to compile the files. Under the Build menu, you can select "Build ch1ex2". You should see "Build: 1 succeeded, 0 failed, 0 skipped" in the Output pane at the bottom of the screen. This won't tell you if you have any warnings, however; this is just the message you get when there are no errors. To see whether or not you have warnings, scroll up in the Output pane; you should see "0 error(s), 0 warning(s)". If you get errors when compiling these files, there may be a problem with your compiler installation, or you may have missed a step in the procedure described. To run the program, use the Debug menu and select "Start Without Debugging".

COMPILING AND RUNNING CODE USING CLASS TEMPLATES

The first example of this book that uses a class template is in folder ch2ex3 at http://www.prenhall.com/childs. We'll assume that you've downloaded these files and placed them in a folder called ch2ex3 on your Desktop.

You follow the same exact procedure for compiling and running code using classes, until you come to the point where you are ready to add files to your project. You use the Project menu and select "Add Existing Item . . . " as before, and you browse to the Desktop folder called ch2ex3, as before. When you open this folder, you won't add all the files to your project, like before. Instead, you should only select checkbook.h and useCheckbook.cpp and add only these files to your folder. If you add the checkbook.cpp file to your project, you will get more compilation errors than you can possibly imagine. After adding the two files to your project, just build and run the project as you did with ch1ex2. If you add the checkbook.cpp to the project accidentally, right click on it in the Solutions Explorer pane and select Remove.

The reason why class templates are handled differently than classes is because with class templates, the specification and implementation files are really just one big header file. The implementation file is included at the bottom of the specification file to make it that way. When you compile classes (not class templates), the .cpp files are compiled individually, but the linker combines the object code for the .cpp files together.

WRITING CODE USING MICROSOFT VISUAL STUDIO 2005

To write code, you can use the exact same process for making a project as described earlier, until you get to the point where you are ready to add files to your project. This time, you would not select "Add Existing Item" from the Project menu, because you are going to write code for the "Items". Therefore, you select "Add New Item" under the Project menu. You can add one new item at a time; if you are going to write a specification file, select "Header File (.h)", and if you are going to write an implementation file or a main program file, select "C++ File (.cpp)". Enter a name, without an extension, for the type of file you chose. If you want to place the file in a folder on your Desktop, click the "Browse" button on the right side of Location, to set the Location for the new file you are about to write. Otherwise, by default, your new file will be placed in the project file under the Visual Studio 2005 folder (which you may want). After you have done everything (selected the file type, typed in a name without an extension, and (optionally) set the location), click the "Add" button. A blank area appears where you can write the code for the file. When you are done writing the file, if you want to write more files, select "Add New Item" under the Project menu, and follow the process again to create more files. You may create files `til your heart's content.

When you're done writing files, in the Solution Explorer pane, remove all files that are the implementation files for class templates; if you don't know what a class template is, don't worry about it. If you are at a spot in the book where you do know what a class template is, to remove the implementation file from the class template, right click on it (in the Solution Explorer pane), and simply select Remove.

At this point, just compile as described before, but expect to have errors, of course. When you click on one of the errors that come up in the Output pane, the compiler will take you to the line of code in which it thinks there is a problem. Once you get the errors out, don't forget to check for warnings by scrolling upward in the Output pane; warnings won't prevent compilation, but many should be heeded. If everything looks clear, you can run the program as described before.

To modify files where you suspect a runtime error is occurring, you can select the File menu, then select the "Open" "File" sequence. You may have to browse around to find the folder that your source code files are in, before you can open the one you want.

OPENING A PROJECT IN MICROSOFT VISUAL STUDIO 2005 THAT YOU HAVE ALREADY CREATED

Make sure that your source code files are where they were the last time that you opened the project. The project files in the project folder will expect them to be there. Then, after starting Microsoft Visual Studio 2005, use the File menu and select the "Open" "Project/Solution" sequence, or select your project from the list shown (if it is there). If you need to open the project by selectng the "Open" "Project/Solution" sequence, you will be in the Visual Studio 2005 folder. Select the project folder you want; it will have the same name as the project name you chose before (if you forgot the project name, select one and cross your fingers). Inside the folder that you select, you should see a file, with the colored, sideways, figure 8 symbol in the lower right corner. Click on this file to open the project.

To open source code files that you would like to change, you can select the File menu, then select the "Open" "File" sequence. You may have to browse around to find the folder that your source code files are in, before you can open the one you want.

WHEN THINGS REALLY GET SCREWED UP

If you have compilation problems you can't solve, or your program runs in weird ways that seems like it has something to do with the planet Neptune, see your instructor.

On the other hand, you might have source code files that you know are good, but somehow the project that they are in just doesn't seem to have that special something. You may have made some error in the standard procedure, and couldn't quite get everything patched up. In this case, you might just want to create a new project from scratch to put your source code files in. You can protect your beloved source code files by making a copy of them and placing them in a folder on your Desktop. Make sure you use the File menu and select "Close Solution", to get back to the main screen of Microsoft Visual Studio 2005. Using the File menu, you can select the "Open" "Project/Solution" sequence, but when you see that loathsome project folder, don't open it. Just right-click on it, select Delete, and wipe that miserable project folder out of your Visual Studio 2005 folder. You might even want to go so far as to remove it from your Recycle Bin, and wipe it from the face of the hard disk. When you feel gratified, you can make a new project from scratch with the same project name to put your wonderful source code files in.

UNIX COMPILERS

A lot of UNIX systems have a compiler called CC. If yours does, we're in business. First, we'll compile and run the ch1ex2 program, in the ch1ex2 folder at http://www.prenhall .com/childs. Assuming that you've downloaded these files to your UNIX account, type the following at the command prompt (in the directory that your files are in):

CC checkbook.cpp useCheckbook.cpp

An executable file called a.out will be created. To run the program, type:

./a.out

To compile a program with a class template, all you need to do is compile the main program file with the other files in the directory. Assuming that you've downloaded the ch2ex3 folder to your UNIX account, just compile by typing:

CC useCheckbook.cpp

Your particular UNIX system may have more sophisticated compilers that you should check into, but this one does the job.

Index